the Universal Computer

Introducing Computer Science with Multimedia

Glenn D. Bank   Robert F. Barnes   Edwin J. Kay

Lehigh University

Mc Graw Hill **Custom Publishing**

Boston Burr Ridge, IL Dubuque, IA Madison, WI New York San Francisco St. Louis
Bangkok Bogotá Caracas Lisbon London Madrid
Mexico City Milan New Delhi Seoul Singapore Sydney Taipei Toronto

The Universal Computer: Introducing Computer Science with Multimedia

McGraw-Hill's Custom Publishing consists of products that are produced from camera-ready copy. Peer review, class testing, and accuracy are primarily the responsibility of the author(s).

3 4 5 6 7 8 9 0 QSR QSR 0 9 8 7 6 5 4

ISBN 0-07-294149-9

Editor: Elizabeth Hunziker
Production Editor: Carrie Braun
Cover Design: Laura Schetzsle and Maggie Lytle
Printer/Binder: Quebecor World

The Universal Computer:
Introducing Computer Science with Multimedia

by

Glenn D. Blank, Robert F. Barnes and Edwin J. Kay

Table of Contents

Preface

This textbook with its accompanying multimedia has two major goals:

(1) To explore the **breadth of computing** as a discipline. A narrow concentration on programming can lead to a misconception that computer science is little more than programming. (The first chapter opens by addressing many common misconceptions.) There's more to astronomy than looking through telescopes: there's *theory*, such as relativity and cosmology, there's *experimental method*, and there's *design* of special-purpose instruments and probes. So there is more to computing than just programming: there's *theory*, such as the study of the limits of computation and the complexity of algorithms; there's the *experimental method* of programming and measuring the performance of programs; and there's the *design* of effective systems in software as well as hardware. Like older sciences and mathematics, computer science emphasizes *abstraction*, or pulling out the essentials. (The *Report of the ACM Task Force on the Core of Computer Science*[1] emphasizes abstraction, theory and design in the study of computing.) This book attempts to follow the recommendations of *Computing Curricula 1991* and *Computing Curricula 2001*[2] by introducing a breadth of knowledge areas of computing, ranging from computer architecture to artificial intelligence. Social, professional and ethical issues are explored in a chapter, as well as in exercises marked "*social/ethical*" throughout the book. Chapters and multimedia also both include many exercises, marked "*explore*", designed to get students to look beyond the book, by exploring the web or library databases. The breadth component of this book makes it suitable for many CS0 courses.

(2) To encourage students to think about and practice **software development as systematic problem solving**. We will make every effort to discourage "blind hacking"—that is, trial and error at a computer terminal. Good programming and problem solving in general requires planning and organization. Chapter 2 examines alternative approaches to problem solving, then gives students an opportunity to practice these approaches using a relatively simple, graphical robot simulation called "Knobby's World." Knobby is a cousin of Karel and Karel++, designed to introduce programming as problem solving. Chapter 4 studies the software development life cycle and a modern, object-oriented approach to problem solving and software development.

A separate book, *A Multimedia Introduction to C++*, introduces programming in C++. In the works another book will introduce programming in Java. C++ and Java are modern programming languages widely used for developing large software systems; Java can also create "applets" that run on the web. The CDROM that accompanies this book also includes multimedia that helps students

---

[1]Denning, Peter, et al. *Report of the ACM Task Force on the Core of Computer Science*, ACM Press, New York, 1988. Also known as the "Denning Report." Reprinted in part in *Communications of the ACM* 32, 1 (January 1989) and in *Computer* (February 1989).

[2]Tucker, Allen B., et al., *Computing Curricula 1991: Report of the ACM/IEEE-CS Joint Curriculum Task Force*, ACM Press, New York, 1991 took a strong position recommending a breadth-first approach to introducing computer science. *Computing Curricula 2001* (www.computer.org/education/cc2001/ steelman/cc2001/chapter7.htm) acknowledges that "Even though the *Computing Curricula 1991* report argued strongly for a broader introduction to the discipline, the majority of institutions continue to focus on programming in their introductory sequence." Nevertheless, the new report notes that a "breadth-first" approach can "provide a more holistic view of the discipline, many computer science educators have argued for a "breadth-first" approach in which the first course considers a much broader range of topics." At Lehigh, we are able to cover both breadth and programming, with the help of multimedia.

learn C++, in parallel with all the chapters of the C++ book, plus the first chapter's worth of multimedia introducing Java in the BlueJ environment (also on the CDROM). Experimental evidence confirms that students can learn Java "objects first" with the BlueJ programming environment, especially with our multimedia.[3] (Interested parties may contact us about the Java manuscript and multimedia in progress.)

At Lehigh, the first author teaches two different first semester courses: 1) a CS0 course for non-majors, based on this book, and 2) a CS1 course for majors and minors, which introduces both the breadth of computer science using this book and Java programming using a different book. Breadth of CS and Java programming may seem like a lot to cover in one semester, but in our experience the multimedia makes it possible to learn enough about the breadth topics without devoting much lecture time to them. Interleaving breadth/problem solving and programming material gives students more time—breathing space, if you will—to learn Java programming by doing. Getting a computer to do what you want it do normally takes time: time for planning a solution, time for coding your solution, and yet more time for stamping out little "bugs"—the errors that lurk in code or even a conceptual solution. We strongly encourage students to get started on programming assignments early! The programming exercises integrated into the multimedia chapters will help students get started. While the Java programming chapters assume a particular order, instructors may cover the breadth chapters in just about any order.

Multimedia

The multimedia which accompanies *The Universal Computer* is complete enough that students can learn from either the book or the multimedia, in either order, depending on their learning styles and/or instructor assignments. The multimedia content explains the salient material of each chapter, then reinforces concepts with interactive exercises, simulations, constructive exercises, and quizzes. Figure 1 shows the user interface and a sample screen. Here are some of the features of the user interface:

▸ The TRACK LIST on the left displays the content of a lesson as a sequence of screens. The menu uses check marks to show progress and highlights the current screen in red. At the bottom of the menu there are progress indicators through the current screen and chapter.

▸ Multimedia **personae** on the lower left model a diverse community of teachers and learners. The personae currently include three professors (one is shown) co-teaching the course, a teaching assistant, a reference librarian, and three students. In addition to graphical images, they speak in audio and/or text boxes. Personae model students and instructors studying material together, working through interactive exercises, and suggest exploratory research on relevant topics using online information.

---

[3] Experimental results in Glenn D. Blank, Willam M. Pottenger, Shreeram A. Sahasrabudhe, Shenzhi Li, Fang Wei and Henry Odi. Multimedia for Computer Science: from CS0/CS1 to Grades 7-12, submitted to *Ed-Media 2003* and available at http://www.cse.lehigh.edu/~cimel/papers/EdMedia03.pdf. While developing *The Universal Machine* (the precursor of this book), the lead author taught CS1 to 70-80 computer science majors and non-majors. From the first year, for which only the manuscript of the book was available, to the second, in which an incomplete version of the multimedia was introduced, mean final examination scores improved about six points. Knowledge of breadth topics showed notable improvement. In the third year, with the complete first edition, mean final examination scores improved another seven points.

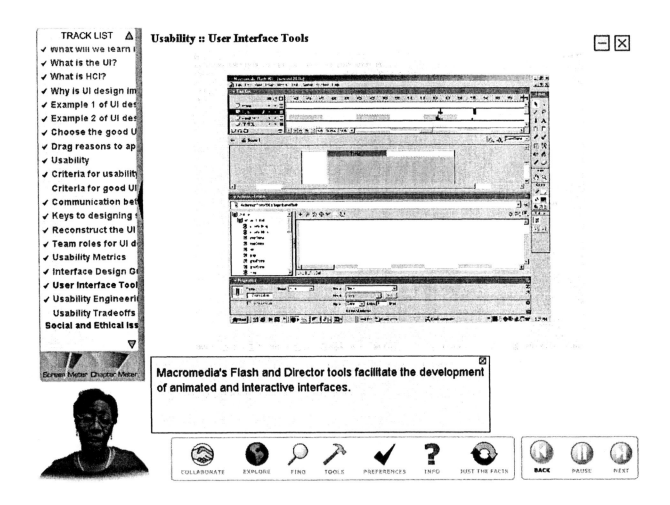

Usability :: User Interface Tools

Macromedia's Flash and Director tools facilitate the development of animated and interactive interfaces.

COLLABORATE EXPLORE FIND TOOLS PREFERENCES INFO JUST THE FACTS BACK PAUSE NEXT

Figure 1: Screen capture from *The Universal Computer*'s multimedia

▸ The COLLABORATE tools will facilitate network-based interaction with instructors, teaching assistants, librarians or other students. Chat, remote-controlled SHOW ME sessions and a multimedia FAQ of recorded SHOW ME sessions will encourage students to get help.

▸ The EXPLORE button facilitates inquiry-based learning, via directed queries on the web, adding to the *exploratory* exercises in the book. A state-of-the-art emerging-trends text mining and visualization tool will help students trace emerging trends as their interest and utility grow over time.

▸ The FIND button lets you find multimedia screens containing specific words.

▸ The PREFERENCES icon presents a panel of options letting the user adapt the environment according to his or her personal learning style, including turning text boxes or audio on/off, toggling auto-advance or wait for next page, setting the timing rate where there is no audio narration, etc. A user may change these settings at any time during a session.

▸ A JUST THE FACTS mode lets users switch to viewing non-interactive content (text and graphics) presented in HTML pages. From there, one can switch back to rich media mode via hyperlinks anchored to the corresponding Flash page. There are also links to interactive screens, which remain in Flash. JUST THE FACTS mode, besides catering to some learning styles, requires less bandwidth, and may be useful for reviewing the material quickly.

The multimedia for *The Universal Computer* has been designed to accommodate diverse learning styles. Do play with the PREFERENCES options to suit *your* style. By giving students different ways to learn material, we hope to attract more novices, especially women and minorities, to computer science. It supplies sound and animation for sensory learners, while letting verbal learners disable sound or switch altogether to JUST THE FACTS mode. Interactive materials include learner-controlled simulations of algorithms, links to programs that students can try immediately after learning related concepts and before exercises that make sure the learner has studied the programs, constructive exercises in which students build programs or models by dragging pieces into place, and inquiry-based exercises in which students learn by doing research, using the web.

While our approach is to present enough didactic material in the multimedia that it can be a stand alone learning experience, interactivity is frequent and rich in *The Universal Computer*. Personae provide feedback to all responses.

The multimedia is deliverable either via CDROM., the internet (cimel.cse.lehigh.edu with a password or www.cse.lehigh.edu/~cimel/prototype.html without), or intranets set up at other institutions by arrangements with the authors. Since all content plays through a web browser (Microsoft Internet Explorer, plus a Macromedia Flash plug-in), it looks the same however it is delivered. An advantage of web-based delivery is that once users log in, their activities may be recorded in a tracking system; instructors and researchers will have access to tools visualizing a learner's activity, or reporting the result of quizzes. An advantage of CDROM-based delivery, on the other hand, is that it removes bandwidth constraints. (The multimedia, especially audio and video, can be sluggish playing through 56K modems; high speed connections or CDROM are strongly recommended.)

The CDROM disk and new web site make this a *multimedia* textbook. Beyond supplementing the textual material presented in this book, the disk includes more illustrations, animations, speech and other sounds, short movie clips, exercises and exercise solutions, bibliographic references to reading materials via the web or in a library, and tools that will help you learn to program in Java. Print text and multimedia can complement each other. The print text presents the core material of the course plus recommended exercises. We have not simply put the print text and source code onto a CDROM. The multimedia software emphasizes what is hard to show in the static medium of text: animating processes dynamically, illustrating abstract concepts concretely, solving problems interactively.

We have designed this book with a particular audience in mind: a class that mixes potential computer science majors with non-majors—because that's the kind of class we teach at Lehigh University. We want to encourage both those with those with little or no computing experience (even those who might be a little intimidated by computers), as well as those with more experience, to explore. We have installed the multimedia in a multimedia-capable computer laboratory which students attend once a week. We devote about one lecture per "breadth" topic and two or three per programming topic. Students can learn the "breadth" material and text without attempting to cover it all in detail in lecture. Multimedia thus allows instructors and students to get the big picture, rather than focusing too narrowly on programming.

Some schools may distinguish between majors and non-majors. A course that is more oriented toward computer science majors may want to put more emphasis on Java programming than we do and devote less class time to the "breadth" material, assigning multimedia chapters for students to study on their own or in labs. An instructor who feels it is urgent to get started with programming even earlier than we do could possibly skip programming in Knobby's World. Students can benefit from the illustration that this world supplies for non-programming concepts later in the book without necessarily having written Knobby's World programs. The multimedia introducing C++ and Java systematically takes students through core concepts, then guides them through study of actual C++ or Java programs (by running them to see what they do, then answering the questions about what happened), then *hands-on* programming of related problems, using a programming environment. We believe multimedia learning is a major advance over getting source code on a diskette—and a lot more work to produce!

On the other hand, a course for non-majors might want to give less emphasis to programming and give more emphasis to the "breadth" material. In a CS0 course, Knobby's World may serve as a "gentle introduction to programming." A recent syllabus for Professor Blank's CS0 course is available at http://www.cse.lehigh.edu/~glennb/cse12/syl1203.htm, and a syllabus for his CS1 course is available at http://www.cse.lehigh.edu/~glennb/cse15/syl1503.htm.

Exercises in the textbook can serve variously as homework assignments, in class demonstration or discussion items (we include many open-ended conceptual exercises for this purpose), and/or examination questions. Answers to all the review questions at the end of each chapter are provided on web site at http://www.cse.lehigh.edu/~glennb/um/book/exsolnew.htm.

Acknowledgments

"Give thanks to the LORD, for He is good, and His love endures forever." Psalm 118:1

A new textbook is a considerable undertaking, but a multimedia textbook must be an order of magnitude more complex! We have learned much and benefitted much from working with a small army of editors, writers, fellow faculty members and students.

First, we repeat our thanks to those who helped with *The Universal Machine*: to Connie Coleman, our multimedia art director, to student multimedia developers John Chapman, Scott Fitch, James Nixon, Lingan Nguyen, Jason Stanford and Beau Sullivan, and to Knobby's World and LOOKOUT programmers Paul Martino, Venkatesh Rao, Louis Tanzos, and Jesse Thilo, and to Denise Gürer, then of Stanford Research Institute, for her extensive comments as well as her contributions to the "Women in Computing" theme in the multimedia. Thanks also to Betsy Jones at WCB/McGraw-Hill, who granted us permission to use the materials of *The Universal Machine* for our new book.

Second, we thank those who are helping with *The Universal Computer*: to the National Science Foundation (grant # EIA-0087977) and the Pennsylvania Infrastructure Technology Alliance (PITA), to student multimedia developers David Goldfeder, Martin Herr, Harriet Jaffe, Sumit Jain, Adam Kinnear, Andrew Mall, Sharmeen Mecklai, Jonathan Morgan, Soma Roy, Shreeram Sahasrabudhe, David Servas, Daniel Shire, Althea Smith, and Fang Wei.

Finally, we especially thank our wives, and our children, extended family and friends, for their love and patience while we buried our heads in this project!

G.D.B.
R.F.B.
E.J.K.

Chapter 1
Introducing ... the Universal Computer

"I wish to God these calculations had been executed by steam."
Charles Babbage, 1822

What is this thing we call a universal computer or universal machine? We would need many books (indeed, a whole computer science curriculum) to explain all the implications of this idea. Alan Turing, a pioneer of computing, coined the term 'universal machine' when he devised a very simple abstract device—now called a Turing machine—which he argued could be programmed to do what *any* computational device could ever do. A **universal machine** is a *general purpose symbol-manipulating machine, capable of solving any problem whose solution can represented by a* **program**—*an organized set of logical operations*. At its heart, a Turing machine is capable of just a few primitive operations such as copying a digit off a piece of paper. Step by logical step, it can solve increasingly complex problems. Though the core of the universal machine needn't be complicated, it does help if it's very fast. A modern computer can perform numerical calculations "faster than a speeding bullet." Equipped with legs, it can also walk around tall buildings. (Note that a universal machine is not the legs but the controller of the legs.) It can also manipulate non-numerical data, such as text or music or speech or images. It can even learn to adapt its behavior.

1.1 Common misconceptions about computer science

The universal machine is a foundational idea of computer science. Many people, however, have many misconceptions about what computer science is about. Computer science explores the kinds of problems that computers can (or cannot) solve, and how to get them solve these problems in ways that are efficient and user-friendly. Yet the misconceptions remain, reminding us of a poem, "The Blind Men and the Elephant." Seven blind men encounter an elephant. Grabbing the tail, one concludes that "An elephant is very like a rope!" Another, walking up against the side, concludes "An elephant is very like a wall." Still another, holding a leg, decides an elephant is like a tree, etc. The poem concludes, "Though all were partly in the right, yet all of them were wrong." Each blind man was misled by limited information. Similarly, we find that many students have misconceptions that lead them to be intimidated or bored or turned off before they even get started. So let's address some of these misconceptions.

Misconception: computer science is for nerds, mesmerized by computer screens

Watch your stereotypes! Real computer scientists are generally bright people, but they are diverse, of both genders and of every race and nationality, with wide ranging talents and interests, both in and outside the field. You will meet some real computer scientists in video clips that come with the multimedia—they are quite diverse and interesting people. And, although it is true that computer scientists often like working with big monitors or the latest laptop, they also do computer science by writing on blackboards or whiteboards, doodling on paper, and especially brainstorming with other people. Computer scientists solve interesting problems. (Hence the second chapter of this book is about problem solving.) Computer scientists solve problems by designing software, or by designing theories or models, as in other sciences. The problems of computer science are wide ranging: from designing really fast computers to designing really appealing web sites, from playing championship chess to understanding human speech, from making it easier to visualize problems to making it easier for people to solve problems cooperatively.

Misconception: computer science is for math whizzes

It is true that computer science started as an offspring of mathematics—Turing's invention of the universal machine was originally research in mathematical logic. And it is true that in many universities, computer science started out in mathematics departments (as is still the case in many small colleges). And it is true that computers are good at computational tasks. Nowadays, though, only a small part of computing is mathematical. Would you believe that back in the 1940's, Thomas Watson, Sr., who ran IBM at the time, thought there would only be a market for at most half a dozen computers? That was because he had this misconception that only a few scientists or engineers would use computers for their mathematical computations. (Fortunately for IBM, Watson's son saw the huge potential of computing!) Today, numerical analysis is just one sub-field of computer science. Case in point: while the third author of this book got a Ph.D. in Mathematics (he *also* got a Ph.D. in Psychology), the second author studied Philosophy, and the first author was originally an English major (and makes no claims that he is a mathematical whiz). Computer science is no longer a sub-field of mathematics, nor is calculus required to study most of computer science. If you are someone who likes solving problems, and you are willing to learn a discipline of systematic and patient problem solving, computer science may be for you.

Misconception: computer science is about computer hardware

Although it is true that some computer engineers have the job of developing faster and more efficient machines, that's just one corner of the field. Most computer scientists see computers as tools, rather than their objects of study. It has been said that "computer science is no more about computers than astronomy is about telescopes, biology is about microscopes, or chemistry is about beakers and test tubes." A better generalization is that computer scientists study *computing*: what is it possible to do with computers? Turing glimpsed some of the possibilities when he first described the universal machine.

Misconception: computer science is about writing programs

As Turing discovered, writing programs is how we get computers to do new and interesting things. Nowadays we call this "software development." A whole branch of computer science called software engineering is concerned with methods for writing (and rewriting) "good" software. Still, many areas of computer science deal only incidentally with software or programming. For example, some computer scientists work on how to facilitate business processes (e-commerce), while still others seek to advance the theory and science of computing.

Misconception: computer science is about the using computers and using computer programs

Many people are first exposed to the field via a course in applications—word processors, spreadsheets, databases, etc. Indeed, computers and programs are put to use in a wide variety of contexts (that's one reason why we called our book *The Universal Computer*), and some computer scientists do develop applications and new tools. As with any science, however, the applications are a minor aspect of the science itself. The applications are tools for solving problems; the science makes it possible to create the tools or to imagine what tools are even possible.

All these misconceptions about computer science indicate that it is a large discipline with many sub-areas for exploration which appeal to people with a wide variety of interests and talents. We hope this text (and accompanying multimedia) will give you a bird's eye view of the whole and maybe spark your interest in further exploring some area or aspect of computing.

Exercise 1.1: Write down any misconceptions you may have about computer science before you began to read this book or multimedia. Discuss why you may have had them. Is the book or multimedia beginning to give you a different idea about what computer science is about? In your own words, what do you think it is about now?

1.2 The universal computer and virtual machines

The universal computer enables us to explore the universe. Indeed, the space program could not have reached the moon without computers. NASA developed the first microcomputer for the Apollo mission to control the complex dockings and landings of the lunar module. Can you imagine the *Star Trek* ship *Enterprise* ever "going where no one has gone before" without computers? It is not only the actual universe that we can explore with the help of these machines. In the next chapter we will investigate *conceptual* universes—"problem spaces" such as arise when one considers the range of alternative moves in a game of chess. As we shall see, an "inner" space can also be vast.

Computers also let us explore *virtual* reality. Computers can extend the senses, projecting images and sounds that change as we move, giving the strong impression that we are moving in a three-dimensional, yet imaginary world. In Japan, prospective buyers use virtual reality to preview variations on a home they might build. In laboratories, scientists use virtual reality to explore the structure of molecules. On the *Enterprise*, officers and crew enjoy virtual reality on the "holodeck"—and occasionally have difficulty distinguishing what is real from what is virtual.

Indeed, the very idea of the virtual is an important elaboration of the idea of the universal machine. While an **actual machine** *implements behaviors in hardware*, a **virtual machine** *simulates behaviors in software, in a program*. An actual machine is tangible; a virtual machine is abstract. Before you get bored with abstractions, let's see just how real they can appear to be. We've mentioned virtual reality—that can *seem* pretty real. Then there's the World Wide Web—believe it or not, it's really a very elaborate network of virtual machines. A web browser is not, after all, an actual machine, it's software—actually a collection of programs, layers and layers of them (we will learn more about these layers of programs in the chapters on computer architectures and operating systems). Are you getting the picture? Virtual machines are powerful—a powerful idea.

Turing's universal machine can, in principle, simulate any other machine—say, one that withdraws cash from a bank account on the Internet. The real beauty of this idea is that it is possible for a rather simple actual machine to simulate a *more complicated* virtual machine. It's rather like an actor (who knows no physics at all), given an appropriate script, being able to play the role of Albert Einstein. Only in computing, things get even more interesting, for it is also possible to create yet another virtual machine from a virtual machine. (Imagine an actor portraying an actor playing Einstein.) Each level of implementation creates new capabilities that the underlying machine does not have, at least not in any straightforward way. For example, an actual machine can send electrical signals across a telephone wire, yet it is unaware of what these signals mean. A virtual machine might interpret a stream of signals as a request to connect to a particular machine (perhaps via other machines) or as a request for a particular document in another machine's file system or even a request to run a program (another virtual machine) on another machine. Watch for virtual machines in this book.

The universal computer is now ubiquitous, showing up on millions of desks, laps and hands. The World Wide Web connects them to multimedia information available on other computers around the globe. Once upon a time, books were chained into libraries, because they were copied by hand. The printing press liberated books from their chains, and revolutionized society—the Reformation spread like wildfire because Martin Luther was able to print his translation of the Bible. Similarly, faxes and computers helped undermine totalitarian regimes behind the old Iron Curtain. Nevertheless, computers are still chained to desks in university computer laboratories. What will happen when the price of computing, which has been dropping exponentially, drops to the price of paperback books? Yet there is a double-edged sword here. Though the universal computer increases communication, it can reduce privacy, enabling information about you to spread without your permission, or even your knowledge. It's the universal gossip. Whom will it tell your medical history, your overdue bills, even your taste in reading material? So the universal computer not only promises, it threatens. (We will explore social and ethical implications in a later chapter, as well as in a few exercises marked "*social/ethical*" throughout this book.)

In the next section, we briefly survey the history of the *idea* of the universal machine. It is not intended to be a full history of computing, which would probably overwhelm you. We just want you to appreciate how these great ideas—the universal machine and the virtual machines it can simulate—came about and came to revolutionize the world we live in. The last two sections will look at the practical machine itself—the hardware and the software.

Exercise 1.2: A personal computer (PC) has a fixed amount of memory. Windows™ acts as if it has a much, much larger amount of *virtual* memory, so that you run program(s) larger than the available physical memory. How does the distinction between actual and virtual memory illustrate the distinction between actual and virtual machines? Why is this useful to you?

Exercise 1.3 (*social/ethical*): Do you think the FBI or other federal agencies should be able to intercept data transmitted on the Internet? (The Justice Department thinks so. After all, spies and thugs can use the Internet, too.) Why or why not? Should there by laws to forbid encryption of data, thus frustrating would be spies from hiding their activities. Why or why not?

1.3 The Very Idea of the Universal Machine

As we have noted, a computer, unlike any other machine, is a universal machine, a general purpose symbol-manipulating machine. A car or a microwave oven or an elevator is a *special* purpose machine, designed to do a particular thing. But there is a huge range of things that a *general* purpose computer can be programmed to do (or even be programmed to *learn* to do).

1.3.1 "Universal Machine" vs. "Number Cruncher"

A general purpose machine is one of the great ideas of computer science. Yet it is hard to shake the idea that computers are essentially "number crunchers." The *Random House Dictionary* (1980) defines 'computer' as "an electronic machine capable of . . . highly complex mathematical operations at high speeds." Even the *Grolier Multimedia Encyclopedia* (1993) defines 'computer' as "an apparatus built to perform routine calculations. . . ." This even though a multimedia encyclopedia depends on a computer's ability to manipulate, organize and search for text, pictures, sounds and movies. Why do you suppose this narrow conception of computers persists?

The word itself gives us a hint. The venerable *Oxford English Dictionary* (1926) defines 'computer' as "one who computes, a calculator, reckoner, specifically a person employed to make calculations in an observatory, in surveying, etc." Of course, the *OED* was compiled before there were any electronic computers, when numerical calculation was done by *human* computers, but the general idea still survives.

What's the difference between a computer and a calculator? A traditional calculator can only perform a relatively small set of numerical operations; a person rather than a program determines which calculations. (Modern scientific calculators do have some computer-like capabilities, with memory, and a limited programmability, yet they are still special purpose devices.) Though many books include a picture of an abacus as a precursor of a computer, an abacus is really an ancient calculator. Similarly, the devices invented by the 17th century philosopher-mathematicians Pascal and Leibniz facilitated numerical operations—addition, subtraction, multiplication, division—calculations, not general purpose computations.

1.3.2 Babbage's Engines

The 19th century mathematician Charles Babbage got so frustrated by errors in human computation that he decided to build a mechanical "computer." He envisioned a steam-powered machine that would automatically compute mathematical tables by adding increments called differences to intermediate results. Just as machines were automating tedious manufacturing operations, Babbage's Difference Engine would automate the tedious mental operations of calculations and looking things up in tables. After completing a prototype, Babbage abandoned the Difference Engine, in order to embark on what he believed was "a better idea." The Difference Engine was, after all, still a special purpose calculator. Babbage's Analytical Engine would be a *general purpose* computer. Instead of a built-in sequence of steps, it would enable a programmer to modify the squence, using punched cards. Earlier in the 19th century, Joseph Jacquard had already introduced punched cards to control the patterns woven by his mechanical looms. Different patterns of holes in the cards led to different mechanical behaviors, thus producing different tapestries. Babbage wanted to mechanize the *logical control* required to solve any formal problem. Though Babbage never did complete the Analytical Engine—if he had, it would have been larger than a steam locomotive—his design anticipated many of the great ideas of computer design.

Born at the dawn of the Industrial Age, Babbage saw first-hand the advantage of automation: a machine performs repetitive tasks without boredom, and thus makes fewer errors than does a person. Babbage enhanced the design of his machine (unfortunately driving up the cost of its implementation) to avoid human errors. Instead of relying on a person to copy the results shown by machine, it would automatically print out its results. **Automation** is a theme of modern computing: *whenever there are tedious, error-prone steps, let the computer do them.*

Exercise 1.4 (*social/ethical*): What are the consequences of increasing automation and the changes it brings for workers in a society moving into the industrial age? What are the consequences for workers in a society moving into the information age? (If you need some background, see the chapter on social and ethical issues for a discussion of these "ages".)
Exercise 1.5 (*social/ethical*): How will increasing automation, especially with computers, affect *your* career? How can you prepare, now, for the changes that automation will bring?

As a general purpose computer, the Analytical Engine would be able to carry out *any mathematical* operation. Lady Ada Byron, Countess Lovelace, who wrote the first computer programs in anticipation of Babbage's machine, wrote enthusiastically about its possibilities:

> The bounds of *arithmetic* were, however, outstepped the moment the idea of applying the cards had occurred; and the Analytical Engine does not occupy common ground with mere 'calculating machines'. It holds a position wholly its own; and the considerations it suggests are most interesting in their nature. In

enabling mechanism to combine together *general* symbols, in successions of unlimited variety and extent, a uniting link is established between the operations of matter and the abstract mental processes of the most *abstract branch* of mathematical science. A new, a vast, and a powerful language is developed for the future use of analysis, in which to wield its truth so that these may become of more speedy and accurate practical application. . . .[1]

She also envisioned *non-mathematical* applications:

Supposing, for instance, that the fundamental relations of pitched sounds in the science of harmony of musical composition were susceptible of such expression and adaptations, the engine might compose elaborate and scientific pieces of music of any degrees of complexity or extent.[2]

Like the Jacquard loom, the Analytical Engine achieved its generality from *stored programs*. One could modify its behavior by altering two boxes of punched cards--one a box of variables, or data, and the other a box of instruction codes. Figure 1.1 shows how Babbage encoded four arithmetic operations as different patterns on punched cards. Thus a box of punched cards might be a program—a sequence of instructions—or it might be data—a table that the engine had already computed and punched. Moreover, Babbage saw the importance of maintaining machine-readable libraries of programs and data, anticipating the idea of *reusable* software.

| Add | Subtract | Multiply | Divide |

Figure 1.1: Four cards for arithmetic operations

Babbage's engine separated a "store" from a "mill." These correspond to the two most important components of a modern computer: *main memory* and *central processing unit (CPU)*. Figure 1.2 depicts a schematic of a modern **stored program machine**, *which can execute any program of instructions stored in its memory*. (Babbage's schematic was somewhat more cluttered with gears and shafts.) A modern machine reads data from an external file into main memory. Similarly, Babbage's machine read punched cards representing numeric data and symbolic variables. His *store* would hold these data. He planned a capacity of a thousand 50-place decimal numbers. Babbage's *mill* read instructions from a separate box of cards. A modern machine reads both instructions and data into the same memory. The underlying principle is still the same: by reading programs which are created externally and are then stored within its memory, the actual machine becomes the virtual machine of the programmer's choosing.

Babbage saw that a few primitive operations, built into the machine, could be combined to create complex programs—different sequences of operations leading to different behavior. In this way, Babbage's mill could perform a variety of mechanical operations upon values brought in from the store. Like Babbage's engine, a modern machine performs only a small number of **primitive**

---

[1]Reprinted in *Faster than Thought*, ed. B. V. Bowden (Pitman, 1953).

[2]*Scientific Memoirs, Selections from the Transactions of Foreign Academies and Learned Societies and from Foreign Journals*, ed. Richard Taylor, F.S.A., Vol. III, Article XXIX, London, 1843.

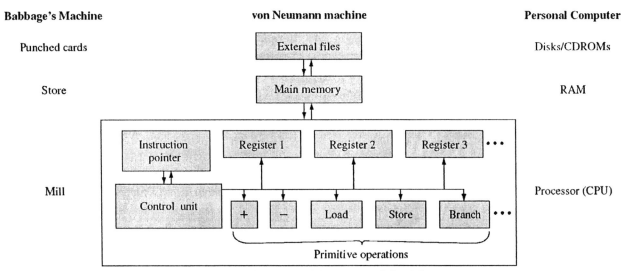

Babbage's Machine	von Neumann machine	Personal Computer
Punched cards	External files	Disks/CDROMs
Store	Main memory	RAM
Mill	Instruction pointer / Register 1 / Register 2 / Register 3 ··· / Control unit / + − Load Store Branch ··· / Primitive operations	Processor (CPU)

Figure 1.2: Stored Program Machine

operations—Add, Subtract, Load, etc.—except they are *"hard-wired" into its electronic circuits.* (The chapter on computer architecture shows just how this is done.) The **instruction pointer** *tells where to find the next instruction in main memory.* The **control unit** *fetches an instruction* from memory, *decodes it* (for example, punched holes in the first three positions of a card meant '+') *and executes the corresponding hard-wired primitive operation the contents of special memory locations called* **registers**. For example, suppose register 1 holds the value 2 and register 2 holds the value 3. Then the '+' operation adds these values and puts '5' in a third register (called the 'accumulator'). In Babbage's machine, this operation was performed by a motion of gears and shafts. In a modern computer, it is performed by an electronic circuit. Though the latter is much smaller and faster, both implement the universal machine.

One important primitive operation is the conditional branch operation. Usually, after an instruction is executed, the instruction pointer is incremented by one so that the control unit just fetches the next instruction from memory (or the next punched card from a box). However, some instructions, called **branch** instructions, *change the value of the Instruction Pointer*, so that instead of getting the next card from the box, the control unit fetches some *other* specified instruction, in effect jumping to another part of the program. Thus, as Babbage realized, a program need not be a rigid sequence of instructions, but can jump from one card to some other card, possibly going back to an earlier one. This type of instruction greatly enhances the flexibility and power of programmable machines. Branching sets up the possibility of making decisions—choosing among alternative behaviors as well as repeating an action. Lovelace defined a "cycle" as "any set of operations repeated more than once" and noted that "the power of repeating instructions ... reduces to an immense extent the number of cards required" (*Ibid*).

Alas, Babbage never completed either of his engines (though there are prototypes of the Difference Engine in the London Science Museum and the National Museum of American History). It was nearly a century before interest in automated general-purpose computation revived—made more feasible by advances in electronics.

Exercise 1.6: In your own words, describe at least three important ways in which Babbage's Analytical Engine anticipates the design of modern computers.

Exercise 1.7: Describe at least three things modern computers can do that Ada anticipated. What does her work imply about the relationship about the great ideas of computing and practical reality?

1.3.3 Electronic computers

By the end of the 19th century, the U. S. Census bureau was using punched cards to process population data. International Business Machines (IBM) and other corporations began manufacturing punched-card data processing machines. These were electro-mechanical devices. Instead of steam, electrical power drove mechanical motion--punching cards and paper tape, sorting cards, and turning the wheels of an adding machine. Yet these machines lacked the generality of Babbage's unfinished Analytical Engine. In the late 1930's Howard Aiken constructed the Mark I, a fully automatic electro-mechanical machine that featured special routines to handle logarithms and trigonometric functions. It was controlled by instructions pre-punched onto paper tape. However, there was no provision for branch instructions, so the *design* of the Mark I was still inferior to that of Babbage's Analytical Engine.

World War II accelerated technological development. Gunners needed tables to predict trajectories for their shells, and each new weapons system called for new tables. So the government sponsored the development of a fully electronic computer which could generate the various tables. The resulting ENIAC (Electronic Numeric Integrator and Calculator) could add 5000 sums or multiply 300 products per second, a thousand times faster than the previous generation of electro-mechanical machines. That was just the beginning: by the turn of the 21st century, a microprocessor could perform over a billion instructions per second, and produce many millions of products per second.

Figure 1.3: Programming the ENIAC

ENIAC used vacuum tubes to store data.[3] A vacuum tube is essentially a wholly electronic switch; getting rid of slow mechanical parts greatly improved the ENIAC's speed. Each vacuum tube could remember a single *binary value* or **bit**: on or off, yes or no, true or false, 1 or 0. ENIAC was a **digital** computer, *representing all information in terms of discrete on/off states*, rather than an **analog** device (such as a mercury thermometer or a volt meter), processing *continuous*

---

[3] A few years earlier John Atanasoff had already used the same ideas in a programmable vacuum tube device he had built at Iowa State College.

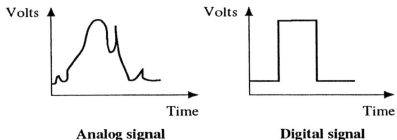

Analog signal   Digital signal

Figure 1.4:Analog (continuous) vs. digital (discrete) signals

quantities. Figure 1.4 illustrates this distinction. ENIAC had over 18,000 vacuum tubes, connected by thousands of wires on boards, and consumed 180,000 watts of electrical power! It was said that the inhabitants of Philadelphia, the location of the ENIAC, knew when the ENIAC was turned on, because their lights would briefly dim.

ENIAC's most glaring flaw was that to program it to perform different computations someone had to unplug and replug hundreds of wires into boards. It was programmable, but tediously so! A mathematician, John von Neumann, looked over the shoulders of the engineers creating the ENIAC and suggested some improvements. Von Neumann demonstrated that a computer with a simple structure (similar to the one depicted in figure 1.2 above) could execute any kind of computation by means of *programs read and stored in memory*—hence, the **stored program machine**. This had two substantial advantages: (1) no longer would reprogramming require tedious modifications of wiring or hardware; (2) instead of accessing a card in a deck, the control unit accesses a location in memory—much faster! Von Neumann also specified a special type of machine instruction, the "conditional control transfer" (a kind of branch), and showed how to invoke subprograms: by interrupting a program, storing the machine's current state in memory, and restoring its state some time later. Frequently used subprograms did not have to be reprogrammed but could be kept intact in libraries of punched cards—just as Babbage had planned a century before—and later read into a computer's main memory. Babbage's dream had come true.

The designers of the first stored-program computer, the EDVAC, used these techniques to radically simplify its design. With just 2500 tubes, it could compute several times faster than and was far more flexible than the ENIAC. ENIAC showed the viability of electronic computing. Users were literally lining up to run scientific number-crunching jobs—only it took many hours to set up each job. Yet few people saw much of a demand for many of these machines. The first computer company—founded by J. Presper Eckert and John W. Mauchly, the two engineers who designed ENIAC—foundered. What market would there be for such expensive number-crunchers?

Exercise 1.8: How were von Neumann's design and the EDVAC an advance on the ENIAC?

1.3.4 Bits and Bytes

ENIAC actually computed with decimal values, but most subsequent computers have used binary values. Computer memory is like a vast grid of switches, each of which can only be in one of two states: on or off, 1 or 0. Each binary value is called a **bit** (short for **bi**nary dig**it**). Strings of bits can represents all manner of things: from numbers and characters to colors and sounds.

Babbage's punch cards illustrate how bit string encoding works. As we saw in figure 1.1, the pattern representing an "add" instruction was three holes followed by a non-hole. We can also represent this pattern as "1110", where a '1' is a hole and a '0' is a non-hole. Similarly, we can represent each of the other instructions by a distinct binary code.

Next, let's consider numbers. You are familiar with decimal numbers, in base$_{10}$. Each position represents a power of 10. So the decimal number $235_{10} = 2*10^2 + 3*10^1 + 5*10^0 = 200 + 30 + 5$. Computers use binary numbers, in base$_2$, where each position represents a power of 10. Consider the binary number 111_2. Each place in a binary represents a power of 2: the rightmost or low order bit is 2^0 (1), the middle bit is 2^1 (2) and the leftmost or high order bit is 2^2 (4). Add them up and you get is $4 + 2 + 1 = 7_{10}$. We can thus decode our binary strings by adding up the value of each place, for each bit that is '1'. Here are some more examples:

$$001 = 0(2^2) + 0(2^1) + 1(2^0) = 0 + 0 + 1 = 1$$
$$011 = 0(2^2) + 1(2^1) + 1(2^0) = 0 + 2 + 1 = 3$$
$$101 = 1(2^2) + 0(2^1) + 1(2^0) = 4 + 0 + 1 = 5$$

How many numbers can we represent with just three bits? The answer is 2^3, or 8. In other words, with bit strings of length 3, we can represent up to 8 distinct values. That's not a lot of distinct values. With four bits, we can represent 2^4, or 16 possible values. The binary number 1011_2 is $1*2^3 + 0*2^2 + 1*2^1 + 1 + 2^0 = 8 + 0 + 2 + 1 = 11_{10}$. With bit strings of length 8, we could represent up to 2^8 or 256 distinct values. Binary $01101111_2 = 0 + 2^6 + 2^5 + 0 + 2^3 + 2^2 + 2^1 + 2^0 = 0 + 64 + 32 + 0 + 8 + 4 + 2 + 1 = 111_{10}$. Because binary or base$_2$ numbers quickly get unwieldy, it is more compact to have computers print out corresponding values in **hexa**decimal or base$_{16}$. A hexadecimal system needs 16 digits, so by convention, the letters A through F represent the hexadecimal digits corresponding to decimal values 10 through 15, e.g., $C_{16} = 12_{10}$ and $1A_{16} = 16_{10} + 10_{10} = 26_{10}$. Figure 1.5 shows some decimal values and their binary and hexadecimal (base$_{16}$) equivalents.

Decimal	Binary	Hexadecimal
1	00000001	1
2	00000010	2
4	00000100	4
10	00001010	A
11	00001011	B
15	00001111	F
16	00010000	10
26	00011010	1A

Figure 1.5: Decimal, binary and hexadecimal number systems

Exercise 1.9: What are the binary equivalents of the following decimal numbers?
a) 5_{10} b) 12_{10} c) 33_{10} d) 515_{10} e) 2050_{10}
Exercise 1.10: What is the decimal equivalent for each of the following binary numbers?
a) 00000111_2 b) 00001001_2 c) 00100000_2 d) 00100101_2 e) 10011011_2
Exercise 1.11: What is the hexadecimal equivalent for each of the binary numbers above?
Exercise 1.12: We said above that 8 bit strings can represent unsigned numeric values in the range 0 to 255. Why not 256? Alternatively it can represent signed numbers from -128 to 127. Explain how the *high order* (left-most) bit can distinguish negative from positive numbers.

Exercise 1.13: Suppose we wanted to represent just the four instructions of figure 1.1 in terms of bit strings. How long would our bit strings have to be? Hint: how many instructions are we trying to represent, in terms of powers of 2?

Exercise 1.14: Invent a binary code for representing the 26 letters of the alphabet. How many bits do you need to distinguish 26 letters? (Hint: what power of 2 is just greater than 26?)Then assign a different pattern of holes and non-holes to each letter. Show how to encode your first name in your code. By the way, how many bits are needed to distinguish UPPER from lower case?

A **byte** is a string of bits of length 8. With a byte, we can represent numbers from 0 to 255, or from -128 to 127 (including zero). Alternatively, a one byte code could represent up to 256 distinct alphabetical characters. As exercise 1.14 suggests, the actual way we encode is arbitrary. Several codes have been proposed, but nowadays everyone accepts the ASCII (American Standard Code for Information Interchange) standard. In the ASCII character set, the character 'A' is 65_{10} or 01000001_2, 'B' is 66_{10} or 01000010_2, and so forth. There are eight bits in a **byte**, enough to distinguish 2^8 or 256 possible values. Figure 1.6 gives a partial table of ASCII codes.

Decimal	Binary	ASCII	Decimal	Binary	ASCII	Decimal	Binary	ASCII
0	0000000	Null	7	0000111	Bell	9	0001001	Tab
32	0100000	Space	33	0100001	!	34	0100011	"
35	0100011	#	36	0100100	$	37	0100101	%
48	0110000	0	49	0110001	1	50	0110010	2
56	0111000	8	57	0111001	9	58	0111010	:
64	1000000	@	65	1000001	A	66	1000010	B
88	1011000	X	89	1011001	Y	90	1011010	Z
91	1011011	[	92	1011100	\	93	1011101	]
97	1100001	a	98	1100010	b	121	1111001	y
122	1111010	z	123	1111011	{	124	1111011		

Figure 1.6: Partial table of ASCII codes[4]

Exercise 1.15: Using figure 1.6, determine the decimal ASCII codes for the character '@', the digit '2', the letter 'Y' and the letter 'y'. Why does ASCII have different codes for 'Y' and 'y'?

Exercise 1.16: Go to a PC, start up an MS-DOS command window, and press the following key combinations: Ctrl-A, Ctrl-H, Ctrl-I, Ctrl-M. Note what happens for each one and explain.

Exercise 1.17 (*explore*): Use a search engine (such as google.com) to find a complete ASCII code table on the web. Discuss two interesting characters encoded by ASCII and one by extended ASCII.

Exercise 1.18 (*explore*): Lest you think a code for 128 or 256 characters is enough, the **Unicode**

---

[4]The first 32 characters of the ASCII are unprintable special codes, some of which are entered by special keys or combinations of keys: e.g., 7 rings a bell, 9 encodes tab (Ctrl-I), etc. You can infer the digits and alphabetical characters from relative order, e.g., the ASCII code for the digit '3' is 51, for the letters 'C' is 67 and 'D' is 68, and the letters 'c' is 99 and 'd' is 100.

international character set uses 16 bits to distinguish 2^{16} possible characters. Why so many characters? Hint: think globally. Use a search engine (such as www.google.com) to investigate Unicode and discuss a few interesting characters that Unicode can represent (which ASCII cannot).

Exercise 1.19: The ENIAC used a ring of 10 vacuum tubes to represent a decimal digit, e.g., to represent 3 the third vacuum tube would be "on" and the remaining vacuum tubes "off." How many vacuum tubes are needed to represent the numbers 0...999? As an alternative, numbers on the ENIAC could have been represented as binary numbers, where each bit would be represented by a single vacuum tube that is either "on" or "off." How many vacuum tubes would be needed to represent the numbers 0...999 in this case?

1.3.5 Turing's Symbol Manipulators

Alan Turing, a British mathematician, envisioned the universal machine as having much greater potential than simply being a "number cruncher." He had the key idea that a computer is essentially a **symbol manipulator**, a device which *represents and processes objects as symbols*. Words and hieroglyphics are symbols, and so are numbers—representable in terms of holes in punched cards or paper tape or switches in vacuum tubes or transistors. In fact, during World War II, Turing helped design a computer that cracked secret codes of the Nazi high command. (The COLOSSUS actually preceded the ENIAC, but was itself a secret for over twenty-five years.) Code-breaking was an early concrete demonstration of arbitrary symbol manipulation.

In the 1930's, Turing and other mathematicians were interested in studying the potential of logical computation as well as its limits. Given a set of mathematical axioms, is it possible to prove computationally whether or not a statement is a theorem? To study such questions, Turing designed a class of simple abstract machines, which have come to be known as *Turing machines*.

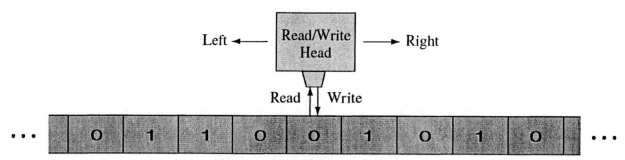

Figure 1.7: A Turing machine

Figure 1.7 depicts a Turing machine. As you can see, it's quite simple: a read/write head pointing to one square on a tape of unlimited length. Each square on the tape either contains one symbol from a specified "alphabet" or else is blank. The head is in one of a number of internal states. The machine is capable of only a few simple operations: 1) *reading* what's written on the square it points to; 2) *writing* a symbol on the current square (or erasing the current symbol); 3) *changing state* from its current internal state to another (which enables it to "remember" what it has just read); 4) *moving* the head one square to the left or the right on the tape; and 5) *halting*. Each Turing machine has a set of instructions—a program—composed from these primitive operations.

Various notations for these instructions are possible; we will present them as "4-tuples": (current-state, reading, new-state, action). So an instruction (state5, X, state3,<-) represents the instruction "if in state 5 and reading an X, then change to state 3 and perform action <-, i.e., move left one square on the tape." When a Turing machine starts (in a specified starting state), it reads the square it is pointing to, then follows whatever instruction is appropriate to that state and that symbol. In most Turing machines (called *deterministic* Turing machines), there is only one instruction for any state and any symbol, but *non-deterministic* Turing machines may have more than one instruction for any given state-symbol combination.

As a simple example, let's create a Turing machine that replaces each '1' in a binary numeral with a '0' and vice versa, using the following five rules.

(start,1,new,0); (start,0,new,1); (start,blank,start,halt);
(new,1,start,->); (new,0,start,->).

Suppose the binary numeral is 001. The machine begins in the "start" state with the head pointing to the leftmost symbol in the numeral. Here's a picture:

001
^
[start]

The second instruction is the only applicable one; it tells the machine to change its internal state to a state we have simply called "new" and replace the '0' with a '1'. The machine is now in state "new" and is looking at a 1:

101
^
[new]

Now the fourth instruction applies and tells the machine to return to state "start", and move one square to the right (i.e., to the next symbol).

101
^
[start]

The machine is again in the "start" state and is looking at the second symbol (also a '0'), so the same actions are repeated. As a result, the machine is once again in the "start" state and is looking at the third symbol (a '1').

111
^
[start]

The first instruction now applies, so the machine goes into state "new" and replaces the '1' with a '0', after which the fifth instruction applies. The machine state is changed to the "start" state again, and the head moves one square to the right.

110
^
[start]

It is now in the "start" state and is looking at a blank, so the third instruction tells the machine to halt. The original symbol string '001' has been changed to '110'.

Turing machines are not limited to binary code computations, since the squares may hold any symbol in the specified alphabet. Here's a set of rules that capitalizes the first letter of each word of a sentence, stopping at a period:

(start,a,new,A); (new,A,new,->); (new,a,new,->)
(start,b,new,B); (new,B,new,->); (new,b,new,->);

...

(start,blank,start,->); (new,blank,start,->)
(start,., start,halt); (new,.,start,->)

The ellipse, ..., implies similar rules for the other twenty-four letters of the alphabet.

Suppose we create a tape that says **a bee sees**. Then we position a head in state "start" at the first symbol on the tape, **a**. The first rule matches the situation, so changes the state to "new" and changes **a** to **A**; the second rule now applies, moving the head to the next position on the tape. The machine is now in state "new" and reading a blank, so the second rule from the last applies, changing the state to "start" and moving to the next position on the tape—i.e., the first letter of the second word. The fourth rule now applies, again changing the state to "new" and this time replacing the **b** with **B**. Now the fifth rule moves the head one position, so the machine is in state "new", looking at **e**. The fifteenth rule applies twice, moving the head to the blank between the last two words. Again, the second rule from the last applies, changing the state to "start" and moving to the next position on the tape—the first letter of the last word. The fifty-fifth rule now applies, changing the state to "new" and changing **s** to **S**. The fifty-sixth rule moves the head to the right, and then the fifteenth rule twice moves the head to the final letter, leaving the machine in state "new". The fifty-seventh rule moves the head to the next position (the period), leaving the machine in state "new". Now the machine reads the period instead of a blank, and the last rule changes the state to "start" and moves the head past the period to a blank. The next to last rule then halts the machine—"**a bee sees.**" has become "**A Bee Sees.**" Also note that this program will move the read head to the right forever if there is no period at the end of the sentence—fair punishment for poor punctuation! (Why does this happen? Hint: look at the third rule from the last.)

Exercise 1.20: Suppose that the first Turing machine is in the "start" state with an initial tape configuration of **1001**, with the head on the leftmost **1**. Trace the activity of the machine, step by step, showing how the state of the machine changes with each step, until it halts.

Exercise 1.21: The multimedia for this chapter includes a Turing machine simulation. After learning how to use it in both novice and advanced modes, implement and test the program described above, inverting binary numbers, with a starting configuration of **1001.**

Exercise 1.22: Discuss at least two things you learn about Turing machines and at least two things you learn about programming from the previous exercise.

Exercise 1.23: Here are the rules for another Turing machine, which inverts any string of **0**'s and **1**'s, as before, but only if the string is preceded by an asterisk. (i.e., if the asterisk is missing, it won't change the string.)

      (start,*,good,->); (start,1,start,->); (start,0,start,->);

      (good,1,new,0); (good,0,new,1);

      (new,1,good,->); (new,0,good,->);

      (start,blank,start,halt);(good,blank,good,halt).

Explain how this works. (Notice the changes from the earlier program. What is their function?)

Exercise 1.24: A Turing machine can use its internal states to "remember" a bit of information. Thus if you wanted to capitalize the initial letter of *every other* word, you could add another pair of states, going from "start1" to "new1", from "new1" to "start2", from "start2" to "new2", and from "new2" to "start1". Modify the program given earlier to do this. Explain how it works.

Exercise 1.25: Create a Turing machine, which given an alphabetic string between square brackets, encodes (or encrypts) it as a secret code. E.g., given an initial tape of **[secret]**, produce **[rdbqds]**. (Each letter is replaced by the previous one in the alphabet, where we assume **z** "precedes" **a**.) You may use the Turing machine simulation in the multimedia to implement and test your solution.

Exercise 1.26: The branch instruction is a crucial component of a general purpose machine, yet a Turing machine does not include branch among the capabilities of the head. How does a Turing machine get the effect of a conditional branch?

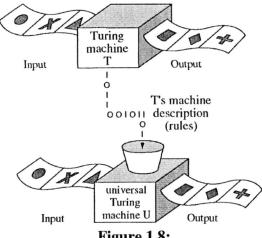

Figure 1.8:
universal Turing machine

Turing argued that these simple machines—which were not so much number crunchers as pure symbol manipulators—were capable of doing anything that is *computable*, just by steadfastly moving symbols on and off the tape. Moreover, he developed the idea of a single computational procedure (which computer scientists now call a *universal Turing machine*) which would be able to perform any computation whatsoever. Figure 1.8 may help you visualize what he had in mind.

Turing's "universal" machine, **U**, can imitate any other Turing machine, **T**. Just encode **T**'s rules onto **U**'s tape. In other words, **U** reads **T**'s rules as a program. **U** can thus simulate anything computable by any other machine **T** as a virtual machine. Turing's thesis (known as the Church-Turing thesis) is that anything computable can be computed by some Turing machine. It therefore follows that a universal Turing machine is indeed universal. It can compute anything computable.

In other words, a universal Turing machine can simulate any other computer—by running a program. It can simulate a von Neumann machine, another fairly simple machine with only a few primitive operations (but made more efficient by storing its program in high speed memory instead of a paper tape). It can simulate the processor of a Macintosh™. The simulation of the von Neumann machine or the Mac is a virtual machine. Machine **U** isn't a Mac; it's simulating one. For that matter, there's a product that lets a Macintosh simulate a PC running Windows. For that matter, both the Windows and the Macintosh environments are actually virtual machines that can run "on top of" various actual machines.

Once you think of these machines as symbol manipulators, you see that they are capable of any procedure programmable in terms of logical operations upon arbitrary symbols. Though the word *computer* still carries the connotation of a number cruncher, one now ought to think of a computer as a general purpose machine, just as capable of manipulating text or graphical images or virtual reality as integers. Indeed, a child first meeting a computer is likely to think of it as a machine that beeps, displays colors, and plays games—not at all merely a device for performing calculations. Turing described many other examples of non-numeric problems that computers could solve, such as solving jig-saw puzzles, or playing chess. Turing speculated in 1947:

> Given a position in chess the machine could be made to list all the 'winning combinations' to a depth of about three moves on either side. This . . . raises the question, 'Can the machine play chess? It could fairly easily be made to play a rather bad game. It would be bad because chess requires intelligence. . . . It is possible to make the machine display intelligence at risk of its making occasional serious mistakes. By following up this aspect the machine could probably be made to play very good chess.[5]

You can buy reasonably good chess programs for your PC today. Just as Turing imagined, much

---

[5]Lecture to the London Mathematical Society, 20 February 1947, excerpted by Andrew Hodges, *Alan Turing: The Enigma* (Simon and Schuster, 1983).

of their skill derives from exploring several "moves on either side." The best chess programs compete with grand masters by examining dozens of moves on either side, evaluating hundreds of thousands of potential configurations. Are these machines intelligent, then? This was another question that fascinated Turing, one that we explore in the chapter on Artificial Intelligence.

1.3.6 A brief history of practical universal machines

The history of the *idea* of the universal machine really ends in the 1940's, once the first actual machines based on the theoretical machines envisioned by Turing and von Neumann had been constructed. (Note that Turing's machines were mathematical abstractions, never intended as actual machines. But his theoretical work laid the foundations for the practical machines that Eckert and Mauchley and others built a decade later.) After that, the history of *computing* as a discipline and an enterprise accelerates, becoming a history of increasingly powerful and practical machines.

Turing recognized that for symbol manipulation to be useful, it has to be cheap and accessible. Programs stored on punched cards or paper tape would be too cumbersome. For the stored program machine to be practical, it needs a lot of cheap, fast, directly accessible storage:

> One needs some form of memory with which any required entry can be reached at short notice. This difficulty presumably used to worry the Egyptians when their books were written on papyrus scrolls. It must have been slow work looking up references in them, and the present arrangement of written matter in books which can be opened at any point is greatly to be preferred. We may say that storage on tape and papyrus scrolls is somewhat *inaccessible*. It takes a considerable time to find a given entry. (*Ibid.*)

In other words, practical computers need lots of **RAM** (*randomly accessible memory*)—a vast, directly accessible store. Instead of having to wind a tape forwards and backwards, a computer can read or write to any cell in RAM at the same very high speed. The first electronic computers started the computer revolution. With each cycle of computer hardware development, the price of RAM drops an order of magnitude (by a factor of 10) and the speed of processors increases an order of magnitude. (See Figure 1.9 for a comparison of orders of magnitude.)

Unit name	Number of bits	Power of two	Range of values
bit	1	2^0	2
byte	8	2^8	256
kilobyte (K)	10	2^{10}	1,024
megabyte (M)	20	2^{20}	1,048,576
gigabyte (G)	30	2^{30}	1,073,741,824
terabyte (T)	40	2^{40}	1,099,511,627,776

Figure 1.9: Comparison of bits, bytes, Ks, Megs and Gigs

The first electronic computers of the 1940's had 1,000 words of memory (each computer "word" can hold a number). By the 1950's, computers had 8,000 words, and in the 60's, IBM came out with a very successful line of **mainframe** computers with a capacity of 64,000 words. This trend accelerated further with the development and increasing availability of **microcomputers**. In the mid-1970's, Intel Corporation fueled the microprocessor revolution by making a complete processor available on a single microchip, the 4004. Until then, computers were very large, intimidating machines kept in air-conditioned inner sanctums and ministered to by specially trained operators. Putting the CPU on a chip enabled hobbyists to configure their own computers. Apple Computer and Radio Shack began introducing microcomputers to a mass market. Early Apples available in the late 1970's had 8 kilobytes of RAM memory. What are kilobytes? A **byte** is a string of eight bits, enough to distinguish 256 numerical or character values. A **kilo**byte or **K** is 2^{10} = 1024—roughly a thousand—bytes. A **mega**byte is roughly a million bytes and a **giga**byte is roughly a billion   When IBM came out with its first PC in 1981, its designers felt 64K was ample. Within a few years most PCs had 640K. There's an urban legend that Bill Gates said, "640K ought to be enough for anybody," though Microsoft's famous founder vehemently denies that now. Engineers figured out how to put thousands and then millions of bytes of memory on single components made out of silicon chips: 64K in 1985, 256K in 1987, 1M ("meg" or million bytes) in 1988, 4M in 1990. By 2000, 64M chips were commonplace, and by 2002, 256MB chips were plentiful.

Meanwhile, processor speed also began to double, and processor prices to halve about every two years. The speeds of input/output devices, such as CDROM drives and graphics screens, have similarly increased. As a result, many things that were at one time only theoretically possible because of the lack of speed or of adequate memory are now becoming practical: digitizing movies, simulating weather patterns, or recognizing human speech. Much of what Turing dreamed about has become reality.

Exercise 1.27: How much memory does your personal computer have, in bytes and in bits? (If it's a Windows PC, you can usually find out by pressing the keyboard combination Windows-Break.)
Exercise 1.28 (*explore*): How much is a terabyte? Why would anyone need that much data? Do a search with a web search engine to find a couple of applications for terabyte storage.
Exercise 1.29: Take a look at Knobby's World—it's accessible from the multimedia for *The Universal Computer* via the Tools button, or the Knobby icon in *The Universal Computer* folder. When Knobby appears on the scene, press the Run button to watch him carry a flag to the top of the mountain. Then press Reset to restore his initial state and press the Step button repeatedly to observe how he accomplishes his task. What sequence of primitive instructions does he use to pick up the flag? How is Knobby's specific program somewhat like the program of a Turing machine? What are his primitive instructions? How are they similar to those of a Turing machine?

1.4 Anatomy of a Computer

We now look at the components and structure of a personal computer. (The multimedia corresponding to this section will help you visualize this material.) The **hardware** or *physical components* of the machine include the central processing unit (CPU), the memory, and the peripheral input and output devices. The **CPU** or **processor** is the heart of the machine: it fetches instructions from memory and executes them, and thus *performs logical and arithmetic computations and controls the flow of data* between main memory and peripheral devices. Looking back at figure 1.2, the inner box—showing the instruction pointer, control unit, data registers and primitive operations—is a simple sketch of a CPU. The **registers** are *high-speed* but relatively expensive *storage*, fast enough to keep up with the processor. Much of the activity of the CPU is transferring data from slower **main memory** (RAM or Random Access Memory) to registers and back. The Analytical Engine had mechanical registers, the ENIAC had vacuum tube registers, and modern computers have very small transistors etched into silicon wafers. Unlike the ENIAC, a von Neuman or stored program machine loads its programs from external files (at first on punch cards and later on disk drives) into memory. Once a program has been loaded into memory, the **instruction pointer** (or program address register) *holds the address of the next machine instruction in memory*. The CPU runs the following cycle:

fetch the next instruction from memory;
decode the instruction (some binary code corresponds to some instruction);
execute the corresponding hardwired primitive operations.

The primitive operations manipulate data in the registers, much as the head of a Turing machine manipulate data in the squares of a tape—the obvious difference is that a modern CPU and its registers are much faster. Faster CPUs run the above cycle more times per second. In the 90's processor speeds were typically in the millions of cycles per seconds (mega-hertz or MHz), but with the turn of the century processor speeds were measured in GHz or billions of cycles per second.

The CPU is connected by a bundle of electrical lines called a **bus** that *allows the transfer of data among the CPU, main memory, and peripheral devices.* **Peripheral devices** are so called because they stand outside the heart of the machine, yet they are the primary means of *getting information into and out of the computer.* Some devices just provide **input** to the machine, including the **keyboard**, which transmits characters to the CPU, the **mouse** and other **pointing devices** (such as trackballs, pens and touchpads), which track coordinates corresponding to locations on a screen, **scanners** and optical character readers (OCRs), which convert images into digital signals, and **microphones** which convert sounds into digital signals. Other devices only produce output, such as **monitors** (also called displays or screens) which display characters or graphical images, **printers,** which provide hard copy of data, and **speakers,** which produce audible output. To help a CPU process increasing amounts and complexity of data from these devices, many computers have special purpose processors (actually small, dedicated computers) such as video and sound cards. Special purpose programs, called *drivers*, help the CPU communicate with these devices. Finally, some devices can go both ways, providing either input or output. A **floppy disk drive** can read from or write to a diskette. These disks let you carry your data around with you. Early versions were called "floppies" because they once were flexible. Nowadays, diskettes are firm and hold 1.44M (megabytes) of data. Before you can use a disk, you must **format** it, preparing it for use. Figure 1.10 depicts how diskettes (as well as hard drives) are formatted.

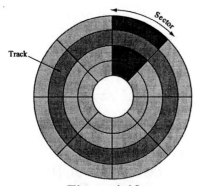

**Figure 1.10:
Format of a diskette**

This simplified drawing shows an organization of four concentric **tracks**, each with eight **sectors**. This organization enables the device to find data as requested. A typical diskette has 40 to 1024 tracks and hundreds of sectors. Once a diskette is in a drive bay, a motor spins it very rapidly, and a magnetic **read/write "head"** *detects the presence or absence of magnetic marks* on the surface of the disk. A **hard disk drive** stores information in a manner similar to diskettes. They are usually fixed inside the machine (though it is now possible to obtain portable hard drives) and contain far more data than floppies: anywhere from 10M to 100G (gigabyte or billion bytes) or more. Instead of just one disk, a hard drive consists of a stack of disks (or platters) and multiple read/write heads. An alternative to the electromagnetic technology of diskettes and hard disks is optics (light). Instead of detecting magnetic charges, optical storage devices detect the reflection of lasers by pits on the surfaces of platters. A **CDROM** (Compact Disc Read Only Memory) is a write-once, read-many disk; that is, a relatively expensive device writes data onto the platter just once, then less expensive CDROM drives can read it as many times as you like. CDROM disks can hold far more data than floppies or magnetic disks—over 600M in the early 1990's; DVDs introduced in the late 90's can hold nearly an order of magnitude more. As with all computer technology, the devices for writing on CDROM disks have dropped in price. At the same time the technology for creating compact disks improved so that they could be rewritten. Now, **CD-RW** (Compact Disk-ReWritable) devices are commonly included with a PC. CDROMs and DVDs are the medium of choice for delivering large amounts of data, such as multimedia.

Other input/output devices enable computers to communicate with each other. A **modem** (modulator-demodulator) transmits a computer's digital information across ordinary analog telephone lines. Figure 1.11 illustrates how modems let a pair of computers communicate. On the sending side, one modem converts digital information into analog form and puts it on the line. The other modem converts analog information back into digital form for the receiving computer. When two modems connect (usually with a loud hiss), the two sides must agree on the speed at which they will exchange data. Newer modems are capable of ever faster baud rates (a **baud rate** measures bits per second), jumping from 300 baud of the mid-80's to 56K baud in the mid-90's.

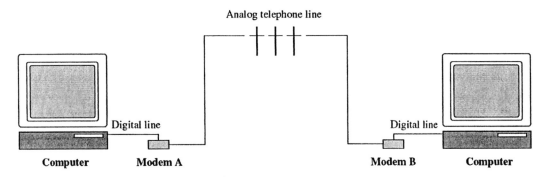

Figure 1.12: Communication between two modems

Even faster communication between machines is possible if high speed lines transmit digital information. Computers connected by high speed wires form **local area networks (LANs)**, allowing them to share relatively expensive resources such as large disk drives, printers or connections to computers elsewhere. Networks of computers talking to other networks of computers give rise to **wide area networks** (WANs). The **Internet** is a very large WAN that spread rapidly around the globe. Another chapter covers computer networks in more detail.

Exercise 1.30: What was a key advance of the stored program machine architecture, realized in the EDVAC? What does the instruction pointer do?

Exercise 1.31: What is the processor speed of your personal computer, in MHz or GHz, and in CPU cycles per second? (If it's a Windows PC, you can usually find out by pressing the keyboard combination Windows-Break.)

Exercise 1.32: After studying the **Anatomy of a Computer** section of the multimedia for this chapter, introduce yourself to a nearby actual machine. Make a list of as many of its components as you can find and describe in a sentence or two what each component can do for you.

Exercise 1.33: Investigate the connection speed of a PC in your house, dorm or campus. You can get an idea of optimal performance, in Windows™, by clicking **Start**, pointing to **Settings**, clicking on **Control Panel**, then **Network and Internet Connections**. To get a better idea of actual throughput, try using a file transfer program such as ws_ftp™, and note its report of how many bytes per second it transfers.

1.5 Faces of the Computer

The "face" of a computer is more than just the screen and keyboard—some of the hardware of the previous section. It's really the **software**—the programs that a computer reads into memory and executes--that enables you to interact with the machine. The earliest computers, despite flashing light bulbs put on some machines for show, were not designed for easy use. Early computers only allowed **batch processing**, processing just one program at a time. Though this was fine for many applications, a need arose for **interactive processing**, in which a machine responds to users while executing a program. With the emergence of personal computers, putting machines on the desks of schoolchildren and salespeople, a need also emerged for "friendlier" interfaces: enter Macintosh, Windows, Linux, etc.

Behind each of these interfaces is an **operating system (OS)**, *a program that manages the resources of a computer system.* An OS is a fairly powerful and complex program, doing everything from managing access to memory and controlling access to input/output devices to running system commands and other applications programs for users and other programs. Even in batch processing environments, there is a need for an OS to efficiently schedule a queue (sequence) of jobs. With interactive programs there developed an even greater need for automatic system management. After all, why should a computer wait around idly while a user is typing with one finger or even just scratching his or her head? It could just as well switch its attention to other tasks—this OS capability is called **multitasking**. Of course, if a machine has too many tasks or too many users, its services will bog down, rather like a waiter in a very busy restaurant, spending more time running between patrons and spending little time actually serving the patrons. You'll learn more about how operating systems work in another chapter.

Larger machines, such as mainframe computers handling airline transactions for hundreds of travel agents around the country, are **multiuser** systems. Workstations running the **Unix™** operating system also allow *many users*—such as students on a college campus—*to "log in" and share their resources* across a network. A personal computer, on the other hand, is usually assumed to be dedicated to a single user. **MS-DOS™** (Microsoft Disk Operating System), an operating system introduced along with the IBM PC (making a fortune for Microsoft and its founder, Bill Gates), assumes a single user will just do one thing at a time. We'll call it "DOS" for short.

Operating systems interact with users via an **interface**, *part of a program that performs tasks at the request of a user.* The multimedia associated with this section will give you a hands-on demonstration of two general kinds of "faces" that you will encounter on computers: command-line interfaces, such as older DOS or Unix systems and graphical user interfaces, such as Macintosh™ or Windows™. Here we will focus on DOS, because it is easier to explain in text than a graphical interface and because it is available from all Windows platforms. A **command-line interface** is *line-oriented, accepting one command per line* (ending with pressing the Return or Enter key).[6]

---

[6]In Windows 2000 or XP, we recommend that you launch DOS by pointing your mouse at the *start* button, then selecting **Run...**, then enter **cmd**. A feature of **cmd** processor is that it lets you cycle

The system displays a **prompt**—*a signal that the system is waiting for user input*—at the beginning of a line, something like this:

```
C:\ >_
```

To get the machine to do something, a user types in a **command** (shown in bold-face type):

```
C:\>format a: _
```

The DOS command interpreter will then attempt to format a floppy diskette in the drive labeled a: (thus preparing the diskette for further use via DOS).

A few years after MS-DOS came out, Apple Computer™ introduced the Macintosh™, with an OS that supported multitasking as well as a **graphical user interface (GUI)**, *in which a user interacts with graphical objects displayed on a screen using a mouse* or similar pointing device. Microsoft™ imitated this "look-and-feel" in the Windows™ system, and X windows (distributed by MIT) provided a foundation for portable GUIs for Unix-based systems. A GUI system displays on its screen (which one may think of as a metaphorical "desktop") a set of **icons**, *small graphical images intended to suggest their association with particular computer functions or applications*. For example, a Macintosh "trash can" icon suggests a place where one can dispose of unwanted data. (Windows 95™ remodeled this icon as a recycling bin.) The mouse activates behaviors associated with icons. For example, clicking on a Macintosh trash can reveals its contents—just in case you want to drag something back out.

The OS controls access to a computer's input/output devices, responds to commands entered via the keyboard, displays responses on the monitor, maintains data on disk drives, etc. Many OS commands enable users to organize information on disk drives into **files**, each of *which names a contiguous block of data*. For example, the file named CMD.EXE holds the DOS command interpreter itself. Since this (and most files ending with the extensions .COM or .EXE) is a **binary**, *computer-executable program*, humans will find its contents quite unreadable. A file named README.TXT (supposing such a file happened to exist on your C: drive) would probably be a **text file**, *containing humanly readable information*, which you could examine by entering the command:

```
C:\>type readme.txt
```

or   `C:\>type readme.txt|more`

The DOS command type displays the contents of a file on the monitor. If your file is too big to be displayed in one screen, the second line above shows how to get type to display one screenful at a time. The vertical bar, |, is a **pipe**, so that the output of one program is input to another; in this case the output of type as the input of more.

Because there may be hundreds of files on a computer's hard drive, modern operating systems provide a way to organize them into **directories** (also called **folders**). This is analogous to how businesses organize printed information: manila folders are arranged into drawers, which are in turn filed in cabinets. Computer files are like the manila folders, subdirectories are like drawers, and directories are like cabinets. In fact, *directory systems allow users to organize data in files hierarchically*, as deeply as one likes, just as one could conceivably organize cabinets into closets, and closets into rooms, and rooms into storehouses.... In DOS, the C:\ prompt tells the user that DOS is currently looking at the root or top-level directory. Here are a few DOS commands showing some things you can do with directories (if you are a DOS novice, you might want to get on a computer and try this):

---

through a history of previous commands by using the up and down arrows, and to edit commands using the right and left arrows.

1	`C:\>dir`	(lists content of root **dir**ectory)
2	`C:\>md mydir`	(**m**akes a new subdirectory called `mydir`)
3	`C:\>cd mydir`	(**c**hanges **d**irectory to `mydir`)
4	`C:\mydir>dir`	(lists content of `mydir`—now, empty)
5	`C:\mydir>md mysubdir`	(creates another subdirectory under `mydir`)
6	`C:\mydir>cd mysubdir`	(change focus to `mysubdir`)
7	`C:\mydir\mysubdir>copy \windows\win.ini`	(**copy** a file from another directory)
8	`C:\mydir\mysubdir>dir`	(now `mysubdir` has one file in it)
9	`C:\mydir\mysubdir>del *.*`	(**del**ete all files in `mysubdir`)
10	`C:\mydir\mysubdir>dir`	(now `mysubdir` again has no files in it)
11	`C:\mydir\mysubdir>cd ..`	(shifts up one directory level to `mydir`)
12	`C:\mydir\mysubdir>rd mysubdir`	(**r**emove **d**irectory `mysubdir`—*must be empty*)
13	`C:\mydir>cd \`	(shifts from anywhere to root directory)
14	`C:\rd mydir`	(**r**emove **d**irectory `mydir`—*cleaned up*)

The `dir` command on the first line will display a list of all the files in the "root" directory. Each line contains additional information about each file: its name, size (in bytes), and time of its creation or most recent modification. A line that says <DIR> indicates that this is the name of a subdirectory. The `md` (or `mkdir`, for "make a directory") command on the second line creates a new subdirectory, whose name shall be `mydir`. The `cd` (for "change directory") `mydir` command changes the active directory down to `mydir`—notice that the DOS prompt changes to show the current directory. The fourth line creates yet another subdirectory called mysubdir under `mydir`, and the fifth line shifts down to that directory. Now the prompt, `C:\mydir\mysubdir>`, shows a "path" down from the root directory, `\`, through `mydir` to `mysubdir`. The `dir` command shows that this new subdirectory has no files yet. The `copy \windows\win.ini` command makes a copy of file `win.ini` from the `windows` directory and puts it in the subdirectory, as the following `dir` command shows. (You could use `type win.ini` or `notepad win.ini` to see what it contains.) Saying `cd ..` goes back "up" a level in a hierarchy of directories; saying `cd \` always returns to the root directory. The `del` command deletes a file or files; the `*.*` uses a "wild card" notation, where `*` matches any pattern. To delete all files in the current directory, type `del *.*`. Careful, this could be catastrophic! The `rd` (or `rmdir`, for "remove a directory") command tries to delete a directory (the `del` command deletes a *file*), but in this case, it will not do so because the directory `mydir` is not empty. You must delete its contents first, and before you can do that you must delete the contents of `mysubdir`.

Needless to say, these commands only scratch the surface of the capabilities of DOS, let alone the more powerful capabilities of other operating systems.

Exercise 1.34: Work through and describe, step by step, two different ways to copy a text file to a new directory or folder on a floppy drive, to view the directory, and finally to print the file, one by using commands in DOS and another by interacting with icons in Windows. What are some pros and cons of these two methods?

Exercise 1.35: After starting DOS from Windows with **cmd**, enter **dir /?** to display a description of the command and its options (or switches). For many DOS commands running in the **cmd** processor, **/?** is an option that displays a helpful description. Describe a few interesting options of **dir** or other commands and how you might use them.

Exercise 1.36: Holding down one key then pressing another key trigger special functions in a GUI. In Windows, what do the following key combinations do: Alt-Tab, Ctrl-Esc? Many Windows PCs come with a special Windows key—what do these key combinations do: Windows-D, Windows-E, Windows-F, Windows-R, Windows-F1? When or why might these short-cuts be useful?

Exercise 1.37: The authors freely admit their bias towards Windows—our bias is not necessarily indicate a preference, just what's most widely available on our campus. If another GUI is available to you, such as Macintosh or a GUI running on top of Linux, how does it accomplish some of the functions described in this subsection? How does it let you create, copy and delete files and folders (or directories)? Is a command-line interface available? Is there an on-line help system and if so what are some things you learn from it? Are there useful short-cuts for common functions? Which GUI do you prefer, and why?

Exercise 1.38: What happens when you put a file in a trash can or recycle bin of a desktop GUI? What's the difference when you use the `del` command in DOS? Why is it important to be aware of this difference? Is there a way to get the effect of `del` in Windows Explorer? (If you don't know, in press Start then Help, or Windows-F1, to investigate.)

Exercise 1.39: Suppose you want to buy a new PC and you are wondering whether to invest in a faster processor or more memory. People who know would usually advise you to get more memory. Why? Hint: think about what a modern OS typically does, such as multi-tasking and virtual memory.

Chapter review. Are the following statements true or false? Explain why or why not.

a) A universal machine can perform any task without anyone specifying how it is done.

b) A universal machine basically just crunches numbers and spits out fractions.

c) Automation is great for tedious, error-prone activities.

d) A stored program machine stores programs in its central processing unit (CPU).

e) A computer is hard-wired to perform thousands of different primitive instructions.

f) A branch instruction stores a value in a machine's instruction pointer.

g) A digital computer stores information in bits, which are on/off states.

h) A Turing machine has a powerful "head" which reads a finite tape faster than a speeding bullet.

i) A universal Turing machine can simulate any other Turing machine as a virtual machine.

j) RAM is a major practical improvement of modern computers over Turing machines.

k) A byte is a string of 2^8 or 256 bits.

l) The CPU executes instructions that are not hard-wired into a machine.

j) A keyboard, mouse, monitor, printer, microphones, modems, etc., are all peripheral devices.

k) A floppy disk is ready for use as soon as you take it out of the box, just like pizza.

l) A CDROM is a write-once, read-many times medium.

m) A modem converts bits into analog form for transfer over a telephone line.

n) The Internet is a LAN.

o) An operating system is hardware that controls the physical devices of a machine.

p) An operating system is just the program that executes commands at the request of a user.

q) A multitasking operating system will let many users interact with a machine at once.

r) A command-line interface typically displays a prompt and waits for a user to enter input.

s) Macintosh™ and Windows™ are convenient command-line interfaces.

t) A file is a unit of data stored on a peripheral device such as a floppy disk.

u) Computers execute programs stored in text files.

v) Directory systems organize data in files hierarchically.

Summary

The **universal machine** is a general purpose symbol-manipulating machine, capable of anything one can express as a program—an organized sequence of logical steps. Babbage envisioned a machine that would perform any logical computation automatically. His machine anticipated the design of a modern computer, distinguishing the "mill" (now called a **central processing unit** or **CPU**) from the "store" (**memory**). He also saw that one built-in instruction should be a **branch**, enabling the machine to make simple decisions that could lead it to different points in its program, possibly looping back to an earlier point. Alan Turing later provided a formal description of a simple kind of program and argued that such programs could perform any computational task. He also showed that a single program of this kind could do the work of any other program, thus introducing the concept of a universal machine and showing both its extraordinary capabilities and limitations. He also emphasized that such a machine could be thought of as more than a mere number cruncher, since it can manipulate anything that can be represented by arbitrary **symbols**. A number is a symbol, but so is a string of letters in a secret code or a mailing address or a position on a chess board. John von Neumann, observing the design of the ENIAC, proposed the design of a **stored program machine**, which would store the program(s) as well as data in memory.

Modern computers are **digital** machines, representing information as discrete on/off states or **bits**. A **byte** is eight bits, enough to distinguish 256 numerical or character values, as it does in the extended **ASCII character set**. The computer revolution has been fueled both by the rapid expansion of memory capacity and by the rapid increase of processing speed. Today's computers have random access memory (**RAM**) capacities on the order of many millions of bytes ("megabytes") and hard drives and CDROMs that can store hundreds of megabytes to gigabytes. Modems of the mid-90's could transmit data across telephone lines nearly 100 times faster than they could ten years earlier. Direct digital connections transmitting data thousands of times faster have become the main trunks of the "information highway," through which networks of machines can share complex data such as formatted chapters of books or continuous video.

Running inside all this physical **hardware** is much more malleable **software**, the programs that a stored program machine reads into memory and executes. The **operating system (OS)** is a program that operates a computer system: managing access to memory, controlling access to input/output devices, and executing system commands and other application programs for users and other programs. Though early OS's emphasized **batch processing**, efficiently scheduling a queue of jobs, **interactive processing** between machine and users has become much more important. These days the first thing you may associate with an OS is its user interface. DOS, like Unix and other earlier operating systems, features a **command line interface (CLI)**. Macintosh and Microsoft Windows have popularized icon- and mouse-based **graphic user interfaces (GUI)**. Behind the friendlier face, much remains the same, such as a hierarchical organization of data into directories of files. Nevertheless, when it comes to the universal computer, expect change! Out of the bit stream emerge symbols and programs, graphical representations of fractal computations and pictures from interplanetary robots, icons and voices and music, and more sound and fury. Who knows what will emerge next out of the bit stream?

Chapter 2
Problem Solving *Before* Programming
"Set up the tabernacle according to the plan shown you on the mountain."
Exodus 26:30

Computers are useful because they help us solve problems. To be effective, though, a computer needs a *program*—a precise description of what it is supposed to do. Getting a computer program to do what you want it to do is another problem! So effective problem solving is probably the most important skill a person needs to use a computer; indeed, it is extremely useful for getting things done in life generally.

Finding a solution to an interesting problem can be compared to a journey: in this chapter, we explore the notion of a *problem space*. You determine what you are starting with (the *givens*), where you are headed (the *goals*), and what resources or moves will get you from here to there. After these preliminaries, we'll examine three distinct approaches to problem solving: *hacking* or trial-and-error, *analytical* or breaking things down, and *analogical* or object-oriented. Along the way, you'll encounter some puzzles and other problems which will provide some food for thought. Along the way, we'll introduce Knobby's World, to give you some practice applying the problem solving strategies of this chapter and also give you a gentle introduction to the art of programming.

But don't skip ahead to programming Knobby! A major goal of this chapter is to convince you that the more time you spend in problem solving *before* you start coding, the less overall time it will take to get the software to work properly.

2.1 Problem solving strategies

People actually have many different styles or approaches to problem solving. We see this, for example, in the different ways in which characters solve mysteries in detective stories. The mystery novels of Agatha Christie exemplify three styles of problem solving. (If you aren't an Agatha Christie fan, just think of similar characters in the mystery genre, such as Perry Mason, Columbo or any of a myriad of imitators of Sherlock Holmes.) Christie's Belgian detective M. Hercule Poirot, like Sherlock Holmes, reasons **analytically**, putting together little clues logically. When he solves a case, he presents a solution by carefully laying out the evidence so that it points with an irrefutable logic at the culprit. Such powers of careful reasoning amaze the reader. Similarly, when Holmes says, "It's elementary, my dear Watson," Watson is nonetheless impressed, wondering not so much at the simple explanation as at the process that led to this solution. You may not be a Poirot or a Holmes, but you can learn some of their skills. It takes patience and discipline.

On the other hand, Miss Jane Marple solves problems by **analogy**. Something about a mysterious case may remind her of someone in her village, St. Mary Mead. "That reminds me of my Uncle Henry..." Then she draws parallels between the new case and the old memory and makes inferences about the new case based upon the similarities and differences between the cases. Analogy guides her problem solving, allowing her to discover the hidden meaning of clues. Similarly, lawyers reason by comparing a new case to old ones that have set precedents. They then reason about the differences between the cases, so that they adapt what they know about the old case to account for the new one. In this way, reasoning by analogy starts with retrieving from memory and continues with structural adaptation to new situations. Like reasoning by logical analysis, it is an acquired skill, developed by building up a memory of relevant cases and learning to adapt them.

Yet a third kind of mystery story plot is one in which the leading characters Tommy and Tuppence Beresford more or less stumble through an adventure, making guesses here and there, and somehow surviving many exciting, life-threatening scrapes, until they finally come to understand what has been going on. This problem-solving strategy is often called **trial-and-error**, or in "computerese," **hacking**. To be fair, it's useful to distinguish between **blind** and **informed** hacking. If you don't know what you are doing, hacking can be dangerous. It's not so bad if you're just trying to hack through a bush, but you might not want to machete through a jungle on your own. Hacking, or just trying out things to see if they work, is OK if you're an Indiana Jones of software (there are a few successful "hackers" who enjoy going where no one has ever gone before) and you're willing to risk lots of time stumbling into dark holes, or if you know you're dealing with a small problem. If the problem is complex, you probably want to plan ahead, take stock of your supplies, and if you don't have a map, make one!

"We don't know WHAT we're makin' yet. We just started."

Figure 2.1: Hacking—no plan, no predicting the outcome

Exercise 2.1: Although people often use all of these strategies, they generally tend to favor one of them or another. What problem solving strategy do you typically use? Think of a problem that you have been working on recently and describe how you went about solving it, step by step. Is your problem solving strategy like any of those just described? If so, which one(s) and how so?

2.2 Algorithms: paths through "problem space"

Before the writing the code for a program to solve a problem one must think of an **algorithm**—*a precise specification of a behavior intended to solve a well-defined problem.* Coding then translates an algorithm into a particular programming language, resulting in a **program**, *an expression of an algorithm that a computer can perform.* As the machine executes a program, it will carry out the described behavior as a sequence of simple steps or instructions. So, many introductory textbooks define "algorithm" using words like "a finite sequence of steps." But a "sequence of steps" is a rather superficial view of algorithms. Beneath the surface of a sequence there is an underlying structure, often a rather complex one, sometimes with as many surprising turns and parallels as a good mystery novel. That's what makes algorithm development challenging and interesting.

Let's illustrate this idea of a structure underlying a sequence by considering a sentence:

Dagwood loves his lovely wife.

Superficially, a sentence is a sequence of words, in this case five of them, separated by spaces or punctuation marks. Yet there is much more behind the scenes. The individual *words* have an internal structure (called morphology); for example, 'loves' is from the stem 'love' plus an inflectional affix '-s'. The *sentence* has yet more unseen structure, based on the order of its words. This is called the *syntax* of the sentence. Grammarians represent a syntactic structure with a tree like that shown in Figure 2.2.

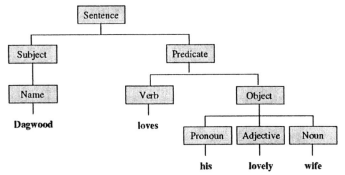

Figure 2.2: A structure ("parse tree")

Something like this structure allows you to understand how these words combine to form the sentence's meaning. Some of this meaning comes from the words in the sentence itself, but much of it comes from inferences from background knowledge. Do you happen to know the name of Dagwood's lovely wife? Finally, some of the meaning comes from the purpose or intention of the person who spoke or wrote this sentence. Maybe it was to point out something, maybe it was to ask or answer a question, etc. But the syntax contributes a great deal to how we understand the meaning.

Exercise 2.2: Draw a syntactic tree for "His lovely wife loves Dagwood." What's the difference in the meanings of the two sentences? How is this related to the difference in the syntactic structures?

So an apparently "simple" sentence actually may possess a quite complicated underlying structure.[1] Similarly, underlying the sequence of steps in a computer program is a more complex conceptual structure. When solving a problem you must develop and design the *purpose* and *structure* of an algorithm before you can generate an actual sequence of steps.

Looking back at our definition of algorithm, take note of the modifiers *precise* and *well-defined*. An algorithm must specify a behavior in such a way that at any point, there is no doubt about what should be done or how to do it. So a recipe instruction that says "season to taste" would fail on these criteria. What seasonings should be used and how much? This is not precise. What does "to taste" mean? This is not well-defined. (Not unless we are specifying for a virtual machine with the palate of a chef!) It is often remarkably difficult to specify a desired behavior in an algorithmic way. Before attempting to describe the behavior which we would like our algorithm to perform, though, we need to clearly define the problem it is supposed to solve.

---

[1]Natural language processing (NLP) is a field of computer science which is related to linguistics. It tries to enable computers to analyze or generate sentences by incorporating these various aspects of grammatical structure. We'll come back to NLP in our chapter on Artificial Intelligence.

Exercise 2.3: Try this one with a friend. Hang a jacket over the back of a chair. Each of you write a precise, step by step procedure for the other to put on the coat. Then each of you play "dumb robot" that only follows explicit, clear, unambiguous instructions. (It's more fun, and instructive, if the robot is very literal-minded.) If your instructions are not fool-proof, try revising them once and running them again. Hand in both versions. (By the way, this exercise is very much a part of real world software development. A **structured walkthrough**—*describing an algorithm out loud to peers*—often helps developers discover possible errors or missing steps in a software design.)

2.2.1 Givens, Goals, and Resources

Even before specifying the behavior that we would like our algorithm to perform, we need to define the problem we want the algorithm to solve. What, then, is a *well-defined problem*? If you ask a friend what one of his or her problems is, you'll typically get an answer like "I can't sleep," or "I'm doing badly in school," or "I can't pay all my bills," and so forth. Notice what all these answers have in common. They are all declarative statements—claims about the way things *are* (or at least the way the problem-sufferer thinks they are). As important as these statements are, they are only a part of a problem, a part we call the **givens** (or *initial conditions*) of the problem. There is more that goes into the definition of a problem than the givens, since there may be many quite different problems in which the given is just that "I can't sleep." Not being able to sleep may not be a problem for a night watchman, and only a minor one for a small child waiting to see Santa Claus, but can be a catastrophe the night before an important job interview.

In fact, a problem arises only when the givens conflict with a problem solver's **goals**, or *desired state*. If the givens describe the way things *are*, then the goals are statements about the way they *should* be. So a problem consists of at least a pair of things—a set of givens and a set of goals, which are different from the givens. (If there's not much difference, it's not very much of a problem.) Achieving the goal(s) is when a problem solver can stop—or go on to the next problem.

Suppose you wake up thirsty one night and you want a glass of water. OK, your solution is just to get up and get a drink. But it's quite a different problem for someone lying all trussed up in a hospital bed! So a third component of a problem is the set of **resources**: *the means or methods that can transform a problem state in order to move, step by step, from givens to goal(s)*. They can be of many sorts: in a game, they are the possible moves; in preparing a meal, they are the available ingredients; in designing an electronic circuit, they are the components and connections. If you are using a machine to do something, your resources are the operations that it can perform. For example, with the nine or twelve buttons on a microwave oven, you can transform raw, cool or frozen into cooked, hot or thawed. In computer programming, the lowest-level resources are the small number of basic instructions that the computer can perform. (As we shall later see, hardware and software engineers assemble these into more complex resources that become building blocks for other problem solvers.) Thus, differences in givens or differences in goals or differences in resources make different problems.

2.2.2 Knobby's World

If you've been able to use the multimedia software, then you've met Knobby the Knowbot. He looks like a cross between a "Cone Head" (friendly and handy for pointing out things) and Mr. Spock (the green-blooded, pointy-eared, very logical science officer of *Star Trek* fame). We introduce Knobby to help you think precisely about problem solving (and elsewhere other computing concepts). Knobby is a relative of *Karel the Robot*, an invention of Richard E. Pattis (John Wiley & Sons, 1981, 1995). Like Karel, Knobby's mission is to give people "a gentle introduction to programming" and great ideas of computing. Knobby is a little different from Karel, however, because Knobby's creators (Blank and Barnes) want him to help them teach a slightly different set of concepts.[2] Knobby and his creators nevertheless acknowledge a debt to Karel and Pattis.

Knobby lives in a simple grid-like world. It does not have much depth. Indeed, it is a flat land, with straight, impenetrable **boundaries** on all sides, and a criss-cross of **streets** (running east and west) and **avenues** (running north and south), along which Knobby may travel. However, Knobby cannot penetrate his north or west boundaries. If you try to make him, he'll just crash (a "run-time error"). As you can see, Knobby himself is currently resting at the corner of 1st Street and 1st Avenue, with his head pointing north.

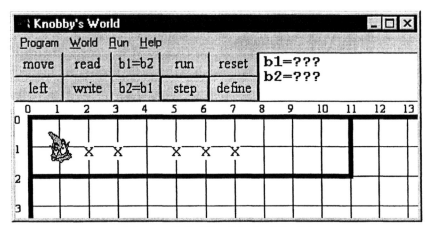

Figure 2.3: Knobby's World

Knobby's World can also have **walls**. Shown as thicker lines (red on the computer), walls are impenetrable to Knobby, like the boundaries of his world. (Knobby may, however, be able to go *around* walls.) Wall sections can line up to form buildings, doors or rough terrain. In Figure 2.3, the wall sections frame the problem space. Also, on occasion, certain **characters** appear in Knobby's World. These simple folk are in fact characters like those on a keyboard. Like Knobby, they always stand at street corners. In Figure 2.3, two sequences of 'X' characters could represent the numbers 2 and 3. As we shall see, Knobby can copy them and carry these characters around to other corners in his world. A Knobby's World program, which you will learn about at the end of this chapter, will enable Knobby to execute a series of instructions that add 2 ('XX') plus 3 ('XXX') to get 5 ('XXXXX'). (You may recognize a Turing machine program from chapter 1 here.)

Since Knobby cannot set up walls, nor create new characters (though as we will see, he can copy them), walls and a cast of characters must appear as *givens* of its initial situation. A **situation** is an *exact description of an initial state* of Knobby's World. You can find various initial situations in files (with extension .sit) that can be set up and loaded into Knobby's World before he starts "knocking about," so to speak. Later on, we'll explain how to create your own situations.

Knobby, like a Turing machine, has only a small number of primitive instructions, including

---

[2]Some of the salient differences between Karel and Knobby are: a) instead of beepers, Knobby has blackboards, which correspond more directly to variables, in order to illustrate input/output and assignment in imperative languages; b) instead of Pascal, the language of Knobby's World is designed to prepare students for C++ or Java; c) Knobby lets students define new "macro" instructions by direct manipulation; and d) Knobby has a graphical user interface.

move, advancing forward one square; **left**, turning 90 degrees counter-clockwise, **read**, copying a character from a corner into one of Knobby's "slate" boards, and **write**, copying a character from his board onto a corner. Yet like Turing machines, Knobby can solve complex problems. For example, even though Knobby has no primitive instructions for arithmetic, he can nevertheless be programmed to add (or subtract, multiply, etc.).

Exercise 2.4: We have suggested that Figure 2.3 represents an addition problem. What are the givens of Knobby's World in the situation shown in Figure 2.3? Try to describe them as precisely as possible. What, precisely, is the goal of the problem of Figure 2.3? What are the resources available to solve problems in Knobby's World?

Exercise 2.5: The addition problem of Figure 2.3 is indeed very similar to an addition problem given with the Turing machine simulation in the multimedia for chapter 1. What are the differences between the way the way we represent the problem in the Turing machine vs. in Knobby's World? Are these differences significant or superficial? Explain your answer. (Note: for this exercise, just focus on the representations of the problem, not the programs that solve the problem.)

Exercise 2.6: Fixed boundaries on all sides makes it easier to implement Knobby's World within a computer's memory. How would eliminating one or two of the boundaries make Knobby's World more like a Turing machine? Hint: think about the Turing machine's tape.

2.2.3 From ill to well defined problems

Many of our daily problems are ill-defined: the givens or goals or resources (or some combination) are unclear. That's what makes them so difficult! Ideally, the problems we need to solve are *well defined*: the givens and goals and resources are all clearly defined. Since life isn't always so neat, the very *first* step in getting a computer to solve a problem (let alone a person) is to make the problem well-defined. In many "real world" programming problems, the givens and goals come from some other source—such as a client who asks a software engineer to develop an application program—while the resources are defined by the computer or the programming language or both. The first job for a software engineer (especially one known as a "systems analyst") is to help clients transform their scruffy problem descriptions into well-defined problem specifications (and then we hope the client doesn't change the specifications, but clients often do).

We can visualize problem solving in terms of the simple diagram shown in Figure 2.4:

Figure 2.4: Problems as "Black Boxes"

What are the **inputs** to a problem? The *givens*. The **outputs** are the *goals*. The box in the middle represents the solution algorithm, whose "inner workings" are a combination of the *resources*. Until we actually define the algorithm, it is a "black box"—we do not know what is inside or how it works. (That's OK for most of its users, so long as it correctly transforms givens into goals.) When we think an algorithm works, we can test it, making sure that it does accept various inputs (givens) and does transform them into expected outputs (goals).

2.2.4 Understanding the real problem

Before one can reasonably hope to develop a solution to a problem, the first task is to make sure one has stated the problem correctly. Sometimes, of course, the problem is ill-defined, so the first task is to define it properly. Often, though, the problem is stated in a way that seems to be well-defined, but in fact depends upon implicit assumptions—which may not even be true. A "blinder" effect can cause problem solvers to look at the givens, goals, and resources too narrowly, perhaps because of implicit assumptions or because we are too familiar with them. "They have eyes but do not see" (Jer 5:2, Matt 13:13). It's been said that a fish never notices the water in which it swims! Ask almost anyone what color snow is, and the answer will be "white." Actually, especially in the shade, snow often appears to have a slight blue tinge. Artists, photographers, scientists, inspirational preachers, inventive engineers, must learn to see familiar things in an unfamiliar way.

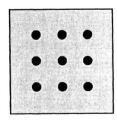

Exercise 2.7: Consider the diagram to the left. Try to draw a single line, without picking up your pen or pencil, consisting of four straight line segments, which connects all nine dots. (Are you stuck? If so, try re-examining your assumptions. Did we say that the lines have to lie *inside* the area within the box?)

Exercise 2.8: How could you connect all nine dots with just one straight line? (Think about your resources. Just what is a 'line'?)

Exercise 2.9: Using six matches or toothpicks, of exactly the same length, without bending or breaking them make four triangles of exactly the same size. (Hint: Think about what assumptions you may be unconsciously making.)

Exercise 2.10: Here's another one. Take an ordinary baseball. If you throw it in just the right way, it will slow down and stop, reverse its direction, and return to your hand. Can you do it?

Exercise 2.11: This one we recommend you do with a partner—and think aloud about what you are doing. Write down 10 uses for a brick, noting how long it takes. Do it again. (This is easy, isn't it?) Write down 10 more, again seeing how long it takes. Which list took longest to write? Why?

Exercise 2.12: Now look at your lists of uses, and write down the *properties* of a brick on which these uses depend. (Typically they will all depend on only three or four fairly obvious features: shape, mass, etc.) Now think of some quite *different* properties of a brick, and write down 10 more uses for a brick based on these properties, again seeing how long it takes. Is it getting harder or easier? Why? Are the uses getting more interesting or imaginative? Why?

Exercise 2.13: Take another look at Knobby's World in Figure 2.3, which shows how Knobby can represent natural numbers like 2 and 3. What about zero? How would Knobby compute 2+0 or 0+3? Modify Knobby's representational system so that there is an explicit way to represent zero, as well as other numbers such as 2 and 3.

Exercise 2.14: People use a positional base$_{10}$ system, apparently thanks to their ten fingers; digital computers use a positional base$_2$ system, thanks to the relative ease of making switches out of tubes or transistors. What kind of system is Knobby using in Figure 2.3?

One of the goals of the above exercises is to help you think about how you think. *Metacognition*—thinking about thinking—is a way to learn to remove the blinders of unconscious assumptions. Once you see that you have been focusing on certain features of a problem, you can look for others you may not have noticed. For the nine dots problems of exercise 2.8, you need to think outside the box—many problems require thinking "outside the box" of initial assumptions. If you have been focusing on superficial features, you can deliberately look for *structural* relationships.

In the brick problem, reflecting about uses of a brick may reveal the limitations of your initial approach, so you can go beyond them. When you're stuck (and sometimes you don't realize you are), take time to step back for another perspective, perhaps in another place, or from another person.

Once upon a time, a king asked the mathematician Archimedes to figure out whether the royal crown was pure gold or not. Shaving even a little bit off and testing it for purity, or damaging the crown in any way, was out of the question. He decided that comparing the volume of the crown with the volume of an equal weight of pure gold would help him learn whether the crown had the same density as pure gold and would thus give him the answer. But how to find the volume of the crown? Finding the volume of a regular solid would be easy, but the crown was of highly irregular shape. Finding the volume of a liquid would be straightforward, but melting a crown was not an option. What other resources were available? Pondering the problem, he took time to go to the local bathhouse. As he got in, he noticed the water, sloshing out the sides of the pool. Then he saw it: his own body's volume was displacing the same volume of water. He ran out into the streets, naked, exclaiming, "Eureka!" (That's Greek for "I found it!"). He'd just discovered how to measure volume by displacement. "Eureka!" has ever since been the cry of problem solvers (usually clothed) who, by re-examining their assumptions and looking at the problem a different way, discover a new resource for solving it.

Often in specifying a problem it is useful to devise a **notation** in which *to represent the givens, goals and resources of a problem explicitly and concisely.* A "fine-grained," detailed notation can often reveal certain crucial features of the problem on which a solution depends. Even when two forms of notation are equal in expressive power, one form may suggest a route to a solution that the other may not—the right kind of notation may help us to see things about a problem that we might not otherwise see. Suppose you got the following word problem: "An unknown quantity multiplied by *a* is nullified by *b;* what is the quantity?" Solving this word problem is difficult. Let's try re-casting it in algebraic notation: *ax + b = 0; what is x?* Now it's easier to see that, in order to find the value of *x*, we can subtract *b* from both sides to get *ax = -b*, and then divide both sides by *a* to get *x = -b/a.* The algebraic notation really makes it much easier to solve this problem, doesn't it?[3] So you can see the importance of a good notation for problem solving.

Exercise 2.15: Invent a notation to explicitly and concisely describe the givens and goals of a Knobby's World situation, then use this notation to describe the situation of Figure 2.3. (After you've come up with a notation, compare yours with the one we created for Knobby's World, described later in this chapter. Which do you like better and why?)

Exercise 2.16: Invent a notation for explicitly and concisely representing the resources available to Knobby. Then use this notation write a procedure to put an 'X' between the "XX" and the "XXX".

2.2.5 Exploring problem spaces

Once a problem is well-defined, we can think of solving it in terms of a spatial analogy. We need to find a *path* that successfully leads from where we are (the givens) to where we want to go (the goals). Finding the right path may require some exploration, since there are many possible steps one could take from any point along a path. The "points" in a problem space are **states**, *each of*

---

[3]In fact, it seems incredible that the solution of the quadratic equation $ax^2 + bx + c = 0$ was discovered before the invention of modern algebraic notation. But today, with the help of algebraic notation, high schoolers can derive the solution as a quadratic formula: $x = (-b \pm \sqrt{(b^2 - 4ac)}) / 2a.$

which is a snapshot of a possible configuration of the objects of interest to a problem. A path is thus a sequence of points. The givens constitute one point in a problem space; the goals constitute another point in the same space. The task for the problem solver is to find a path from the given state to the goal state, using only the resources at hand. In a well-defined problem, we know the given state, the goal state, and the resources at hand. A **problem space** is *a complete set of possible states*—generated by exploring possible steps or moves, which may or may not lead us from a given state to a goal state. A problem solver's task is to discover the path—out of a myriad other possible paths—that actually leads from the given state to the goal state. Discovering the right path for an interesting problem usually requires knowledge and forethought.

2.3 Preliminary analysis

Consider a taxi-driver's problem, depicted in Figure 2.5. Its task is to go, say, from the corner of 7th Street and 2nd Avenue to the corner of 4th Street and 3rd Avenue.

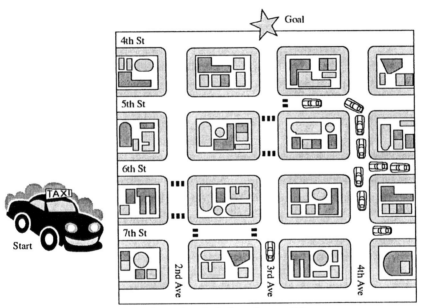

Figure 2.5: Taxi-driver's problem

The driver's resources are to go a block north, a block east, a block west, or a block south. Some of these resources may be applicable at any time, but some of them may be applicable only in certain conditions—for example, if 2nd Avenue is torn up between 6th and 7th Streets, the driver cannot apply the resource "go one block north" at the corner of 7th and 2nd. This everyday example illustrates a few points we can make about many problems: (1) there may be many solutions (and even more partial solutions), so that it is not necessarily obvious what to do; (2) some solutions are better than others, possibly because they involve fewer steps; and (3) constraints on the problem space can help guide the problem solver to a solution.

Observations like these constitute a second step in the process: a **preliminary analysis**, in which we try to determine any constraints that will be faced in developing a solution. Having laid out the problem, preliminary analysis starts by asking a series of questions, such as those shown in Figure 2.6, in order to clarify the givens, goals and resources.

What are the *givens*? Do we really have all of them?
>> Are the givens specific to a particular situation or can we generalize?
>>> (For example, does it matter what street corner the cab starts on?)
>> Is there a notation that represents the givens and other states succinctly?
What are the *goal(s)*?
>> Is there a single goal, or are there several?
>> If there is a single goal, can it be split into pieces or not?
>> If there are several goals or subgoals, are they independent or are they connected?
>> Are there obstacles to overcome to reach a goal? How can they be overcome?
>> Are there any constraints on developing a solution?
>>> (For example, do "near misses" count?)
>> Is time a factor or is it not? Space or memory? Dollars?
What are the *resources* (moves, operators, procedures, rules, transformations)?
>> For each resource, are there constraints (*preconditions*) to be met before applying it?
>>> If so, are there other (possibly simpler) resources that meet the preconditions?
>> When you apply a resource, what changes? (*Variants* are the things a move changes.)
>> When you apply a resource, what stays the same (*invariants*)?
>> Are there more powerful resources for this problem? Would someone else know?

Figure 2.6: Questions for preliminary analysis

Exercise 2.17: For the taxi-cab problem shown in Figure 2.5, ask yourself the questions in Figure 2.6 to find as many likely constraints about the givens, goal(s), and resources as you can establish, without actually developing a solution.

Exercise 2.18: For the Knobby's World problem of Figure 2.3, ask yourself the questions in Figure 2.6 to find as many likely constraints about the givens, goal(s), and resources as you can establish.

Now, after the preliminary analysis, comes the actual development of an algorithm. The problem of developing a solution algorithm to a well-defined problem is, unfortunately, not itself a well-defined problem. To be sure, the **goal state** is clear—to have a solution to the original problem. The **givens** are also clear (if we have done a good job on the earlier part of the process). But the **resources** we have for *developing* the solution (which are generally not the same as the resources we can *use* in the solution)—the steps we can take along the way—are by no means clear. However, there are some general approaches that often prove helpful, and in the remaining sections of this chapter, we discuss some of them.

Here's another problem to consider. You are walking through the forest, with a fox, a bag of corn, and a goose, and find your way blocked by a river. Fortunately, there is a small rowboat on the shore but it's too small to take the four of you—only two will fit at a time. Your first thought is to row back and forth, perhaps taking the fox, the corn, and the goose over one at a time, but you soon realize that the problem is not that simple. Leaving the fox alone with the goose means that the fox will eat the goose, and leaving the goose alone with the corn means that the goose will eat the corn. Even worse, leaving all three alone means that (since foxes are clever), the fox will first allow the goose to eat the corn, and then eat the now-fatter goose, and finally probably run away, leaving you with nothing. What to do?

Let's analyze this problem by asking the questions of preliminary analysis in Figure 2.6. *What are the givens?* You, the fox, corn, goose and boat start out on one side of the river. That's the initial state. *Are the givens specific to a particular situation?* Yes: all players must start together or else we cannot play the game.

Is there a way to represent the givens succinctly? A good representation system not only helps to keep things clear, it can sometimes even suggest what to do next. Let's assign each of the four characters a unique character code: yourself (Y), the fox (F), goose (G), and corn (C). We don't really need to represent the boat, since it will always be with Y. We do need to represent where everybody is vis a vis the river, which we will represent as |. All the players start out on one side of the river, so the initial (given) state is YFGC|. *Will this notation represent other states?* Yes, it will: the various states in the problem space are the possible arrangements of all the players on one side of the river or the other. For example, YF|GC represents the (undesirable) state where you and the fox are on the left bank of the river and the goose and the corn are on the right bank of the river.

Exercise 2.19: How could you represent states of this problem in terms of binary numbers (1's and 0's)? Do you need to represent the boat or the river as a binary number? Why or why not?

Exercise 2.20: There are $2^4=16$ possible states in this problem. Can you explain why? List them.

What is the goal of this problem? When can the problem solver proclaim "case solved"? Try putting it in your own words now. Next, can you represent the goal state in terms of our representation notation? If so, jot it down in the margin now.

Is there a single goal, or are there several? Just one: everybody on the other side of the river. *If there is a single goal, can it be split into pieces (subgoals) or not?* Not really: if you simply try to move any one player at a time, some other player may get eaten! *Are there obstacles to overcome to reach a goal?* Yes: you need to avoid letting one player eat another. How can they be overcome? By never leaving a pair of enemies (one will eat the other) on the opposite shore. We have just described an important constraint on the problem solution. There are no "near misses"—our players are too hungry to be trusted! Another constraint is only Y can row, so F, G and C cannot cross the river without Y. Time is not a fixed factor, but we would like a reasonably quick, inexpensive solution.

What are the resources? The resources consist of four pairs of moves (for a total of eight moves): you can row yourself across the river (Y->) or you can row yourself back (<-Y); you can row yourself and the fox across the river (YF->) or you can row yourself and the fox back (<-YF); and similar pairs for the goose and the corn. A solution will be a sequence of moves that begins with the given state and ends with the goal state. The *precondition* for each move is that the right players must be available in the right place; for example, YF-> will only apply if you and the fox are both on this side of the river. In addition, there are the obvious eating constraints to observe.

Exercise 2.21: Devise a notation that describes these preconditions on applying resources. One possibility is if-then rules: if (preconditions) then (move). Using your notation, list all possible moves and their preconditions. Another possibility might be similar to the notation we used for Turing machines in chapter 1.

The **variants** (*things that vary or change*) for each move are the positions of the players that move. There are many **invariants** (*things that don't vary*). Specifying variants and invariants can help identify and constrain the resources of a problem. Our notation for the fox-goose-corn problem highlights variants implicit in each move: Y-> and <-Y are both moves involving Y; the other resources each move two players. Many invariants are implicit in the notation, but needed to be discovered before we could be sure the notation would be correct. For starters, the moves all leave the *unmentioned* players where they were. Also, the river is invariant, unaffected by any moves—so our representational notation can ignore the river. Moreover, though the boat moves, it's always on the same side of the river as you (we assume that it won't just float away down the river!); this relational invariant is why our notation can also ignore the boat. Finally, the very association of characters with codes (e.g., F=fox) is invariant. It's tempting to take all these invariants for granted, but stating them (writing them down during your preliminary analysis of a problem) and preserving them (making sure your solution takes these constraints into account) makes our problem description much clearer and our problem solution much easier. (The study of variants and invariants will be a recurring theme in our study of programming. "Therefore keep watch.")

Here's another example. Suppose you and a friend are playing a game on a square table, 25" by 25", ruled off in one-inch squares, with the center square removed, for a total of 624 available squares. You have 312 black 1" square pieces and your opponent has 312 1" square white pieces. You place a piece first, then your opponent places a piece, etc. Can you play so as to put the last piece on the table? The givens, goals and resources of this problem are straightforward enough, but let's look at the invariants. Consider your choice and your opponent's response together as a single move—*ply* is the technical term for a move/counter-move pair . The *parity* (*evenness or oddness*) of the number of unplayed squares is an invariant of each ply. Furthermore, the number of unplayed squares in the initial state is even (624). Therefore, after every ply, the number of unplayed squares will always be even. So, when it is your turn, there can never be a single unplayed square. You cannot win! Discovering an invariant will save you some trouble.

Exercise 2.22: What are some of the variants and invariants of the moves in checkers or chess? How could you use these to specify a notation for the game?

Exercise 2.23: What are the variants and invariants in all Knobby's World problems? Can specific Knobby's World problems set up additional variants or invariants? Discuss an example problem, such as the addition problem or one of the others posed later in this chapter.

2.4 Hacking through a jungle?

Our preliminary analysis of the fox-goose-corn problem leads us to discover a number of important constraints. To appreciate them, let's consider what happens if we try to apply moves without considering the constraints. Starting with YFGC|, we could try Y->, but <-Y is not possible, since Y is on the wrong side of the river. Similarly, it is impossible to row Y and another player anywhere if the two of you are not on the same side of the river. Thus, of the eight conceivable moves, there are only a maximum off four *possible* moves— moves allowed by their preconditions—in any state.

Figure 2.7 shows how one might visualize all the possible moves in a problem space as a **search tree**. Like the parse tree of Figure 2.2, this tree grows upside-down, with its **root**—the initial state (YFGC|) in which all the players are on the left bank— at the top. Each possible sequence of moves is a **branch** growing down from the root. For example: on the far right, the branch from YFGC| to FG|YC then YFG|C is one possible sequence of moves. This tree shows all the move sequences up to depth 2, in other words, two moves or levels down from the root.

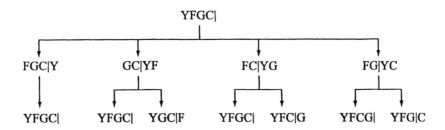

Figure 2.7: Search tree for fox-goose-corn problem to depth 2

Exercise 2.24: In Figure 2.7, how many states are there at depth 1? At depth 2? How many would there be at depth 3? How would you characterize the way the number of states is growing? Suggest one or two ways to slow down its growth.

As the previous exercise suggests, the number of possible move sequences grows very rapidly. This rapid increase of states is called a **combinatorial explosion**. If unchecked, the population of possible states will explode out of control. If a problem has **m** (say, 5) possible moves from each state and the solution path requires **p** (say, 7) moves from the given to the goal, then solving the problem will generate as many as **m^p** (here, 78,125) states. For this reason, uninformed or blind search for a solution can be a huge waste of time and resources. Here's the moral: novice hackers trying things at computer terminals usually grope in a blind search space. Skillful hackers, on the other hand, may be able to ignore most of the possibilities and concentrate on productive ones.

Informed search exploits knowledge about a problem. For this problem, as you may have observed already, some *possible* moves are unwise. Consider the constraints on our resources. For example, if from the given state, you row yourself and the fox across the river, then the goose will eat the corn. The same move is OK, though, when the goose and the corn are on *opposite* sides of the river, States in which the fox cannot eat the goose and the goose cannot eat the corn are *permissible states*. Moves that lead to permissible states are *permissible moves*. Restricting attention to sequences of only *permissible* moves simplifies the problem. Also, if you have just rowed across the river (alone or accompanied), it is both possible and permissible to row back the same way, but it's a stupid move. A global constraint of avoiding duplicate states will cut down the possibilities tremendously. So from among the permissible moves, we must sometimes choose the *productive* moves. Informed search thus *prunes* many useless branches from a search tree.

Exercise 2.25: Copy figure 2.7 and circle the *permissible* states. How many permissible moves are there for the first step? All the nodes beneath the non-circled nodes can be cut away, or pruned. How many permissible states are there in the second step? How much have you reduced the overall search tree with just pruning at the this level? A move back to an earlier state is not productive. How many *productive* moves are there at depth 3?

Figure 2.8 shows another, more compact way to represent the complete state space of the fox-goose-corn problem—as a **state space graph** (rather than a tree). Though a tree only grows in one direction (computer science trees usually grow down!), this graph has bi-directional branches, in this case showing succinctly that it is possible, though not productive, to revert to an earlier state. Also, graphs permit multiple nodes to converge on one node lower in the tree—for example, there appear to be three different ways to reach the goal, at the bottom of the graph. But is that really true? Look carefully: which of the three states immediately above the goal state are permissible?

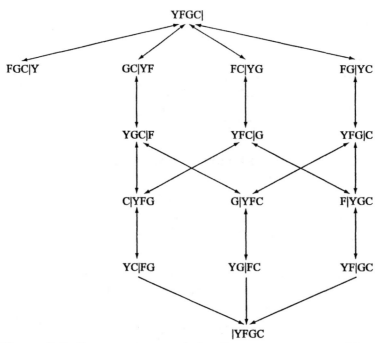

Figure 2.8: State space graph for fox-goose-corn problem

Exercise 2.26: Copy figure 2.8 and cross out the states that are not permissible. How many possible paths are there from initial to goal state now? What does this exercise tell you about the importance of knowledge about the constraints on a problem? In exercise 2.21 we stated that there are 16 possible states, yet Figure 2.8 only list 15. What is the missing 16th state? Why do you think we made this error in the first place?

2.4.1 Hacking from givens to goals

Hacking *keeps trying resources (operators or rules) that apply to the current situation, step by step, until it reaches the goal.* Each time a resource or rule applies, you take a step, possibly toward a solution (or possibly away from it); you also change the situation (you have a new state). Hacking *forward* begins with the givens, chooses a first step (producing a new state), then a second, and so on until the goal is reached. Blind hacking, lacking knowledge about the right resources to apply, is more likely to choose an unproductive move that leads away from the solution than a productive one that leads towards it. Wasteful and frustrating!

Here is a tree of *productive* moves, now drawn length-wise, from left-to-right, to depth 3:

$$YFGC| \rightarrow FC|YG \rightarrow YFC|G \begin{cases} C|YFG \\ F|YGC \end{cases}$$

Figure 2:9a: Tree of moves to depth 3

Now we have a choice about how to continue. We can either pick a *single* branch and extend it to its end, successfully or unsuccessfully; or, we can make a single move at a time on *all* branches. The first strategy is called **depth-first** search: follow a single branch of the tree and dive as deep as you can go; if you can't go any further, you back up to next highest level, look for an alternative, and dive again. The second strategy is **breadth-first**: consider all possibilities, across one level at a time. Since our *informed* search tree isn't branching very profusely, let's do breadth-first, to see the whole search space expand in parallel. Breadth-first search has an additional advantage of finding the *shortest* solution, from the root of the search space tree.

From state C|YFG, only moves <-Y, <-YF, and <-YG are possible. Only the latter two moves are also *permissible* (otherwise the fox eats the goose). Only the last option is productive—taking us to state YGC|F (otherwise we go back to the previous state). Similarly, from state F|YGC, moves <-Y, <-YG, and <-YC are possible; only the last two are permissible; and only move <-YG is productive—resulting in YFG|C. Our tree is now:

$$YFGC| \rightarrow FC|YG \rightarrow YFC|G \begin{array}{c} \rightarrow C|YFG \rightarrow YGC|F \\ \rightarrow F|YGC \rightarrow YFG|C \end{array}$$

Figure 2.9b: Productive moves to depth 4

Now, let's consider the top branch, from state YGC|F. Moves Y->, YG->, and YC-> are possible, but only YC-> is permissible and productive, leading to state G|YFC. On the lower branch, from state YFG|C, moves Y->, YF-> and YG-> are possible, but only YF-> is permissible and productive, and this also leads to state G|YFC. Here's what the space of productive moves looks like now:

$$YFGC| \rightarrow FC|YG \rightarrow YFC|G \begin{array}{c} \rightarrow C|YFG \rightarrow YGC|F \\ \rightarrow F|YGC \rightarrow YFG|C \end{array} \rightarrow G|YFC$$

Figure 2.9c: Productive moves to depth 5

Because the two branches have converged to the same state, G|YFC, it's more convenient to represent the situation as a graph rather than a tree. Now the only possible, permissible and productive move is <-Y, which goes to state YG|FC. That's fine, because from here the only productive move is YG->, which winds up in the final state |YFGC. Our final search diagram is:

$$YFGC| \rightarrow FC|YG \rightarrow YFC|G \begin{array}{c} \rightarrow C|YFG \rightarrow YGC|F \\ \rightarrow F|YGC \rightarrow YFG|C \end{array} \rightarrow G|YFC \rightarrow YG|FC \rightarrow |YFGC$$

Figure 2.9d: Graph reaches goal!

This graph shows us that there are actually two different solutions; it also tells us that in terms of number of steps required, neither is better than the other.

This problem has characteristics that make informed hacking from givens to goals a good approach. First, this was a well-defined problem, with clear and simple givens, goals and resources. Just the details—discovering the permissible and productive constraints on moves—make it tricky. In any one state, there are only a few possible moves—at most four, sometimes less. The permissible and productive constraints further cut down this number—for example, from the initial state, there was only one permissible move. Knowing these constraints, we can go directly to the solution. Recall that for a five step solution the original tree had the potential of having $4^5 = 1024$ states at depth 6. However, using constraints, we pruned this very dense tree to the graph of Figure 2d. As Francis Bacon observed, "knowledge is power." But knowledge is also work!

Imagine, however, a problem (a chess game, for example) in which there is a much larger number of permissible initial moves (20 in a chess game). Of course restricting attention to productive moves may help considerably, but even the number of productive moves may grow exponentially. Chess games do not rule out the possibility of repeated states (board configurations). Of course, master chess players, using considerable knowledge about the game, usually only consider *very* productive moves! In such a problem, the givens-to-goals approach is less appropriate, unless we can find some additional ways to prune the tree substantially (such as chess master-level knowledge). Hacking from givens to goals is most successful when one already has a lot of knowledge about how to solve the problem (hence "*informed* hacking").

Exercise 2.27: Describe how the givens-to-goals approach would apply to the game of checkers. Does this seem like a good strategy? Why or why not?

Exercise 2.28: Imagine yourself standing very sleepily before your bathroom mirror one morning very early, needing to brush your teeth. Outline an algorithm (of at most 8-10 instructions) to program yourself how to brush your teeth, using an informed hacking problem solving approach. Note: you get to determine what counts as "primitive" moves (resources) for the problem!

2.4.2 From goals to givens

Reverse givens-to-goals and you get a "goals-to-givens" strategy. Rather than begin at the beginning (the given state) and proceed in a step-by-step fashion to the end (the goal state), this approach begins at the end, so to speak, and "backs up" in a step-by-step fashion until it reaches the beginning. More precisely, one imagines oneself at the goal state and asks "What might the *final move* to the goal state have been, and what state might it have been made from?" Choosing one of these possibilities, one then asks the same question to obtain a next-to-the-last move from the next-to-the-next-to-the-last state, etc., etc., until one arrives at the given state. If we've kept a record of our backward moves, we can run the solution by simply reversing them.

Figure 2.10: A maze problem

Exercise 2.29: You want to get through the maze shown in figure 2.10. Intuitively, do you try to solve this problem givens-to-goals (starting from the entrance), or goals-to-given, or some combination, or neither? Describe your problem-solving process, step by step. (Cognitive scientists who study human problem solving actually get subjects to record what they are doing in informal protocols. Introspecting about your own problem solving processes can help you to refine them.)

Exercise 2.30: By asking the questions of preliminary analysis of Figure 2.6, make the givens, goals and resources of the maze problem above explicit.

Exercise 2.31: Develop a search tree representing your solution to the maze problem.

Because we can represent both as a search for a path between two states in a problem space, goals-to-givens and givens-to-goals are abstractly the same strategy. For example, the fox-corn-goose problem is the same whether you start with all on the left bank or the right bank. Goals-to-givens is particularly useful when there are a relatively *small* number of possibilities for the *final* move or when there are a *large* number of possible *initial* moves. On the other hand, some people find goals-to-givens be a bit more difficult for some people to do, since it requires one to be able to back up, to see how to reverse a move. Once one gets used to thinking in reverse, it becomes easier.

Another variation of the givens-to-goals approach involves searching from the goal and from the given simultaneously. One has found a solution when the two searches have found a state in common. Solution of the problem then consists of a path from the given-state to the common state and thence from the common state to the goal-state.

2.4.3 Drawbacks of hacking

Both forward and reverse hacking methods treat algorithm development as discovering a sequence of steps. Such strategies work best when there are not too many steps, not too many possible moves (or resources, operations, rules, etc.) at each step, and not too many dependencies between steps. If there are too many steps, problem solving gets tedious and humans tend to make errors. Humans have a limited short term memory capacity—we can keep track of seven "chunks" of information at a time, plus or minus two. (Telephone numbers were designed with seven digits rather than twelve or fifteen for this reason!) If there are too many choices, a combinatorial explosion kicks in (as we saw when we considered all possible moves for the fox-goose-corn problem), causing a memory overload for a problem solver keeping track of too many alternative branches. The simple problems we have studied so far only have a few primitive moves. A little practical knowledge (also known as **heuristics**, or *rules of thumb*) enabled us to limit the alternatives drastically and only use permissible and productive moves.

Many real world problems (such as finding a job or designing a house or a software system) require far more primitive moves as well as more difficult analysis to discover the practical knowledge of a problem domain. If there are dependencies between steps—an early choice of one step may force an undesirable step later—a problem solver may simply get stuck in a "catch 22."

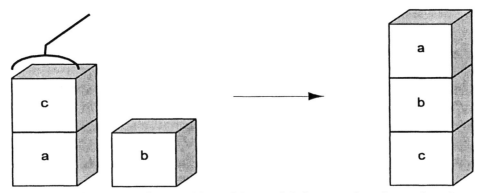

Figure 2.11: A blocks world problem with interacting dependencies

In the "blocks world" of figure 2.11, a robot has a gripper that can put one block at a time on another block or the table. The figure depicts a seemingly simple problem: transform the given state on the left (with block C on block A) into the goal state on the right (a stack of three blocks). Suppose a robot planner decomposes the task of building a stack with A on B and B on C into two sub-tasks: put A on B and B on C (or vice versa). An overly linear-minded planner will, however, get stuck. Suppose it tries to put block A on top of block B first: then it will have to take block A off again in order to put block B on block C. On the other hand, suppose it starts by putting B on C: then it will have to unstack B and C in order to get to block A! The two sub-goals—put block A on B and put block B on C—turn out to *interact*.[4]

Exercise 2.32: Show a sequence of *three* steps that solves the problem of Figure 2.11.
Exercise 2.33: Can you think of interacting dependencies in a "real world" problem? (How about when you are planning your courses for a semester or trying to find that dream car you can afford

---

[4]Researchers in robot planning (a branch of Artificial Intelligence) have developed programs that notice and solve problems with interacting sub-goals. One, called "Hacker" (now isn't *that* an interesting name!), recognized and fixed such "bugs" after stumbling into them. Another, called "NOAH," tried to avoid such bugs in the first place, by taking a "least commitment" approach, i.e., not committing to any sequence of moves until it sees that constraints make it obvious.

or designing an engine or an earring?) Describe the interacting sub-goals, then suggest how to avoid the interacting dependencies to solve the problem.

Exercise 2.34: What is the problem space for Figure 2.11? Develop a notation for the states of this space. How many possible states are there? Often, after we have solved a problem we are asked to solve a similar problem, but the original solution is inflexible and not easily adapted to the new problem. Can you adapt your solution of the problem of Figure 2.11 to a problem with four blocks? With five blocks?

2.5 Analytical reasoning

Sherlock Holmes solves problems by analysis. One form of analysis, particularly useful for complex problems, is **top-down decomposition**, or as Caesar called it, "divide and conquer." Subdivide the overall problem into several sub-problems such that solving the sub-problems would guarantee the solution of the overall problem. Then divide each of the sub-problems into sub-sub-problems in the same way, etc., until you get down to simple steps. Generally, by the time you've done this several times, the sub-...-sub-problems are small enough that they are relatively easy to solve. "*Elementary*, my dear Watson."

For example, how does one plan a menu for a meal? One can approach this in a givens-to-goals fashion, deciding the first dish, then the second, then ..., etc. You might prepare lunch this way, grabbing whatever looks appealing out of the fridge. French chefs and others are more systematic. Though he is a detective and not a chef, M. Poirot is rather fussy about his food—his menu must complement the main dish—the *pièce de resistance*! As an analytical problem-solver, he instead first breaks the menu down into courses: the main course, the preceding courses, and the following courses. Then, since the main course is the most important, he subdivides that into: (1) the main dish, and (2) the accompanying dishes. "Well, my main dish is to be Cornish game hen *a l'orange*, and for accompaniments I want creamed spinach and wild rice, and of course a beverage, but we'll wait a bit on that. Now, what is to precede the main course? Well, we'll want a soup course, and a fish course. And after? umm—a salad course and a dessert. The soup? Well, the game hen sauce is pretty robust, so I want something somewhat bland—say, cream of lettuce soup. And ditto for the fish, but a little punchier—filet of sole Veronica (a cream sauce with white grapes)—and a dry white wine for the beverage. And back to the soup course for a beverage—small glasses of a light, delicate sherry. The salad? simply assorted greens, with a nice raspberry vinaigrette dressing. And the dessert—a recapitulation of the orange flavor...a mandarin orange tart, and with it a somewhat sweeter, heavier white wine. That's it. Wait—the wine for the game hen! A red wine here, since the sauce involves orange and garlic, but not too heavy for the bird. *Voila*! Now we've done it! *Bon appetit*!"

2.5.1 Outlining as top-down decomposition

The top-down approach is very helpful in writing an outline. In fact, the top-down approach is the very idea behind an outline. In olden days B.C. (before computers), writing an outline by hand went something like this. You selected your first major topic (I), and then your first major sub-topic (I.A.), and then your first sub-sub-topic (I.A.1), and then your three sub-sub-sub-topics (I.A.1.a., I.A.1.b, and I.A.1.c). Then to the second major topic (II), and to its first sub-topic (II.A), etc. And so on. But here's the rub—though the *concept* of an outline is top-down, the *procedure* for creating an outline was typically givens-to-goals! Now, however, with the magic of word-processors, you can construct an outline exactly the way it should be constructed. First, put down all the major topics:

                    I.
                    II.
                    III.
Then insert the sub-topics:
                    I.
                                A.
                                B.
                    II.
                                A.
                                B.
                                C.
                    III.
                                A.
Now insert the sub-sub-topics:
                    I.
                                A.
                                            1.
                                            2.
                                B.
                    II.
                                A.
                                            1.
                                B.
                                            1.
                                            2.
                                C.

And so on. *This* is the way to make an outline—top-down decomposition! There is an important moral here for problem solving in general. For many of us, the task of writing an essay is like facing the great unknown. Outlining is an excellent way to get started, because it helps you see your main point, then break it down into supporting ideas, etc. Similarly, *top-down decomposition is an excellent way for one to tackle problems about which one has little knowledge.* Better than hacking!

Exercise 2.35 Depict M. Poirot's menu, described above, as an outline. Also, point out any interacting subgoals that he encountered and resolved while designing the menu.

Exercise 2.36: Construct the outline of the first chapter of this book. By the way, do you plan your expository compositions this way?

Exercise 2.37: An earlier exercise in this chapter invited you to imagine yourself standing very sleepily before your bathroom mirror one morning very early, needing to brush your teeth. Develop an algorithm (of at most 8-10 instructions) to program yourself how to brush your teeth, using a top-down decomposition approach.

2.5.2 An Automatic Teller Machine Problem

Here's another problem, with a "real world" flavor. The Real World Software Consulting firm has been hired to design an automatic teller machine (ATM) for the First Virtual Bank. After confirming a customer's PIN (personal identification number), it should allow withdrawals and deposits to access that customer's checking and savings accounts.

Let's begin our preliminary analysis by first defining some terms:

ATM: a machine that provides access to individual bank accounts
- card: has a magnetic strip containing unique account information
- PIN: personal identification number, serves as password to account
- account: individual checking or savings
- transaction: withdrawal or deposit
- balance: current amount in an account
- withdrawal: subtract amount from account balance and dispense cash
- deposit: accept envelope of money and add amount to account balance

The givens are:
- the PIN associated with a card
- the balance in each account before any transactions

The goals are:
- withdraw cash from a checking or savings account, or
- deposit an envelope of money into checking or savings account

There are a couple of important constraints between the givens and goals:
- the user must enter a PIN that matches the PIN associated with the card
- withdrawals must not exceed an account's balance, excluding today's deposits

OK, now we are ready to design an algorithm, using a top-down decomposition approach:

    ATM machine
        Read card
        Verify PIN
            Ask user for PIN
            Make sure PIN matches PIN associated with card
        User requests transaction
            Deposit to checking
            Deposit to savings
            Withdraw from checking
            Withdraw from savings
        Make transaction
            ...
        Another transaction?
            Yes: go to "User requests transaction"
        Return card and say good-bye

Exercise 2.39: There are interacting sub-goals in this problem. What are they? (Hint: it has to do with one of the constraints.) How should the ATM system resolve these sub-goals?

Exercise 2.40: Flesh out the decomposition of the above algorithm (i.e., insert steps where you see the ellipses, ..., in the above outline).

Exercise 2.41: First Virtual Bank has just added money-market accounts, with withdrawal and deposits. They also want to allow users to make transfers between accounts and request the current balance at any time. Do a preliminary analysis and design an algorithm for the new system.

Exercise 2.42: Do you notice any redundancies in the top-down analysis shown above? If you did (or were to do) either of the previous two exercises, would there be even more redundancies? How could these redundancies be avoided?

2.5.3 Bottom-up composition

Another analytical technique, working in the opposite direction as "top-down," is working "bottom-up". Start with the very smallest pieces available, the basic or primitive resources, and combine these into "chunks" that we expect to be useful in a solution of the problem. Then we combine these into larger chunks, and these into still larger chunks, until finally we have an overall "super-chunk" which is the solution to the problem. Top-down *decomposes* a problem into subproblems. Bottom up *composes* resources into super-resources.

Consider, as an example, the taxicab driver problem mentioned earlier. Its task is to drive from some corner to another—say, 7th and 2nd to 4th and 3rd. Suppose now that the only primitive actions it can perform are "drive forward one block" and "turn left." We surely know beforehand that in many tasks, the driver will need to turn right. And so, knowing this, even without knowing the specific task the driver has, we might begin assembling a chunk called "turn right," consisting of three applications of the left-turn instruction, and perhaps even one called "turn around," consisting of two left-turn instructions. Now, given the specific task at hand, assembling these and perhaps other small chunks—"face north" (by turning left while facing east)—and the primitive instructions, we could then combine them into even bigger chunks: e.g., "move far enough north" and "move far enough east," and then to an overall solution: "(1) face north; (2) move far enough north; (3) face east; (4) move far enough east." If it were advantageous, we could even define even larger chunks: "go north," consisting of "(1) face north; (2) move far enough north." And similarly, "go east." We could then make the overall solution consist of only "(1) go north; (2) go east."

Exercise 2.43: Using primitives and the smaller chunks ("turn right" and "turn around"), construct the larger chunks "go east," "move far enough north" and "move far enough east."

Of course, this is a rather simple task, with only four overall parts, so it is not difficult to see how the chunks can be made larger and larger. In fact, we already know that in the absence of blocked streets, any path which moves the cab north and east can be accomplished by first going north and then going east. It should be clear that for a bottom-up approach to be successful, we must have at least two sorts of knowledge from the very beginning. (1) We need a very good sense of exactly what our basic resources are. (The top-down method can defer consideration of all "bottom-level" resources until it gets the task broken down into fairly small pieces. These small pieces may be either already known or newly discovered primitives.) (2) We also need some sense of what "chunks" are likely to be useful in attacking the overall problem. Otherwise, we may find that our assemblies of chunks don't fit together all that well. This would be as if, in assembling a skeleton from individual bones, we put together the finger-bones from two distinct fingers into one chunk, then another finger-bone and three hand-bones into a second chunk, then the rest of the hand-bones and a forearm bone into a third, etc. Even if the pieces managed to assemble together, the structure would be artificial; the "parts" would have no clear functional relation to each other. In larger, more complicated problems, there may be a real danger that we have assembled our chunks in ways that are not useful or practical.

A bottom-up approach is more effective when it reuses resources that have been built up from more primitive ones. Reusing higher-level resources can solve common sub-problems in short order.

It is often useful to combine the bottom-up and the top-down approaches. Building up from the bottom can create more powerful resources; breaking down from the top leads to subproblems that can use these new resources more effectively.

Exercise 2.44: Re-examine the solution to Knobby's addition problem, bottom-up, in order to discover any reusable resources. Describe other problems or sub-problems that could possibly use these reusable, high-level resources.

2.6 The analogical approach

In much of our thinking we reason by analogy. Analogical reasoning starts by noticing a similarity between a new problem and an old case. Our expectations for today are based on our memories of a day much like this one. Little children, having learned to identify their fathers as "Daddy!", often employ the term upon seeing some entirely unrelated man, having noticed the general resemblance. Even animals learn to generalize, and react to some particular stimulus in ways like their reactions to other similar stimuli.

Often multiple comparisons are helpful, especially in cases in which several similarities exist. John Stuart Mill laid out several methods of analogical reasoning, now called *Mill's methods*. The Method of Agreement compares a number of similar cases in which some particular phenomenon occurs and attempts to explain it in terms of the other features the cases have in common. The Method of Difference compares a case in which a phenomenon occurs and a case in which it does not occur, and attempts to explain the phenomenon in terms of the other differences the cases have. In more complicated cases, these methods can be combined (as in exercise 2.44).

Exercise 2.45: Sam has reported in sick with vomiting, no abdominal pain, no fever, but an elevated pulse rate. Checking your notes, you notice a number of cases in which a new drug mycosporin has been tried.

A: vomiting, abdominal pain, no fever, normal pulse, drug was successful;
B: vomiting, abdominal pain, high fever, elevated pulse, drug was successful;
C: vomiting, no abdominal pain, high fever, normal pulse, drug was unsuccessful;
D: no vomiting, abdominal pain, high fever, elevated pulse, drug was unsuccessful;
E: no vomiting, no abdominal pain, high fever, elevated pulse, drug was unsuccessful;
F: vomiting, abdominal pain, no fever, elevated pulse, drug was successful.

What (if anything) do you see common to all the successful cases? The unsuccessful cases? How do these differ? Given that in no cases did the drug do any harm to the patients, would you prescribe the drug for Sam? Why or why not?

Figure 2.12: Another maze

2.6.1 Copy and paste

A simple and practical application of analogical reasoning is **copy and paste**. Rather than re-invent a solution to a problem, you might be tempted to just copy a solution that already exists, perhaps on the CDROM that comes with this book. Go for it! However, you may well find that the nearest snippet in the book is not exactly what you want. Simply copying is rarely sufficient to solve a new problem. You have to observe the differences as well as the similarities between the old case and your new one and adapt the old snippet to your new problem.

Exercise 2.46: In Exercise 2.29, you developed an algorithm to solve a maze problem. Figure 2.12 shows another maze problem. How is this maze different from the earlier one? What changes (if any) in the algorithm would this difference require?

Exercise 2.47: Two earlier exercises had you programming yourself to brush your teeth. Develop an algorithm for using mouthwash instead. (How does an analogical approach suggest itself?)

2.6.2 Object-orientation

Object-oriented programming generalizes the copy and paste technique *by making it possible to reuse and extend existing classes of objects*, without actually having to copy or modify old code. For example, drawing geometric shapes on a computer screen involves lots of details having to do with putting pixels (tiny dots of color) on a graphics screen. Suppose all these details were hidden in classes like Circle, Triangle, Line, Shape and Point? Suppose a program could draw figures on the screen by just constructing new objects out of these general classes and moving them wherever as needed? Much easier than plotting pixels yourself! Just as automotive engineers look to reuse existing components, such as batteries or transmissions or even engines, that were successful in earlier designs, so object-oriented software engineers look to reuse existing software components.

A **class** *specifies the properties and behaviors that a set of objects have in common.* The properties are data values, while the behaviors are operations that a class can perform. For example, all objects belonging to the class Circle share the following features:

*   properties: a center point and a radius,
*   behaviors: compute my circumference, compute my perimeter, draw myself around my center point, move myself to a new center point, etc.

The first task of object-oriented problem solving is identifying the classes of a problem domain (some of which may already have been implemented). The second task is determining the properties and behaviors of a class.

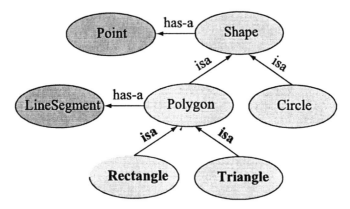

Figure 2.13: A Shapes inheritance hierarchy

The payoff of reusable classes of objects motivates object-oriented software to look for more abstract classes which capture commonality. For example, as figure 2.13 suggests, classes Circle, Triangle, Rectangle, etc., all have some common properties (such as a center point) and behaviors, such as having an area, a perimeter, can draw and move themselves on a screen, etc., all of which can be collected together in a common class, Shape. Common properties may figure in common behaviors: when its center Point moves, the whole Shape moves. Once a software engineer has discovered the common class, it becomes much easier to create new sub-classes—such as Parallelogram and Pentagon—which **inherit** the *common properties and behaviors.* To take another example, robins, canaries and eagles all inherit common properties and behaviors from the abstract class, bird: they all have feathers, wings, beaks and warm blood, lay eggs, and so forth. Each subclass in turn extends the superclass in more specific ways: a robin has a red breast while a canary is yellow; a Triangle has three sides while a Hexagon has six. Extensions may override the way abstract behaviors work: all Shapes should draw, but a Circle draws by extending its radius from a center point while a Pentagon draws by connecting its five points. Note, however, that *requiring* that all Shapes be able to draw themselves is still useful. It sure would be disappointing if you asked an Octagon to draw itself and it said "I don't do that," or worse yet, the whole program crashed!

This habit of looking for generalizations from particulars, then deriving new particulars and taking into account their divergences from generalizations, is another form of analogical reasoning. It comes naturally to people, who learn to recognize categories of objects as infants. Nevertheless, it needs to be refined and formalized to deal with complex systems. The art of "object-think"—like just about every problem solving technique—gets better with practice and knowledge.

Reusing and extending code without actually copying it means that a supplier does not have to provide all the details of the code, only enough to make it understandable and usable. Since software systems typically reuse components from many different classes of objects, object-oriented software typically involves a combination of analogical reasoning and bottom-up composition—and may involve some top-down decomposition and even informed hacking as well.

Exercise 2.48: Design a class Square. What are its properties? What are its behaviors? Where would you insert it in the class diagram of figure 2.13? Think carefully about the properties and behaviors it will inherit.

Exercise 2.49: Design a class Ellipse. What are its properties? What are its behaviors? Where would you insert it in the class diagram of figure 2.13? Think carefully about the properties and behaviors it will inherit.

Exercise 2.50: Design a class Bicycle. What are its properties and behaviors? What other classes can serve as *parts* of objects of this class (for example, a Bicycle *has-a* pedal)?

2.6.3 An object-oriented analysis of the ATM problem

Earlier (in section 2.4.2), we designed an ATM machine using top-down analysis. Let's take another stab at this problem using an object-oriented approach. Instead of thinking in terms of actions that decompose in terms of other actions, an object-oriented approach first looks for classes of objects, then analyzes their properties and behaviors.

A good place to start looking for classes is in the definition of terms for the problems. Classes should have a few interesting properties (representing the state of an object) and behaviors (representing the actions that an object can perform). So let's take another look at terms we defined earlier, making notes about whether they might make good classes:

- ATM: maintains state of user's interaction, performs transactions—class
- card: maintains PIN, reads PIN—class
- PIN: a number or a string—probably just part of card
- account: abstracts over checking, savings (or money-market,...)—superclass
- transaction: abstracts over a deposit, withdrawal (or transfer,...)—superclass
- balance: a number—probably a property of an account
- withdrawal: has amount, verifies sufficient balance, subtract from account—class
- deposit: has amount, adds to account—possibly a class

Looks like we've got an interesting collection of classes here! Notice how some terms (deposit, withdraw) that looked liked actions (or functions) from the point of view of top-down analysis suddenly look like potential classes from an object-oriented perspective. Either point of view could provide a reasonable solution for this problem (and we'll explore both approaches to programming in subsequent chapters of this book). But the object-oriented approach has a couple of advantages. (1) It considers both data (properties) and actions (behaviors) together. Packaging data and properties together provides more organization and will make reuse easier. (2) It facilitates inheritance of common features from superclasses. Looking for commonality will avoid writing or even copying redundant code and of course will support even more reusability. Figure 2.14 shows a first cut at a class diagram for this problem. You should especially note that the arrows in this diagram each have one of the two labels "is-a" and "has-a." An arrow from A to B marked with "is-a" indicates that A is a subclass of B. An arrow from A to B marked "has-a" indicates that class A has an instance of class B as part of its data.

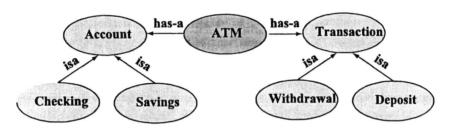

Figure 2.14: A class diagram for the ATM problem

Besides fleshing out all the properties and behaviors of the classes, we also need to consider the constraints discovered in our earlier preliminary analysis (in section 2.4.2). In an object-oriented analysis, such constraints become questions of *responsibility*. Which class is responsible for observing the sufficient balance on withdrawal constraint? Probably class Withdrawal. Another possibility might have been class ATM, which has to manage transactions. But it's a better idea to localize responsibilities as much as possible. After all, this constraint is irrelevant to class Deposit.

Which class is responsible for observing the PIN constraint? Oops! None of the classes in our first-cut analysis handles this constraint—we forgot to include a class for Card! Note that responsibility-driven analysis can help us catch mistakes like this one. Better to catch these mistakes early in the game (during analysis) than late (while coding). Much better! Folks at Real World Software and elsewhere have learned this lesson: there really is a big payoff in time and money saved by catching bugs early!

Exercise 2.51: Fix the class diagram of Figure 2.14 and flesh out the properties and behaviors of all the classes in the diagram. Are you ready to start writing Java programs? Do you feel better prepared than if you had started coding without having done this analysis?

Exercise 2.52: Extend the class diagram of Figure 2.14 to allow for money-market accounts and also allow for transfers between any two accounts. What new responsibilities emerge with these modifications and whose are they?

Exercise 2.53: Having successfully delivered the ATM software analyzed above, the Real World Software firm has just landed another contract: a mortgage servicing company wants to support transactions over the phone: after checking a customer's PIN, the system will let the customer either make a payment from another bank account (prearranged) or check the current balance on the mortgage. What aspects of the ATM software can be reused? What needs to change?

Exercise 2.54: Proponents of object-oriented software emphasize a *bottom-up* approach to problem solving. Why might a bottom-up, compositional approach seem to go hand-in-hand with reusable classes of objects?

Exercise 2.55: Are you up for an ambitious and fun term project? Take a look at the following games. You can start by developing a use case analysis (see chapter 4) and requirements specification for one of them. You might want to work in pairs, with one student playing the role of a customer and another as an analyst; the customer's role is to make sure the analyst describes the proposed system in a way that characterizes how a customer would actually be satisfied to use it. Your mission now is to understand the problem, not implement the solution. Implementation will be the responsibility of programmers who know how to use a modern programming language and reuse ready-made software, including various kinds of collections and random number generators.

1.   The Game of Life is about simple "organisms" that live in a two-dimensional world laid out like a checker board, where we call each square on the board a "cell.". There are a few simple laws of life, death and survival from generation to generation: 1) spontaneous generation: an empty cell with three living neighbors will come to life in the next generation; 2) loneliness: a cell with one or zero neighbors will die; 3) overcrowding: a cell with four or more neighbor will die; 4) survival: a cell with two or three neighbors will live into the next generation. All births and deaths appear to occur simultaneously. Though the laws are simple, the "game" can be fascinating because some initial populations give rise to interesting patterns that will repeat, grow or move across the board. Like Turing's machine and Knobby's World, it's amazing what you can do with a few simple rules! Write a program that plays this game. Let the user specify the locations of the initial population.

2.   In the game of Hangman, a user tries to guess the word that the computer is "thinking". (The program maintains a list of possible words in memory.) For each turn, a user guesses a letter. If that letter happens to be in the word, then the computer will show at what positions that letter (and any other letters the user has guessed right) is in the word. For example, if the word is "guess" and the user guesses 'e' and 's', then the program will display:

    `__ess`

On the other hand, if the user guesses a letter that is not in the word, the computer will add another part of a hanging stick figure, typically a head followed by a trunk, followed by two legs (one at a time) and finally two arms. The user wins if she guesses the word first and loses if the whole stick figure is hanging first.

3.   MasterMind is another back-seat of the car favorite. To win the game one guesses the sequence of four colored pegs. Player #1 sets up the sequence of four pegs, using any one of six colors for each of the pegs. Player #2 guesses a sequence of four colors for the pegs, and Player #1 responds by displaying a black marker for each peg with a correct color in the correct location and by displaying a white marker for each of the remaining pegs having the right color (but not in the right position). Player #2 wins by guessing the correct sequence within seven guesses. (Variations on the game allow for different numbers of pegs, whether duplicate colors are allowed, and the number of guesses.) Let the computer be Player #1. (If you want to dabble in Artificial Intelligence, let the computer be Player #2!)

4.   Many card games make interesting projects. For example, in the card game War, two players are dealt all the cards in a deck, then each player draws the top card from his pile. The player whose card has the higher face value wins both cards. If they draw the same card, then there is a "war": each player draws three cards face down, then one more card, for which the same rules as above apply. If a player runs out of cards during a war, this his last card plays against the opponent's card. When a player has no more cards, the opponent wins. Or maybe you know the rules for another card game, such as Fish, Hearts, Euchre, Pinochle, or Poker?

For these problems, it is recommended that you ignore most user interface issues. A simple command-line interface is a good place to start. A principle of modern software design is separation of concerns: keep the design of a user interface separate from solving the core problem itself. Make sure you've done the analysis right before you go on to the next step.

2.7 Problem solving and programming in Knobby's World (optional)

As you saw earlier in this chapter (and the multimedia of chapter 1), Knobby lives in a simple grid-like world. In the rest of this chapter, we will explore the world of Knobby and the things he can do in it. We'll show you the simple things Knobby can do and how they can be combined to allow him to accomplish more complicated tasks. Knobby will thus give you an opportunity to practice what you've learned in this chapter: especially problem solving by decomposition and analogy. Knobby's World is also a "gentle introduction" to computer programming—once you've learned concepts in one language, it's fairly easy to learn them in others—such as Java.

From Knobby's perspective, his World is a grid of streets and avenues, with walls blocking his way, and inhabited by himself and other characters on street corners. From your perspective, as Knobby's programmer, his World is a simple integrated programming environment (IDE). You can get to this environment either by clicking on the button marked **Knobby** on the ship's console, or if you don't want to start up the whole spaceship, you can just click on the Knobby icon in the Universal Machine folder. The IDE has some buttons and menu options, which let you control Knobby's behavior and create, modify and run Knobby programs. By default, Knobby starts off in a situation which puts him next to a "mountain." Ready to climb?

2.7.1 How Knobby moves

In Knobby's world, his philosophy of life is simply to follow instructions. He is quite docile and obedient, unless you ask him to do something that violates the laws of physics of his world, such as walking through walls. Knobby has only two primitive instructions for movement. The **left** instruction (click on the `left` button or press **L** on the keyboard) causes him to rotate 90 degrees to the left. To get him to face any other direction, just keep telling him to turn left.

The **move** instruction (click on the `move` button or press **M**) causes him to advance one block in the direction that his head is pointing. However, if Knobby is facing a wall or a boundary when he tries to carry out a move instruction, then he won't move, but will instead "crash"—that is, issue an error-message and stop whatever he is doing.

Believe it or not, you are now ready to program Knobby to do certain simple tasks. Your first exercise will involve manipulating Knobby directly, as described above. "Hands-on" programming!

Exercise 2.58: Start up Knobby's World. By default, it should load the situation file `mountain.sit`. By using `move` and `left`, navigate Knobby to the other side of the mountain.

Think about how you developed the sequence of instructions for Knobby to climb to other side of the mountain. What problem solving technique did you use? With direct manipulation, it's tempting just to work forward, from givens to goals: take the first step, then take the second step, then ... and so on, without planning ahead. However, if there are complications in the task, even with direct manipulation it may be important to use an analytical or an analogical approach (or some combination). People who play direct manipulation video games often develop strategies and plan ahead even as they are jiggering the controls. With Knobby, too, you can think what sort of maneuvers, like turning around, Knobby is likely to need to do, and plan them out ahead of time.

Exercise 2.59: How can you instruct Knobby to take three steps *backward*? When or why might you want Knobby to do this?

2.7.2 How Knobby interacts with messages

Knobby can also read and write with a couple of electronic "blackboards" (actually, "whiteboards"), b1 and b2. These boards and their contents appear above the northern boundary of Knobby's world. Each board may contain a character. (When Knobby begins a situation, however, his boards are **uninitialized**—*their initial contents are undefined*, appearing as **???**) Knobby has a few instructions that manipulate the contents of these two boards. He can change their contents by copying a character from one board to the other. Clicking on the b1=b2 button or pressing **1** tells Knobby to place a copy of whatever character is in board b2 into b1 (replacing whatever may have been in b1); similarly, clicking on the b2=b1 button or pressing **2** tells Knobby to place a copy of whatever character is in b1 into b2 (thus replacing whatever may have been in b2). Note that the buttons imply that *copying goes from right to left*, e.g., the instruction b1=b2 copies *from* b2 *to* b1. Note also that *a board can only hold one value at a time*, so copying replaces whatever that board had been holding before the copying.

So far the two boards are alike, but there is also an important difference. Board b1 is connected to the outside world in a way that board b2 is not. Knobby can also take in a character from the corner on which he is standing onto b1, but not onto b2. When he does this, although a copy of the character appears on board b1 (replacing whatever had been there), the original character still remains on the corner—it does *not* vanish. This behavior, called **reading input**, occurs when you click on the read button or press **R**. In a similar way, Knobby can put a character onto the current street corner. When he does this, the character is copied from board b1 onto the current corner. This behavior, called **writing output**, occurs when you click on the write button or press **W**. Reading and writing are alike in that afterwards the same character appears both on b1 and also on the corner. Figure 2.15 summarizes Knobby's primitive instructions.

instruction name	behavior	key
move	moves one square forward	'M'
left	turns 90 degrees left	'L'
read	read character into b1	'R'
write	write character out from b1	'W'
b1=b2	copy from b2 to b1	'1'
b2=b1	copy from b1 to b2	'2'

Figure 2.15: Knobby's primitive instructions

Exercise 2.60: How can you instruct Knobby to take three steps forward, pick up a character, and return to his original position?

Exercise 2.61: What happens if Knobby attempts to perform a write at the beginning of a task? Why? How can a Knobby program avoid this behavior?

Exercise 2.62: What happens when Knobby performs a read from a corner that appears *not* to have a character on it? How can you use this behavior to *erase* other characters? Is there any situation where it is impossible to erase characters? Is there any situation where it is impossible to write characters?

Exercise 2.63: Now for some action! Press the `reset` button, so that Knobby is back where he started, ready to start a task. Knobby's goal is to pick up a copy of the flag, 'F', climb up to the top of the mountain (where it should find '^'), plant the new flag there, then climb down to the other side of the mountain. What problem solving strategy might you well use to solve this problem?

Exercise 2.64: There is no single command to copy a character from a corner to board b2 or vice versa. How, then can these tasks be done? Afterwards, how are the characters on b1, b2, and the current corner related?

It is often useful to consider these characters as *messages*. Physical objects can only be in one place at a time. Messages, on the other hand, can be transmitted to many places at the same time, by means of copy machines, conference calls, or electronic mail. Knobby is not just a taxi-driver—he is an electronic messenger boy. How many messages can Knobby carry? The answer is, just two: one on each board. If Knobby picks up (reads in) a message, the new one replaces whatever old message was already on his board. Similarly, when Knobby puts down (writes out) a message at some corner, his message replaces any old message that may happened to have been at that corner.

Exercise 2.65: Suppose we want Knobby to carry two *different* messages. (E.g., suppose Knobby is at 1st Street and 1st Avenue, and we want him to pick up two messages—one at 1st Street and 2nd Avenue, the other at 1st Street and 3rd Avenue.) How can he do that?

Exercise 2.66: Without actually doing it, what do you suppose would happen if you sent Knobby to the flag, had him read it, and then copied b2 into b1? Why? Now perform the experiment to see if your analysis was correct. (Don't forget to `reset` the world first.)

Exercise 2.67: `Reset` again. This time plant a copy of the flag on top of the mountain, then come back down and erase the (original) flag you've left at the bottom. How can Knobby "empty" board b1 in order to erase the flag? Hint: see exercise 2.62.

Exercise 2.68: Let's make a more realistic simulation of picking up an object. `Reset` again, and this time erase the original flag *before* carrying the copy up to the mountain top. Warning: this is tricky—why? Does this remind you of any problem from the previous chapter? Hint: some top-down decomposition should help.

2.7.3 Defining new instructions as macros

So far you've been programming Knobby by direct manipulation, pressing buttons and watching Knobby react. This style of programming is great for short and simple sequences. Often, though, you may find yourself repeating certain sequences of instructions. In fact, we've remarked above that it may be useful to think out some such sequences ahead of time. But things are even better than that! Knobby can be taught to remember such sequences of instructions as new user-defined instructions. For example, you could teach Knobby that turning *right* can be accomplished by making three `left`s. Click `Define` or press **D** to **define** an instruction. Knobby will ask you to name the new instruction. You might call it **right**. Then lead Knobby through the sequence of instructions that you will want him to perform. After the last instruction, click `Define` or press **D** again to end the sequence. Knobby will confirm that you have recorded a new instruction. To see if Knobby has indeed learned the new instruction correctly, press **E** to execute your instruction.

Knobby will ask for the name of the instruction to execute. Give the name of one you have defined, and Knobby will execute it (starting from his current state). If you mistyped the name, Knobby will complain that there is no such instruction. If Knobby does execute the instruction, you should make sure that he does exactly what you wanted him to do. If not, you have a **logical error**: *a syntactically well-formed sequence of instructions which nevertheless does not correspond to the behavior that the programmer intended.* Welcome to **debugging**: finding errors and fixing them!

Exercise 2.69: Define instructions `right` and `reverse` (direction). Then send Knobby through the task of planting a flag on a mountain, using your new instructions. (Remember, you perform a `left` or a `move` as before; you perform a `right` or a `reverse` by pressing **E**, then telling Knobby which new instruction to execute.)

Exercise 2.70: Now that you have used the defined instructions `right` and `reverse`, define *one* new instruction for the complete flag-moving task. (Test it to make sure that it works correctly.) In what sort of circumstances might this new instruction be part of a solution to a larger problem?

You've now learned to teach Knobby new instructions defined in terms of more primitive ones. You'll find that many editors, word processors and programming environments let you record sequences of instructions directly as *macro-instructions* ("macros", for short). A **macro** is *an instruction composed of a sequence of simpler instructions.* Macros can be great for developing a personal short-hand. Yet they have limitations. For one thing, Knobby's macros cannot *branch*, so they cannot select among alternative behaviors nor can they repeat a sequence of behaviors (we'll talk about these later). So in defining a macro you must know exactly what steps are to be taken. For example, to define a macro for climbing a mountain, you must know how many steps high each "peak" of the mountain is.

User-defined macros can helpfully serve as building blocks in problem solving. Recall that top-down decomposition involves breaking a problem down into smaller, easier to solve problems. When you are solving problems for Knobby, the subproblems you identify can become user-defined instructions which you can implement subsequently. A user-defined instruction can call other user-defined instructions (so long as they have been defined already), so you can break a problem down this way. Once you have broken a problem down to the level of Knobby's primitives *or previously defined macros*, you have an algorithm.

Consider the mountain climbing problem again. Let's start by asking the questions of preliminary analysis (figure 2.6). *What are the givens?* Knobby's initial location, the mountain configuration of walls and ledges, the flag 'F' to the left of the mountain and the top of the mountain, '^'. *Is there a way to generalize?* The mountain could conceivably be at a different position, and have ledges of different heights, and we should still be able to solve this problem in the same general way, while still taking account of the differences. *Is there a notation that represents the givens and other states succinctly?* Knobby's world itself provides an explicit representation: the givens can be defined by their coordinates which are the world's streets and avenues. *What are the goals?* To carry the flag 'F' to the top of the mountain, where there is a '^' character. This single goal can be subdivided into several subgoals. Here is an initial draft of subgoals:

> walk to the flag
> pick up the flag
> climb the mountain, a ledge at a time, until reaching the top
> plant the flag at the top of the mountain

Are these goals independent or connected? There are dependencies having to do with the flag. As you saw earlier, picking up the flag actually involves two steps: reading the 'F' into board b1 and erasing it by writing out a blank—a ' ' character. The connection arises because both the reading and the writing can only be done via board b1. Knobby needs not only to *read* the flag into b1, but also to *write* a blank out of b1. Recall that Knobby's boards start out uninitialized. So how does Knobby obtain a blank? By reading a blank from an *empty* corner, such as the one he starts out on. That way, when Knobby reaches the flag, he'll have a blank to write out. There is, however, another problem. If Knobby writes the blank out first, he'll erase the flag before he's had a chance to read it; but if he reads the flag first, he'll remove the blank in b1 before he's had a chance to write it! Do you see a solution to this dependency?

Are there obstacles to overcome? Yes, the ledges of the mountains. They may be overcome by devising a way, preferably a general method, to climb them. And so forth.

Knobby programming will let you practice your problem-solving skills. You should refine our initial set of subgoals, which in turn may decompose into other subgoals, and so forth, until you are down to the level of Knobby's primitive instructions. Then you can write an algorithm as a sequence of instructions, many of which are macro-instructions which call other more primitive instructions.

Exercise 2.71: Finish developing an algorithm for the mountain climbing problem by designing macros, then implement it. You may encounter limitations of macros that prevent you from generalizing a bit. If so, describe what you'd like to be able to do but cannot, at least with macros.

2.7.4 Knobby's programming language

A more powerful way to teach Knobby new behaviors is to describe them in Knobby's *programming language*. A Knobby **program** *defines one or more instructions in terms of other instructions*. Here is a simple Knobby program that defines three instructions:

```
define move3 as        //move 3 blocks
{ move   move   move }
define square3 as       //traverse a 3x3 square
{ move3  left   move3  left  move3  left  move3  left }
define main as   { square3  move   square3 }
```

Exercise 2.72: To use the Knobby program editor, press **Ctrl-e** or select <u>E</u>dit Program from the <u>P</u>rogram pulldown menu. Using the editor, enter the above program. When you're done, select <u>F</u>ile then <u>S</u>ave to save your program as file squares.kno (by convention, Knobby programs end with the .kno extension). Back in Knobby's World, select <u>P</u>rogram and <u>L</u>oad your new program squares.kno (Knobby won't be able to run your program until you load it), then run it. Because there is an instruction named main, Knobby will start executing this instruction, which in turn executes square3, etc. (What happens if Knobby is too close to a boundary or a wall?)

The Knobby programming language has a **syntax**, *a system of rules which define the form of valid Knobby programs.* Lest you think that rules are boring or inhibiting, remember that most games have rules, too. If you follow the rules of a game, there are penalties or you lose. If you try to run a Knobby program that does not conform to the rules of its language, you will get an error message. Figure 2.15 summarizes the rules:

1. A program consists of one or more instructions, which must take the form
   define *instruction-name* **as { *instructions* }**
2. The words and symbols in bold-face, such as **define** and **}**, must appear as is, literally.
3. The words in italics, such as *instruction-name*, will be defined by other rules.
4. An *instruction-name* consists of one or more letters or digits, starting with a letter.
5. The *instructions* are one or more of either *primitive-instruction* or *instruction-name*.
6. A *primitive-instruction* is either **move** or **left** or **read** or **write** or **b1=b2** or **b2=b1**.
7. You must **define** *instruction-name* before it can appear in other *instructions*.
8. The last (and possibly only) *instruction-name* in a program must be **main**.
9. A *comment*, beginning with **//**, followed by any other characters, may appear anywhere.

Figure 2.15: Rules for Knobby's World programs

For now, that's all the rules we'll need. (In the next chapter, we'll formalize these rules, and learn additional ones that define more complicated programs.) The rules define the *form* of Knobby programs. Now let's talk a bit about what programs that follow these rules *mean*:

1. A program begins execution at **main**.
2. When Knobby encounters an *instruction-name*, it begins executing its *instructions*, starting with the first instruction after **{** until the last instruction before **}**.
3. When Knobby encounters a *primitive-instruction*, it executes it.
4. Knobby ignores everything on a line following **//**. These comments are not for Knobby—they are for human comprehensibility. Comments allow a reader of a program to understand what its author intended. Moreover, writing comments can help you to avoid errors—if you make sure that your program actually does what the comments say it does! Comment *early* and *often*!

Exercise 2.73: Knobby's World automatically loads a program, written using Knobby's language, that accomplishes the task described in exercise 2.55 (the first Knobby's World exercise). Pull down the Program menu and select Edit to view the source code of program `mountain.kno`. Then, pressing the `step` option to observe Knobby's behavior one step at a time, write down the instructions that Knobby actually performs while executing this program.

Exercise 2.74: Think about it: how does Knobby's language support the problem solving strategy of top-down decomposition? Hint: to what part of a top-down decomposition does a `main` instruction
correspond? Draw a diagram (an outline or a upside-down tree) that shows the decompositional structure of the `mountain.kno` program.

Exercise 2.75: In `morning.sit`, Knobby wakes up every morning when a newspaper **N** lands loudly on the porch just outside his bedroom. Write a program so that Knobby will get out of bed, go out and pick up the paper and bring it back to bed. (The newspaper should act like a physical object, i.e., after Knobby picks it up and brings it in, it should no longer be outside!)

2.7.5 Creating initial situation files and libraries

For a reason we'll see in a moment—or just to pose Knobby new problems—it will be useful to be able to define new situations. That's not so hard. If you study `mountain.sit`, you'll see that it's a text file that specifies wall segments. For example, the first line in the file—

```
Wall 8,4   6,4
```
—specifies a wall segment from 8th street and 4th avenue to 6th street and 4th avenue, i.e, two blocks north and south on 4th avenue. Situation files can also specify the initial location of characters, each as a `Thing`, and Knobby himself. Study one of these files to see how it initializes Knobby's world, then try any of the following exercises.

One more remark: in several places you have seen the use of simple examples of defined instructions—such as `right` and `reverse`—which are re-used in many different contexts and programs. If you make it a practice to notice when this occurs, you are on the way to constructing a **library** of useful *instructions which can be re-used again and again*, either directly or with slight modifications. This is the idea behind "bottom-up" problem solving. As programs become larger and larger, they are written by teams of programmers, rather than by single individuals. To prevent each member of the team from "re-inventing the wheel," it becomes increasingly important to develop these libraries of routines. Object-oriented software provides more organization to libraries, further promoting reusability of software components.

Exercise 2.76: Situation `maze.sit` shows Knobby sitting at the entrance of a maze. Navigate him through the maze by hand. Introspect a bit: what problem solving strategy are you using?

Exercise 2.77: `Reset` the world and solve the maze problem again. Wait a moment though. What user-defined instructions would make it easier? If you've defined any of them in a program before, you don't need to rewrite them now! Make a copy of that program and get rid of that program's `main` instruction (and any others you don't think you'll need). (What problem solving strategy does this activity involve?) When you load that program file, it won't run (since there is no `main` instruction), but you can still perform the instructions you loaded. How? By pressing **E** to execute a user-defined instruction. Moreover, even if you load another program, any instructions that you do not explicitly redefine in the new program will still be in memory, so you can perform them, or call them in your new instructions. You have just begun to create a library of reusable instructions. Why is this a good idea? Create a small library and use it to help guide Knobby though the maze.

Exercise 2.78: If you like mazes, have some fun by creating your own maze situation files. (A couple of exercises earlier we explained what maze files look like.) Try to make yours more difficult! Does your maze program escape a different maze? If not, you could create a new program that specializes on your new maze.

2.7.6 Decomposition of an arithmetic problem

Though Knobby has no primitive instructions for arithmetic, he can nevertheless be programmed to add (or subtract, multiply, etc.). Figure 2.3, if you'll recall, showed a world in which Knobby is standing next to two numbers: XX (2) followed, after an empty corner, by XXX (3). In general, any number **m** will consist of the character 'X' on **m** successive corners of 1st Street. For *two* numbers, we separate them by an empty corner.

Before adding, Knobby goes to a "home base"—facing north (up) on 1st Avenue and 1st Street—then goes to work.

Now, what does Knobby need to do to add two (XX) and three (XXX) in order to get five (XXXXX)? Three things (notice the decomposition):

(I) fill in the empty corner after the first string of X's representing 2, so that the final configuration will consist of just one number, with one string of X's;

(II) erase the 'X' at the end of the second string of X's representing 3; and

(III) go back to his home base, showing that he has completed the task.

OK, how does he do the first subtask? (Let's break it down further.)

> (I)
>> (A) go to the empty corner;
>> (B) write an 'X' on it.

How does he do this? (That's right, we need to keep breaking the problem down until we reach the level of instructions that Knobby already knows how to perform.) In order to reach the empty corner:

> (I)
>> (A)
>>> (1) turn right — but Knobby doesn't know how to turn right, so:
>>>> (a)-(c) turn **left** (three times);
>>> (2) go to the empty corner:
>>>> (a)-(c) **move** ahead (three times).

Now on to (I)(B), writing an 'X'. Hmm... to write an 'X', Knobby needs to have an 'X' in board **b1**, which means he first needs to read it. But he can't read it now, because now he's on a blank square. As in the blocks world problem of Figure 2.10, subtasks (I)(A) and (I)(B) *interact*.

Let's assume Knobby has completed the first major subtask. The second was to erase the last X. How does Knobby find the *last* X? He goes to the first blank and moves back a square. How does Knobby erase something on a corner? It turns out that he can read a blank character from any "empty" corner. Then, *writing* a blank onto a corner "erases" what was there. Since Knobby is now on a corner with an X, he will need to get the next available blank by going one block *beyond* the last 'X'. Now the second major subtask breaks nicely into pieces, too:

> (II)
>> (A) go to the next blank corner
>>> (1)-(4) **move** ahead (four times)
>> (B) **read** a blank (into **b1**)
>> (C) return to last X
>>> (1) reverse course
>>>> (a)-(b) turn **left** (twice)
>>> (2) **move** once
>>> (3) erase corner
>>>> (a) **write** blank (from **b1**)

Now, with the exception of the third task (see Exercise 2.88), we're ready to code up a solution—you'll find it in the Knobby's World program, `adder.kno`. Try stepping through it.

Exercise 2.79: How can Knobby avoid this interacting subgoals problem above? Hint: plan ahead!

Exercise 2.80: Knobby's third task (going back to home base) is fairly easy—it has two main parts. What are they? How are they done?

Exercise 2.81: Construct a complete top-down tree for Knobby to perform his task. Label the "root" (i.e., the top node) "2+3". Use the three first-level subtasks noted above, labeled appropriately, as coming out from the root. Then sub-divide each of these as discussed. Keep subdividing each subtask down to the primitive instructions move, left, read, or write.

Exercise 2.82: Modify the above algorithm so that Knobby can add 3+4. Think analogically: what are the similarities and differences? What opportunities are there for reuse? Implement your 3+4 program (you may want to copy `adder.kno` first).

You may be scratching your heads about now. Why is it so much trouble to get Knobby to add two numbers? Well, in part it's because he's only capable of representing *unary* numbers directly. Still, it seems wasteful to have to "hard-wire" the addition of 2 and 3 into a particular program! It sure would be nice if we could persuade Knobby to add *any* two numbers, wouldn't it? Well, with an instruction for repetition and with a test for equality, operations we introduce later, we could generalize Knobby arithmetic. How? The key to the generalization is to discover the parts of the outline that need to be generalized. Go ahead: look for any "hard-wired" repetitions in the algorithm outline, then generalize them by a repetition instruction with an equality test.

There you have it! Using some analytical and analogical reasoning, we have discovered how Knobby can add any two numbers! And if Knobby can do addition, maybe he can do all sorts of arithmetic—subtraction, multiplication, exponentiation, logarithms? Why not? Knobby may have a cuter head than the universal machine, and he may be able to move in two dimensions instead of just one, but he actually has a lot in common with Turing's great idea.

Exercise 2.83: The Turing machine simulation in the multimedia for chapter 1 also included an addition program. Compare the Turing machine and Knobby's World solutions for this problem. Are they equivalent? Do you think one is clearer or easier to understand than the other? If so, why?

Exercise 2.84: How is Knobby's World like a Turing machine? Point out the things that are the same and the things that are different. Do any of the differences allow a Turing machine to do things that a Knobby's World program could not ever do, or vice versa?

Chapter review. Are the following statements true or false? Explain why or why not.

a) "Elementary, my dear Watson," alludes to Holmes' analytical approach to problem solving.

b) Hacking is a common but not a recommended problem solving strategy for novices.

c) Analogical reasoning involves breaking a problem down into smaller problems.

d) A recipe is analogous to a well-defined solution to a problem.

e) Sentences and programs are both essentially sequential structures.

f) Famous detectives and expert hackers ignore considering the givens and goals of a problem.

g) Turing kept the resources of Turing machines in his head.

h) The resources of Knobby's World are its walls and characters.

i) The givens of Knobby's World are defined in its situation file.

j) Real world problems usually start out well-defined.

k) A "blinder" effect can cause us to miss important givens, goals or resources of a problem.

l) Preliminary analysis begins the implementation of a program.

m) In the fox-goose-corn problem, the location of the boat is a variant, accounted for in our notation.

n) A blind hacking approach can get "blind-sided" by a combinatorial explosion.

o) Informed hacking relies on knowledge of a problem domain to get through a problem space.

p) Interacting subgoals is something that only happens in toy "blocks world" problems.

q) Decomposition is an excellent way to tackle problems about which one has little knowledge.

r) Analogical problem solving is just copying an old solution, as is, into a new problem.

s) Object-oriented programming combines analogical and bottom-up problem solving strategies.

t) The first task of object-oriented problem solving is decomposing down to primitive actions.

u) Knobby's macros can facilitate either top-down decomposition or bottom-up composition.

v) A Knobby program can have one `main` instruction, appearing at the top of the program.

x) Knobby keeps some handy, reusable instructions for composition of programs in his head.

Summary: How to Solve a Problem

After all this, you may well be waiting with bated breath for the general secret of how to solve any problem. Sorry—the "secret" is that there *is* no such secret! Problem solving takes knowledge and practice. If that doesn't bother you, you might really enjoy computer science. What we have tried to do in this chapter is to give you a set of concepts and approaches which can be applied in various ways to various sorts of problems. As we continue to explore computer programming, we will have many occasions to return to these concepts and approaches, so you should get to understand them now. As we explore other areas, keep them in mind to learn where, when, and how they apply.

When you get a problem, first do some **preliminary analysis**, which determines its:

givens—facts or state of the world that you start with,

goal(s)—statement(s) about a desired state of the world, and

resources—means or methods or moves that can transform a state of the world into another one, hopefully a step closer to a goal.

In **well-defined** problems, solving a problem involves formulating an **algorithm** (a precise specification of a behavior that will solve a well-defined problem) which will lead from a given state to a goal state. We have supplied a list of questions that a software systems analyst should ask about the givens, goals and resources in order to clarify the specification of the problem. Asking these questions can help you transform the problem from an ill-defined one to a more well-defined one.

We've also looked at three major problem-solving styles:

1) **Hacking**, in which one just dives headfirst into the problem and chains forward, one step at a time. Hacking often requires that one **search** for a solution: if a particular sequence of steps fails, one may need to back up to a previous state and try another sequence. A hacker may start to wander or jump around in the problem space. Hacking is OK if you have a pretty good idea where you are going ("**informed hacking**"), either one has expertise in a problem domain or the problem or subproblem is small, but it is not recommended for novices and/or more complicated problems.

2) **Analytical**, in which a sleuth or a software engineer approaches a problem logically and systematically. A classical (and highly recommended) analytical method is **top-down decomposition**, where you start with the goal and break it down into smaller subgoals (subproblems), until reaching elementary steps. A variant is **bottom-up composition**, in which a sleuth starts with the pieces of evidence and tries to put them back together to explain the mystery. A mixture of top-down and bottom-up is also possible. Analytical problem solving is highly recommended for tackling unfamiliar problems, because it doesn't assume as much knowledge about the domain.

3) **Analogical**, in which the solver notices that the new problem is similar to an old case (in a memory or library of cases). Then, taking into account differences as well as similarities between the cases, one adapts the solution for the old case to the new problem. Analogical reasoning can be as simple as copying and pasting code that worked before or as complicated as reasoning about the structure of atomic physics by analogy with the structure of the solar system—the analogy is a starting point. It may have flaws, yet even the flaws can be instructive.

For some real-live, concrete practice applying the techniques of this chapter, you can design algorithms and real-live programs that solve problems in Knobby's World. As you do, remember that thinking about thinking—reflecting on your assumptions and problem solving methods—can often help you break free of assumptions and biases, discover novel solutions, and even identify and correct "bugs"—errors in your nearly perfect algorithms.

Chapter 3
Programming Languages and their Translators
"... to another diverse kinds of tongues; to another the interpretation of tongues ..."
1 Corinthians 12:10

Wouldn't you need a translator to understand Swahili or Hebrew? Likewise a computer, which only speaks in a low level machine language, needs a translator to understand a high-level programming language. We say that a programming language is **high-level** *if it helps people focus on creating algorithms that solve problems, rather than the details of how a machine actually works.*

When you learned about the universal Turing machine in chapter 1, we made much of its potential—capable of solving any problem whose solution can represented by an organized set of logical operations. Impressive though that is, you may have noticed that it takes a lot of logical operations to solve problems with a Turing machine—nine rules to add two numbers, 29 rules to multiply. Why not just build addition or multiplication right into the machine? Indeed, most modern processors do have these operations hard-wired in (you'll learn how in chapter 5). But hard-wiring more operations into a machine does not necessarily go far enough, from the point of view of a person who wants to use a computer to solve a problem.

You may wonder, why not just talk to computers in English (or Chinese)? The answer to this question is that machines need instructions to be precise, while human or natural languages tolerate ambiguity. Words can have many meanings—for example, *ring* can mean a circular object or a resonant sound, among other things. Because of ambiguities, a computer program once translated *The spirit is willing but the flesh is weak* into Russian as *The vodka is good but the meat is rotten*! Natural languages help people describe the openness and unpredictability of the wide world. Programming languages, on the other hand, help machines solve problems in ways that are dependable and predictable. That's why, once you learn how to use a program, you can count on it to keep behaving the same way, given the same inputs.

The previous chapter introduced a simple programming language for Knobby's World. In this chapter, we'll start by taking a closer look at Knobby's relatively simple language, while introducing ideas commonly found in richer languages that you may have heard about, such as Pascal, C++ or Java. Then we'll look at the development of these ideas in several succeeding generations of languages. Finally, we'll look at how modern programming languages get translated into machine language, the code that a machine can actually execute.

3.1 Language structures

The previous chapter introduced Knobby's World as a way of reviewing different ways to solve problems. Knobby's programming language has the virtue of simplicity: it was designed for beginners. The goal of this section is to survey basic structures common to most programming languages. We will take a closer look at the language of Knobby's World, and along the way we'll expand our discussion to explore related, common structures in other languages.

3.1.1 Syntax diagrams

The previous chapter described the form of Knobby's language with rules in English. We hope they were clear, but as we said above, English is open to ambiguities. So computer scientists have developed formal notations to describe the structures of programming languages precisely. **Syntax diagrams** use a graphical notation, consisting of *labeled nodes* (circles or squares) *connected by directed arcs* (arrows). Figure 3.1 shows diagrams describing how to spell an *instruction-name*.

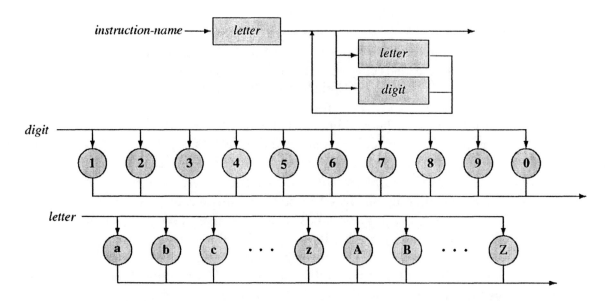

Figure 3.1: Syntax diagrams for *instruction-name* (identifier)

The diagrams show the flow of program elements by following arcs from node to node. So the diagram for digit can flow through any of the nodes labeled 1, 2, ... 9, 0 and out. Notice that there are two different shapes for nodes:

1) Circles are **terminal symbols**, corresponding *directly to symbols that may appear in the source code of a program*, such as the digits. A terminal symbol is also known as a **token**, something like a word or a punctuation mark in English.

2) Rectangles are **non-terminal symbols**, which *expand to other diagrams*. Whenever you see a non-terminal symbol in a rectangle node, such as *letter*, you switch to a diagram with this name, and when you exit this diagram, return where you left off in the original diagram.

Suppose you want to generate the *instruction-name* go2. The diagram for *instruction-name* starts with a non-terminal symbol, *letter*. So we switch to the diagram for *letter*. Though you don't see it, the ellipses (...) assume that you know that g would be a letter between c and z. After generating the token g we are done with the *letter* diagram, so we return to *instruction-name*. After *letter*, this diagram can branch either to *letter* again or to *digit*. If we choose *letter*, we transfer again to the *letter* diagram, this time generating an o. Back in *instruction-name*, the arc from *letter* flows back to the top line, where we can again choose either *letter* or *digit*. This time we choose *digit*, so we can generate 2 . Then we exit the diagram for *instruction-name*. Voila! We have generated go2.

Exercise 3.1: According to the diagrams of figure 3.1, which of the following strings are valid instruction-names, and which are not? Explain why or why not.

    a) abba b) comeToDaddy c) come-to-daddy d) 3blindmice e) Apollo9

Exercise 3.2: Here's how we first tried to describe the rule for *instruction-name* in English:

    "An *instruction-name* consists of one or more letters or digits."

What's wrong with this definition? Hint: Look at the first syntax diagram in figure 3.1. Can you rewrite it so that it is correct, in English? What's the moral of this exercise?

Exercise 3.3: When you switch from a non-terminal node in one diagram to another diagram, what do you have to remember or keep track of? Do you think this remembering capability is really needed to generate or recognize *instruction-names*? Why or why not?

3.1.2 Identifiers, numbers and operators

Other languages have a greater variety of tokens than does Knobby. An *instruction-name* is a special case of an **identifier**, *which gives a name to any programmer-defined object*. Many languages permit underscores (_) anywhere in an identifier, so instead of using capital letters, some programmers use _ to form readable identifiers, e.g., `pick_up_flag` is a single token in many languages, such as Pascal, C or C++. Java and C# also permit '$' in identifiers.

Most identifiers are defined by programmers when they write a program, but a few are defined by the programmers who designed a language in the first place. For example, when the lead author designed the language for Knobby's World, he chose to use the identifiers `define` and `as` to describe how programmers would define instructions. Such built in identifiers are called **reserved words** or **keywords**: since they are *built into the language*, programmers cannot use reserved words as identifiers elsewhere in the program. For example, `define read as` is illegal in Knobby's World, since `read` is a reserved word in this language.

Most languages also treat numbers as tokens. Numbers may be **integers** or whole numbers, such as `212` or `-459` (note that a negative sign can be part of a number). Or they can be **floating point numbers**, which are how computers approximate real numbers, such as `650000.0` (in decimal notation), or `6.5e5` (the same value in exponential notation); `0.000123` or `1.23e-4`. The notation *e5* means "move the decimal point five places to the right" (to get `650000.0`); the notation *e-4* means "moves the decimal point 4 places to the left."

Just as English has punctuation marks, most programming language treat some special characters as tokens. For example, most languages treat +, -, * and / as built-in arithmetic **operators**, denoting add, subtract, multiply and divide, respectively. Many languages also use special two-character tokens. For example, the token <= means "less than or equal" in many languages. You cannot have a space between the < and the =, since separately these are two different tokens.

Exercise 3.4: In which language(s) are the following identifiers—Knobby's language, Java, C++ or none of the above? Explain your answers.

    a) `go_for_it`   b) `goForIt` c) `go$4`   d) `go4it`   e) `4score`   f) `go+4`

Exercise 3.5: Why do most languages require that an identifier *not* start with a digit? Knobby also has this rule, but is it really necessary in Knobby's language?

Exercise 3.6 (*explore*)**:** Using a search engine such as www.google.com in a web browser, find lists of keywords for Java and C++. Which of the following are keywords in one or both languages?

    a) `class`   b) `catch`   c) `break`   d) `bool` e) `boolean`

From this exercise, what inference can you make about the relationship between these languages?

Exercise 3.7: Java and C++, like Knobby's World, use { and } to open and close a block of code, whereas Pascal uses the keywords `begin` and `end`. Which pair of tokens do you prefer and why?

3.1.3 Blackboards, variables and assignment

In Knobby's World, several primitive instructions have to do with copying characters from between the world and blackboards. For example, `read` copies a character from a corner of the world to blackboard `b1`, and `b1=b2` copies a character from blackboard `b2` into `b1`. A constraint of this copying activity is that a corner or blackboard can only hold one character at a time. So if you `read` a character, say 'F' from one corner, then `read` another character from another corner, say '^', then `b1` now contains a '^'—the 'F' it once contained has been clobbered.

The single value constraint is why it was a bit complicated for Knobby to "pick up" a flag

'F', which implies both reading it from a corner and writing a blank to the same corner. First Knobby has to `read` the 'F', then use `b2=b1` to copy the 'F' to the other board, `b2`, then move to another corner and `read` a blank character into `b1`, then move back to the 'F' corner, then write the blank, then use `b1=b2` to restore 'F' to `b1` for writing.[1] Why so complicated?

Here's why. Most programming languages have **variables**, *data objects whose values can vary while a program is executing.* Variables can hold just one value at a time. Similarly, as you learned in chapter 1, CPUs have **registers**, which can hold one value at a time. In the underlying machine, registers just have numbers, but programming languages make these things more convenient by giving them names. Just as Knobby's instruction `b1=b2` copies a value from one blackboard to another (right to left), the **assignment** operator of other languages *copies a value into a variable.* C-style languages (C++, C#, Java, JavaScript, etc.) denote assignment with an "=" operator, as in this expression:

```
pounds = 205
```

Assignment changes the value of the variable `pounds` to `205`. Variables in computing are not like variables in mathematics. One "solves" an algebraic equation, such as $X = Y / Z$, by substituting values for variables on either side of the equation. In C, on the other hand, "=" means assignment, not equality (which C denotes by "==", a *comparison* operator). Assignment *changes* the value of a variable on the left-hand side.

Exercise 3.8: Why is the expression $Y / Z = X$ illegal in C-style languages?

Exercise 3.9: Pascal and Ada express assignment with a slightly different syntax: `pounds := 205` How does this form avoid possible confusion with the form of assignment in C-style languages?

3.1.4 Data types

In Knobby's World, the blackboards and corners of the world only hold single characters. More powerful languages let you manipulate different types of data, using different operations. For example, it wouldn't make sense to multiply or divide characters. Even among the numeric data types, there are subtle differences. For example, integer division yields a whole number result— $5 / 2 \rightarrow 2$ (lopping off the remainder); real division keeps a fractional result, e.g., $5 / 2 \rightarrow 2.5$. To make sure the computer applies the correct operation, many languages require different notations to describe data in source code. A common convention is to surround single character data in single quotation marks, e.g., `'Q'` or `'5'`, and string data in double quotes, e.g., `"fun"` or `"76"`, so they won't be confused for integers. Besides different operations, the different types represent their data in different ways. For example, in C++ a single character is always represented by one byte, whereas a string refers to a array of zero or more bytes: `""` is a string of length zero, `"Q"` is an string of length 1, and `"fun"` is a string of length 3. Because of the generality of strings, `"Q"` and `'Q'` are represented differently in memory and so are not directly interchangeable.

Many languages require that programmers write a **declaration** *for a variable, specifying its type,* before using it in code. Here's how you can declare some variables in C-style languages:

```
int pounds; double kilos;
```

---

[1] Karel, another instructional robot world language similar to Knobby, carries around a bag which can contain any number of beepers. So another beeper doesn't clobber earlier ones that Karel has picked up. Karel's bag is like a **list**, while Knobby's blackboards are like single variables.

Figure 3.2: Visualizing Variables

Figure 3.2 depicts what these variable declarations tell the program to create. As you can see, a variable has an identifier, which a programmer uses to refer to this object, and a type, which determines the representation of the data and constrains the operations on it.

Why does an `int` get a smaller box than a `double`? In mathematics, there is an infinite range of integers, but a computer must define an `int` as an object in memory with some specific size. In Java, an `int` always gets 32 bits. Since the "box" allocated for a `int` has a fixed size, its range of values must be finite. With 32 bits, an `int` can range from -2137483648 to 2137483647. For a `double`, which represents a floating point number, Java allocates 64 bits. These bits are divided in two segments: some for the *exponent* (how many places to move the decimal point right or left) and the rest for the *mantissa* (the value). For example, the floating point number `0.123e-3` has a mantissa of `0.123` and an exponent of `-3`. Allocating a fixed number of bits to a `double` has a slightly unfortunate consequence: it limits the accuracy of the `double`. Because floating point numbers are only approximations of the real numbers of mathematics, floating point operations won't always produce accurate results. For example:

```
double a = 1000.43; double b = 1000.0;  a - b;
```

The result of the subtraction is not `0.43`, as you might expect, but `0.4299999999995`—close, but no cigar! It turns out that the number `1000.43` is not precisely representable in floating point format, which is after all a finite number of bits (10 for the exponent, 53 for the mantissa and 1 for the sign).[2] We call this short-fall of floating point arithmetic a **round-off error**. So computers aren't 100% accurate! Since the `float` type allocates half as many bits as `double`, it offers less precision.

The above two declarations also initialize the variables a and b, to the values `1000.43` and `1000.0`. **Initialization**, like assignment, gives a variable a value. Without initialization, variables may start out undefined. In Knobby's World a blackboard is initially `???`, reminding you that it is undefined; in programming languages undefined means whatever happened to be in that location of memory when the program creates your variable. It's usually a good idea to initialize a variable, unless you know that it's going to get a variable from an input source soon after it is created.

Many languages let programmers define new data types, constructing them out of the primitive ones built into the language. Here's how we define an `employeeType` in Visual Basic:

```
Type employeeType
      firstName As String * 30
      lastName As String * 30
      age As Integer
      wage As Single
End Type
```

Our new type has four parts, sometimes called **fields** or **data members**. The first two fields are strings of length 30, allowing for names of up to 30 characters. The last two fields are an integer and

---

[2]The IEEE (the Institute for Electrical and Electronics Engineering) developed a standard to provide some consistency between machines. If each manufacturer has a unique way to represent floating point numbers in terms of bits, programs might yield different results on different machines!

a single-precision floating point number. We can now define a variable using this new type:

```
Dim employee As employeeType
```

The keyword `Dim` (short for "dimension") introduces a variable declaration in Basic. We can then use a period to access the fields or members of this variable:

```
employee.firstName = "Jennifer"
employee.age = 24
```

Pascal uses the keyword `record` and C uses `struct` to define similar structures. (Once you learn how to represent something in one language, it's not hard to understand how to represent something similar in another language, albeit with a slightly different notation.)

Another common and useful data structure is an **array**, representing a block of values of the same type. Here are a couple of array declarations in Basic:

```
Dim scores(0 to 9) As Integer
Dim employees(0 to 999) As employeeType
```

The first declaration creates an array called `scores` containing 10 integers; the second declares an

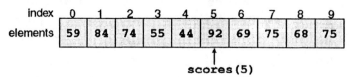

Figure 3.3: Array of scores with integer element values

array of 1000 `employeeType` records. (In Basic, we say "the dimension of `scores` is 10," hence the keyword `Dim`.) Figure 3.3 depicts the `scores` array, with 10 elements. Note that arrays are **homogeneous**, *each element having the same type*, whereas a `TYPE` or `record` is **heterogeneous**, since *each field may be different in type*. Because arrays are homogeneous, languages use a uniform **indexing** scheme to access elements, e.g.:

```
scores(5) = 92
employees(15).wage = 8.0
```

The value between the parentheses is an index or subscript, accessing an individual element of an array. The first line assigns 92 to the element at index 5 (the sixth element) of `scores`, while the second assigns 8.0 to the `wage` field of the element at subscript 16 of the `employees` array.

Exercise 3.10: The definition of `employeeType` above has `wage As Single`. To what Java or C++ type does `Single` correspond? Why do you think so?

Exercise 3.11: The **modulo** operator, `%`, produces the *remainder* left from an integer division. For example, 11 % 3 leaves a remainder of 2. What does 19 % 4 produce? What should 5.5 % 2 produce? (It typically does different things in Java and C++.)

Exercise 3.12: Given the following code: `double x,y; y = x / 7;`

A Java translator will complain: "`variable x might not have been initialized`." Why? How could the code fragment be changed to avoid this error message?

Exercise 3.13: Assign your last name to the variable `employee` declared above.

Exercise 3.14: Why do we say that 92 is the sixth element of `scores`, when its subscript is 5?

Exercise 3.15: Given the `scores` array shown in figure 3.3, what does `scores(1)` produce? What about `scores(9)`? What about `scores(10)`? (There a couple of possibilities for the last one.)

Exercise 3.16: Define a Visual Basic `Type` for a complex number, consisting of a rational and a imaginary value, both real numbers.

3.1.5 Instructions, statements and functions

There is a Chinese proverb, "Great things can be reduced to small things, and small things can be reduced to nothing." In Knobby's World, programs can be reduced to programmer defined instructions, and defined instructions can be reduced to primitive instructions. This is the way of decomposition that we learned about in the previous chapter. All programming languages support this way of breaking large problems down into smaller ones.

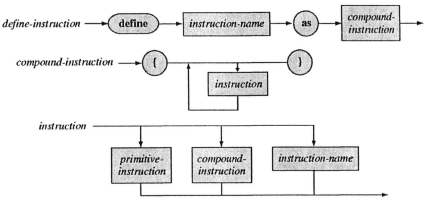

Figure 3.4: Syntax diagrams for *instructions* in Knobby's World

Figure 3.4 shows the syntax diagrams for defining an *instruction* in Knobby's World. The **body** of an instruction is a *compound-instruction*: zero or more instructions between { and }. In Knobby's World, instructions are effectively atoms. Even b1=b2 and b2=b1 are indivisible, though they are meant to resemble assignment expressions of other languages.

Things are a bit more complicated in languages that permit expressions built up from **operators** (tokens denoting instructions that an actual or virtual machine can perform) and **operands** (data that operators use to produce results). In C-style languages, b1=b2 would be an expression consisting of an assignment operator between two variables. Expressions can have many operators, e.g.: x=3+4*5. How does a translator know when an expression ends? Some possibilities are the end of a line (as in FORTRAN), a closing parenthesis, or a punctuation mark, such as a semi-colon. As figure 3.5 shows, the syntax for a *statement* in C-style languages is simple.

Figure 3.5: Syntax diagram for *statement*

Knobby's instructions also simplify what happens when a program transfers from one part of a program to another. Consider a simple Knobby program:

```
define right as { left left left }
define main as { right move }
```

Knobby transfers control from the **caller**, main, to the first instruction in the **callee**, right. Then it proceeds to execute all the instructions in the callee (in this case, three lefts), then transfers control back to the next instruction in the caller, move. Of course, things can get more interesting, if the callee itself needs to transfer control to yet another instruction. But so long as Knobby can keep track of where he left off, everything should work fine. This model of instruction call is common to all high level languages, except that instead of instructions, the building blocks of programs are variously called **subprograms**, **procedures** or **functions** or **methods**. The Knobby snippet above is equivalent to the following snippet in C or C++:

```
void right() { left(); left(); left(); }
void main() { right(); move(); }
```

Instead of define and as, we substituted void and (), and everything works about the same. But these new tokens are the simplest form of richer structures. In addition to transferring *execution*, most other languages also permit transfer of *data* from caller to callee. As the diagram of figure 3.6 shows, a C-style **function** has a return *type* (preceding the *identifier* naming the function) and a *parameter list* (between the parentheses following the function name).

In mathematics (and in most functions in a C++ math library), a function produces a value. A void function like those above is the exception: void means this function does *not* return a value.

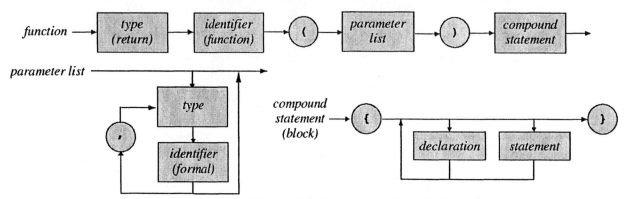

Figure 3.6: Syntax of C-style functions

Some programming languages, such as Pascal and Ada, distinguish procedures, which do not return anything, from true functions, which always return a value. C and C++ (as well as C# and Java) let you indicate the type of object that a function returns, or possibly nothing, as part of its declaration. A return *type* may be void or any built-in C++ type or programmer-defined class. If it is not void, the function can participate in expressions, including assignments, that expect an object of this return-type. Here is an example of a function that returns a value:

```
int cube_three() { return 3 * 3 * 3; }
```

The reserved word return indicates when the function will return a value to its caller. Function cube_three() always returns the result of the expression 3 * 3 * 3, which is of course 27. The result produced by a function can in turn be part of an expression in its caller. For example:

```
int cube_four() { return cube_three() * 3; }
```

This snippet returns the result of cube_three(), 27, to an expression, which multiplies it by 3; the value of *this* expression—81—in turn becomes the value returned by function cube_four(). Two things happen when a program reaches a return statement:

(1) the value of the expression to the right of return gets sent back to the caller

(2) control transfers from the callee back to its caller

Item (1) is optional: it's possible to omit a return value, when the function's return-type is void.

If a return type provides a way to get a data value *out of* a function, how do we get data *into* a function? The answer is through **parameters**, which appear between the parentheses after a function-name. For example:

```
double energy(double mass)
{ return mass * 186030 * 186030; } //c == 186030 == speed of light
```

Now you see what those parentheses after the function name were for. Function `energy` gets one input parameter, `mass`, of type `double`. Another function can call this function, like this:

```
double e = energy(3);
```

To follow what happens to parameters, it is useful to distinguish between the parameters in caller and callee. The **actual parameter** is *the variable or expression in the caller*, in this case, 3. The **formal parameter** is *the identifier declared and used in the callee*, in this case, `mass`. When we call a function, the actual parameter from the caller gets copied into the formal parameter of the callee. So in this case, the actual parameter value 3 gets copied into the formal parameter `mass`. The expression `mass * 186030 * 186030` produces the rather large value `103821482700.0`. Function `energy` returns this value to its caller, which in turn assigns it as the value of variable `e`.

Calling the same function with different actual parameters will cause the function to produce different results. For example,

```
double e = energy(4);
```

returns the value `138428643600.0` and assigns it to `e`. Thus parameters and return types allow functions to generalize the data that they manipulate. You can call a function from many different parts of a program, to use it in different ways.

This sort of generalization of program units is an important idea in computer science. A **library** is *a repository of many common functions* that software developers have tested and made available to other programmers. For example, many programming environments come with a math library providing functions such as `sqrt`, `round`, `sin`, etc. Programmers who want to use a library function just need to learn its **signature**: its *name, return type and parameters*, and perhaps a bit of documentation about what it does. For example, if we tell you that `sqrt` has a return type of `double` and takes one `double` parameter, you could figure out how to use it. You don't need to know how `sqrt` actually computes its result to use it. Libraries of functions illustrate the power of **procedural abstraction**: *hiding the details of code of in order to emphasize the essentials of what it does*. Libraries hide the details of implementation, letting other programmers concentrate on finding the program components they need to do their job.

Exercise 3.17: The syntax diagrams for Knobby instructions in figure 3.4 include *instruction* as a possibility within a *compound-instruction*, and *compound-instruction* as a possibility within *instruction*. How is this kind of definition more complex than anything we saw in the definition of *instruction-names* in figure 3.1?

Exercise 3.18: Functions are a bit more complicated than shown in figure 3.6. C-style languages also allow optional *qualifiers*, such as `static` or `volatile`, before the return type. Modify the syntax diagram for function in this figure to allow for optional qualifiers.

Exercise 3.19: Given what we just told you about `sqrt`, declare a variable n and initialize it to the square root of 25. What is the resulting value of n? (You may use a calculator to find the result.)

Exercise 3.20: Write a C++ function which returns the square root of the square root of a number. Write an expression that calls this function and explain what each function returns.

Exercise 3.21 (*explore*)**:** You can browse documentation for the Java Development Kit (JDK) on the web. Go to http://java.sun.com/j2se/1.5.0/docs/api and investigate some other interesting methods (in Java, functions are called **methods**). Describe a couple of interesting methods from the **Math** class and a few other interesting methods from any other classes in the JDK.

Exercise 3.22: After doing the previous exercise, reflect for a moment. What do you now know about these methods? What don't you know? Why don't you need to know everything about these methods to use them? Why is this a very good idea?

Exercise 3.23: How is a microwave oven panel another good example of the power of abstraction?

3.1.5 Control structures

So far, our Knobby's World programs have used the simplest control structure—so simple as to be almost invisible—the **sequential** control, executing statements in sequential order, one by one. Sequence alone produces a rather rigid kind of behavior—the sort of thing that led to the phrase, common in the early days of the Industrial Revolution, "the inexorable machine." Ada Lovelace and other pioneers of computing saw that other kinds of control structures would give a machine the ability to let the details of one action govern the nature of subsequent actions. This is crucial to a flexible, universal machine.

High level languages feature essentially two kinds of control structures—namely, **conditionals**, which *select* on some condition, and **repetitions**, which *loop* on some condition. Knobby's World expresses these two structures with the `if` and `while` instructions. Other languages provide many other structures, but conceptually they all boil down to select and loop.

Figure 3.7 shows the syntax diagrams for *conditional-instructions* in Knobby's World.

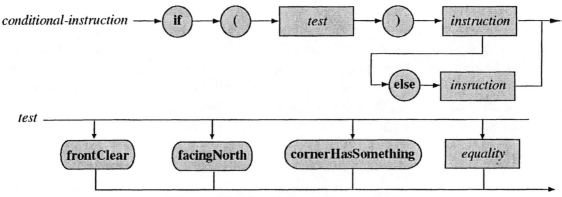

Figure 3.7: *Conditional-instruction*

Knobby's sensors allow a program to make simple *tests*, each of which furnishes a value of either **true** or **false**, depending on what a sensor is detecting. These are Knobby's tests:

> `frontClear`—true if there is no wall or boundary directly in front of Knobby, else false
>
> `facingNorth`—true if Knobby is currently facing north, else false
>
> `cornerHasSomething`—true if Knobby is on a corner with non-blank character, else false
>
> *equality*—true if b1==b2 or b1=='c' or b2=='c' where 'c' is any character, else false

Let's consider an example:

```
if  (facingNorth) write
else { move  left }
```

If the test `facingNorth` is true (Knobby's head is facing north, i.e., up), then Knobby will write the contents of b1. Otherwise, he will make a diagonal move to the left.

Knobby can also test for the **negation** of a predicate's truth value, with a **not** operator. E.g.:

```
if (not cornerHasSomething) read
```

If the test `cornerHasSomething` is *false* (the corner is empty), then Knobby will read that corner.

Exercise 3.24: The second example above has no `else` part. Is that legal, according to the syntax diagrams? Why or why not?

Exercise 3.25: Knobby's World comes with an example program called `ifwall.kno`. Load it, run it and examine its source code. What does it do and how does it work? What's a bit arbitrary about the way it's written?

Exercise 3.26: Write a *conditional-instruction* which tests to see whether there is a wall is directly in front of Knobby, and if so, he turns left, otherwise he moves ahead one square.

Exercise 3.27: Write a *conditional-instruction* which tests to see if `b1` is holding `'F'` and if so writes it on to the current corner.

Exercise 3.28: Write a *conditional-instruction* which tests to see if the current corner is empty **and** `b1` is holding `'F'` and so writes it on to the current corner. Note: Knobby's language has no `and` but it's still possible to express this idea.

Exercise 3.30: In Knobby's World, load the situation file `hurdle.sit`. In this scenario, Knobby has joined a track team. For the hurdle event, he must run as fast as he can to the goal 'G', "jumping" over any hurdles along the way. After developing an algorithm on paper first, code a program in Knobby's language which runs Knobby through the course shown in `hurdle.sit`. (For this version, *do not use a loop*; that's another exercise, below.)

As you might expect, conditional-*statements* in C-style languages are very similar to Knobby's conditional-*instructions*. There are two differences: 1) instead of *instructions*, they have *statements* (see Figure 3.5) and 2) instead of a *test*, they have a *conditional-expression* between the parentheses. These two differences allow a greater variety of possible forms.

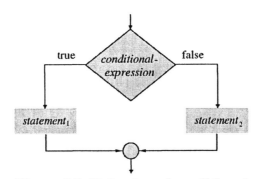

Figure 3.8: Behavior of conditional

So much for the form; what about the meaning of behavior of conditional-statements. For this, see figure 3.8. As you can see, at the heart of this control structure is a **branching** behavior. If the *conditional-expression* (like the *test* of Knobby conditionals) yields the value `true`, then the program will perform *statement₁*; if the *conditional-expression* yields `false` and there is a statement following an `else`, the control passes to *statement₂* and then to the statement following the conditional statement. If the *conditional-expression* yields the value `false` and there is no statement following an `else` the control passes immediately to the next statement following the conditional-statement.

Knobby has just a few built-in tests; the range of conditions in other languages is much greater. In Java and other C-style languages, an equality operator can compare the values of any two variables (e.g., `x == y`) or expressions (`x+1 == y+2`). These operators are applicable not only to numbers, but to objects of other types, such as characters. For characters, the lexical order derives from their ASCII codes, described in chapter 1 (see figure 1.6). Since the ASCII code for `'A'` is 65, `'B'` is 66, etc., `'A' < 'B'` is true.

The **boolean operators** *negation* (written `not` in Pascal or Basic, `!` in C-style languages), *conjunction* (`and` or `&&`), and *disjunction* (`or`, `||`) are the glue for putting together compound tests in boolean logic. George Boole's logical connectives express operations on the truth values "true" and "false". Figure 3.8 shows the meaning of the boolean operators in terms of **truth tables** (where T stands for "true" and F stands for "false"):

not (!)			and (&&)			or (||)		
α	!α		α	β	α && β		α	β	α || β
T	F		T	T	T		T	T	T
F	T		T	F	F		T	F	T
			F	T	F		F	T	T
			F	F	F		F	F	F

Figure 3.8: Truth tables for boolean operators

The columns headed by α (alpha) and β (beta) stand for any input expressions that produce truth values. The truth table for `not` (`!`) shows that, whatever α is, the result is the *opposite* value. The truth table for `and` (`&&`) produces T when *both* its operands are T, otherwise F. Finally, the truth table for `or` (`||`) gives F when *both* its operands are T, otherwise T.

One way to understand the evaluation of an boolean expression is to construct an evaluation tree, like those shown in figure 3.9.

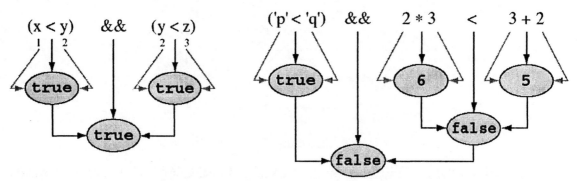

Figure 3.9: Two evaluation trees

We grow an evaluation tree topside-down, corresponding to the order in which the expression will evaluate. Let's consider the example on the left. First we evaluate the innermost, higher precedence operators—in this example, the parenthesized relational operators, which both yield `true`. These values in turn combine in outer, lower-precedence operators—here, `&&` yields `true`. The root of the tree, where all evaluations for an expression converge, yields the value for the complete expression. The tree on the right evaluates the relational operator > before the logical operator &&, because in C-style languages relational operators have higher precedence than binary logical operators.

Exercise 3.31: What is the truth value of the following C/C++ expressions? Explain why.

```
a)  3 == 7          b)  3 == '3'        c)  3 >= sqrt(3)
d)  'A' < 'Z'       e)  3 < '3'         f)  2 != round(2.3)
```

Exercise 3.32: Construct evaluation trees for the following expressions, assuming that the values of x, y and z are 1, 2 and 3, respectively:

```
a) (x > y) || (y < z)     b) !(z <= y)     c) z <= y || y >= z
```

Exercise 3.33: The truth table for or (||) above is for *inclusive* disjunction, since it is true if either or *both* operands are true.. There is also another kind of disjunction—*exclusive disjunction*—which is true just when one or the other of the components is true, *but not both*.) Construct a truth table for the *exclusive* sense of **or** ("xor").

Repetitions are familiar from nature. Many mundane human tasks also involve repetitions: whipping cream, washing clothes, sawing a board. Indeed, an advantage of machines is that they perform such repetitions without boredom. What makes repetitions interesting is that conditions *are not quite the same* during each iteration. The cream gets thicker, and when it's thick enough whipping can stop. Getting a loop right requires that we specify correctly when the loop must stop.

Knobby has only one form of *repetition-instruction*:

Figure 3.10: Syntax diagram for repetition-instruction

The effect of a *repetition-instruction* is similar to that of a *conditional-instruction*: both begin by performing a *test*. However, with the *conditional-instruction*, after *test* is performed, and the appropriate instruction executed, the process then goes on to the next instruction in the program. But with the *repetition-instruction*, as long as *test* evaluates to true, the "while-loop" will keep executing *instruction* (which may be a *compound-instruction*). For example:

```
while (frontClear) move
```

No matter where Knobby is, as long as his front is clear, he will move. Note that this version does not move just a fixed number of steps. Here's a simple program illustrating the while instruction:

```
//loopgoal.kno -- a simple program illustrating loops --
//    Knobby keeps going until he finds a goal, G
define reverse as    //turn around
{ left left }
define gotoGoal as  //go to the goal
{ while (not cornerHasSomething) move
}
define main as
{ reverse  gotoGoal }
```

With this program, Knobby turns around and scouts for a corner with a character, then stops. (You can try this program yourself; step through it to see how it works.)

The rules for while-loops in other languages are very similar, replacing Knobby's simple test with the same range of conditional-expressions possible for if-statements. As with Knobby, the loop body keeps executing as long as the loop condition remains true. (Each time through the loop body is an **iteration**, as in re*iterate*.) Like Knobby's *instruction*, the *statement* can be either a single statement or (more likely) a block or compound statement between curly braces.

Exercise 3.34: Write a Knobby's World loop that moves him ahead until he confronts a wall.

Exercise 3.35: Implement a Knobby's World program that gets Knobby to go to 1st Street and 1st Avenue (assuming there are no obstacles).

Exercise 3.36: Implement a solution to hurdle.sit (see exercise 3.30) using a while loop.

Exercise 3.37: C-style languages also have repetition statements with the form do *statement* while (*repeat-condition*). For example:

```
do n=n+1; while (n < 100 );
```

At a minimum, how many times must this instruction execute? Contrast the while form:

```
while (n < 100 ) n=n+1;
```

What's the minimum number of times this loop can execute? Which form is more general (i.e., using which form can we express the logic of the other)?

Exercise 3.38: Pascal has a "repeat-until" loop. For example:

```
repeat n=n-1; until (n == 0);
```

It executes until the conditional-expression is true. At a minimum, how many times must this instruction execute? How is it similar to the "do-while" form described in the previous exercise? How is it different? Rewrite the above example as an equivalent while-loop.

Exercise 3.39: Declare n as a integer and initialize it to 0. Then write a C-style while loop that increments (adds 1 to) n until n is 100. This is an example of a **definite** loop, *because it iterates a predictable number of times*. How many times does this loop iterate?

Exercise 3.40: Similar to the previous exercise, write a C-style while loop that counts *by 2*. Is this also a definite loop? How many times does this loop iterate?

Exercise 3.41: Many languages have syntactic forms expressing **definite** loops. For example, the following statements in Pascal and Java print the numbers 1 to 10, one per line.

```
for i:=1 to 10 do writeln(i);
for (i=1; i < 10; i++) System.out.println(i);
```

In both languages, a for statement does three things: 1) *initialize* a counter variable (in this case, i) 2) *test* to see whether it has reached a *final* value (in this case, 10), and 3) *increment* the counter variable. The loop keeps executing its body (in this case, an output statement), then incrementing the counter, until it reaches the final value, whereupon it exits, going on to the next statement. Rewrite the above loop as a C-style while loop. Rewrite the problems of the previous two exercises as C-style for loops. Which form do you like better for these problems, while or for? Can the previous exercise be written as a Pascal for loop? If so, how? If not, why not? What lessons do you learn from this exercise about the purpose and design of different syntactic forms for loops?

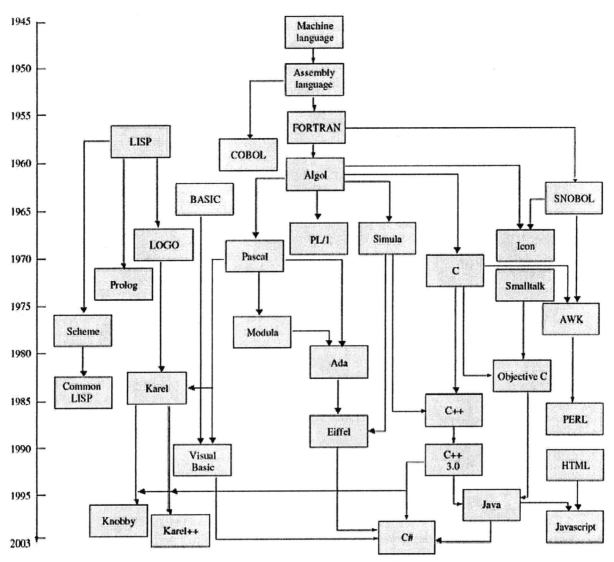

Figure 3.11: A family tree of programming languages

3.2 Languages for solving problems

We have reviewed enough common language structures that we can now ready to look at why computer scientists have developed so many languages. Why, in half a century, have computer scientists created more languages for computers than all the languages that people speak? Because there are many different kinds of problems and many different ways to solve them. Figure 3.11 shows a family tree of programming languages—despite how dense it appears, there are many more cousins and in-laws we haven't included. We'll examine them in terms of the kinds of problems they were designed to solve.

3.2.1 Machine language and assembly language

The universal machine and Knobby's World give you some idea how a computer works. A relatively small number of operations are hard-wired into the electronic circuitry of a machine. It gets instructions from a program loaded into memory, decodes these instructions one at a time in terms of its hard-wired operations, and executes them. Back in chapter 1, we also saw how bit strings can represent in binary code the different primitive instructions that a machine's circuitry can perform. Suppose a particular machine has 16 operations hard-wired into its circuitry—modern processors usually have more, but let's suppose. We assign a number to each operation. Operation #1 *halts* a program. Operation #2 *loads* a value from memory into a register. Operation #3 *stores* a value in a register back into memory. The last two operations also need to provide additional information: which register (another number) and which location in memory (another number). Operation #4 *adds* the contents of two registers together. (Note that we are now assuming that addition is hard-wired into our processor.) And so forth. Here's what a snippet of our **machine code** might look like to our lean and mean machine:

```
0010000110100100
0010001010100001
0100000100000010
0011000110100010
0001000000000000
```

Now a computer would find these 16-bit operation codes perfectly decipherable, but to you and me it's nearly gibberish! Maybe it would help if we had the computer "pretty print" the code, inserting spaces between parts of the code:

```
0010 0001 10100100
0010 0010 10100001
0100 0001 00000010
0011 0001 10100010
0001 0000 00000000
```

The first four bits distinguish 16 (2^4) possible operations, the next four bits are 16 possible registers and the remaining eight bits are either a machine address or a second register number. A little better? OK, not much. Suppose the computer displays the above code using decimal values (actually they are more likely to display machine code in hexadecimal or base$_{16}$):

```
2 1 164
2 2 161
4 1 2
3 1 162
1 0 0
```

Believe it or not, this is close to the machine code that the first programmers wrote! A few thousand headaches later someone began to associate mnemonics with the numeric codes (e.g., HLT for halt, LD for load, ST for store, and ADD for addition) and got:

```
LD   1 X
LD   2 Y
ADD  1 2
ST   1 Z
HLT
```

The two values (called operands) to the right of the operation symbol represent memory locations or registers. For example, LD 1 X means "load the contents from memory location X into register 1." This symbolic notation--associating symbolic names with operations, registers, and memory locations--is an **assembly language**. An **assembler** *translates an assembly language program into actual machine code*. Assembly language programming is still with us, especially for applications that require finely tuned hardware control or efficiency.

Since different machines have different primitive machine operations, assembly languages and programs written in assembly lack **portability**—i.e., a program for one machine won't work on another machine. Also, assembly languages force programmers to think at the level of a machine rather than at the level of problems. That's why higher-level programming languages were invented. For example, with Knobby's World, you don't have to worry about manipulating the graphics of the robot or its world; these details are taken care of for you by the programming environment.

Exercise 3.43: Write a simple arithmetic expression equivalent to the above assembly program.

Exercise 3.44: Why are programs written in high-level programming languages usually more portable than those written in assembly language? Why might one write code in assembly anyway?

Exercise 3.45 (*explore*): Using a web search engine, discover and describe a few applications using assembly language programming.

3.2.2 FORTRAN and COBOL for engineering and business problems

FORTRAN, the Methuselah of the family, still surviving after all these years, was designed primarily for solving scientific and engineering problems. A major goal of the IBM computer scientists who developed FORTRAN was simply to convince programmers, loathe to waste precious computer cycles, to use a programming language translator at all. The emphasis was on efficiency, which kept it close to machine code (for a particular IBM model of that era). They were *so* successful in designing for efficiency that FORTRAN remains in widespread use for engineering applications. Sticking close to the machine, however, led to code which conceptually still resembled machine code. Subsequent versions of FORTRAN have sought to add ideas borrowed from newer languages.

Though the first applications of computers were primarily for science and engineering, data processing applications for large businesses soon began to emerge. Grace Murray Hopper, in the late 1950's, invented a programming language called FLOW-MATIC that was the first business-oriented programming language. FLOW-MATIC was the basis for the development of COBOL (COmmon Business Oriented Language). COBOL's designers, including Hopper, sought to make COBOL's syntax somewhat English-like, though many programmers find it somewhat verbose. By introducing general data and control structures for manipulating files of records, COBOL became the language of choice for large data processing applications. Though COBOL is now considered a dinosaur by many, a huge legacy of COBOL code remains in use.

Figure 3.12: Grace Hopper

3.2.3 Algol-like languages for general-purpose programming

Elegance and generality in language design were goals of ALGOL (**Algorithmic Language**). ALGOL's generalized language structures were no longer tied to a particular machine architecture. (IBM did not see the wisdom of such generality and chose to stick with FORTRAN rather than support ALGOL.) ALGOL introduced machine-independent control structures such as **if-then-else** and **loops**. ALGOL also introduced **hierarchical structures** as a way to organize code. Similarly, Knobby's language lets you group many instructions together as a compound instruction, and you can **nest** one instruction inside another as deeply as you like, for example:

```
if (not frontClear)
        if (not facingNorth)
                if (not cornerHasSomething) { reverse move }
                else { left move }
        else { right move }
```

Let's appreciate the elegance of this structure by considering what the actual machine would have to do instead of using branch instructions. Suppose Knobby comes to the beginning of the fragment and finds its front *is* clear. Then it would have to branch past all the nested structures, to whatever instruction follows both else parts. The interpreter figures out where the branch should "go to" for us. On the other hand, if Knobby finds obstacles in front, right and left, then it executes the compound instruction—which here consist of the two instructions but could consist of any number—then also branches past both else parts. FORTRAN programmers used to have to code all these branches as explicit GOTOs, like this:

```
        IF (FRONTCLEAR) GOTO 30
        IF (FACINGNORTH) GOTO 20
        IF (CORNERHASSOMETHING) GOTO 10
        CALL REVERSE()
        CALL MOVE()
        GOTO 30
10      CALL LEFT()
        CALL MOVE()
        GOTO 30
20      CALL RIGHT()
        CALL MOVE()
30      CONTINUE
```

Pretty hard to read, isn't it? Fortunately, not even FORTRAN programmers have to code this way any more, because more recent standardized dialects of FORTRAN have incorporated ALGOL-like control structures. Spaghetti programs led one computer scientist, Edsgar Dijkstra, to write a now-famous letter to the *Communications of the ACM*, called "Go To Statement Considered Harmful." He argued that "the **go to** statement should be abolished from all 'higher level' programming languages," on the grounds that programs with many GOTOs create a "conceptual gap" between the static structure of the program (as one views it on the page) and the dynamic structure of the corresponding computations (as one traces the execution of the program). Dijkstra didn't quite get his wish. Many high level languages (including Basic and C++ but *not* Java) still have GOTOs. However, Dijkstra did help create the impetus for **structured programming**, which avoids GOTOs and instead *promotes the use of clear, comprehensible control structures*. It is most defensible to use GOTOs when dealing with errors, when the execution of the program must be terminated. More modern languages, including Ada, Eiffel, C++, and Java, provide language structures for **exception handling**, *which eliminate the need for GOTOs in response to errors*.

Exercise 3.46: What are GOTOs and why did Dijkstra consider them dangerous? Do you think it's a good idea to ban GOTOs from high-level programming languages? Why or why not?

Exercise 3.47: Studying the two code snippets on the previous page, from Knobby's World and FORTRAN, what GOTOs are eliminated from the Knobby code? Are these branches implicit in the Knobby code, and if so, do you think the Knobby interpreter will actually execute these branches? Why is it a good idea *not* to show these branches in the Knobby source code?

Exercise 3.48: Why would programmers typically use GOTOs to handle errors, such as invalid input data, during the execution of a program? Why have programming language designers introduced exception handling forms for thus purpose? Why not just use GOTOs?

ALGOL sired a large family of "ALGOL-like" languages in the late 60's, including PL/1, Pascal and C. Nicklaus Wirth designed Pascal, naming it after the 17th century French philosopher/mathematician. Intended as an instructional language, Pascal's design *emphasizes simplicity, security and structure*. Its *simplicity* (compared to more elaborate languages of its era, such as IBM's PL/1) makes it easy to learn as well as to implement, so that Pascal soon became the instructional language of choice on most college campuses in the 1980's. Its *security* model insists that programmers declare the types of all objects before using them, so the machine will not perform illegal operations. Its *structure* exploits the generality of hierarchical structures and emphasizes simple control structures that force the dynamic behavior of programs to flow *down* the page.

On the other hand, researchers at Bell Labs developed C (so called because it succeeded language *BPML*) as a **systems** programming language. Its design *emphasizes efficiency and flexible control over the resources of actual machines*. Indeed, C is known as "a structured assembly language." Unlike standard Pascal, C provides access to machine addresses and binary, bit-manipulating operations. Though C has high-level control and data structures comparable to those of Pascal, it also provides plenty of ways to subvert its type system, so that systems programmers can do what they need to do. For example, in Pascal,

```
n: integer;
```

declares the variable n to be an `integer`. Therefore, the statement

```
n := 'c';
```

is illegal, because it attempts to assign a character to a variable of type `integer`. In C, though—

```
int n;
n = 'c';
```

—the equivalent variable declaration and assignment are legal. A C translator figures that the programmer must want to assign the ASCII value of the character `'c'` (99) to n, and makes it so.

Like Pascal, C was widely adopted during the 70's, but for different reasons. Because it provides access to machine features yet is relatively machine independent, C became the language of choice for implementing operating systems, system utilities, and translators for other programming languages. Writing all but a fraction of the Unix operating system in C, then bundling C with Unix, helped make Unix (and later Linux) easier to develop and more portable.

Exercise 3.49: How does the type system of Pascal make it more suitable for beginners than C? If we told you that Java has a stronger type system than C++, which would you prefer for instructional purposes, and why? Which might an expert systems programmer prefer, and why?

Exercise 3.50: Why do systems developers implement most of their programs in C rather than assembly language on the one hand or Pascal on the other?

3.2.4 Improving general-purpose languages with modularity

Despite the popularity of these third generation languages like Pascal and C, computer scientists began to point out their flaws. While elegant control structure preserved a correspondence between dynamic behaviors and static code, the same could not be said for data. Wulf and Shaw wrote an article warning that "Global Variables Can Be Dangerous." Their title was obviously a take-off on Dijkstra's earlier letter, and the danger is analogous. Let's illustrate the danger with a fragment of code in Pascal:

```
count: integer; {declaring a global variable}
{ many hundreds of lines of code later, define procedure Max... }
function Max(x: integer; y: integer)
   count: integer; {declaring a local variable}
   begin
      count := count+1; {accumulate # of times program calls Max}
      if x > y then Max:=x else Max:=y;
   end;
{ many more lines of code later, we initialize count ... }
count := 0;
```

The first line declares a variable count near the beginning of the program. As the comment between curly braces suggests, it's a **global variable**, *a data object that is accessible throughout the program*. It would be accessible within function Max, too, except that we have also declared another, local variable with the same name within this function. In a **block-structured** language like Pascal, a **local variable** *declaration takes precedence over a non-local or global variable declaration*. So,

```
count := count+1;
```

in Max refers to the *local* version of count. That's probably not what we want, though, since the local variable will exist only while the program is executing function Max. That is, every time the program enters Max, it creates the local variable count again, then destroys it when it exits Max. So count will never accumulate a running count of times the program calls Max. On the other hand, if we eliminate the local declaration of count, then the statement in Max must refer to the global variable. The statement at the bottom of the code fragment initializes the global count to zero, then the statement in Max accumulates a count as desired.

Now our program fragment works, but Wulf and Shaw point out that this typical use of global variables permit changes to global variables to occur *anywhere* in a program. Like tracing the control flow of GOTOs, tracing the *value* of a global variable is also rather like following a strand of spaghetti through a bowl. It gets initialized in one place, incremented in another place, and probably displayed in yet another place. Programmers will need to jump all over the source code to figure out what is happening to such variables. If programs are thousands of lines long with hundreds of procedures, global variables can make programs very hard to understand and maintain.

These observations led to the development of the Modula and Ada languages, which introduce **modules** or **packages** that *more carefully limit access to data objects*, facilitating programming in the large, that is, developing systems with a thousand or more lines of code.

When Bjarne Stroustrup moved from Sweden to Bell Labs in the late 1970's, he wanted to graft some of the best ideas of the Simula programming language (developed in Sweden) onto the

C programming language (developed at Bell Labs). The strength of C was, and is, systems programming. On the one hand, it has high-level language structures (if-then-else, loops, etc.) that make it easier to describe algorithms. The high level structures are also much more portable than machine-specific instructions, so systems implemented in C are able to migrate to other machines more easily. On the other hand, C gives a programmer access to low-level instructions, such as binary logic and machine addresses, so that he or she can write efficient code. Systems programmers like this mix of high level structure and low level flexibility. Beginners and others may find the mix less desirable. Mucking around with machine addresses can be mysterious and potentially quite hazardous. Indeed a C program can quite easily damage the operating system, creating problems that might not manifest themselves until long after the C program has ceased running. Moreover, like Pascal, C is a block-structured language, permitting arbitrary access to non-local variables.

C++ is a **hybrid** language. It preserves all the capabilities of C, but provides ways to make it more secure and less obscure. However, C++ is a very rich and complex programming language. In addition to being a "better C," C++ adopts Simula's support for classes and object-orientation, building on the strengths of modular languages. Simula, as the name implies, was a language designed for implementing simulations of objects and their behavior. Suppose, for example, you want to simulate an airport control tower. Take a look at Figure 3.13.

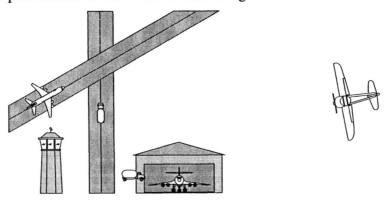

Figure 3.13: Identifying objects at an airport

It's fairly straightforward to think of objects in this domain, isn't it? Airplanes, landing and takeoff strips, gates, the tower, etc., are all objects. A simulation language should make it possible to model these objects and their behaviors. It's also natural to organize objects into categories or classes. There are many particular airplanes, but they all have many properties and behaviors in common. Simula, and later other object-oriented languages such as Smalltalk, Objective-C, C++, Eiffel, Java and C#, make it possible to describe a general **class**, such as `Airplane`, and then construct from individual objects from a class, all sharing the common properties of the class. The data or properties of an object are *local to that object*, rather than global to a program.

Exercise 3.51: Modifying a global variable in a local function or block is called a **side effect**. In terms of the example code fragment above, discuss why side effects are a bad idea, especially for software projects that involve programming in the large.

Exercise 3.52: Why would many programmers recommend capitalizing global variables—e.g., `COUNT` instead of `count`? Is this enough to avoid the dangers discussed above?

Exercise 3.53 (*explore*): Using a web search engine, investigate the idea of "namespace" in C++ or C#. How well do you think it addresses the problems with global variables?

C#. How well do you think it addresses the problems with global variables?

Exercise 3.54 (*explore*): Using a web search engine, investigate the idea of "packages" in languages such as Ada or Java. How well does it address the problems with global variables?

3.2.5 Solving problems with strings, symbols and lists

FORTRAN was designed to be especially good at number processing. It even has a built-in type for complex numbers, rarely needed outside of scientific or engineering applications, and not included in business-oriented COBOL or any of the more general purpose Algol-like languages. On the other hand, other languages have emerged that specialize in string or symbol processing. For example, SNOBOL, Icon, AWK and PERL have many built-in string-manipulating operations. Here is a code snippet of Icon code:

```
str := "line upon line"
every str ? write(find("line")) || " "
str ? while t := t || move(4) || "-" || move(1)
write(t)
```

prints 1 11 line- upon- line-. The first line creates a string, str, containing the sequence of characters "line upon line". The second line uses Icon's scanning operator ? to scan across the contents of str, and also uses the find operation to returns positions at which the substring "line" begins—in this case, at positions 0 and 11. The third line scans across str again, this time creating a new string t: the move(4) operation grabs four characters of str, the || operator concatenates two strings together and the move(1) operation gets one more character. It keeps doing this while there are more characters in str, then the last line writes out everything concatenated into t: line- upon- line-. String processing features like these facilitate processing of ASCII text files, such as web pages or program source files.

Shortly after IBM started developing FORTRAN, John McCarthy started inventing a very different language, in order to explore how to get machines to model artificial intelligence. Instead of numbers, LISP emphasizes lists and symbols, hence **LIS**t Processing. Symbols have names, and can store values or lists. Let's consider an example of symbol and list processing:

```
(reverse (list 'Pam ('Adam 'Abby)))
```

Let's analyze how this works from the inside out. The single quotation marks tell LISP to use the symbols Pam, Adam and Abby literally (otherwise, LISP would try to get a value associated with each symbol). The function list then constructs a list from what follows (a symbol followed by a list), producing (Pam (Adam Abby)). Finally, the function reverse produces another list that reverses the list produced by list: ((Adam Abby) Pam)

LISP, based on Alonzo Church's lambda calculus, is the first language to support **functional programming**, or *programming by combining functions*. In his ACM Turing lecture in 1978 for his work on FORTRAN and Algol, John Backus argued for functional programming as a new paradigm for programming languages. A *paradigm* is a systematic way of seeing things; for example, the way people viewed the relationship between earth and the heavens when the Copernican system superseded the Ptolemaic. The von Neumann machine creates a paradigm for most programming languages. But the von Neumann machine has bottlenecks that cramp the potential of computing. All instructions must flow, one at a time, through the instruction pointer, forcing serial flow and making GOTOs all too easy to implement. All data must eventually get loaded into a small number of high-speed data registers, leading to an emphasis on assigning values to variables. As a result, the von Neumann machine paradigm makes **parallelism**—*programs which execute more than one* *strand of instructions at the same time*—hard to think about, and also leads to excessive emphasis on structures that control access to names, so they won't get tampered with accidentally or otherwise.

Backus developed a notation to make programming more like mathematics. Functions produce results. In functional programming languages, such as LISP and ML, more complex behaviors are the result of functions that apply the results of other functions. For example:

```
>(mapcar 'add1 '(1 7 5 3))
(2 8 6 4)
```

Function `mapcar` applies another function to a list. In this case, the function being applied is `add1`, which increments its argument by 1. So (`add1 1`) produces 2. In turn, `mapcar` keeps applying `add1` to a list of arguments (in this case (`1 7 5 3`)), producing another list of incremented arguments, shown on the second line above. Function applications avoid storing values in variables and so can bypass the von Neumann bottleneck. To date, however, functional language interpreters have been implemented only on machines with von Neumann architectures. Old paradigms die hard!

Logic programming also tries to break away from the procedural paradigm. Ideally, one just provides a collection of axioms and theorems, then lets the built-in logical inference machine prove, deductively, what you want to know. Whereas the **procedural** paradigm emphasizes *how* to solve a problem, i.e., algorithm development, the **declarative** logic paradigm emphasizes *what* is known. Prolog implements logic programming by letting the programmer supply a database of facts and rules and then reasoning via the logically sound rule of resolution. Here is a simple database:

```
teaches(john,biology).  teaches(laura,physics).
teaches(fred,english).  teaches(sue,english).  teaches(sue,music).
science(biology).  science(physics).
science_teacher(P) :- teaches(P,S) and science(S).
```

Each of the seven facts in the database is a unit clause or fact, consisting of the name of a predicate, e.g., `teaches`, followed by a list of arguments, e.g., `john` and `biology`. We can read the first fact, in English, as "John teaches biology." The last line is a rule, consisting of a head, a `:-` operator (read "if"), followed by a body of clauses. We can read this particular rule as a backwards if-then rule, that is, "if P teaches S and S is a science then P is a science teacher."

Given this database, one can pose queries (goals) which the inference engine will attempt to prove. Here are a few examples:

```
?- teaches(laura,physics).
yes
?- teaches(laura,math).
no
?- teaches(laura,X).
X=physics
?- teaches(T,english).
T=fred ;
T=sue
?- science_teacher(P)
P=john ;
P=laura
```

The first query produces `yes` because it matches a fact in the database; the second produces `no` because there is no proof of it from the database. The third query produces a more specific solution:

it succeeds, with X bound to physics. The fourth query produces two possible answers—Prolog backtracks to find alternative solutions. Finally, the fifth query uses a rule, succeeding because the body of the rule, teaches(P,S) and science(S), produces a solution, with P bound to john and backtracking produces a second answer, with P bound to laura. As you can see, a Prolog program consists of database of facts and rules, with no explicit control structures. However, Prolog is not a pure declarative logic; because of backtracking, Prolog programmers still have to think about and often take control of the order in which the inference engine attempts to prove things. Nevertheless, logic programming has also motivated the design of new machine architectures that break free of von Neumann machine architecture, with its bottleneck of executing one instruction at a time through the program address register.

Exercise 3.55 (*explore*): Using a web search engine, discover a couple of interesting string-processing features of AWK or PERL, and describe how they might be used, practically.

Exercise 3.57: Given (list (last ('mom 'dad)) (last 'Gladys 'Albert))), what would LISP produce? As you might expect, last produces the last element of a list.

Exercise 3.58: A little more obscurely, car produces the first element a list, while cdr produces the rest of a list. So what does (list (car (1 2 3)) (cdr (4 5))) produce?

Exercise 3.59: If (abs n) returns the absolute value of n, what is the result of the function (mapcar 'abs '(-1 7 -5)? Contrast the way a typical von Neumann machine and a parallel processing architecture might evaluate the mapcar function.

Exercise 3.60: Given the database above, what does Prolog produce from the following queries?

```
?- teaches(laura,Subj).
?- teaches(T,Subj).
```

Exercise 3.61: Add a rule for humanities_teacher to the above database, then show the results of querying for humanities_teacher(T).

Exercise 3.62 (*social/ethical*): Can languages affect how people think about problems? How has the von Neumann machine—with its emphasis on pumping instructions through a program address register and data through a small number of data registers— affected the way people think about solving problems with computers? How has it affected the design of many programming languages, especially procedural languages such as FORTRAN, Algol, Pascal, C++, etc.? Hint: think about constructs such as statements and compound statements, variables, and assignment. How do procedural languages possibly limit the way people think about solving problems with computers? How might non-procedural languages be liberating or empowering for some people?

Exercise 3.63 (*social/ethical*): Certain programming languages develop a following in particular communities. For example, most Artificial Intelligence researchers like LISP or Prolog (each with its own sub-community), systems programmers like C, many engineers stick with FORTRAN, many business or government executives stick with COBOL, World Wide Web developers are buzzing about Java, while Microsoft is promoting C# as an alternative to Java within its .NET framework. What kind of attitudes would you expect a community to have about its language of choice vs. those of other communities? How can these attitudes affect the way members of these communities relate with each other? What would you recommend to improve relationships between these different communities and why?

3.3 Language translators

There are generally two kinds of programming language translators: interpreters and compilers. At the United Nations, human interpreters provide simultaneous translation from a speaker's language into a hearer's language; afterwards, more meticulous translators (the analogue of compilers) can produce transcripts of entire speeches. An **interpreter** for a language is *a virtual machine for that language.* It translates and executes each line of a program as the line is encountered. For example, when you get into LISP and enter an expression such as

```
> (car (cdr (glenn blank)))
```

the LISP interpreter immediately analyzes it and produces

```
blank
```

So LISP provides virtually immediate translation, which is very useful for exploratory programming and **rapid prototyping,** or *quickly producing a running program that shows what a finished product might look like.* One reason Basic became a dominant language for education is that its interpreter gives students quick feedback and facilitates hands-on programming. (On the other hand, these features can encourage hacking!)

Compilers, on the other hand, *translate programs into lower-level machine code* which can later run on the target machine. FORTRAN, ALGOL, Pascal, C, Ada, C++, etc., all have compilers that translate their source code into actual machine code. A compiler translates C++ source code into machine code that a processor such as a Pentium can actually execute. Because it runs directly on an actual machine, compiled machine code is typically many times faster than equivalent interpreted code. On the other hand, while interpreting is almost instantaneous, compiling from source to machine code takes time, from minutes to hours, depending on the size of the program.

To complicate matters, some languages feature the best of both worlds: *first compiling* source code into code in an *intermediate* language, *then interpreting* the intermediate code. The immediate code runs on a virtual machine, simulated by a program, rather than an actual machine. For example, Knobby programs are compiled into instructions written in the Knobby's World program (a virtual machine) rather than in terms of your computer's machine code (an actual machine). We'll take a look at Knobby's intermediate code later in the chapter and the multimedia. Java, C# and some other languages work the same way. The javac command translates programs into instructions that a Java Virtual Machine (JVM) can interpret. The java command actually invokes the virtual machine. So, Java compiles source code to intermediate code, which in turn executes in a JVM. One advantage of this hybrid approach is faster translation time, since it's usually easier to translate to intermediate than actual machine code. Another is portability: once a JVM has been ported to another actual machine, all Java programs will also run on the target machine. Java has been successful in part because the JVM has been installed in many web browsers. Java thus supports rapid prototyping and easy porting of interactive Web pages.

Interpreters also have the advantage of being able to perform more checks at **run-time** (*while your program is running*) to prevent and more easily diagnose errors. For example, the Knobby interpreter prevents Knobby from crashing into walls. Or consider what happens when a program tries to divide x by y. An interpreter can check that x and y are both numbers, and may even make sure that y is not 0. Few actual machines make these checks (since the checks would make the processor slower and much more complicated). With such errors a compiled program will "crash"—i.e., stop running, often mysteriously. An interpreter which stops with an intelligible error message is surely preferable to a program that stops running without any explanation!

Compilers try to prevent such disasters by performing more checks at **compile-time** (*while it is translating your program*). To do so, compiled languages usually require that programmers provide more information. C++, Java, C# and other compiled languages require that programmers specify type information about variables in advance, for example,

```
float x,y;
```

Here, the compiler is being told that x and y are floating point numbers. Thus the compiler can perform **type checking** to be sure the operations used on x and Y are legal. It's all right to multiply x and y because they are of type float (and not, say, strings of characters). But a C++ compiler that sees x % y will flag the modulo (remainder) operation, which is legal for values of type int (integers) but not float, as an error. After all, floating point division does not leave a fractional remainder. Thus compilers can catch some errors in a program's intended meaning before they have a chance to occur, whereas interpreters won't catch them until they actually do occur. To spare users from strange run-time error messages, software engineers generally prefer as much compile-time error checking as possible.

Exercise 3.64 (*explore*): Java (and C#) usually compile to code for a virtual machine (VM). What is a drawback of running VM code instead of actual machine code? What is "Just-In-Time" (JIT) compiling and how does it help overcome a drawback of running VM code?

Exercise 3.65 (*explore*): While C and C++ programming environments usually translate to actual machine code, there are a few interpreters available. Use a web search engine to investigate and write a short report discussing the purported advantages of interpreters for these languages.

Exercise 3.66: Knobby will warn you if you try to write out the contents of an uninitialized blackboard (i.e., if a program has a write before doing a read). Why is this check easier for an interpreter than a compiler? (Explain how each would catch such an error.)

Exercise 3.67: Suppose x and y were defined as string (strings of characters). Why would it be a good idea for a translator to check the type of x and y before allowing the operation x * y? Why is it necessary in order to translate the operation x + y correctly?

Exercise 3.68: Unlike C++, a Java compiler will accept x % y, by first converting the operands to int, then producing the result of the integer modulo (remainder) operation. Which design do you think is better? Is a Java compiler still using information about the types of the operands? How so?

Exercise 3.69: A compiler might object to the first statement below, but not the second:

```
x = y / 0;  x = y / x;
```

Some compilers will flag the divide by zero error in the first statement. A divide by zero error could be lurking in the second statement. How could this happen? Why can't a compiler catch this error? What would an interpreter do to catch this error?

3.3.1 How C++ and Java compilers produce machine code

Most C++ compilers go through the sequence of steps shown in figure 3.14.[3] Java compilers go through similar stages; we will note differences below. Nowadays most compilers automatically

---

[3] One exception is a translator that Bjarne Stroustrup et al. developed at AT&T Bell Labs. This program actually translates C++ code into C, then invokes a C compiler to do the rest.

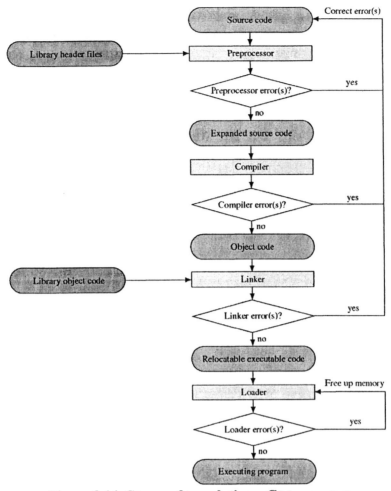

Figure 3.14: Stages of translating a C++ program

run as many of the stages of translation as possible (unless for some reason a stage must halt because of an error in the program). The **preprocessor** (itself a program, usually called cpp) *goes first, scanning your program for any compiler (or preprocessor) directives.* These special instructions always start with the '#' character. Here, for example, is a line you will find in most C++ programs:

```
#include <iostream>
```

The preprocessor sees the #include command and processes it by including the contents of file iostream into your source code at this point in the program. The angle brackets, <..>, are a hint to the preprocessor to look for this file in a directory associated with the compiler. Most compilers supply iostream. Such files are known as **header files**, because they usually appear at the head or top of C++ source code files. At one time, header files always had the extension .h—for example, iostream.h. This file supplies information about the input/output ("I/O") library. After the preprocessor has done its work, it produces an intermediate file (which you will rarely ever see) in which all the preprocessor instructions have been replaced by C++ code that the rest of the translation process will understand. The compiler is now prepared to accept code that refers to names declared in the header file, such as cout. The preprocessor may, however, find errors in your compiler directives. Suppose it cannot find the file iostream (either because it has not been installed or the compiler cannot find its directory). Then the preprocessor will issue an error message complaining about this unknown file.

Java, on the other hand, has no preprocessor step. You may be thinking, "But aren't Java's `import` statements rather similar to C++'s `#include` directive?" Indeed, they both do include source code from other files, but Java's `import` is handled by the compiler rather than a preprocessor. Notice that `import` needs to end with semicolon, while the `#include` directive has a special syntax known only to the preprocessor. The `import` statement is a bit "smarter" because the Java compiler knows more about the structure of the Java language than the preprocessor knows about C++. The **compiler** takes source code (in the case of C++, expanded source code from the preprocessor) and *attempts to translate it* into something a machine can almost (but not quite) execute. If it succeeds, a C++ compiler will produce a file of **object code**, *consisting of actual machine instructions in binary format*. A Java compiler, on the other hand, will produce a file of **byte code**, *consisting of Java virtual machine code in the form of a long string of bytes*. (We will learn more about byte code later.) C++ object code files typically have an extension `.obj` on PCs (and `.o` on other platforms), while Java byte code files have an extension `.class` on all platforms. If your source C++ program has the name `myprog.cc` or `myprog.cpp`, then a successful compilation will produce the file `myprog.obj`. Not so fast, however! The compiler may notice errors in your program. Its error messages are (sometimes obscure) hints about what you need to fix.

Exercise 3.70: Error messages may seem like a nuisance. Nevertheless, why are error messages a good idea? What do you think would happen if a translator did not issue error messages?

Exercise 3.71: Why does Java generate byte code instead of actual machine code? Do you think it might be possible for a Java compiler to generate actual machine code instead? What would be the advantages and disadvantages of doing so?

Though C++ object code is binary machine code, it is not quite executable. Usually it needs other object code, from libraries. It's the same with Java `.class` files; their virtual machine code depends on a lot of code from libraries. A software **library** is *a repository of code* that's already been designed, implemented, tested, compiled, and maintained for you. Remember `iostream`? That was a header file, an interface to a library. The **interface** describes how to use the library; a compiler also uses the interface to ensure that you use library code correctly. For example, `iostream` describes an object called `cout`. This header file declares that `cout` is of type `ostream`. If a program doesn't `#include iostream`, then the compiler won't know the type of `cout` (indeed, `cout` will be undeclared) and you'll get more error messages. The machine code corresponding to `iostream`, including the definition of `cout`, is kept in a library of object code maintained by the compiler. Similarly, `java.awt.*` refers to packages already compiled into Java byte code.

Exercise 3.72: A library consists of *object* code that has already been compiled. Can you think of a couple of reasons why it's a good idea to store object code rather than source code in a library?

Exercise 3.73: Can you think of a couple of good reasons why it might be a good idea to store *source* code rather than object code in a library? Why do you suppose this is *not* the usual practice?

The next step involves the **linker**. With C++, the linker takes your object file, *combines it with object code from other files including libraries*, and produces an executable program (with extension `.exe` on a PC). The linker resolves references to objects and declared (mentioned) but not defined in your source code, such as `cin` and `cout`, which have already been pre-compiled into object code libraries by your compiler vendor. The linker may also produce error messages, if it cannot find a definition of some object that was declared in your program or a header file it includes. Java also has a linker, which also combines code—byte code instead of object code—including code in libraries. An important difference, though, is that the Java linker is **dynamic**—it does its work at run-time, finding any code it needs on the fly. As a result, Java programs can be more flexible, adding capabilities as they are needed. Also, Java avoids the need for large executables that contain everything that might be needed. (Actually, the idea of dynamic linking has its counterpart in the C++ world, in the form of dynamic link libraries, with the extension `DLL` on Windows platforms.)

Finally, the **loader** takes an executable program file, *loads it into main memory*, and begins executing it. If your operating system permits more than one program to run at the same time, it also has to decide *where* in memory to load your program. In this case, the linker assumes that the executable code it creates will start at address zero. An operating system can then load the program anywhere it can find enough memory. The actual starting address where the program loads into memory is called the **base address**: *all other addresses are relative to this address*. The system automatically adds any addresses in executable code (the **relative offset addresses**) to the base address. For example, if a relative offset address is 200 and the base address is 12000, then 12200 is the actual machine address when the program is running.

Many integrated programming environments will automatically attempt to load your program for you. You can also load an executable program by typing its name at the OS prompt. Loading can also fail, for example, if there is not enough memory currently available. If that happens, you may need to "unload" other programs from memory (by closing them), and try, try again. There seem to be so many obstacles to success when writing a program, but success is readily achieved.

Exercise 3.74: If a relative offset address of a variable in a program is 128 and the base address for the program is 6400, what is the actual machine address of this variable?

Exercise 3.75: How does *loading* illustrate von Neumann's idea of a stored program machine?

Exercise 3.76: Why do you need to run Java applications, such as the `Hello.class`, by typing `java Hello`, rather than just `Hello`?

3.3 Inside Knobby's programming language translator

At the heart of Knobby's World is a simple machine rather like the universal Turing machine or the von Neumann stored program machine that were introduced in chapter 1. How is Knobby like a universal machine? Knobby's world is like Turing's tape, only with two dimensions instead of just one. Also, just a small set of instructions move Knobby (his pointy head is like the universal machine's read/write head), and read, write, erase symbols in his world. How is Knobby also like a von Neumann machine? They both have design features that make them more suitable for programming. They both can read programs from a file, store them in memory and execute them. Also, Knobby's two boards are like registers and Knobby's interpreter is like a control unit, decoding and executing sequences of instructions.

Instead of being hard-wired into the silicon of an **actual machine**, Knobby's instructions are executed by another program. Thus Knobby's World is a **virtual machine**, a machine implemented in software. (Java's "world" is also a virtual machine.) Like a von Neumann machine, Knobby has a current instruction pointer (program address register) and an **interpreter** that fetches, decodes and executes its primitive instructions. Knobby's blackboards are analogous to registers—both hold small amounts of data. The mouse (or keyboard) input and screen output are connected to but not part of the essential Knobby machine (it maintains an *internal representation* of Knobby's world). When the mouse clicks on a `move` button, the user interface sends a one character (or byte) code, in this case 'm', to the Knobby machine. The interpreter gets the byte 'm', decodes it as a `move` and executes the corresponding primitive instruction. The `move` instruction modifies Knobby's position in the internal representation of its world stored in memory, then signals the Knobby's World interface to redisplay itself with the Knobby icon in its new position.

3.3.1 Knobby "machine code"

Knobby programs, as you know, consist of sequences of these primitive instructions. Similarly, von Neumann machine programs consist of sequences of primitive instructions, stored in memory from an external file, then decoded and executed, one at a time. Knobby can execute primitive instructions stored in memory. Recall that the user can define new instructions as sequences of other instructions and can ask Knobby to execute these new instructions. Knobby stores the definition as an association between the name of an instruction (e.g., `right`) and a **byte code**—*a sequence of bytes, or characters, in which each byte encodes an instruction.* For example, the byte code for `right`—"LLL"—encodes three `left` instructions. When the Knobby interpreter executes a `run` instruction, it gets the name of the instruction it is to run, finds it in memory, then decodes each byte (e.g., 'L' is a `left`) and executes it.

Knobby also gives us a higher level way of describing behaviors than the primitives. Instead of defining new instructions interactively, we can define them using a programming language. The Knobby language also include control structures: `if-else` branching and `while` loops. Programming languages make it easier to express ideas—particularly algorithms that solve problems. Knobby's six primitives constitute a low level language which is represented in a byte code more meaningful to machines than humans. Higher level languages meet us halfway.

The Knobby translator transforms a Knobby program, consisting of a collection of instructions, into byte code. If translation succeeds, Knobby immediately begins executing the byte codes, starting with the one associated with the instruction called `main`.

Exercise 3.77: Knobby program `mountain.kno` defines several instructions, including:

```
define initializeBoard2 as { read b1=b2 }
```

Invent reasonable single-character byte codes for the primitive instructions `read` and `b1=b2` (which means "copy `b2` into `b1`") then translate the body of this instruction into a byte code sequence.

Exercise 3.78: The compiler for Java translates programs into byte code. Why does translation to byte code (rather than actual machine code) facilitate portability of Java applications?

3.3.2 Stages of translation

Translating a program is more complicated than simply responding to button presses. Figure 3.17 illustrates the stages of translating a programming language: scanning tokens, parsing syntactic structures and either generating executable code or directly executing it.

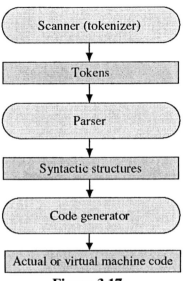

Figure 3.17:
Stages of translation

A **scanner** (also known as a **tokenizer** or **lexical analyzer**) *recognizes the words* (or **tokens**) of a language. Some of Knobby's tokens are **keywords**, *defined as part of the language*, such as `define`, `while`, `if`, etc. Other tokens are numbers, user-defined identifiers and special "single character" tokens, such as { and }. Every programming language has rules of token formation which a scanner uses to recognize the tokens of a language. The rules for Knobby, as we saw in figure 3.1, are fairly simple: a token is sequence of one or more alphanumeric characters (letters or digits) ending with a 'white space' character (where white space is a space, tab or new line). A white space character is called a **delimiter**, since it *indicates the end of a token*. So `pick up flag` is three tokens, whereas `pickUpFlag` is just one. Single character tokens, such as { and }, do not need a white space delimiter, and can act as delimiters for multi-character tokens. For example, {move} is three tokens.

By letting spaces, tabs and new lines all delimit or separate tokens, most modern programming languages are **free format**: *programmers are free to arrange tokens as they choose*. Only the order in which they appear is significant. Here's a Knobby code fragment:

```
if (frontClear) move else if (leftClear){left move} else if
(rightClear){right move} else reverse
```

which is equivalent to this one:

```
if (frontClear)       move
else if (leftClear)   { left move }
else if (rightClear)  { right move }
else reverse
```

While these two code fragments are equivalent as far as the Knobby interpreter is concerned, the second makes the multi-branching structure more obvious to humans. Software engineers have developed conventions like this, exploiting free format, to promote greater readability, making programs easier to understand and maintain.

In languages requiring **fixed format**, the positioning of program elements in particular parts of a line or page is significant. FORTRAN programs, originally punched onto 80 column cards, one card for each line of code, reserved columns one through five on each line (or card) for numeric labels, column 6 to indicate whether a line continues the statement on the previous line, columns 7 through 72 for program instructions, and columns 73 through 80 for line numbers—in preparation for the time when you inadvertently shuffle the cards by dropping them, giving new meaning to a program that seems to behave randomly! For reasons more obvious to programmers than keypunch machine manufacturers, most modern programming languages opt for the flexibility of free format.

A scanner recognizes sequences of characters as tokens of a language. A **parser** recognizes those sequences of tokens which are well-formed structures in the language. In chapter 2, you saw a tree structure for the English sentence, "Dagwood loves his lovely wife." Programming language parsers create similar tree or graph structures. (You may never actually get to see these structures, but parsers form them in computer memory.) Like natural (human) languages, programming languages have **grammars** or **rules of syntax**. These rules tell the parser (and programmers) which sequences of tokens form valid structures. Earlier in this chaper, we introduced syntax diagrams as a way to describe these rules. John Backus and Peter Naur, two computer scientists who developed it for the ALGOL programming language in the late 1950's, developed a text-based notation for describing these rules, which is now known as **Backus-Naur Form** (or **BNF** for short). BNF describes a grammar for a language in terms of formal rules like these:

conditional-instruction => **if** (*test*) *instruction*

conditional-instruction => **if** (*test*) *instruction* **else** *instruction*

Each of these rules consists of a left-hand-side, an arrow, and a right-hand-side. The symbol on the left "expands to" (or "rewrites to") the symbols on the right. The bold faced tokens, **if**, **else** and the parentheses, are terminal symbols, that is, they do not expand any further, since they are tokens of the language. The italicized symbols are non-terminals, expanded by other rules. Syntax diagrams are a simply a more visual notation for describing the same structures. Syntax diagrams and BNF have the same **expressive power**; that is, *any structure that one notation can express, the other can as well*. The equivalent of terminal symbols (tokens) are ovals and the equivalent of non-terminal symbols (which implicitly expand into other diagrams) appear as squares. **Extended BNF** adds a bit more notation: '*' (called the Kleene star) indicates zero or more repetitions of the given symbol(s), and 'l' indicates alternative choices. This additional notation makes our rules a bit more compact without adding any expressive power.

Exercise 3.79: Some programmers prefer to put the instructions, e.g., { left move }, on a separate line rather than on the same line as the if. Try rewriting the multi-branching structure above this way. Which convention do you prefer and why?

Exercise 3.80: Try rewriting the syntax diagrams for *instruction-names* in figure 3.1, as BNF rules.

Exercise 3.81: When you switch from a non-terminal node in one rule to another rule, what do you have to remember or keep track of? Do you think this remembering capability is really needed to generate or recognize *instruction-names*? Why or why not?

Exercise 3.82: Rewrite the syntax diagram for repetition-instruction, in figure 3.11, as a BNF rule.

Exercise 3.83: Describe the form of telephone numbers, such as (800)-123-4567, using BNF rules.

Exercise 3.84: Write BNF rules that can parse the sentence "Dagwood loves his lovely wife" and similar sentences, but won't accept ungrammatical sequences such as "Wife lovely his loves." Hint: *noun, verb, pronoun*, etc., categorize words (lexical categories), whereas *NP* (noun phrase), *VP* (verb phrase), *S* (Sentence), etc., categorize structural groups of words (phrases and clauses).

Exercise 3.85: The extended BNF rules defining the Knobby's World language can be found as an option of `Help`. Using these rules, find and explain the errors in the following code fragment.

```
define move3 { move   move   move }      //move 3 blocks
define main as
{ read write move 3 write move3
```

To a machine, the meaning of a program is executable code. (Computer scientists call this view of *meaning* an **operational semantics**.) In this sense, the byte code into which a Knobby's World program gets translated represents its meaning—a virtual action corresponds to each byte. Richer programming languages call for more complex translation into actions. A Java compiler, for example, parses expressions into expression trees, then generates machine instructions as it traverses the leaves of the tree. It also has to take into account the types of the operands—that is, using integer operations if both operands are `int`, floating point operations if both operands are `float`, etc.

   Code generation *specifies how to transform syntactic structures into primitive instructions.* The simple language of Knobby's World is relatively easy to map into primitives. So far, we already know that Knobby represents primitive instructions as byte codes; for example, move is 'm', `left` is 'L', `write` is 'w', etc. A user-defined instruction is a string of bytes. The `reverse` instruction, whose source code body is `{ left left }`, is byte code "LL". What about user-defined instructions that include other instructions? Suppose the Knobby's World translator numbers each successfully defined instruction 0 through 9. (Actually, it allows more instructions, but that's a little more complicated to explain.) For example, suppose it encodes instruction `reverse` as instruction #3. A `reverse` instruction therefore translates into two bytes—"r3"—where 'r' denotes a run (user defined) instruction and 3 is instruction #3. (Why #3? Because the byte code for the user-defined instruction `reverse`—"LL"—is stored in the *third* slot of the table of user-defined instructions.) Suppose another user-defined instruction, `runAway`, has a source code body of `{reverse move move move}`, then its byte code is "r3mmm". When the interpreter encounters the 'r', it looks up the instruction at the next byte (instruction #3) and begins executing its byte code--in this case, "LL" of `reverse`. After completing the byte code of the *callee* instruction (`reverse`), control returns to the *caller* instruction (`runAway`) in order to execute the rest of its byte code—"mmm". That's a bit confusing, so let us look at the example again in more detail. Suppose the user-defined instruction `runAway`, `{reverse move move move}`, gets stored in the fifth slot of the table of user-defined instructions. So `runAway` translates into a two-byte code "r5". When the interpreter encounters "r5" it looks up the code for `runAway` and starts to execute the byte code "r3mmm". Then it encounters "r3" and starts to execute the byte code for `reverse`. When it finishes executing the byte code for `reverse` it then finishes executing the rest of the byte code for `runAway` (mmm).

Exercise 3.86: From your experience problem solving with Knobby, why might it be a good idea to describe an algorithm in a language independent of Knobby's *before* programming? Why might a formal, unambiguous notation be better for describing algorithms than English?

Exercise 3.87: What byte code will the Knobby translator create for the `main` instruction of program `mountain.kno`? What happens, step by step, when the Knobby interpreter executes this byte code? (You don't need to define the byte codes for all the instructions that `main` invokes!)

Exercise 3.88: Suppose that the byte codes for `reverse` and `runAway` are stored in the table of user-defined instructions as described above. Further suppose the user defined instruction `shuttle`, given by {runAway runAway runAway} is stored in the eighth location in the table of user-defined instructions. What is the byte code for `shuttle`? What happens, step by step, when the Knobby interpreter executes the byte code "r8m"?

3.4 Exploring programming languages

As you can see, programming languages are a rich area of computer science research and application. Special-purpose languages have been invented for many different purposes. Many languages have been designed to introduce programming, such as Basic, Logo, Karel, and Knobby. SQL (Structured Query Language) helps get information out of databases. Other languages, such as HTML or HyperText Markup Language, JavaScript, and ActionScript (all of which we will discuss in chapter 8) control how pages appear in web browsers. Most of these languages share a core of ideas that we have discussed in this chapter. Once you learn an idea, it is usually easy to learn how to do the same thing in other languages. New concepts are what make new languages more interesting and more challenging to learn. Meanwhile, if you would like to explore programs in various languages, the multimedia includes tutorials for Java, JavaScript, and Flash/ActionScript.

Exercise 3.89: Why is a high-level language usually machine independent?

Exercise 3.90: What is the difference between a machine language and an assembly language?

Exercise 3.91: Rewrite the following spaghetti code as a single `if-then-else` statement:

```
        IF X < Y GOTO 10
        X=X+1
        GOTO 20
10      X=Y
20      CONTINUE
```

Exercise 3.92: In early versions of C, there was no type checking on function parameters. So, for example, you could declare a function

```
double foo() double p; { return p + sqrt(p); }
```

This function expects a parameter of type `double`, but you could pass in something quite different:

```
foo("Jennifer");
```

Why is this a bad idea? What might happen when a computer tries to execute the above code?

Exercise 3.93: Later, the ANSI standard version of C, learning from the design of C++, changed the language to include stronger type checking on function parameters. So, for example:

```
double foo(double p) { return p + sqrt(p); }
```

Now the compiler function will give you an error message if you try to pass in anything that is incompatible with the type of the parameter. Why is this a good idea? But consider this case:

```
foo(7);
```

Since 7 is not a `double` but an `int`, what do you think the C or C++ compiler should do?

Exercise 3.94: Does the syntax diagram of figure 3.6 describe the early or ANSI form of function parameter lists (see the above two exercises)? Explain your answer.

Exercise 3.95: Some languages include a run-time **garbage collector** that *scavenges for any memory that is no longer in use.* So, for example, LISP, after interpreting the expression

```
(reverse (list 'Pam ('Adam 'Abby)))
```
leaves in memory the list structure that it produces, (Abby (Adam Abby) Pam), even though it is no longer needed anywhere. Before the LISP environment runs out of memory, a garbage collection routine will scan for all the inaccessible list structures, destroy them, and make all that memory available for further processing. Why are garbage collectors especially important for languages that generate lots of list or object structures? On the other hand, why are garbage collectors inconvenient for programs that need to run in predictable, real time?

Exercise 3.96 (*explore*): Do a search on the web to find out whether garbage collection is built into C++ or Java. Why or why not?

Chapter review. Are the following statements true or false? Explain why or why not.
a) High-level programming languages help people focus on different kinds of problems.
b) Both syntax diagrams and BNF rules have non-terminals as well as tokens, but they look different.
c) Pascal and C express assignment differently, but either way they modify the value of a variable.
d) Using the double type guarantees that floating point computations will have no errors.
e) In C-style languages, functions always return a value.
f) Assembly language associates symbols with a numeric code for an actual machine.
g) FORTRAN and COBOL, two of the oldest high level languages, are still widely used because of the elegance of their design.
h) Structured programming avoids GOTOs by promoting functional decomposition.
i) Pascal and C were both designed as instructional languages.
j) C++ is a hybrid language, combining the systems programming features of C and the business processing strengths of COBOL.
k) Interpreted languages with reusable resources in libraries facilitate rapid prototyping of software.
l) Functional and logic programming both try to break free of a bottleneck in the dominant von Neumann machine architecture.
m) Compiled code runs faster than a speeding bullet, or at least equivalent interpreted code.
n) Compilers provide better support for rapid prototyping of experimental software.
o) Interpreters usually provide stronger type checking to make sure source code is correct.
p) An advantage of compilers is that they perform more checks on code at run-time.
q) Preprocessor directives perform type checking early.
r) A compiler generates nearly executable machine code, nearly since it won't quite execute as is.
s) A linker combines information in header files with object code.
t) A loader has to adjust any machine addresses in a program's machine code.
u) A Java compiler translates source code into actual machine code.
v) Knobby's World translates instructions into byte code, a form of actual machine code.
w) Translation to byte code is part of the reason for the success of the Java language on the Internet.
x) A scanner (or tokenizer) recognizes keywords, identifiers, numbers and subway tokens.
y) A free format language simply ignores all space characters (including tabs and newlines).
z) A parser analyzes syntactic structures of a language, according to the grammar of English.

Summary

Machine code consists of strings of binary values, encoding the primitive operations that a machine's circuitry can perform. To make programming the machine easier for human programmers, an **assembly language** associates mnemonic names with each binary machine code for operations, registers and memory locations. Each assembly language is tied to the instruction set of particular machine, so these programs are not very portable. Also assembly languages tend to force programmers to think at the level of the machine. For these reasons, **high-level** programming languages were invented, so that programmers could focus more at the level of the problem.

FORTRAN, the first successful **high-level language**, emphasized efficiency for engineering applications. It provided instructions that translated directly into the primitives of IBM computers of the 1950's, including several different kinds of GOTOs. Observing that prolific use of GOTOs led to "spaghetti programs," computer scientists designed a more elegant language, ALGOL, which provide **control structures** that allow a closer correspondence between the static layout of a program and its dynamic run-time behavior, spurring an emphasis on **structured programming**. Despite the popularity of structured languages like Pascal and C, computer scientists noticed their flaws, particularly with respect to their weak control over access to data. **Global variables** are to data what GOTO statements were to flow of control, making the dynamic behavior of programs hard to follow. Languages such as Modula and Ada try to correct these problems by providing **modules** or **packages** that control access to objects. **Object-oriented languages** such as Simula, Smalltalk, Eiffel and Java, support modularity in **classes**, which closely associate code with data.

The designers of ALGOL invented the Backus-Naur Form (**BNF**) to formalize the rules for the grammar of a language. **Syntax diagrams** provide a visual representation of these rules which is equivalent to BNF rules in expressive power.

An **interpreter** translates source code and immediately executes in a virtual machine. A **compiler** translates source code into machine code, which may either be an actual machine or a virtual machine. Programs for Knobby's World (and Java) are **compiled** into byte code; an interpreter then executes this intermediate code. On the other hand, a compiler for languages like C++ translate programs into actual machine code which can then be run on an actual machine.

Translation from C++ into machine code goes through several stages. A **preprocessor** responds to compiler directives by modifying the actual source code before the compiler itself sees it. The **compiler** translates source code into object code for an actual machine. The **linker** combines the object code with code from other modules or libraries, producing an executable program. The **loader** takes an executable program, loads it into main memory, and begins executing it. At each stage of translation, errors may occur, perhaps because a compiler directive refers to a file that cannot be found, or because part of a program is syntactically ill-formed, or because a program refers to an object that the linker cannot find in a library. Error messages provide hints about what the programmer must do to get the program to compile correctly.

A language translator has a **scanner**, which combines characters into the tokens of the language and a **parser**, which combines tokens into syntactic structures. **Code generation** either produces machine code or directly executes behaviors. Each of these components follow and enforce formation rules; for example, what counts as a **token** (a word or punctuation mark) of a language.

While compilers produce more efficient code, interpreters avoid the last few stages of translation to machine code, and so facilitate faster turn-around and software development. So they are often preferred by researchers and developers more interested in experimental prototypes than commercial products. LISP, one of the oldest and widely used interpreted languages, supports a **functional programming** approach to program composition. Prolog implements **logic programming**. The declarative logic paradigm emphasizes *what* is known, whereas the procedural paradigm emphasizes *how* to solve a problem, i.e., algorithm development.

Chapter 4
Software Engineering
"Managing change is like trying to hold 400 ping-pong balls in your arms."
Bill Clinton

If you've tried Knobby's World or another programming language, you've gotten a taste of programming. Writing small programs is fairly easy, once you get the hang of the **edit-compile-run-debug cycle**: creating a program in an editor, compiling it, finding any errors, making more changes to your source code, etc., until either it works, or you give up for the day (or night)! Because of the conceptual gap between the way people think and machines operate, this programming cycle is pretty hard to avoid. Nevertheless, if the cycle starts spinning rapidly, that is probably a warning that you are hacking blindly. We urged you, in the chapter on problem solving, to *plan before you code*. This "before" already implies distinguishable stages of development. A better appreciation of these stages will help you to develop a view of software development as a systematic engineering discipline.

4.1 Programming-in-the-large

For a beginner, or even for those who have some programming experience but are learning new computing concepts, even several dozen lines of working code may seem a bit complex. After all, it takes time to learn the resources of a programming languages and to develop the error-free instructions that computers require. In the "real world," however, complexity multiplies as programs get large. To give you an idea how large programs can get, and the bugs that can cause catastrophic failures, consider:

- Denver airport's automatic baggage handling system had bugs that delayed the opening of the new airport for two years, with a $27 million cost overrun for software, and $360 million for the delay.
- The NASA Space Shuttle system has about 3 million lines of code (about 100,000 lines in the shuttle itself). The first scheduled launch of the shuttle Columbia, already three years late and costing millions of dollars more than planned, was canceled before launch because of a software timing error. The space shuttle system is still known *not* to be error-free.
- Software in the Therac-25 radiation system had an error which gave patients overdoses—some of which were fatal!

The complexity of software has come to dominate the *cost* of computing. Figure 4.1 traces a trend in the relationship of the cost of computing hardware and software. In the 1960's, expensive hardware was over 80% of the bill, but by the 1970's software was over half the bill and projected to reverse the earlier ratio. Computer scientists of the 1970's warned about an impending "software crisis." To some extent, this crisis has been averted by advances in software engineering and with newer programming languages. Nevertheless, software development has become a major industry. The worldwide cost of software more than tripled in the ten years since the mid-1980's. The cost of developing software is not the whole story. There are also the costs of errors in software already deployed, sometimes disastrous or nearly so: a $5 million loss by the Bank of New York in one day, a gridlock in the AT&T telecommunications system, a defense system interpreting the rising moon as a nuclear attack.

Exercise 4.1 (*explore*): Search the web to learn more about a software catastrophe (one mentioned above or a different one). Explain what happened, *why* it happened, and any lessons learned.

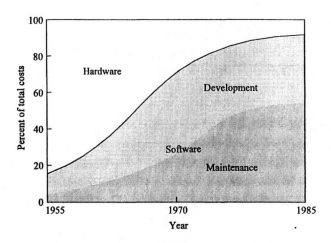

Figure 4.1: Relative proportion of software vs. hardware costs[1]

You may be thinking, "Well, I'm not planning to write millions of lines of code." You won't. These software projects—and most non-trivial, real world projects—involve *teams* of programmers. Indeed, a good definition of software engineering as "multi-person construction of multi-version software."[2] If you wind up developing software for a living, you're more than likely going to be working on a team. Therein lies much of the complexity—getting machines to understand humans is hard enough, let alone getting people to understand each other. You may or may not work on a team project in this course. Nevertheless, there is much you can learn from putting into practice principles that software engineers have honed for **programming-in-the-large**—the *analysis, design, implementation and maintenance of large-scale software systems*. Even relatively small programs—or other endeavors in life, such as writing an essay or planning a wedding or putting together a small business—can benefit from a systematic approach.

4.2 The "Waterfall" Life Cycle

Here is a semi-official definition (from the *IEEE Standard Glossary of Software Engineering Terminology*):

> **Software engineering** is the systematic approach to the development, operation, maintenance, and retirement of software.

By now the word 'systematic' should be ringing in your ears. It implies planning, mapping out where you are going, rather than blind hacking. The four stages in the above definition are analogous to stages in a life. Development is like conception (someone has a bright idea) and childhood (figuring out to how to get it to work), operation and maintenance are like adolescence and adulthood, and retirement—to mix metaphors—is the sunset of a program's life. This sequence of stages makes an important point about software. As you can see by taking another look at the lower half of figure 4.1, the majority of the effort and cost of software happens *after it has been deployed*.

---

[1]B. W. Boehm, "Software engineering," *IEEE Transactions on Computers* C-25, 12 (1976), 1226-1241.

[2]D. L. Parnas and D. M. Weiss, "Active design reviews: Principles and practices," *Journal of Systems and Software*, 7(4): 259-65, December 1987.

A virtue of software is that it is relatively easy to change—otherwise it might as well be hardware. Nevertheless, the more complex a software system gets, the harder it is to change. There are several reasons for this. For one, larger software systems are harder to understand. One way to alleviate this difficulty is to organize these systems into separate **modules** or **classes**: *software components that are relatively independent of each other*. That way one can localize change to a particular module or small set of modules. Modules can also promote reuse of software components in new systems. Another problem is that the more changes get introduced into a system, the more it tends toward entropy and chaos—that is, its internal order breaks down. Making a change in one part of the program often causes unpredictable changes in other parts. Software engineers try to alleviate this problem by planning for change. Nevertheless, often the only way to reestablish order in a system is to retire an old version and redesign it from scratch.

Exercise 4.2: How can good comments reduce the cost of software maintenance?
Exercise 4.3: How can modules reduce the cost of software development and maintenance?

Figure 4.2 depicts the stages of the software life cycle, providing more detail for the development stage in the above IEEE definition:

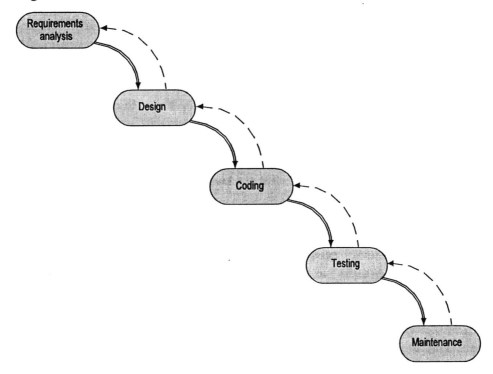

Figure 4.2: The "waterfall" model of the software life cycle

In the classic **waterfall model**, *software development progresses from one stage to the next only after the previous stage is complete*. Gravity only allows the waterfall to go down; there is no going back to a previous, "higher" level. This is the ideal. Managers would like development to be as predictable as possible. It certainly would be simpler and cheaper if no one could change the requirements of a system once they have been determined. In many software shops, there are actually different people associated with different stages: a systems analyst does analysis, designers design, different teams of programmers do the coding, then the testing, then the system upgrades and other maintenance. The reality is that not only does software change, but change happens during the process. A customer may want to change the requirements (just a little!) even after the software developer is ready to deliver a system. That's why figure 4.2 also allows for salmon swimming *upstream* (the dashed arrows). The process is not strictly linear, but allows for cycles. Most software engineers argue that this cyclical pattern is essential to the development process, rather than something to avoid. On the one hand, complex software requires much *re*-analysis and *re*-design before they are truly reusable. The highly reusable Java Development Kit (JDK), for example, has undergone many substantial revisions since its first release in the mid-1990's. On the other hand, more cycles mean more costs, so many software *managers* remain fond of the predictability of the waterfall model. Software engineers also know that the more effort a development teams puts into getting things right early, the much more costs are saved further downstream in the process.

Let's examine each of these stages. To make the process concrete, we will trace the development of a program for a relatively simple problem:

> The Megabyte Company has an initial service charge of $32 plus $16 per hour to repair a computer. The manager wants a program to show the revenue generated by a repair person per week. For example, if Minnie Bits takes 35 hours to fix 24 machines, then she generates $1328 that week.

Exercise 4.4: Perform the calculation for Minnie Bits' revenue. What are the inputs and outputs?

4.3 Analysis of requirements

Working with the customer(s), a system analyst seeks to describe a system that will solve the problem. The questions for preliminary analysis shown in figure 2.6 are a good place to start. The analyst produces a document called the **requirements specification**, which should explain *what* the program will do, under what system constraints (but not *how*). Ideally, the requirements specification is a contract between user and systems analyst about what the analyst will deliver. A specification should include at least the following:

- A statement of the **purpose** of the proposed system.
- A statement of its **scope** (system-wide limitations or constraints).
- **Definitions** of terms in a problem's domain.
- A description of **input values** and their sources.
- A description of **output values** and their destinations.
- A description of the system's **behavior** (from a user's point of view).

Restating the **purpose** attempts to make it more explicit, often discovering gaps or even errors in a user's initial description of a problem. (Get used to this—there may even be gaps and errors in assignments from your instructor!). Try doing the following exercise before reading further.

Exercise 4.5: Write a purpose statement for the Megabyte Company problem. In writing this statement, do you see any remaining issues that need to addressed?
Exercise 4.6 (*explore*)**:** On the web, find other possible elements of a requirements specification.

A statement of **scope** spells out system-wide limitations or constraints. For example, are there performance requirements—i.e, if there are numerical calculations how precise and how fast do they need to be? Will the program be interactive and/or produce printed reports? Does the user require specific platforms—i.e., particular computer(s) and/or operating system(s)? The statement for the Megabyte Company problem doesn't deal with these issues, so the analyst would need to go back to the manager to have these spelled out. For example, can a repair person work fractions of hours? If so, how accurate should the degree of precision be? (The analyst may already be thinking about whether to use integer, float or double precision calculation, though really the focus of a requirements should try to remain on *what* the system will do, not *how*.) Let's suppose the manager says that his shop simply rounds off time spent to the nearest half hour.

English language descriptions can be slippery. **Definitions** of key terms can really help avoid confusion between the user and analyst as well as between analyst and programmers. The analyst should at least make sure the manager of Megabyte agrees with the following definitions:

- *service charge*: amount the customer pays for a repair person to examine a computer.
- *repair rate*: rate of dollars per hour spent repairing a computer, including the first hour.
- *machines repaired*: number of computers a repair person works on during a week.
- *hours billed:* time a repair person works on repairs, rounded to half hour.
- *weekly revenue*: (service charge * machines repaired) + (repair rate * hours billed).

An analyst looks at a problem as a black box, with inputs going in and outputs coming out, as shown in figure 4.3 (reproduced from chapter 2):

Figure 4.3: Analyzing a "black box"

The analyst must now give understandable names to all the inputs and outputs to the proposed system, and make sure they are well defined. It turns out that we have already specified the inputs and outputs for the Megabyte Company problem in the definitions given above: the first four items are inputs (givens) and the last item is the output (goal).

Finally, we analyze the system's **behavior**, emphasizing the user's point of view. Users usually see a system as a black box. So we want to emphasize what the behavior is, not how it does it. The core of the behavior for the Megabyte Company program is to calculate a weekly revenue.

Exercise 4.7: Draw a diagram similar to figure 4.3, indicating the purpose, inputs and outputs of the Megabyte Company problem.

Exercise 4.8: The Megabyte Company also needs a payroll system. It pays its employees weekly, based on the number of hours they work. Given a number of hours of work in a week and an hourly pay rate, the payroll program should compute a weekly pay. In addition, it should compute pay at the overtime rate (1.5) for the first 10 hours in excess of 40, then double-time rate (2.0) for any extra hours beyond 50. Produce a requirements specification for this problem.

4.3 Use cases

A good way to describe the behavior of a proposed system is to describe it from the point of view of a user who might eventually use the system. A **use case** *describes one or more scenarios for using a system, tied together by a common user goal*. In plain English (and use cases should be written in plain English), use cases give descriptive answers to questions that start with "What does the system do if ...." For example, "What does the auto-teller do if a customer has just deposited a check within 24 hours and there's not enough in the account without the check to provide the desired withdrawal?" The use-case model then describes what the auto-teller does in this situation.

Here's an example (from Fowler and Scott, *UML Distilled*, Prentice-Hall, 2000, p. 40):

Use Case: Buy a Product

1.   Customer browsers through catalog and selects items to buy
2.   Customer goes to check out
3.   Customer fills in shipping information (address; next-day or 3-day delivery)
4.   System presents full pricing information, including shipping
5.   Customer fills in credit card information
6.   System authorizes purchase
7.   System confirms sale immediately
8.   System sends confirming email to customer

Alternative: Authorization Failure
At step 6, system fails to authorize credit purchase
Allow customer to re-enter credit card information and re-try

Alternative: Regular customer
3a. System displays current shipping information, pricing information, and last four digits of credit card information
3b. Customer may accept or override these defaults
Return to primary scenario at step 6

The title of the use case is a short descriptive name of the scenario, in this case, "Buy a Product." The next eight lines describe the main scenario, in which everything goes as expected, from the customer finding a product in a catalog to the system confirming the transaction. These eight steps look like an algorithm, but they are written in a user's language, not a machine's. The rest of the use case consists of two alternative scenarios, which branch off the main one. The first alternative branches off at step 6, if the authorization fails, and the second branches off at step 3, if the system recognizes a regular customer (and can therefore save the user a few steps).

Because a use case is written from a user's point of view and in a user's language, it can be very useful as a means of communication between an analyst and a user. Once the analyst is confident that she understands what the user wants, she can specify the requirements of a system.

Exercise 4.9: Develop a use case for the Megabyte Company problem described above.
Exercise 4.10: Write a use case for the behavior of the payroll system described in exercise 4.6.
Exercise 4.11: Write a use case describing the behavior of the **Move** button in Knobby's World.
Exercise 4.12: Write a use case describing the behavior of the **Step** button in Knobby's World.
Exercise 4.13: For one of the game problems described in exercise 2.55, develop a requirements specification and use case(s).
Exercise 4.14 (*explore*): On the web, find another example of a use case. What does it describe? Does its form differ from the above example? How well does it communicate to non-technical users?

4.5 Design

The second stage shifts to *how* to solve the problem, though still not necessarily in terms of a particular programming language. Among other things, **design** looks more closely at the inputs, outputs and behavior. Ferret out additional information about each data object manipulated by the program, such as its data type and range (for example, *cents* must range between 0 and 99). For each input item, ask about its source: does it come from the *user* interactively, or a *file* on a disk, or is it a *constant* built into the program? For each output item, determine its destination: does it go to the user interactively or to file? There may also be layout constraints: for example, if input items come from an interactive menu, specify the layout of the menu, or if output items go to a printed report, specify the layout of the report. (Note that the questions and issues for design expand the questions for preliminary analysis given in figure 2.6.)

Here are the input items for Megabyte Company problem:

- *service charge*: integer constant, $32
- *repair rate*: integer constant, $16.
- *machines repaired*: integer variable from user, ranging from 0 to 99
- *hours billed*: float variable from user, ranging from .5 to 100.0.

There is just one output for this problem:

- *weekly revenue*: integer variable displayed on screen, following a '$'

Now we are ready to design the algorithm: how the black box will perform the desired behavior. But don't rush to start coding in a programming language! Those who code early code often, code more often, and to less good effect, than those who proceed more carefully. Instead, let's design our algorithm as **pseudocode**, *a notation which describes an algorithm as an outline or a recipe in intelligible English*, using programming language structures (such as expression syntax and control structures) only when they are clearer than saying the same thing in English. As we discussed in chapter 2, most algorithms, like sentences or automobile engines or musical compositions, have a structure that can be decomposed into parts, often hierarchically, or top-down. So designing an algorithm as pseudocode (before you actually implement it) is like outlining a composition (before you actually write it). Here's our pseudocode algorithm for the Megabyte Company problem:

> get input items *machines repaired* and *hours billed*
> > get *machines repaired*
> > > (1) prompt user for the number of *machines repaired*
> > > (2) read *machines repaired* as an integer
> > get *hours billed*
> > > (3) prompt user for the number of *hours billed*
> > > (4) and read *hours billed* as a float
> adjust input value *hours billed*
> > (5) round off *hours billed* to nearest *half hour*
> (6) calculate *weekly revenue*:
> > (*service charge* * *machines repaired*) + (*repair rate* * *half hours billed* / 2).
> (7) report *weekly revenue* to user

The numbered steps correspond to a sequence of statements in actual program code. (Note that the higher levels in the pseudocode outline do not correspond to statements of code, but we will soon see how they can appear in a program.) Such a skeleton of an algorithm is similar to what you might find in a recipe book. (Some software engineers prefer a pseudocode notation that simply lists a recipe-like sequence of steps.) The remaining lines (and indentation) reveal the top-down hierarchical structure of the program. Breaking a program down into bite-sized chunks will make it easier to understand, easier to debug, and easier to maintain.

Step (5) introduces the sort of detail that emerges when one looks more closely at a problem. The designer noticed, from the requirements specification, that *hours billed* comes in units of half an hour. What happens if the user types in some decimal other than .5 or 0? Good question. So the designer went back to the analyst and asked. (Recall the analogy of a salmon swimming upstream: sometimes the process must revert to previous stages.) The analyst said, "Just round off any fractions to the nearest half hour." So the designer included step (5) in the algorithm. The designer tried to anticipate questions from the programmer, such as, how will this rounding off work? So the designer introduced an intermediate data object, which is neither input nor output:

- *half hours billed*: result of calculating repair time rounded to nearest half hour

The designer figures this is enough of a hint to the programmer. In step (6), dividing *half hours billed* by 2 gives the *number of hours* for the *repair rate*.

4.6 Classes and UML

The Megabyte Company problem is fairly simple. For more complicated ones, it's useful to identify many separate components. For example, Knobby's World has many buttons (two of which were the subject of use case exercises earlier), menus, an editor, a parser, an interpreter, and of course Knobby and his grid world. Rather than view all this as one monolithic program, it's better to analyze and design these components as distinct modules or classes. Actually, other engineering disciplines have already learned this lesson. Computer engineers and plumbers work with **self-contained units** such as motherboards or fixtures. Ideally, software developers should work with off-the-shelf software components, rather than constantly re-invent the wheel. Just as there are standardized and relatively simple ways of attaching cards to motherboards and plumbing fixtures to pipes, so software components need **simple and explicit interfaces**. By insisting that all connections between software components go through these interfaces, we get **weak coupling**: modules exchange as little information as possible, without side effects or hidden dependencies, making them easier to develop and maintain, independently. But unlike hardware, software components can still support change, through **inheritance** (introduced in chapter 2): a subclass can inherit properties and behaviors without modifying its superclass, then add new properties or behaviors of its own. For example, Polygon extends Shape (without altering Shape) by adding a list of sides and a function computing its perimeter from the length of the sides.

Class diagrams represent the relationships between classes in an object-oriented system. Figure 4.4 shows a class diagram for Knobby's World (left a bit incomplete for simplicity and exercises). The diagram uses a standardized notation for class diagrams which is part of **UML (Unified Modeling Language)**. In this notation, each box represents a class. Each box has three compartments: on top the class name, in middle its data attributes (properties), and at the bottom its operations (behaviors). For example, at the top of the diagram is a class called `ByteCodes`, an attribute `table`, whose type is attribute `HashTable`, and an operation `getCode`, which given a parameter `InstructionName` (whose type is `String`) returns a `String`. (A `HashTable` looks up names efficiently; we'll discuss how it works in the chapter on algorithms.)

This figure is a nice review of some of the concepts we discussed in the previous chapter.

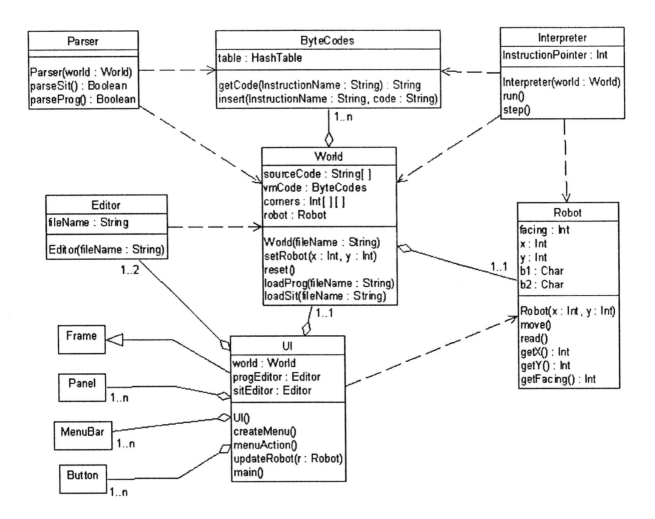

Figure 4.4: UML class diagam for Knobby's World

Since class `UI` (the user interface) contains the `main` operation, we know the program starts execution here. Between `UI` and `Panel`, `MenuBar` and `Button` you'll notice lines with a diamond on one end. These represent **composition** relationships—a UI *contains* these user interface components. The menus and buttons are in one panel and Knobby's grid-world is in another panel. Since there is one user interface with many user interface components, these relationship each have a cardinality of `1..n`. Between `UI` and `Frame` is a line with a triangle at one end, representing an **inheritance** relationship: `UI` is a *subtype* of `Frame`, which already exists in a standardized class library. The `UI` also contains a `World`. The first operation of `World` is its constructor—a **constructor** has the same name as its class and initializes the attributes of instances of this class. In this case, `World` invokes `loadProg` to initialize its `sourceCode` and `loadSit` to initialize its `corners` and `robot`. Operation `loadProg` constructs a `Parser` to translate the `sourceCode` into `vmCode` (virtual machine `ByteCodes`). The `Interpreter` (responding when the user presses the Run or Step buttons in the `UI`) then executes the `vmCode`. The dashed arrows between classes represent **dependency** relationships: for example, `Parser` and `Interpreter` depend on `ByteCodes`; if the latter changes, we must modify both of the former.

If you think this design is complicated, well, we actually simplified it a bit to make it easier for you to understand (and to leave some missing pieces for you as exercises, below). We could use

UML's **sequence diagrams** to depict the typical flow of control through a program more explicitly and completely than our prose description above. We could also use UML's **package** notation to separate the user interface, parser/interpreter and robot/world clusters. Modularity and separation of concerns makes it easier for several developers to work on different units of a system independently, then put the system together later.

Exercise 4.15: Why does operation `getCode` in class `ByteCodes` return a `String`? Hint: what are the elements of a `String` and what do these elements represent in Knobby's World?

Exercise 4.16: What does the attribute `InstructionPointer` in class `Interpreter` represent? What does operation `step()` do with this attribute?

Exercise 4.17: As you learned in the previous chapter, a scanner or tokenizer identifies the tokens of a program. How would you add a scanner to the above class diagram?

Exercise 4.18: What kind of relationship does the diagram show between `Editor` and `UI`? Why?

Exercise 4.19: What attribute(s) does operation `move` in class `Robot` affect and how?

Exercise 4.20: Knobby can also turn left. Where should this capability go in the class diagram? What attribute would it affect?

Exercise 4.21: Knobby can also write from a blackboard to a corner of the world. Where should this capability go in the class diagram? What attributes would it affect?

Exercise 4.22: Why is it a good idea to access or modify operations only through operations in the same class? Hint: think about interfaces and coupling, discussed above. Discuss at least two examples of classes, attributes, and operations in the class diagram that follow this design principle.

Exercise 4.23: The diagram doesn't show much detail for classes `Frame`, `Panel`, etc., because we figured these would already exist in a class library. Is this a good idea? Why or why not?

Exercise 4.24 (*explore*): In fact, something like classes `Frame`, `Panel`, etc., do exist in the Java Development Kit. Use a search engine such as www.google.com to learn more about them. From what class do they both inherit and what is different about the way they inherit from this common parent? Discuss at least two operations (methods) of each of these two classes.

Exercise 4.25: Figure 2.14 shows an object-oriented analysis of the ATM problem. Recast this as a UML class diagram. (Don't sweat all the attributes and operations; just show a few representative ones as we did for Knobby's World.)

4.7 Implementation and testing

The next stage is **implementation**: coding data objects and algorithm in a programming language, then testing it to make sure it works. The CD-ROM supplies a couple of different examples of the Megabyte program in Java and C++. (In this section, we use Java for the sake of concreteness, though the details of Java are not crucial here.) In some ways, the code is simply a highly stylized way of articulating the analysis. If you look at our code, you'll notice that our analysis of the problem appears in comments at the top of the program, and various parts of our design appear in the comments mixed in with the body of the program. Comments are evidence of forethought and planning. Comment *before* you code and whenever your code diverges from your plan; comment *as* you code. You should be able get the gist of the code because of the comments.

Coding is rarely as simple as mixing some ingredients, dropping some batter on a griddle, and *voila*, a pancake! Even with good planning, coding involves that **edit-compile-run-debug cycle** which we mentioned at the beginning of the chapter: writing source code, compiling it, finding any errors, making changes to your source code, compiling it, etc. Analysis and design helps the programmer to understand the problem *before* coding—indeed, we include our analysis and pseudocode as comments in the code. More problem solving starts when we *test* the code.

Compiler error messages usually have to do with structures that do not conform to the syntax of the language or with type clashes. Other messages may have to do with inconsistencies, such as code that a program can never reach during execution. Unreachable code wastes space and indicates a flaw in the structure of a program. Here is a simple example of unreachable code:

```
if (x*x < -1)
    y = x;
```

Because $x*x$ can never be negative, $y = x$ will never be executed.

Linker errors occur when the source code declares an object which the linker cannot find. Such errors may occur when a programmer refers to objects from some library but the linker cannot find the library. For example, a Java program might refer to `Input.getInt()`, but the linker will complain if it cannot find the library defining the `Input` class. (It comes with *The Universal Computer* if you elect to install Java.) Correcting linker errors may involve fixing a misspelled declaration so that it matches the name of a definition or telling the compiler where to find a library.

Run-time errors stop the program unexpectedly while it is running, hopefully with an error message explaining what went wrong. For example, computers lack the ability to divide by zero, so when this occurs they stop, sometimes mysteriously. Alas, a compiler cannot anticipate division by zero when expressions include variables, since it cannot know ahead of time what the values will be. For example, the simple expression $y=x/v$ can cause a run-time error if v happens to be 0 when the program runs and unexpectedly stops. A debugger (which look at one in a moment) can help you locate where and why a program crashes. You may need to sleuth around, though, to figure out what caused the program to "bomb" unexpectedly.

Logic errors occur when a program runs without crashing, but does not perform as expected, producing erroneous output. These are perhaps the hardest to debug, because the program never actually fails. You have to make sure it works *as specified*. The best way to track these errors down is by thoroughly testing the program, making sure its outputs are correct.

After coding the Megabyte program to the Java compiler, it gave us several error messages, all syntax errors. Each line begins with the source file name (`Megabyte1.java`) followed by a line number in that file. The first error messages refers to this line:

```
Megabyte1.java:19: ';' expected
    final int repairRate=16:    //hourly rate for repair
                        ^
```

You have to look closely to see the flaw (get out a magnifying glass): there's a colon (':') after the '16', which does not belong here. Once spotted—the compiler inserts a ^ below it, on the next line, to help you—there's an easy fix: there should be a semi-colon(';') to delimit the statement. Since the Java compiler was expecting a ';' at the end of a statement (rather than a ':'), it goes ahead and assumes that you intended a ';' after all, so it can continue translating the rest of the program. (This assumption may be wrong, in which case the error messages appearing later in the program might not make sense. You may have to ignore compiler error messages triggered by its erroneous guesses about what you actually intended.) The next error message appears at line 36:

```
Megabyte1.java:36: ')' expected
    int weeklyRevenue = (service charge * machines repaired)
                                ^
```

Sure enough, the program has not declared a symbol `service`. When we copied the pseudocode from our design document, we forgot to modify the name of this variable, so that it is one token rather than two . The next error message refers to line 24:

```
Megabyte1.java:24: cannot resolve symbol
symbol  : variable machinesRepaired
location: class Megabyte1
    machinesRepaired = Input.getInt();
                       ^
```

The message `cannot resolve symbol` usually suggest a linker error, discovered after the compiler has already made one pass through the program. The fix is to add the line,

```
import ucomp.Input;
```

near the top of the file. Assuming the `ucomp.Input` has been installed properly, the linker should now be able to find the class `Input`.

Once we have diagnosed and repaired these syntax errors, we are ready to resubmit it to the compiler. Don't be surprised, however, if the compiler finds still more errors. Try not to get frustrated. Why didn't the compiler find these before? We mentioned above that when a compiler gets confused by a syntactic error, rather than give up altogether, it attempts **error recovery**. It tries to skip to a reasonable place, such as to the next recognizable statement. When you correct it, the compiler will now be able to analyze code that it may have skipped before. People do this, too, recovering from stammers and restarts in fluent speech. Machines simply aren't as good at it yet.

Exercise 4.26: The first version of our program is in `\ucomp\chap4\megabyt1.java`. Edit and recompile it until you've gotten all the compiler error messages out of the program.

For experienced programmers, correcting syntax errors is the easy part. You soon learn what the messages mean and how to fix them. But you still have to make sure that the program is *correct*. You may think, look, the program produces output. Can't I hand it in now? Whoa. Are you sure it's the *right* output? Good software engineers try to *verify* that the output conforms to the requirements specifications. They also *validate* that the program really does what the user wants. There is a subtle distinction here. **Verification** asks the question: *Have we built the system right?* **Validation** asks the question: *Have we built the right system?* To answer these questions, you need to **test** the program thoroughly.

There's a well-known story among software engineers about an executive who got a computer-generated bill for $0.00. After a good laugh among friends about "idiot computers," he tossed the bill away. A month later a similar bill arrived, then a third. The fourth bill came accompanied by a message hinting at possible legal action if the bill for $0.00 was not paid at once. The fifth, marked 120 days, threatened all manner of legal actions if the bill was not immediately paid. Concerned about his organization's credit rating in the hands of a maniacal machine, the executive called a software engineer acquaintance. Trying not to laugh, the software engineer told him to mail a check for $0.00. This had the desired effect: a receipt for $0.00 was received a few days later, and the executive carefully filed it away.

There's a sequel.[3] A few days later the executive was summoned by his bank manager. The banker held up a check and asked, "Is this your check?" Yes, the executive said. "Would you mind telling me why you wrote a check for 0.00?" asked the banker. The executive retold his story. And the banker said to him quietly, "Have you any idea what your check for $0.00 did to *our* computer system?"

---

[3]Related in Stephen R. Strach, *Classical and Object-Oriented Software Engineering*, Richard D. Irwin, 1995.

Computer professionals laugh nervously at this story, because they know that thorough testing should have caught this bug. But thorough testing—validating (clearly a system that bills for $0.00 is not the *right* system) as well as verifying software—is a hard problem. Many companies have a separate team that tests a program as brutally as possible.

Good testing takes planning. Develop a **test description**—*a set of sample test data and expected outputs*—before you begin testing. The starting point for planning a test description is the specifications, which describe the expected behavior of your program. To make sure that the Megabyte program's output does meet its specifications, we use a calculator to predict several correct outputs. **Core values** test typical values. For example, the revenue from repairing 24 machines, for 35 hours of work should be $1328 and for 36 hours should be $1344. So far, the program checks out OK. Much as a civil engineer performs stress tests on connections in steel structures, under both normal and extreme conditions, a good software engineer also checks out special cases. Though this is a fairly simple algorithm, we know there is one slightly complicated part—the way it adjusts (rounds off) the repair time. So our test description should check **boundary values** for repair time, such as 35.1, 35.9, 35.4, and 34.6. The first two values look at extremes near whole numbers; the last two check out rounding off to the nearest half hour. Take a moment to look carefully at the results shown below. Do you see a flaw?

```
How many machines did you repair this week? 24
How much time did you spend working on repairs this week? 35.1
Weekly revenue is $1328

How many machines did you repair this week? 24
How much time did you spend working on repairs this week? 35.9
Weekly revenue is $1336

How many machines did you repair this week? 24
How much time did you spend working on repairs this week? 35.4
Weekly revenue is $1328

How many machines did you repair this week? 24
How much time did you spend working on repairs this week? 35.6
Weekly revenue is $1336
```

Have you found the flaw? Two of the outputs are incorrect. The output for 35.9 should have rounded *up* to produce the same output as 36 ($1344) and the output for 35.4 should also have rounded *up* to the next half hour, for $1336. (The other outputs are OK, but the company is losing money here!) We just found a logic error. Note that a compiler won't catch logic errors, because compilers understand little about the *semantics* (meaning) of a program, other than type information. Some computer scientists are trying to build formal verification tools, but these are generally not practical due to the complexity of non-trivial programs. For now, only thorough testing (or a disappointed or angry customer after the program has been delivered) catches most logic errors.

Debugging (fixing errors) is yet another problem solving activity. The methods covered in chapter 2 apply here as well. Generally, the givens are the incorrect output (and in this case some correct output as well) and the goal is getting this output right (while still preserving the other output). A primary activity of debugging is *isolating* the site of the error. In this case, reasoning that the error had something to do with the round off calculation, we figured that the culprit was the calculation of `halfHoursBilled`, in this line:

```
halfHoursBilled = (int)(hoursBilled * 2);
```
The `int` cast truncates the remainder of the `double` expression. (We wanted an answer in whole numbers.) If you do the math, 35.9 * 2 is 71.8, and `int` cast truncates to 71. Similarly, 35.4 * 2 is 70.8, which truncates to 70.

Exercise 4.27: Explain why the above calculation produces correct output for values 35.1 and 35.6, but not for 35.8 and 35.3.

How do we fix this error? Checking Java's `Math` package again, we discovered that it does include a true `round` method. (For some reason, it's not included in the equivalent C++ library.) So we made this change:
```
halfHoursBilled = Math.round(hoursBilled * 2);
```
Apparently, this fix isn't quite enough, because we get another compiler error:
```
Megabyte2.java:35: possible loss of precision
found    : long
required: int
    halfHoursBilled = Math.round(hoursBilled * 2);
                      ^
```

Apparently, the Java compiler still wants us to use that `int` cast before assigning the result:
```
halfHoursBilled = (int)Math.round(hoursBilled * 2);
```
This version produces the right results for all our test cases.

Exercise 4.28: Verify that the above fix works, by correcting `Megabyte2.java`, then testing it with several boundary cases.

Sometimes isolating the site and cause of an error is not so simple. There are a couple of techniques for narrowing down to the site of an error. One is to insert output statements in the code to print out the values of variables before and/or after they change. For example:
```
halfHoursBilled = int(hoursBilled * 2);
System.out.println(" halfHoursBilled=" + halfHoursBilled);
```
Now the output of the program will show us explicitly what we had reasoned for ourselves: if the `hoursBilled` is 35.4, then `halfHoursBilled` is 70 (rounding down).

Another way to narrow down to the site of an error is to use a **debugger**, *a program that provides information about the run-time states and behavior of a program.* We briefly describe the debugger that comes with the BlueJ environment. (The BlueJ tutorial gives more details.) To get started, open the project `debugShapes` (in folder `ucomp\chap4\debugShapes`), then double-click on class `Circle` to edit it. Normally a program simply runs until it completes, or fails due to a bug, but we can use a debugger to get it to stop at some point so that we can inspect its state. To get it to stop, you need to set a **breakpoint**, *a statement where the program will pause its execution* so that you can control the debugger. To set a breakpoint, click on a statement, such as any statement in the constructor, then press `Ctrl-B`. A stop sign appears, as shown in figure 4.5, to the left of this statement—execution will stop at this point. Now go back to the main BlueJ window and run the constructor, by right-clicking on the `Triangle` class box and selecting `new Triangle()`.

```
public Circle()
{
    diameter = 30;
    xPosition = 20;
    yPosition = 60;
    color = "blue";
    draw();
}
```

Figure 4.5: Breakpoint

Because you set a breakpoint in the constructor, BlueJ stops execution here and opens up its debugger, shown in figure 4.6.

The Call Sequence box gives a **trace** showing the methods that have been called to get to this point. So far, it's just `Circle`'s constructor. The Instance Variables area shows the values of the variables for this object. So far, `diameter` has been initialized to 30, but not yet `xPosition`, etc. Of course, that will happen when get to the next statement after the breakpoint. The buttons at the bottom give us ways to continue processing. The **Step** button advances to the next statement; the **Step into** button will, if the next statement is a method call, go into the first statement in that method; the **Continue** button will resume execution without stopping until the next breakpoint, or until the program finishes executing on its own. The **Terminate** button just finishes execution of the program here. At each step or breakpoint, the program displays any changes to the state of the

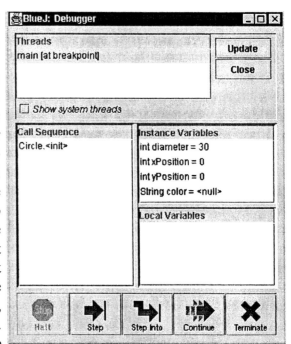

Figure 4.6: Debugger at breakpoint

object. Thus we can observe how the program changes the state of objects, statement by statement. (Tracing a program in a debugger is a very good way to learn how a Java program actually works.)

Exercise 4.29: In BlueJ, tokens like `public` and `"blue"` appear in different colors. Why is this feature of the BlueJ editor (called **syntax coloring**) useful?

Exercise 4.30: If you have BlueJ installed, open the project `ucomp\chap4\debugShapes` and investigate the way the program works. Set a breakpoint at the beginning of the constructor for class `Square`, then run the program up to your program. When and how do the values of the instance variables `size`, and `color` change? Step into method `draw()`. What does it do? When `draw()` is done, what happens?

Exercise 4.31: Two bugs have been planted in class `Circle` of `ucomp\chap4\debugShapes`. To see one, notice what happens when you select method `moveLeft`—where does it move instead? Use the breakpoint facility and debugger to determine the nature of the bug and correct it. Once you've done that, notice what happens when you select construct an instance of `Circle` with a diameter of 5, then you select method `area`—do you get the right result? If not, fix the logic error. Write a short report describing the bugs, how you fixed them to produce correct behaviors, and how the debugger helped you.

As we've mentioned, debugging is a form of problem solving. Stepping through the program one line at a time starting at the top is forward hacking. That's fine for small programs. But it can get impossibly tedious for larger programs or repetitive cycles of debugging. A decomposition approach breaks the problem down into smaller pieces. You can divide the source code roughly in halves, then quarters, etc., or better yet, identify likely pieces of a program. For example, you could put a breakpoint half way through a program's execution, or better yet, just before the place where you suspect it has misbehaved.

Another application of divide and conquer debugging uses comments to disable code. Suppose you know that there's a logic error somewhere in your program but you're not sure where. Try putting multi-line comments (/* ... */) around *parts* of the program, disabling them temporarily. When you recompile the program, the commented-out code will not execute. Here's where Holmesian deduction comes into play. If the remaining, uncommented code does what it is supposed to do correctly, then you can infer that the bug must have been caused by the commented-out part. Or vice versa. Either way, you can use more comments to further isolate the cause of the problem.

Testing and debugging may also involve reasoning by analogy. Once you have stamped out a bug, you are more likely to smell it out quickly the next time. Building up a knowledge of cases is crucial to troubleshooting.

Thorough testing is essential to program validation. It's unclear, however, what counts as thorough testing. Exhaustive testing of all parts of a large program, and all the ways they might interact with different combinations of input values, etc., may not be feasible. Instead, software engineers *plan* for testing as part of the design. Indeed, experiments have shown that every hour of testing during design—by having peers review the design before programming begins—saves about eight hours of program testing. In a **structured walkthrough**, *a designer or programmer explains an algorithm or code to peers*, who are more apt to notice design flaws that the author himself may overlook. As we have seen, a plan for test cases should emphasize boundary values.

There are a couple of different ways to look at testing. **Black box testing** treats the program as an opaque object, making no assumptions about how it works. The tester should just look at the requirements specification and use cases and *validate* that the system meets the requirements. **Glass box testing** treats the program as a set of transparent units. The tester can *verify* that every function or method performs correctly. For large, object-oriented systems, glass box testing comes early, to make sure units are working property before combining them. Black box testing comes later, to make sure the whole system behaves as required.

Another important aspect of software validation is **regression testing**, *testing the changed program against previous test cases*, to ensure that new changes don't cause more bugs. Regression testing also requires planning: what systematic tests will be sufficient to make sure the program is still working correctly?

The goal is not just programs that work sometimes, but programs that are reliable. If you are an apprentice software developer, plan on documenting your test results. Don't just hand in the source code. Also hand in a document showing how you have tested the program, with a wide enough range of test data to inspire confidence that it actually works according to specification. If you discover a "bug" but don't know how or don't have time to figure out how to fix it, include a "bug report" with your program explaining the problem. Respected system software may come with bug reports explaining known limitations. Honesty is good policy.

Exercise 4.32: How can a decomposition approach help you make better use of a debugger? Hint: where should you set a breakpoint?

Exercise 4.33: In terms of the waterfall model, when should developers plan testing? Why?

Exercise 4.34: How can structured walkthrough save time, even though it takes time to do it?

Exercise 4.35: What is the relationship between black box testing and validation? What is the relationship between glass box testing and verification?

Exercise 4.36: Why is it often a good idea to perform glass box testing before black box testing?

Exercise 4.37: When and why should developers do regression testing?

4.8 Delivery and maintenance

When the program appears to perform acceptably, it goes into **delivery**, *making it available to its users*. Of course, users expect more than an executable program. Delivery includes a printed user manual (instructions for installing and using the program) as well as online documentation ranging from `readme` files to web-based help.

The life cycle of a student's program typically ends at this point. You hand it in; we all hope you've learned by doing. The life time of a program for a real world application, however, is just getting started. If it's successful, not only will users run it, but analysts and programmers will remain actively involved in its continued development for many years.

Maintenance of software involves four different kinds of activities, shown in figure 4.7[4].

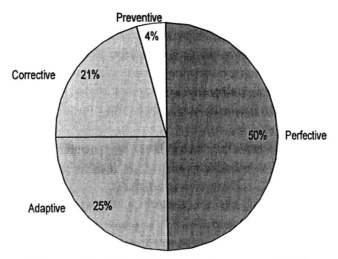

Figure 4.7: Effort for maintenance activities

Corrective maintenance, fixing errors found by users after delivery, alas, is a fact of (software) life. Annoying though it may be, all commercial software have bugs that survive the most thorough testing. Software companies usually warn about this, for example, in a limited warranty agreement to which customers implicitly assent before they break the seal around a product. Bug fixes may appear in subsequent versions (more money), new releases or patches (usually free). **Adaptive** maintenance responds to changes in a program's environment, such as new or upgraded operating systems, or other software or hardware on which the program depends. **Perfective** maintenance improves the behavior or performance of a system, such as extra functions that may be desirable to users, or enhancements to the user interface, or faster processing speed. **Preventive** maintenance increases future maintainability by updating its internal documentation or improving its modular structure. Figure 4.7 shows the relative proportion of effort for maintenance activities. With the advent of object-oriented software engineering, which emphasizes *reuse* of software components, preventive maintenance is getting more emphasis.

4.9 Alternatives: Iterative and incremental models and eXtreme Programming

Maintenance makes a software development process necessarily cyclic. Minor bug fixes may just require re-coding, but significant enhancements may require re-analysis and re-design. We have

---

[4]B. P. Lientz and E. B. Swanson, *Software Maintenance Management*, Addison-Wesley, 1980.

talked about salmon jumping back upstream in the waterfall model. Computer scientists have proposed alternative models of the software life cycle that explicitly allow for progressive cycles. A software shop may produce many releases—where a release is a usable version of a system. **Incremental development** partitions a system into subsystems by functionality. An early release starts with a small, functional subsystem, then later releases add more functionality. **Iterative development** delivers a full system in the first release, then changes the behavior of each subsystem with each new release. For example, suppose a customer wants to develop a new word processing package. An incremental approach could provide just creation functions in release 1, then all organization features in release 2, and finally add formatting in release 3. An iterative approach, on the other hand, would provide primitive forms of all three functions in release 1, then enhance them (by making them faster, improving the interface, etc.) in release 2, etc. In practice, many organizations use a combination of iterative and incremental approaches. Many software companies release a **beta version**, a preliminary version not quite ready for prime time, to a segment of the intended audience, to get feedback (both positive and negative), leading to further fixes and improvements, before releasing a final, **production version**, to a wider market.

Exercise 4.38: A hacker's approach to software development is a **build-and-fix model**: build a first version, then keep modifying it until you've got a satisfied customer, who puts it into operation. Draw a diagram depicting the build-and-fix model. Critique its potential strengths and weaknesses. **Exercise 4.39:** Compare the build-and-fix model described in the previous exercise with the waterfall iterative and incremental models, discussing both similarities and differences.

  XP (eXtreme Programming) emphasizes keeping the customer involved in the development process. Suppose you have to design a system for a customer who only has a vague idea of what their new system should do. (Imagine that!) Traditional models insist that the customer and analyst agree what is required up front. Extreme programming acknowledges that customers may find this difficult, or may want to change their mind. So a guiding principle is that a customer should stay involved throughout the development process, as part of the team. Instead of a formal specification, the customer writes **user stories** describing how they would like a system to behave, which provide enough detail to let the team make a reasonably low-risk estimate of how long the story will take to implement. Then the team creates a **release plan** of small units of functionality that will be delivered, not all at once, but incrementally, in successive releases of the software. A release plan explicitly allows for iterative development, dividing a development schedule up into a dozen or more releases of new features, each taking maybe a week (rather than months) to deliver. To prevent new releases from breaking code that was already working, XP emphasizes **test planning**: every unit of code must have a test plan and no new unit is accepted until it passes *all* tests, both for the new unit and all those that had previously passed. Instead of working in isolation, XP requires **pair programming** (see figure 4.8). Working at a single console, one person is the "designated driver," actively entering code, while the "non-driver" constantly reviews and critiques the code to point out deficiencies, ranging from confusing style to errors in logic. After a time, the partners reverse roles. Though it may seem counter-

Figure 4.8: Pair programming

intuitive to have two people doing the same work, it has been shown that pair programming improves software quality without delaying time to deliver—not only for expert programmers, but for beginners.[5] Think about it. The second person can catch a lot of mistakes and help improve the readability (and maintainability) of the code. Working in pairs can also help beginners (as well as experts) learn from each other.

No matter what method a software house uses for development, maintenance will likely involve different programmers from those responsible for the original development. All the more reason for software developers to be concerned about **documenting** programs, both externally (in technical manuals that include a system's requirements specifications, design and test description) and internally (in comments). All the more reason for software managers (and instructors) to insist that documentation be part of the development process, *not an afterthought*. All the more reason for students of software development, even in an introductory course, to start learning and practicing good problem solving and programming habits—for the long haul.

Exercise 4.40: How is eXtreme Programming different from the hacker's build-and-fix model described in exercise 4.9?

Exercise 4.41: Discuss the tradeoffs of eXtreme Programming, with respect to customer involvement. When and why might it work well and when and why might it not work well?

Exercise 4.42: Why might pair programming be a good idea for students? When and why might it not work well? What commitments would students need to make to make pair programming work?

Exercise 4.43 (*explore*): On the web, learn what *Open-Source* is and discuss examples of how some of these projects use eXtreme Programming techniques. How effective is this combination and why?

Exercise 4.44 (*explore*): Research software testing tools such as Junit. What are they do and why should software engineers use them? Why are the especially useful for eXtreme Programming?

4.10 Software development exercises

You can apply what you have learned about analysis, design, coding and testing in this chapter, to tackle your programming exercises. A possibility is that you may tackle a more ambitious project, such as one of the games outlined in exercise 2.55 (the Game of Life, Hangman, Mastermind, or card games like War or Fish). To be sure, you may have not learned enough to implement any of these programs, but you can begin to work on the requirements, analysis and preliminary design, including use case analysis and class diagrams with UML design. The following exercises introduce more problems for analysis and design which you may or may not implement.

Exercise 4.45: Go through the first four stages of software development for the Megabyte Company problem that will calculate the *average* revenue of an employee per computer: a) Write a requirements specification. b) Draw an input/output diagram for the design. c) Write the code (you may of course modify the program developed in this chapter). Test to make sure that the program runs correctly. Keep a log of any errors, causes of those errors, and corrections that you make.

Exercise 4.46: Computers may be more than number crunchers, but they sure are good at it. The Real World Software company wants to include a calculator application in their ATM, letting users

---

[5]C. McDowell and L. Werner, "The Effects of Pair-Programming on Performance in an Introductory Programming Course," *Proceedings of the 33rd SIGCSE Technical Symposium on Computer Science Education*, 2002, pp. 38-42.

sum up their deposits or double-check transactions, by entering numbers and touching keys corresponding to four arithmetic operators plus equals to show a final result. Take this problem through the analysis (include a use case description) and design stages.

Exercise 4.47: RWS wants to develop another application for FVB: an electronic checking account. It should enable users to record the usual information on checks: check number, date, amount, to whom the check was made out, and memo lines. In addition, it should maintain budget codes distinguishing different categories of checks, such as telephone, taxes, tithes (contributions), and be able to list checks by particular budget codes and report totals for budget codes for specified time periods. Of course, it should also handle deposits as well as check withdrawals. Take this problem through the analysis (include a use case description) and design stages.

Exercise 4.48: RWS and FVB are talking about another project: a bank-by-phone system. Using touch-tone telephones, customers can dial up a BBP system, which will first verify their PIN. Then customers can request the balance on either their checking or savings accounts, transfer funds between accounts, request that checks be sent to recipients (with pre-arranged codes that they can enter easily with a touchtone phone), and set up new recipient codes (with their addresses and recipient account numbers). The BBP system will respond with a combination of pre-recorded and digitized audio messages. (A rapid prototype could simulate audio with text string output.) Take this problem through the analysis and design stages. (Feel free to reuse any of the analysis done for the ATM problem that might be relevant to this one!)

Exercise 4.49 *(social/ethical)*: Suppose Real World Software, thinking they could knock off this ATM problem in a short time, uses a hacking approach to implement the ATM system for First Virtual Bank. When RWS delivers the software, it does not quite perform according to FVB's requirements; moreover, it is poorly documented and its structure hard to understand. RWS points out that FVB's requirements did not specifically mention anything about design or implementation documentation; they simply provided a short description and agreed on a bottom-line for delivery. What do you think is the responsibility of the software supplier and that of the client in this case?

Exercise 4.50 *(social/ethical)*: A student is having difficulty getting a program to work, so he or she goes to the instructor for help. The instructor sees that there are no comments in the code indicating what the student had in mind, so the instructor refuses to help debug the program until the student rewrites it with comments including preliminary analysis and pseudocode design. The student points out, desperately, that the assignment is due the next morning. Do you think the instructor is justified in not giving immediate help? Why or why not?

Chapter review. Are the following statements true or false? Explain why or why not.
a) Much of the complexity of programming-in-the-large is communication.
b) A virtue of hardware components is that it's relatively easy to get them to do new tricks.
c) Modules, such as Java classes, can help manage change and maintain order in software.
d) Comments on the meaning of variables and functions can reduce the cost of software maintenance.
e) A "waterfall" model of the software life cycle encourages frequent re-analysis or re-design.
f) A use case describes a problem solution or algorithm from a system's point of view.
g) A use case describes one scenario.
h) A requirements specification explains how to implement a program.
i) Definition of key terms is an important activity of the analysis stage.
j) Design shifts from analysis ("what") to implementing a program in Java ("how").
k) It's a good idea to have strong coupling and dependencies between modules or classes.

l) In UML, composition and inheritance relationships are always 1 to many (1..n).

m) Pseudocode is fake Java code—pretty useless!

n) Linker errors occur when a header file is missing or in the wrong directory.

o) If a program runs without crashing unexpectedly, then it's correct and you can hand it in—hooray!

p) When a compiler attempts error recovery, it may skip over some source code in a program.

q) It's a good idea to test with boundary values, not just core values.

r) Debugging is another problem solving activity, only more fun.

s) A breakpoint is where a program crashes, even more fun.

t) A structured walkthrough can help discover flaws in the design before implementation.

u) Newer models of the software development life cycle allow for re-analysis and re-design.

v) In the context of software engineering, XP refers to a release of a popular operating system.

w) Pair programming reduces productivity because two people are working at the same thing.

x) Pair programming promotes cross learning.

y) Planning tests before writing code is a good idea.

z) Documentation should be done after a software project is complete.

Summary

The complexity of software has come to dominate the cost of computing. To tackle complexity, software engineers have honed principles for **programming-in-the-large**, the analysis, design and implementation of large-scale software systems. A **software life cycle** models the stages through which these systems progress. In the **waterfall model**, software developers progress from one stage to the next only after the previous stage is complete. Typical stages include: (1) **requirements specification**, which describes, to both the customer and systems analyst, *what* the program will do, under what constraints; (2) **design**, which shifts to *how* to solve the problem, looking more closely at the inputs, outputs and behavior, and developing an algorithm in **pseudocode**, a notation that outlines an algorithm in intelligible English with some programming language constructs; (3) **coding** the data objects and algorithm in a programming language; (4) **testing** to make sure that the program performs according to specifications and debugging any logic errors; (5) **delivery**, making a well-documented program available to its users, and (6) **maintenance**, correcting newly discovered errors, adapting a program to new environment, improving its functionality or performance, or increasing its future maintainability. **Use cases**, describing the behavior of a system from a user's point of view, are one way to communicate user requirements. **Object-oriented** software emphasizes modular design in self-contained units called classes with simple and explicit interfaces, and inheritance of a way to extend existing classes without changing it. **UML (Unified Modeling Language)** provides a standardized notation for object-oriented analysis and design, including **class diagrams**, which depict a system of classes and their relationships graphically. Software engineers have proposed newer models of the software life cycle, such as **eXtreme Programming**, which put more emphasis on iterative and incremental development, and keeping the customer more involved throughout the process.

Chapter 5
Peeling the Onion: Computer Architecture
"Contrariwise," continued Tweedledee, "if it was so, it might be; and if it were so,
it would be; but as it isn't, it ain't. That's logic."
Lewis Carroll, *Through the Looking Glass*

The time has come to tell you a secret. *Your personal computer isn't real.* "What do you mean--*isn't real*!?" you say. "I can see it, feel it, even *hit* it sometimes. It *has* to be real!" Relax, you are not hallucinating. It's just that the machine you've been using—whether it be Windows PC or Macintosh or Linux—is actually a *virtual* machine. Remember, we introduced the idea of a virtual machine earlier, pointing out that the power of the universal machine is that it can act as if it were another machine by *simulating* that machine's behavior—thus creating a "virtual" machine. So one virtual machine can be created on another virtual machine. In fact, when you start up Windows or a Macintosh, you're actually starting up a virtual machine called an *operating system*. The actual machine doesn't know anything about windows or menus or even files. When you then proceed to start up a word processor or spreadsheet or web browser, in effect you're creating yet another (even more specialized) virtual machine.

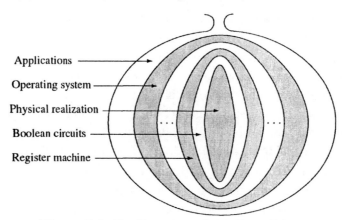

Figure 5.1: Peeling an onion of machines

Like an onion, a computer actually has many layers. The surface layer is almost always a virtual machine, such as the Flash player running *The Universal Computer*. Below that is a web browser, and below that is an operating system. Each of these layers is a virtual machine, created by software running on the machine one layer "down". Several layers below the OS is a *stored program processor* similar to a **register machine**. Below that is a complicated **boolean circuit**, implementing the logic of a register machine, and below that are the transistors and wires which implement the boolean circuit. These last two inner layers are the subject of this chapter.

5.1 The Register Machine

Much as a universal Turing machine can be programmed to simulate any computational device, everything you can do on your computer is accomplished by a **register machine**—'RM' for short. In what follows, we will describe an RM incrementally, by starting "barebones" and adding functionality. Our RM simplifies von Neumann's stored program machine, depicted back in figure 1.3—which is itself an idealization of the processors (such as a Pentium™, Athlon™ or PowerPC™) that you actually find in computers. As you know, a universal Turing machine can simulate an RM, but an RM is more efficient—because an RM stores programs in memory instead of on a paper tape, an RM has registers for high speed computation, and an RM has instructions designed especially to exploit its stored programs and registers.

A **register** is *a high-speed storage device* of a specific fixed size (in bits). Each one has an identifying number, from 1 to *n*—for example, the RM in figure 5.2 has registers 1 through 7. An RM is thus similar to a simple, hand-held calculator, which has a certain number of memory registers in which it can store numbers up to some maximum size. To keep things simple, we will consider an RM which only stores positive integers and only does numerical calculations.

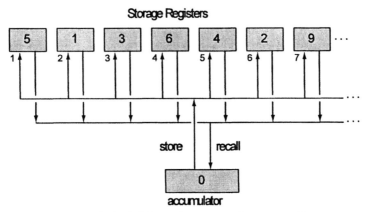

Figure 5.2: RM registers and accumulator

In addition to a collection of numbered storage registers, an RM has a special register called an **accumulator**, which *holds the results of each computation*. The accumulator is where all the numerical "action" happens—other registers are only for fast storage and retrieval of data. Think of a simple calculator: it has a window onto a register in which computation occurs—in effect, an accumulator—and at least one memory register into which you can store values. Typically, to perform some operation on data stored in a register, you must recall it to the accumulator, perform an operation that puts a new value in the accumulator, then re-store the result in the original register. (These days many calculators appear to perform calculations directly in the memory register, by means of M+ and M- keys, but we'll keep our RM simple.)

5.1.1 Register machine instructions

So far, the "hardware" of an RM consists only of an accumulator and a collection of storage registers, numbered from 1 to n. An RM's "software" resources consist of a small number of machine instructions. Our first few instructions move values around between the various registers. The STO (for "store") instruction copies the contents of the accumulator into a register. Since there is more than one register, the STO instruction takes a parameter specifying the destination register. For example, 'STO 5' copies the value in the accumulator into register 5, replacing whatever may have been in the accumulator. RCL (for "recall") copies the contents of a designated register into the accumulator—so 'RCL 8' copies the contents of register 8 into the accumulator, replacing whatever may have been there. (If either of these instructions gets a parameter whose value is not a register number, a "fatal error" occurs—the machine "crashes.") Obviously, these instructions do nothing more than simply move numbers around—no "calculation" yet. Suppose an RM's accumulator and registers are as shown in figure 5.2 above. Then figure 5.3 shows the state of the RM after successively performing the instructions STO 1; RCL 4; STO 3.

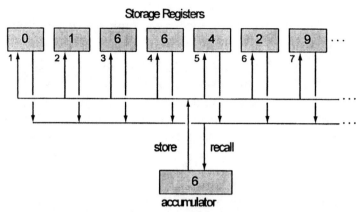

Figure 5.3: The RM after `STO 1, RCL 4, STO 3`

Exercise 5.1: Find the differences between figures 5.2 and 5.3 and explain how they happened, step by step.

Exercise 5.2: What would be the effect on the RM shown in figure 5.3 of each the following instructions (in sequence, each instruction changing the state of the machine): `STO 7`; `RCL 2`; `RCL 3`; `RCL 5`? What would be the effect of the instruction `STO -7`?

Exercise 5.3: Knobby's world is similar to a Register Machine with a single register. What two objects does Knobby's world have that are essentially equivalent to the accumulator and a register, respectively?

Exercise 5.4: What Knobby instructions are analogous to `STO` and `RCL`?

Exercise 5.5: How does assignment (in Pascal, `x:=2`) ultimately execute `STO` and `RCL`?

Exercise 5.6: Recall that an RM is a von Neumann machine, which has external memory. What in Knobby's world is equivalent to a Register Machine's external memory? Hint: Where else can Knobby store things that he can't get to as quickly?)

You might be wondering, why does a RM use cryptic three letter names, such as `STO`, for its instructions? Actually, these names are a luxury. As far as the RM is concerned, these instructions are distinguishable by binary numbers, e.g., `STO` might be instruction code 001, `RCL` is instruction code 010 (decimal 2), etc. An **assembler** *translates these mnemonic three letter symbols into machine code numbers*—making machines a bit more comprehensible for humans.

5.1.2. Arithmetic and input/output instructions

Though hand-held calculators have addition, subtraction, multiplication and division built in, our register machine's arithmetic resources are simpler. Indeed, to emphasize simplicity, our RM has fewer primitive instructions than most. `ZER` (for "zero out") enters a value zero into the accumulator—thus "clearing" its contents. `INC` (for "increment") *adds* one to the contents of the accumulator; `DEC` (for "decrement") *subtracts* one from the contents of the accumulator. Here's one way to enter a value of 5 into the accumulator is: `ZER, INC, INC, INC, INC, INC`.

Suppose the registers can store positive numbers ranging from 00000 to 99999. What if the accumulator has already reached its upper (or lower) limit, and executes an `INC` (or `DEC`) instruction? (Exceeding an upper limit is known as an **overflow**; decrementing below a lower limit is an **underflow**.) Here a computer engineer has a design choice: she could posit that *nothing* happens in the accumulator, or she could posit that the values "cycle around"—going from 99999 to 00000 with one INC, or from 00000 to 99999 with one DEC. Either choice represents a potential error, sometimes called an **exception**. A third design choice might be to signal an exception by putting a non-zero code in some specially designated register. To keep things simple, our RM will just do nothing, so that 99999 + 1 = 99999 and 00000 - 1 = 00000.

Exercise 5.8: What problems would face a programmer if ZER, INC and DEC were the only way to enter data into the accumulator?

Exercise 5.9 *(social/ethical)*: Something like an overflow could have occurred in many computer programs on January 1, 2000. Why? What problems would have resulted? Why were programs designed that would have this flaw in the first place? Who was responsible if such programs were not corrected in time?

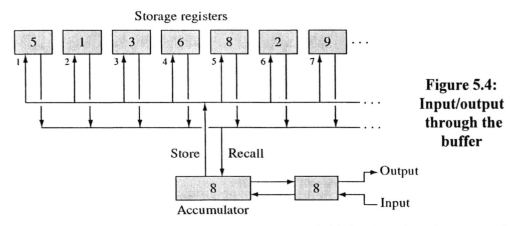

Figure 5.4: Input/output through the buffer

The ZER, INC and DEC give us one way to put initial values into the accumulator, but it's clumsy. We really need a way to receive or send values from or to the "outside world." So our RM also has a second special register called a **buffer**—*connecting the accumulator with the input/output devices*, shown in figure 5.4. I/O devices tend to be slower than processors, so it's efficient to store values in a buffer register, then let the RM continue processing. Later we'll learn more about how the I/O devices and main memory interact with the processor.

To *input* a value to the RM, the accumulator must receive a value from the buffer. Similarly, to *output* a value from the RM, a value must be sent from the accumulator to the buffer. For this purpose, our RM has two input/output instructions. INP reads a value from the buffer into the accumulator; we assume there is some arrangement for feeding *keyboard* or other input sources into the buffer. On the other hand, OUT writes a value from the accumulator into the buffer; again, we assume some arrangement then feeds buffer contents to a monitor or other output device.[1] Finally, a program, however short or long, has to have a beginning, middle, and end. The beginning is simply the first instruction in a program. The end is not necessarily the last instruction in the program; rather, it is the last instruction executed—a HLT (halt) instruction. (You'll see how a program might end someplace other than the last instruction shortly.)

With these instructions, we can write programs for the RM to perform simple

---

[1]The buffer accounts for some puzzling behavior. A "write" instruction sends data to an output buffer, but the data doesn't appear on the monitor until the buffer is *flushed*, emptying the contents of the buffer. The *next* "write" instruction flushes the buffer. But what happens to the data for the *final* "write"? It doesn't appear—novice programmers sometimes conclude that the final part of the output has been "lost".

calculations. Here's a program that computes the value of *n+3* for the input *n*:

```
INP
INC
INC
INC
OUT
HLT
```

The RM gets a value of *n* from the user, increments it three times, outputs the result, then halts.

Exercise 5.12: Write the RM code that will receive an input value, add two to it, store the result in register 1, subtract four from the current accumulator value, store the result in register 5 and output the two values—first, the value in register 1, then that in register 5.

Exercise 5.13: Suppose, in the previous exercise, you had wanted to subtract 4 from the *original input value* instead of the current accumulator value. How would your code look? Hint: is it enough simply to perform the operations in the reverse order? Why or why not?

5.1.3 Control instructions

As in von Neumann's design, an RM stores its programs in memory and retrieves its instructions, one by one, from consecutive memory locations. Each instruction in a program has an **instruction number**—its relative address in memory. The **instruction register** (also known as the **program counter**) *holds the memory address of the next instruction to perform*. The RM *fetches* an instruction from the memory location given in the instruction register, *decodes* it (figures out which machine instruction it is), then *executes* it. Then it fetches the next instruction, and so forth. We call this *fetch-decode-execute* loop a **machine cycle**. Immediately after fetching an instruction from memory, the RM automatically increments the value of the instruction register, so that it will usually fetch the next consecutive instruction from memory.

With the instructions we've seen so far, an RM can perform only rigid sequences of instructions. A branching capability makes it more flexible. The RM has two **branch** instructions: BRZ ("branch on zero") and BRN ("branch on non-zero"). Each of these also takes a parameter: an instruction number. For the BRZ, if the current value of the accumulator is *zero*, then it puts the parameter (an instruction number) into the instruction register, so it will branch to that instruction in the next cycle. If the accumulator value is not zero, the machine just continues to the next instruction as usual. The effect of BRN reverses the test: if the value in the accumulator is *non-zero*, it puts its parameter in the instruction register. (As with the STO and RCL instructions, if a parameter is invalid, the machine crashes.)

Figure 5.5 shows the machine just after it has executed instruction #6. Let's go back and replay a couple of steps. Instruction 4, RCL 2, had recalled a value 1 from register 2 into the accumulator. Instruction 5 then decremented the accumulator, making its value 0. Since the value in the accumulator was in fact 0, instruction 6, BRZ 12, placed the value 12 into the instruction register. This move will cause the RM to "jump" to instruction 12 in the program.

In addition to conditional instructions, an RM's branch instructions also allow the execution of repetitions, though their construction is somewhat different from while loops. In the first place, the only tests available are whether the accumulator value is zero or non-zero. (This limitation is less drastic than it may seem; indeed it only makes it more clumsy to obtain the same effect.) In the second place, an RM test typically occurs as a post-test, at the *end* of the

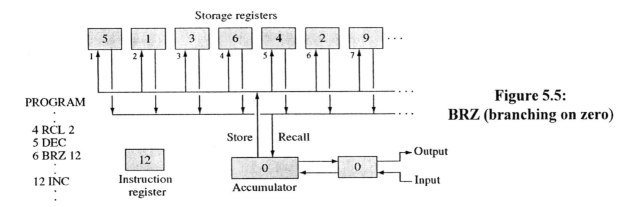

Storage registers

Figure 5.5:
BRZ (branching on zero)

PROGRAM
.
4 RCL 2
5 DEC
6 BRZ 12
.
12 INC
.

12
Instruction
register

Store   Recall

0
Accumulator

0

Output

Input

loop rather than at the beginning. That is, a BRZ or a BRN instruction appears *after the last* instruction in a loop and the branch instruction's parameter goes back up to the *first* instruction in the loop. When this construction is used, the RM always performs a loop at least once. If the branch test succeeds—the repeat condition—the machine returns to the first instruction in the loop; if not, it goes on to the following instruction.

Exercise 5.14: The BRZ and BRN instructions are analogous to the if control structure. How can an RM get the effect of the if-else control structure? Write an RM program fragment which reads an input value and stores it in register 2 if the accumulator value is zero, but recalls the value from register 5 and outputs it if the value is non-zero. (Hint: where does the program control go from there?)

Exercise 5.15: Recall that the body of a while loop will not be executed at all if the test condition is not initially true. Suppose you want a similar sort of loop for the register machine--e.g., a loop which would be expressible in Java syntax as

```
while (accumulator != 0) DEC
```

How can this be done? Hint: Where should the initial test be made? What should the test be? What should be done if it is satisfied? If it is not satisfied?

Branching (and looping) lets us implement more general programs. Instead of just adding a fixed number to an input value, we can add *any* two input values.[2] Rather than explicitly perform INC a fixed number of times, it would be more general to use a loop. In fact, since neither input value is fixed, we *have* to use a loop. How do we do this? The idea is that we have two values, and we repeatedly decrement one value (until it reaches zero) and increment the other. In such a loop, the sum of the two values will be an *invariant*. Thus, when the one value has been decremented to zero, the other value has been incremented to the sum of the two original values. Here is our algorithm in pseudocode:

1. Input the two numbers
2. Perform a loop until the first number is zero.
    a.   decrement the first number
    b.   increment the second number
3. Output the second number as the sum of the two input numbers.

---

[2]Again, real RM's also generally have at least addition as a primitive operation. But, partly for simplicity's sake, and partly because you should see how *very simple* primitives can be combined to make more complicated operations, we limit our arithmetic instructions to INC and DEC.

Exercise 5.16: Is this analysis adequate for all cases? Hint: What will happen if the first number is zero to begin with? What should the algorithm do in this case?

Exercise 5.17: Recall the HLT instruction. Why is a HLT instruction necessary, rather than just stopping at the end of a program's code? Hint: Think about branch instructions.

We are now ready to write our algorithm in RM code (with Knobby-style comments):

```
1     INP
2     STO 1    //Why is this necessary before the second INP?
3     INP
4     STO 2    //What is being done here? Why? (See pcode outline)
5     RCL 1
6     BRZ 14 //What is being done here? Why?
7     DEC
8     STO 1    //What is being done here? Why?
9     RCL 2
10    INC
11    STO 2    //What is being done here? Why?
12    RCL 1
13    BRN 6    //What is being done here? Why?
14    RCL 2    //What is being done here? Why?
15    OUT
16    HLT
```

Exercise 5.18: Answer the questions posed in the comments above.

Exercise 5.19: Look at instruction 13. Improve it.

Exercise 5.20: Reflect on what happens in the addition program when the input numbers are 18 and 2 (in that order). Considering the previous exercise, improve the program.

Exercise 5.21: Write a program to output the *smaller* of two input numbers, assuming that all RM numbers are non-negative. (If they are equal, output their common value.) Hint: In terms of the register machine's capabilities, what does it *mean* to say that one number is less than another? In the program given above, what kind of problem-solving approach are we using?

Exercise 5.22: Write a "subtraction" program for the RM, still assuming that RM numbers are all non-negative. Which of the two input numbers should be subtracted from the other? Why?

Exercise 5.23: Think of a way to do *genuine* subtraction, which may involve negative numbers, on an RM. Hint: How could you represent negative numbers?

After addition and subtraction come multiplication and division. How can an RM perform these more complicated operations? (You are now treading in the footsteps of the famous mathematicians Pascal, Leibniz, and Babbage.) Well, remember that multiplication is simply repeated addition, and division is repeated subtraction. Since we can write programs for these, we can embed them as **subprograms** in larger programs and call on them. However, a lowly RM does not have a built-in ability to define and call instructions. When Knobby calls a defined instruction, control branches to the beginning of the instruction, and when the instruction terminates, control reverts *back* to the point after that instruction call. The RM will do something much simpler. To call a subprogram is to branch to its first instruction number. The last instruction of a subprogram is also a branching instruction, but it will always send control back to the main program (in fact, to the specific instruction referred to in the branch instruction). So a subprogram can be called in *different* places, but only if in each case we wish the **flow of**

control always to revert to the very *same* instruction after the subprogram is finished. If this is satisfactory, we can treat subprograms in either of two ways: (a) renumber a *copy* of the subprogram appropriately, and physically embed it into the main program (this is called **inlining a subprogram**), or (b) renumber the subprogram itself as a separate set of instructions, branch to the beginning of the subprogram and later back from it to the appropriate point in the main program. For an example of the latter approach, suppose we take our addition program and renumber its instructions and addresses from 101 to 113. We can branch from another place in the program--say instruction 56—to instruction 101; instruction 114 will then be a branch instruction returning to the appropriate instruction in the calling context—e.g., instruction 92.

Exercise 5.24: Notice, however, that our RM's branch instructions are *conditional branches*, not *unconditional* "GOTO's". What we *may* need in order to call the subprogram and what we *will* need at the end of the subprogram in order to return to the main program is a branch which is executed *no matter what* is in the accumulator. How can an RM accomplish this?

Exercise 5.25: What are the advantages and disadvantages (if any) of inlining vs. explicit subprogram calls? Which approach strikes you as better? Why?

Exercise 5.26: Suppose, however, that when the subprogram is called from instruction 56, we wish control to revert to instruction 57 after the subprogram terminates, *but* when it is called from instruction 121, we wish control to revert to instruction 122. What difficulties does this pose? Hint: How does an RM "remember" where to branch back to when the subprogram is over? (We'll come back to this issue later.)

So the process of multiplication goes roughly as follows: we read the two numbers, and if either is 0, the answer is 0. If not, we add the second number to zero to get a (temporary) sum. We then decrement the first number and see if it is now 0. If so, the value of the sum is the answer. If not, we add the second number to the sum. We then decrement the first number again and see if it is now 0. If so, the value of the sum is the answer. If not, we add the second number to the sum again And so on ... Here, then, is the general outline for a multiplication algorithm:

1	Read the first number.
2	Branch on zero to output the value 0 and halt.
3	Store the number in register 1.
4	Read the second number.
5	Branch on zero to output the value 0 and halt..
6	Store the number in registers 2 and 3.
7	Recall and decrement the contents of register 1. //why do this?
8	Branch on zero to output the contents of register 3 and halt.
9	Add what's in register 2 to what's in register 3. //the subprogram
10	Store the result in register 3.
11	Branch on non-zero back to step 7.

Exercise 5.27: What happens in line 11 if the accumulator value is 0? (Think carefully—this is a bit of a trick question!)

Exercise 5.28: Compare lines 2 and 5 with line 8; think of a way to make the program structure simpler by placing a different initial value in register 3. Suppose we do that. What does that do to the order of the instructions in lines 7-11? (Try it out by computing 1*2.) Correct the program by moving line 8.

Exercise 5.29: Now notice the "awkwardness" of the last pair of instructions in the changed program. How could you improve the program? Write an improved version. Test your program by using it to compute 0*n, and n*0 (for some small non-zero value of n). Cases like the "0-case" are called **boundary value** cases, and it is at such values that errors often occur.

Exercise 5.30: Recalling the difference between the addition and the subtraction programs, write an outline for a division algorithm, outputting *both* the quotient and the remainder. What will you want to do if the divisor is zero?

Exercise 5.31: Write a complete division program for the RM.

5.1.4 New data types and operations

We have seen the basic structure of a register machine and how it works. But what we've seen it do so far is basically pretty simple–addition, multiplication, subtractions whose answers are positive values. As a popular song of some years ago went, "Is that all there is?". Since we claim that the virtual computer you are accustomed to using is based on a register machine, there had better be more!

Indeed there is. First, let's look at how the register machine can deal with data other than positive integers. Certainly, to have real subtraction, we need to be able to represent negative numbers. An earlier exercise touched on how to achieve this capability in an RM. One way to achieve this is to have an additional register to keep track of whether the number in the accumulator (or any other register) is positive or negative. (Suppose the entries in the registers are in binary notation. Can you see another way to represent negative numbers without using another register?) Arithmetic can then carry on very much as usual: [+]5 - [+]3 = [+]2, [+]3 - [+]5 = [-]2, etc. Notice that the absolute values of the differences are the same. The sign is determined by whether the first number or the second is larger. So we could accomplish any subtraction of two positive numbers in much the same way we did subtraction earlier—decrementing each value until one of them becomes zero. The other one provides the absolute value of the answer; the sign is determined by which of the two values is now zero.

Exercise 5.32: How would we compute [-]5 - [-]3? [-]3 - [-]5? (Hint: what happens if you keep decrementing a negative number?)

Exercise 5.33: Notice, these cases, as well as the ones above involve two numbers with the same sign. What about, say, [+]5 and [-]3? Or [-]5 and [+]3? How would we compute subtractions involving these numbers?

Exercise 5.34: For that matter, how would we do addition of a pair of "mixed numbers"?

How about real number arithmetic? In fact, quite a number of real computers actually do real number arithmetic by simulating it in terms of complicated integer arithmetic. (That's right, another virtual machine.) Recall the way real numbers are expressed in exponential notation–as the product of a mantissa and some power of 10 (thus, 3.25 = 325e-2). A pair of registers can store these two parts. So any real number (within the machine's limit of accuracy) can be represented with an integer mantissa and an integer exponent. Recall, though, that each number has many such representations: 3.25 = 325e-2 = 3250e-3, ... etc. This means that to add numbers, the addends must first be manipulated so as to have a common exponent. Thus 101 + 3.25 + .0006 = 101e0 + 325e-2 + 6e-4 = 1010000e-4 + 32500e-4 + 6e-4 = 1042506e-4, the last step involving ordinary integer addition.

Exercise 5.35: On an RM, how could the addends be manipulated to have a common exponent? (Hint: How would one change 3.25e0 to 32500e-2? What is done to the mantissa and what to the exponent?)

Exercise 5.36: Write an outline of how to add two real numbers given in exponential form, but not necessarily with the same exponent.

These examples show how the RM as we have defined it can do a surprising number of things. We can also enrich the RM by providing it with means of **indirect access** to registers. Recall the way that STO and RCL access registers. Each of these instructions is supplied with a numerical parameter which gives the address of a data register. This is **direct access**—sending data directly to or bringing data directly from a register. In indirect address, a parameter also provides a register address, but the data in this register is *another register address*. (The intermediate register providing another register address is called a **pointer**, and the address that the intermediate register holds is called a **stored address**.) Our indirect access instructions are ISTO (indirect store) and IRCL (indirect recall). Figures 5.6a and 5.6b illustrate the difference between STO and ISTO.

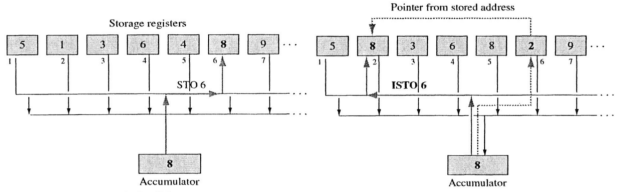

Figure 5.6a: Direct access   **Figure 5.6b: Indirect access**

In the direct access case (figure 5.6a), the instruction STO 6 sends the value in the accumulator (namely, 8) to R6, changing its previous contents to 8. All other registers remain unchanged. Contrast ISTO 6 (figure 5.6b). It goes to R6 and reads its contents (here, 2). So the stored address is 2, making R6 a pointer to R2. ISTO 6 then sends the content of the accumulator (8) to R2. In this case, ISTO 6 has the same net effect as STO 2, where 2 is the value in R6.

Exercise 5.36: In your own words, explain what STO 3 and ISTO 3 would each do.

Exercise 5.37: In your own words, explain what RCL 6 and IRCL 6 would each do.

ISTO is somewhat like having your mail sent to a fixed address while you are traveling and letting that person forward your mail to you, rather than having it sent directly to whatever address you may be at. As a more computer-oriented analogy, indirect address is also somewhat like the program register providing an address rather than data—more specifically, the address of the next instruction to be executed. In fact, we can exploit this analogy even further by applying the principle of indirect access to the branching instructions BRZ and BRN. Whereas BRZ 2 would tell the machine to go to instruction 2 if the accumulator value is 0, IBRZ 2 would tell the machine to go to *the instruction whose number is in register 2* if the accumulator value is 0.

An advantage of this flexibility in access can be seen if we consider using subprograms. Recall that a subprogram is a certain set of instructions which may be called from any point in a program. The difficulty is that whenever this is done, as soon as the last instruction is executed, control cannot return to the point at which the subprogram is called—the only flexibility would be branching according to the accumulator value. But we *can* return to the call point easily if we have indirect branching rules. Here's how: before calling the subprogram, put the number of the next instruction in a designated register, say R100. Then at the end of the subprogram, use an indirect branching rule, say IBRZ, to access that register. Thus, if the accumulator value is 0, IBRZ 100 will send the control to that instruction whose address is in R100—i.e., the instruction immediately after the instruction that called the subprogram.

Another advantage of indirect access is that it can support more complex data structures such as arrays, records, and objects. What all these structures have in common is that a RM first uses a stored address to access a **base** address, then computes an **offset** from that base. For example, the base address of an array is a pointer to its first element. The RM can then compute the offset address as: base+subscript*element-size (in machine "words"). So on a machine with 16-bit words, if a is an array of 32-bit integers, whose base address is k, then a[5] is at $k+5*2$.

Exercise 5.37: For the employeeType described on pp. 65-66, describe how to compute the address of each field. Explain your assumptions about String and Integer types.

5.2 Boolean Circuits

Underlying all the dazzling stuff you can do on any computer is a register machine. You may be wondering, how do those operations and registers actually work? Well, one could say that it's all done by manipulating 1's and 0's. Of course, you rarely actually see binary numbers flashing around, since you're almost always looking at a virtual machine. In fact, what's really happening *isn't* that 1's and 0's are moving around. Rather, an actual machine has components that switch between one of two states (hence these binary components are said to be **bi-stable**). In principle, binary components could be anything which could represent two states. You could have people—standing up or sitting down. You could have soda cans—full or empty. You could have circuits—with current flowing or not flowing. You could have magnets—pointing north or south. Present-day computers use a combination of electronic transistors, electro-magnetic and optical disks, but computers of the futures may use DNA or atoms.

Exercise 5.38: Suppose you had a network of pipes, with pumps that could force water to flow in various ways through the network. If each individual section of pipe is an element of the system, what are its two states? (Assume that water is always flowing in the system, so the states are not *water flowing* and *water not flowing*.)

In the ENIAC, these binary components were vacuum tubes, which changed state much faster than mechanical relays, but still were bulky and generated a great deal of heat. The invention of the transistor enabled engineers to design machines with much smaller components. Nowadays, VLSI (Very Large Scale Integration) designers etch millions of microscopic transistors into chips made of silicon (an element which happens to be low cost, since it's found in sand, and which is also a semiconductor of electricity). In the future, computers may go back to using light bulbs—or rather, laser optics—to store trillions of binary states. (CDROMs already use laser optics to retrieve bits from shiny platters.)

Although the two states may be a variety of things, it is convenient to designate them as 1's or 0's. It is also convenient to think of the basic parts as devices with inputs (1's and 0's) and outputs (ditto) which are connected as electric circuits are connected. Since this is not a book about electronics, we'll abstract away from electric circuits a bit, and talk about **boolean** circuits. They get their name from the nineteenth century English mathematician George Boole, who first set down their underlying principles. Boole invented a logical calculus which bases its calculations on boolean values (true and false) rather than 1's and 0's. A digital computer represents these two boolean values as true (for when the electric current in the circuit is flowing) and false (for when the electric current is not flowing). This calculus (called **boolean algebra**) can determine the truth or falsity of complicated logical expressions. So a boolean circuit describes how to implement a logical or boolean expression in hardware (in terms of transistors and electrical lines); the input(s) to boolean circuits are boolean values, and the output(s) are boolean values also. Boolean algebra is represented at a lower level of abstraction by current flowing or not flowing, and at a higher level of abstraction by calculations on a number system with only two numbers, 0 and 1. That certainly makes life simple.

5.2.1 The basic building blocks

The elementary components of boolean circuits are **gates**: units that direct current flow in different directions depending on the input and their internal circuitry. We can build a computer from just three basic types of gates: **not-gates**, **and-gates**, and **or-gates.** A **not**-gate is the simplest: it is a device with a single boolean input and one boolean output which is always the exact *opposite* of the input. Or to put it another way: the output is **1** (current flowing) if the input is **0**, and is **0** (current not flowing) if the input is **1**. An **and**-gate is a bit more complicated. It is a device with two (boolean) inputs and one (boolean) output which has the following behavior: when both inputs are **1**, its output is **1**; otherwise, its output is **0**. An **or**-gate is also a device with two inputs and one output, but a quite different input-output relationship. Its output is **1** if one *or* the other (or both) of its inputs is **1**; otherwise, its output is **0**. It should be clear that these gates realize the behavior of the three boolean connectives from the previous chapter—hence the names. (In speaking English we often think of 'or' as meaning "one or the other, *but not both*"—that is the *exclusive* sense of the word. In computer science we prefer the **inclusive** meaning of 'or'. Especially when offered pie or ice cream—we take pie *and* ice cream.) Figure 5.7 gives truth-tables reviewing the behavior of the three gates, where we use the letter 'i' to denote an input (remember, you can think of **1** as **true** and **0** as **false**).

i	not-i		i1	i2	i1-and-i2	i1-or-i2
1	0		1	1	1	1
0	1		1	0	0	1
			0	1	0	1
			0	0	0	0

Figure 5.7: Boolean truth-tables

Exercise 5.39: For the exclusive sense of the word 'or', the compound is true when exactly one of its constituents is true. This sense is denoted by **xor**. Write a truth table for **xor**.

Exercise 5.40: Another kind of gate is the **equ**-gate, with an output of **1** if the two inputs are equal, and 0 otherwise. Write a truth table for **equ**. How are **xor** and **equ** related?

As Figure 5.8 shows, you can think of the boolean gates as simple electrical circuits. In each case, we have inputs in which current is either flowing (**1**) or not (**0**). The **and**-gate, in the middle, is the simplest; it consists of two switches, each connected to an input, which are connected in *series*. When a current flows through an input, it *closes* its switch—allowing current to flow through it. When *both* input currents A and B flow (**1**), both switches are closed, allowing current to flow through them; then current flows through the circuit as a whole (**1**). On the other hand, if current is *not* flowing in an input (**0**), then its switch springs *open*, blocking the flow of current through it; then no current flows through the circuit as a whole (**0**). We can extend this analogy, comparing an **or**-gate to an electric circuit with two switches in *parallel*. As seen at the right in figure 5.8, when *either* input current flows (**1**), its switch is closed and current flows (**1**); if neither input current flows (**0**), both switches are open, and no current flows (**0**). The **not**-gate at the left in figure 5.7 is slightly different. When the input current *flows* (**1**), it forces the switch open, *preventing* current from flowing through the gate (**0**). When no current flows (**0**), the switch remains closed, allowing current to flow through the gate (**1**). Reference to the truth-tables above shows the correctness of these analogies. From just these three building blocks, we can build any boolean circuit. (In fact, as we will see in Exercise 5.41, not even all three of these are needed.)

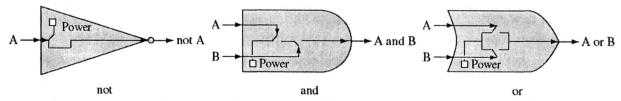

Figure 5.8: Boolean "gates" as electrical circuits

Exercise 5.41: Show how an **or**-gate can be constructed from an **and**-gate and three **not**-gates. Hint: First try to construct a circuit which is the *opposite* from an **or**-gate--an output of **1** for two **0** inputs, and **0** otherwise; then use another **not**-gate. Similarly show how to construct an **and**-gate from an **or**-gate and three **not**-gates. Now, with fewer hints do the harder task of showing how to construct an **exclusive-or**-gate from two **and**-gates, an **or**-gate, and two **not**-gates.

5.2.2 Building boolean circuits

Now we are ready to put these simple gates together to form more complicated circuits, by connecting outputs from one gate (or circuit) as inputs to another. As we shall see, there are two ways to look at this process of constructing machines out of gates—as connecting physical wires or designing truth tables—and these two are logically equivalent.

At this point, given a table showing the behavior of a boolean circuit, we want to be able to construct a circuit with just that behavior. In effect, the table specifies the behavior of a black box. Our task is to determine just what's in the box. In doing so, it will be useful to use *generalizations* of **or**-gates and **and**-gates. A **generalized or-gate** allows not just two but *any number of inputs*, while retaining the defining property that *its output is **1** if any of its inputs is **1**, but **0** if all of its inputs are **0***. The value of a generalized **or**-gate depends on a generalization of an interesting property of a simple **or**-gate: when *either* of the inputs of a simple **or**-gate is **0**, its output is equal to the *other* input. The corresponding version for the generalized **or**-gate is that when *all but one* of its inputs are **0**, its output is equal to the one remaining input.

Exercise 5.42: Use a truth-table to verify that an **or**-gate does have aforementioned "interesting property." Do the same to show that, say, a four-input **or**-gate has the generalized property.

Exercise 5.43: What is the corresponding "interesting property" of **and**-gates? Use a truth-table to verify that an **and**-gate has the property.

Exercise 5.44: What is the corresponding definition for a **generalized and-gate**? What is the corresponding property for generalized **and**-gates?

Exercise 5.45: *Any* generalized **or**-gate can be put together from standard **or**-gates in a fairly straightforward way. Can you discover what it is? Hint: what about a three- or four-input gate?

Exercise 5.46: Describe how to construct any generalized **and**-gate. Hint: what method of problem-solving is involved here and in the last four exercises?

Now that we have gates as our basic components, we're ready to construct circuits. We'll base our constructions on truth tables. The columns show the inputs or outputs; the rows each map a unique combination of input values to output values. If there are n inputs, each taking two possible values, there should be 2^n rows. For example, in figure 5.7 below, there are 3 inputs, so there are $2^3 = 8$ rows. Row 3 handles the combination i1=**1**, i2=**0**, i3=**1**, yielding o=**0** as output.

i1	i2	i3	o
1	1	1	1
1	1	0	0
1	0	1	0
1	0	0	1
0	1	1	1
0	1	0	1
0	0	1	0
0	0	0	0

Figure 5.8: A three-input truth table

Let's call each row's *input* combination its **signature**, and call each row whose *output* is a **1** a **1**-row. For each **1**-row, we'll construct a sub-circuit—it should output **1** when the actual inputs match that row's signature, and **0** for all other actual input combinations. If an input value is **0**, then sending it through a **not**-gate will convert it to **1**. Thus if the signature for row 4 in figure 5.8—i1=**1**, i2=**0**, i3=**0**—is sent through the gate combination i1, **not**-i2, **not**-i3, the resulting values are all **1**s. We then route these values through a generalized **and**-gate. Thus if the original input was (**1,0,0**), it is converted to (**1,1,1**) and the final output is **1**. If you look at the circuit in figure 5.9, you can trace i1 going directly into the second **and**-gate, while i2 and i3 each first go through a **not**-gate before going to the second **and**-gate. That takes care of the fourth row in figure 5.8. See if you can trace the sub-circuits for other **1**-rows (1, 5 and 6) through the circuit. (Input lines and their negations are horizontal lines, while vertical lines flow down into **and**-gates. Large dots at line intersections can be thought of as soldered connections, while other intersections are insulated, crossing without making an electrical junction.)

Finally, we use a generalized **or**-gate to combine the outputs from the four **and**-gates. Thus the circuit as a whole will produce **1** only if one of the four **1**-row sub-circuits is true, and **0** otherwise. Similarly, *any* logical behavior specifiable by a truth-table can be realized by a boolean circuit.

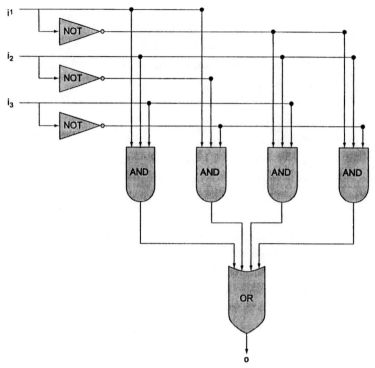

Figure 5.9: Boolean circuit for truth table of figure 5.8

Exercise 5.47: Explain in your own words how the circuit in figure 5.9 accounts for row 5 in the truth table of figure 5.9.

Exercise 5.48: Explain in your own words how the circuit in figure 5.9 accounts for row 6 in the truth table of figure 5.9.

Exercise 5.49: Explain how the circuit in figure 5.9 rules out the four 0-rows.

Exercise 5.50: Create a truth table with three inputs (in the same order as in figure 5.9) and whose 1-rows are rows 2, 4 and 8. Then draw a boolean circuit corresponding to this table.

The circuit of figure 5.9 has three inputs but just one output. Can we construct a circuit with more than one output? Sure. For example, figure 5.10 shows a truth table with two outputs.

i1	i2	i3	o1	o2
1	1	1	1	0
1	1	0	0	0
1	0	1	0	1
1	0	0	1	0
0	1	1	1	0
0	1	0	1	1
0	0	1	0	0
0	0	0	0	0

Figure 5.10: Truth table with three inputs and two outputs

Here's how to construct a circuit for this table. Each output column gets its own **or**-gate, for which the inputs flow from **and**-gates representing each 1 in that column. So the **or**-gate in

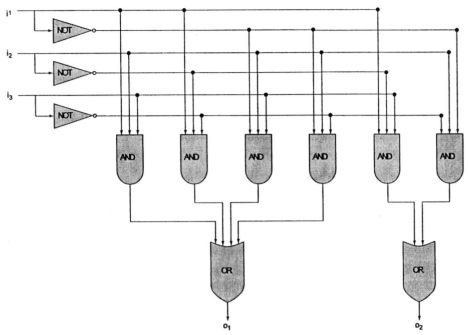

Figure 5.11: Boolean circuit with three inputs and two outputs

figure 5.11 is true if either one of two **and**-gates is true. The left **and**-gate accounts for the 1 in the third row, when i1 is true, i2 is false (through a **not**-gate) and i3 is true.

Exercise 5.51: Explain in your own words how the circuit in figure 5.12 accounts for row 6 in the figure 5.11.

Exercise 5.52: Add an output column to the table in figure 5.9 with **1**'s in rows 2, 5, and 8. Then construct a boolean circuit representing the new truth table.

5.3 Making a register machine from boolean circuits

Given truth tables and boolean gates as building blocks, we can construct a circuit for various practical devices—such as a register machine. First of all, the register machine deals with positive integers. Back in chapter 1, you learned how to represent integers in binary notation. So all integers up to some maximum limit can be represented by bit strings (1's and 0's)—as either multiple inputs to or outputs from a circuit. If we use 4 bits to represent our numbers, we have a range from 0 to 15. (Bit widths for integers in PCs have jumped from 16 in the 80's to 32 in the 90's to 64 in the 2000's, giving machines the capability of handling larger numbers—for arithmetic, larger memory addresses, and other uses.)

What about registers? A register is just a *multiple-output circuit*, whose outputs at any time collectively represent the value that it is currently storing. Thus a register which contains the number 9, for example, would be circuit with four outputs, whose output values are 1, 0, 0,1 (since 9 in binary is 1001).

What about the *operations* on register contents? For example, the instructions ZER, INC, DEC, and RCL affect the contents of the accumulator, while STO, OUT, BRZ, and BRN affect other registers. In order to incorporate these instructions into a boolean circuit, we must first represent each one as an arrangement of boolean values. Here's something else to consider: the behavior of some instructions, such as INC and DEC, depends not only on the logic of the *instruction* itself, but on the *contents* of the registers upon which they operate. So, we must somehow construct circuits with some inputs representing instruction codes while other inputs represent the current register contents. (Remember Babbage's "mill" and "store"? Back in chapter 1, we compared the mill to a computer's CPU and the store to memory. At the level of boolean circuits wiring up an RM, the logic of instruction codes is the mill and the gates representing a register's contents is the store.) Moreover, the *outputs* produced by such instructions as ZER, INC, and DEC represent *new* contents of registers. These new register contents may in turn feed into other instructions. What this requires is the recirculation of register *outputs* back into *inputs*, resulting in new outputs which themselves become inputs, etc.

5.3.1 Sub-circuits for ZER, INC, DEC, and HLT

Let's look at a simple case. Suppose we have an accumulator whose capacity is only two bits. So it can contain one of the values 0, 1, 2, or 3 (in binary, 00, 01, 10, or 11). An accumulator is therefore a circuit with two outputs whose values represent one of these four numbers. Since an accumulator needs to retain its value until an operation changes them, it will also need two inputs to recirculate its two bits. It will also need inputs to distinguish instructions which affect the accumulator. For the moment, let's consider only ZER, INC, and DEC. We can distinguish four instructions with two bits of information. So we'll also consider HLT as a fourth instruction, though it doesn't affect the accumulator. Inputs i1 and i2 represent the *instruction*; inputs j1 and j2 represent *recirculated* inputs from previous outputs; and outputs o1 and o2 represent the new, current contents of the accumulator. In each case, '_1' represents the "high (left) bit," and '_2' represents the "low (right) bit."

INSTRUCTION NAME	INSTR CODE		PREVIOUS CONTENTS		NEW CONTENTS	
	i1	i2	j1	j2	o1	o2
ZER	1	1	1	1	0	0
ZER	1	1	1	0	0	0
ZER	1	1	0	1	0	0
ZER	1	1	0	0	0	0
INC	1	0	1	1	1	1
INC	1	0	1	0	1	1
INC	1	0	0	1	1	0
INC	1	0	0	0	0	1
DEC	0	1	1	1	1	0
DEC	0	1	1	0	0	1
DEC	0	1	0	1	0	0
DEC	0	1	0	0	0	0
HLT	0	0	1	1	1	1
HLT	0	0	1	0	1	0
HLT	0	0	0	1	0	1
HLT	0	0	0	0	0	0

Figure 5.14: Input-output relations for the accumulator

For example, if the input is 10 (binary for 2), then i1=**1** and i2=**0**. Figure 5. displays the effect on the accumulator values as an input-output relation.

What does all this mean? Columns i1 and i2 distinguish four instruction codes. If i1=**1** and i2=**1** then the instruction is ZER, i1=**1** and i2=**0** encodes instruction INC, etc. Columns j1 and j2 give the *previous contents* of the accumulator, before executing the instruction. Lines o1 and o2 show the *new contents* of the accumulator, after executing the instruction. Let's read the first four lines. They all show that if the instruction number is 11 (the code for ZER), then no matter what the previous contents of the accumulator may be, the new contents will always be 00. So ZER always puts zero in the accumulator.

The next four lines recognize instruction number 10. They add 1 to the previous contents, using binary arithmetic: $00 + 1 = 01$; $01 + 1 = 10$; $10 + 1 = 11$. What if the accumulator is already full—i.e., its previous content is 11? Adding 1 to it should produce the value 100, but as this is beyond the two-bit storage capability of our example, the machine has an *overflow condition*. As discussed earlier, the response of our simple RM to overflow is no response. So the fourth line for INC leaves the accumulator in state 11.

Exercise 5.53: In what rows are the inputs i1=**0**, i2=**1**? What instruction does this combination encode? Describe what the outputs for these rows accomplish. Which row should produce an *underflow* condition, and what does is it do about it?

Exercise 5.54: What instruction does i1=**0**, i2=**0** encode? What effect does this instruction have on the accumulator?

Having specified the table of input-output relations for these four instructions, our next step is to realize it as a circuit. (You can think of the table a "black box" specifying what the circuit inside the box must do.) The circuit's behavior decomposes into four parts corresponding to the four instructions. So we'll construct an accumulator circuit by first constructing four sub-circuits, then joining them up. (By the way, what problem-solving technique are we using?)

Let's work on the ZER sub-circuit. Its output has to be **00**, no matter what the current accumulator inputs may be. What sort of circuit would do this? Let's break this problem down further. If we could get a single constant value **0** as output, then we could just split that into two outputs—o1 and o2—to get **00**. But how to get **0** as a constant output, regardless of input? Hmm... Logical **and** requires both its inputs to be **1** to produce an output of **1**, right? So, any input and its *negation* always produces **0**. Feeding a value and its negation into an and-gate will always produce **0** as output. You get a negation of a value by feeding the value into a not-gate. But which value should that be? Actually, it really doesn't matter. It could be i1, i2, j1, or j2—let's pick j1. Now we have enough information to wire up a circuit, shown in figure 5.15.

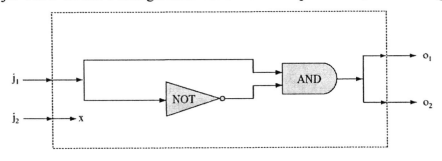

Figure 5.15: ZER **instruction as a boolean circuit**

Inside the black box, the circuit just ignores j2 (by wiring it to a ground), so that it only needs to consider the remaining input line, j1. Then the line splits into two lines. One of them runs through a **not**-gate, which produces **not**-j1. Then both lines converge again at an **and**-gate, to compute j1-**and-not**-j1, which is of course always **0**. Finally, that output splits into two equal outputs for o1 and o2. The resulting two outputs are always **0**, no matter what the value of j1 and j2 are, so the overall output is thus **00**.

Now, looking at INC in the truth table above, you can see that the values for o1 are logically j1-**or**-j2. Getting the right value for o2 is a bit more complicated. We want the output to be 1 when either the value of j1 is 1 or the value of j2 is 0. That's j1-**or-not**-j2: we want to use an **or**-gate to combine j1 with **not**-j2. Now we just need to create one sub-circuit for o1 and o2. First, we'll split j1 and j2 each into two inputs—one for o1 and one for o2. Then we'll run j1 and j2 through an **or**-gate to get j1-**or**-j2 for o1. Then we'll run j2 through a **not**-gate to get **not**-j2, and run j1 and **not**-j2 through an or-gate to get j1-**or-not**-j2, for o2. Got that? Try tracing our reasoning out by studying figure 5.16.

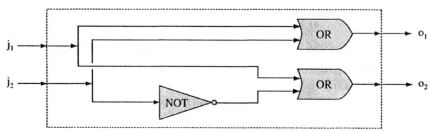

Figure 5.16: INC instruction as a boolean circuit

Exercise 5.55: What problem-solving method did we use to design the ZER sub-circuit?
Exercise 5.56: Explain how the ZER sub-circuit works, in your own words.
Exercise 5.57: Explain how the INC sub-circuit works, in your own words.
Exercise 5.58: Create a boolean circuit for the DEC sub-circuit. Hint: use analogical reasoning. (Isn't this instruction similar to one we just discussed?)
Exercise 5.59: Create a boolean circuit for the HLT sub-circuit. (Note that HLT has no effect on the contents of the accumulator.)

Once we have designed these four sub-circuits, how do we join them together? Our four sub-circuits should each operate *only* with the appropriate instruction code. That is, when i1 and i2 are both 1, the machine only needs the outputs from the ZER sub-circuit, not the outputs of the other sub-circuits. However, looking at the ways in which the sub-circuits were constructed shows that their behaviors depend only on j1 and j2, so they will each behave in the same way *regardless* of the values of i1 and i2. All we need is a way to use the values of i1 and i2 to "select" the right sub-circuit and "ignore" the others.

Here's an opportunity for more reasoning by analogy. Recall how we realized the truth table with two outputs as the circuit of figure 5.11. The circuit used a conjunction of inputs and their negations to "select" the desired output. In much the same way, we can "select" the outputs of each instruction's sub-circuit. When the machine needs to execute a particular instruction (some combination of i1 and i2), selection wiring will force the two outputs of all the other instruction sub-circuits to become **0**. On the output side, generalized **or**-gates can serve as the glue for joining all the outputs of our individual circuits together. Then the accumulator circuit will produce a single set of outputs transmitting the output of the selected sub-circuit.

The circuit in figure 5.15 uses four **not**-gates on the left to select the right combination of values from input lines i1 and i2. It also uses two four-input **or**-gates, one each to join the four outputs for o1 and o2, from each instruction sub-circuit. What is the result of the complete circuit? First, when the instruction code is **11**, selecting ZER, its output (and for that matter, that of all the other sub-circuits) is **00**, so the **or**-gates always yield **00**. Second, when the instruction code is **10**, the INC sub-circuit produces its result (shown above), and all the other three sub-circuits produce **00**, so the final output is just that of the INC sub-circuit. Similarly, when the instruction code is **01** or **00**, the final output is just that of the DEC or HLT sub-circuit, respectively. As a result, *no matter what* the instruction code input, the contents of the accumulator are changed (or left the same) in just the way they should be.

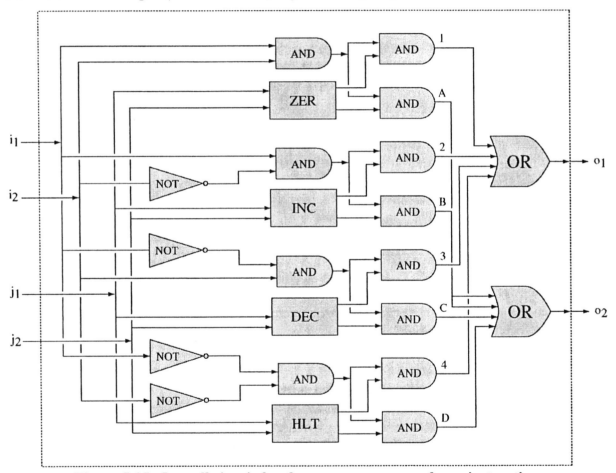

Figure 5.15: Overall circuit for the ZER, INC, DEC, and HLT instructions

Exercise 5.60: Explain in detail how the logic of the circuitry surrounding the ZER circuit always produces **00**.

Exercise 5.61: Explain in detail how the logic of the circuitry surrounding the INC circuit produces the desired result when instruction **10** is input, and otherwise outputs **00**.

Exercise 5.62: Explain in detail how the logic of the circuitry surrounding the DEC circuit produces the desired result when instruction **10** is input, and otherwise outputs **00**.

5.3.2 More complicated parts of the register machine

Let's consider how boolean circuits can effect *storage to* and *recall from* a register. Suppose we have an accumulator and only one storage register, each with a two-bit content. We can distinguish instructions STO and RCL with just one input bit. Figure 5.16 below, though it seems large, is our minimal input-output truth table just for these two instructions.

INSTR NAME	INSTR CODE	PREVIOUS ACCUMULATOR CONTENTS		PREVIOUS REGISTER CONTENTS		NEW ACCUMULATOR CONTENTS		NEW REGISTER CONTENTS	
	i1	j1	j2	k1	k2	o1	o2	p1	p2
STO	1	1	1	1	1	1	1	1	1
STO	1	1	1	1	0	1	1	1	1
STO	1	1	1	0	1	1	1	1	1
STO	1	1	1	0	0	1	1	1	1
STO	1	1	0	1	1	1	0	1	0
STO	1	1	0	1	0	1	0	1	0
STO	1	1	0	0	1	1	0	1	0
STO	1	1	0	0	0	1	0	1	0
STO	1	0	1	1	1	0	1	0	1
STO	1	0	1	1	0	0	1	0	1
STO	1	0	1	0	1	0	1	0	1
STO	1	0	1	0	0	0	1	0	1
STO	1	0	0	1	1	0	0	0	0
STO	1	0	0	1	0	0	0	0	0
STO	1	0	0	0	1	0	0	0	0
STO	1	0	0	0	0	0	0	0	0
RCL	0	1	1	1	1	1	1	1	1
RCL	0	1	1	1	0	1	0	1	0
RCL	0	1	1	0	1	0	1	0	1
RCL	0	1	1	0	0	0	0	0	0
RCL	0	1	0	1	1	1	1	1	1
RCL	0	1	0	1	0	1	0	1	0
RCL	0	1	0	0	1	0	1	0	1
RCL	0	1	0	0	0	0	0	0	0
RCL	0	0	1	1	1	1	1	1	1
RCL	0	0	1	1	0	1	0	1	0
RCL	0	0	1	0	1	0	1	0	1
RCL	0	0	1	0	0	0	0	0	0
RCL	0	0	0	1	1	1	1	1	1
RCL	0	0	0	1	0	1	0	1	0
RCL	0	0	0	0	1	0	1	0	1
RCL	0	0	0	0	0	0	0	0	0

Figure 5.16: Input-output relations for the STO and RCL instructions

Though it looks complicated, a general explanation is rather simple. First of all, with only two instructions, the instruction codes are just one bit—**1** for STO and **0** for RCL. However, we must consider the effect of these instructions on *both* the accumulator and a numbered register, and each of these has two bits of content—thus, two input columns and two output columns for each of the two registers. That's why we need thirty-two lines in all—sixteen lines for each instruction, covering all the possible combinations of values.

Now for the table values. In the sixteen lines on which the instruction is STO, the instruction input is **1**. Remember that the effect of this instruction is to leave the accumulator unchanged, and to copy its contents into the register. Thus on the first sixteen lines, both the *new accumulator output* and the *new register output* are the same as the *current accumulator input*. (Note that the previous contents of the register have been lost.) Similarly, the effect of the RCL instruction is to leave the register unchanged and to copy the register contents into the accumulator. Thus, on those sixteen lines on which the instruction input is **0**, the *new accumulator output* and the *new register output* are the same as the *current register input*.

You can construct the STO and RCL circuits in a manner similar to the way we wired up the ZER-INC-DEC-HLT circuits above. Practice your problem-solving strategies of decomposition, looking for matches with truth tables for the three basic gates, and analogies.

Exercise 5.63: What is the relationship between the number of bits of input information and the number of lines in the truth table for STO and RCL above?

Exercise 5.64: Construct a STO circuit--one which has the correct output values of o1, o2, p1, p2 for all input values of j1, j2, k1, k2 *assuming* that the input value of i is **1**.

Exercise 5.65: Combine the STO circuit with appropriate gates so that it has the desired input-output relation when the value of i is **1**, but always has an output of **0** whenever the input value of i is **0**.

Exercise 5.66: Do the same for the RCL instruction.

Exercise 5.67: Now construct the entire circuit for both the STO and the RCL instructions.

Of course, these are only "local" views, of specific parts of the RM. For the entire RM circuit, all these partial views would have to be incorporated together, making for a very large input-output table! Since there are 11 instructions (note that with only one register, ISTO and IRCL make no sense), instruction codes from 1 to 11 would be needed, so four input columns would be needed to satisfy just this requirement. Even with only two-bit registers, two input columns and two output columns would be needed for the accumulator, numbered register, and buffer— adding twelve more columns. The resulting table would consist of 65,536 (2^{16}) rows! Assuming a larger capacity for the registers and more storage registers, the size of the table would be astronomical for mere mortals. Since the effect of the branching instructions depends on the specifying a parameter for an instruction register, still more input columns would be required. The size of the total table would be truly cosmic! Modern processors typically have more instructions than our simple RM, such as instructions to handle integer arithmetic more efficiently than with just INC and DEC instructions, as well as floating point (real number) processing. Just how many instructions to include in a processor is a matter of some debate among computer architects. **CISC** (Complex Instruction Set Computer, pronounced "sisk") designs feature large sets of instructions, making for very complicated circuits. Another approach is **RISC** (Reduced Instruction Set Computer); these designs reduce architecture to a smaller set of instructions. Besides simpler designs, an advantage of RISC is that it avoids hard-wiring relatively slow instructions, so that overall cycle time per instruction can be faster. A disadvantage of RISC is that programming these machines can be more cumbersome. Architects continue to explore these tradeoffs.

In any case, you can see from the relatively simple RM, let alone more complicated processors, why **VLSI (Very Large Scale Integration)**—*the design of chips in which millions of logic gates and circuits connecting them are etched into silicon*—is so important to modern computer architecture. What we have shown here are only tiny sections of the whole, but enough (we hope) to show how the entire behavior of the register machine can be brought about by simple bit-manipulation.

Missing from our description is an explanation of how the RM executes a sequence of instructions in a step-like fashion. Suffice it to say (again, we are simplifying a bit), that each computer has an internal clock which synchronizes the operations of the computer. Each 'tick' of this internal clock corresponds to the execution of one instruction. The faster the clock ticks, the faster the computer can run.

Exercise 5.68: Why do we need four input columns to handle 11 different instruction codes?

Exercise 5.69: How many rows would the table require to handle 8-bit registers?

Exercise 5.70: How many rows would the table required to handle 8-bit registers plus branching instructions?

Exercise 5.71: The earliest processors for PCs could not perform floating point processing. Why not? How could these early PCs process real numbers without direct hardware support? Why was floating point processing added to the core processor for PCs by the early 90's?

Exercise 5.72: The processor for modern Apple Macintoshes features a RISC architecture. Do a little research on the web to learn more about how it works and its advantages.

5.3 Connecting the processor

You've surely noticed that for simplicity, except for a single very simple connection to some sort of input-output device, we've ignored any device outside the central processor. The register memory, remember, consists of a relatively small number of high-speed memory units. But even personal computers have vastly greater main memories, as well as various kinds of auxiliary memories. Moreover, there are often several input-output devices–keyboard, mouse, microphone, etc. for input and monitor, speakers, printer, etc. for output. And today, there may be multiple processors connected in a small network. In this section, we'll take a necessarily brief look at those aspects of computer architecture.

5.3.1 Cache memory

Just as the registers of the RM had individual addresses, each main memory location has a unique address, which the CPU uses to locate information. (Recall that the RM's instruction register holds instruction addresses in memory.) Other instructions exchange information between memory and numbered data registers. However, this can be a bottleneck, since it is slower to get data from main memory than from registers. One solution is to use **cache memory**, an intermediate memory between register memory and main memory—slower than registers, but faster than main memory (RAM). Swapping data in and out of cache from main memory results in faster processing as it allows the CPU to access data in the faster cache memory.

5.3.2 Bus and controllers

A CPU (such as the RM) connects with its peripheral devices through a collection of lines called a **bus,** in effect a high-speed superhighway, off which interchanges lead to the individual peripherals. Between the bus and peripheral I/O devices are intermediary devices known as **controllers**, devices analogous to a modem. Just as a modem changes digital data from the computer to analog data transmitted over telephone lines, and vice versa, controllers handle the transfer of data between devices of different physical natures—electronic (CPU, main memory), magnetic (disk drives), or optical (CD or DVD drives).

Even high-speed highways can have traffic jams, though, and a similar phenomenon known as a **von Neumann bottleneck** can arise as traffic from the CPU and the peripherals overcrowds the bus. A number of techniques are available to minimize the bottlenecks. The CPU should not constantly have to check slower I/O devices. **Interrupt-driven I/O** lets an I/O device notify the CPU with an interrupt signal when it is ready to receive or send data. That way the CPU can do other things while the I/O device is occupied, rather than simply waiting. Another technique is **direct memory addressing (DMA)** which maps data in a device directly to memory (e.g., from disk to main memory) without having to go through the CPU at all. The CPU contacts the controller with information about what data to transfer, then lets the controller conduct the actual transferring, freeing the CPU to continue its operations during the transfer period. This gets the CPU out of the bottleneck, but the bus can still get crowded, since this involves two periods of bus usage—CPU-controller and controller-memory—rather than one. A way to bypass the bus is to let devices have their own memory. Nowadays, graphics cards, such as those supporting 3D graphics for the latest games and virtual reality, have to manipulate millions of bits of data for every frame (up to 30 frames per second). A solution is to let graphics cards come with their own local memory as well as special purpose processors, so that they can map most of their data directly between their own processors and memory without going through the central bus at all. That's why you might want to invest in buying a graphics card if you want run these kinds of applications.

Earlier PCs used IDE (integrated drive electronics) controllers, in which the controller is integrated into the drive, but more recent ones use EIDE (enhanced integrated drive electronics), which supports higher capacity and DMA. SCSI (small computer system interface, pronounced "scuzzy") allows several devices to be chained, rather than connecting each separately to the computer. It's faster than IDE/EIDE controllers but this more powerful controller system usually requires adding a SCSI card to your computer. The USB socket is common on newer PCs, enabling "plug and play" applications, rather than having to install a driver program for each new device. FireWire also supports chaining and has a much faster throughput rate than USB, making it a popular interface for digital video cameras and other data-intensive applications.

Exercise 5.74 (*explore*): Use the web to learn more about differences between IDE and EIDE.
Exercise 5.75 (*explore*): Use the web to learn about FireWire and/or improvements to USB.

5.3.2 Multiprocessor architectures

First generation computers and PCs assume a single processor. Speed enhancements have been achieved only by speeding up the processor and devices. Another direction is to use multiple processors. Different processors can solve different problems—for example, special purpose processors can be dedicated to handling graphics or other complicated information (signal processing devices). Or multiple processors can work together to solve the same problem. The latter takes us into the design of multiprocessor machines and parallel processing, which can perform several activities at the same time. (In the next chapter, we'll learn how operating systems can make it appear than a single processor can preform several activities at the same time, by switching between them very quickly, but a single processor can really only execute one instruction at a time. There's that von Neumann bottleneck again.)

For "high performance" applications requiring lots of computation, architects design **supercomputers** that exploit the possibilities of parallel processing. Differences between single processor machines and two types of multiprocessor machines can be seen in an instructive way by looking at the instructions they perform and the data they manipulate. A single processor machine, with a single instruction set and a single set of data, is said to have **SISD** (single instruction stream, single data set) architecture. A multiprocessor system may either be **MISD** (multiple instruction streams, single data set) or **MIMD** (multiple instruction streams, multiple data sets). MISD can speed up processing of multiple operations on the same data—such as large arrays or databases. MIMD is more natural for applications involving large computations on disparate data, such as modeling global climate from thousands of changing variables.

Exercise 5.76: Using analogical thinking, name these two types of multiprocessor architecture.

Chapter review. Are the following statements true or false? Explain why or why not.
a) A *virtual machine* is a machine that seems to exist, but really doesn't.
b) A *register machine* (RM) has a lot in common with a cash register.
c) In an RM, the *accumulator* accumulates the results of all the computations performed so far.
d) The instruction STO copies the contents of the accumulator into all the registers.
e) The instruction RCL 5 moves the contents of register 5 to the accumulator.
f) The instruction INC requires a parameter to say which register is being incremented.
g) The instruction DEC always subtracts 1 from the contents of the accumulator.
h) The instruction sequence INC DEC leaves the contents of the accumulator unchanged.
i) The *buffer* is used in the instruction INP, but not in OUT.
j) The *instruction register* holds the number of the next instruction to be performed.
k) After each instruction is executed, the RM increments the instruction register.
l) The RM instruction set has three *branching* instructions.
m) STO and RCL involve *direct access* to a register; ISTO and IRCL involve *indirect access*.
n) Direct access uses registers called *pointers*.
o) *Boolean circuits* are certain electric circuits that were invented by George Boole.
p) The three basic building blocks of boolean circuits are **and**, **xor**, and **not**.
q) An **or**-gate represents the exclusive sense of the word 'or'.
r) An **or**-gate can be constructed from an **and**-gate and two **not**-gates.
s) The overall behavior of any boolean circuit can be represented by a truth-table.
t) Any truth-table can be realized as the behavior of a boolean circuit.
u) Most, but not all, RM's can be realized as boolean circuits.
v) All the RM instructions except STO and RCL can be realized as boolean circuits.
w) The truth-table for even a very small RM would be pretty enormous.
x) *Cache memory* is the fastest part of register memory
y) A *bus* is a special part of the CPU which carries data to and from registers.
z) SISD, MISD, and MIMD architectures are really just different names for the same thing.

Summary

The computer you interact with is a virtual machine which runs on several layers of virtual machines which ultimately run on an actual machine. Lower in this hierarchy is something like a **Register Machine**, which exploits a small number of **registers**, or high-speed storage areas. The **accumulator** is a special purpose register where computation takes place. The **buffer** is another special purpose register whose values can be "swapped" with the accumulator. The remaining numbered registers store temporary values. A RM has a small set of **primitive instructions**, designed to exploit its registers: STO (*store* the contents of the accumulator into a designated register); RCL (*recall* the contents of a designated register into the accumulator); ZER (clear the accumulator by entering *zero* into it); INC (*increment* the contents of the accumulator by one); DEC (*decrement* the contents of the accumulator by one); BRZ (*branch on zero* to a designated instruction if the contents of the accumulator are zero); BRN (*branch on non-zero* to a designated instruction if the contents of the accumulator are not zero); ISTO (*indirectly store* the contents of the accumulator into that register whose address is stored in a designated register); IRCL (*indirectly recall* into the accumulator the contents of that register whose address is stored in a designated register); and HLT (stop the computation). The branching instructions allow the construction of both *conditionals* and *loops*. With the stored addresses accessible via ISTO and IRCL, an RM can also handle *subprogram calls*, by storing a pointer to an instruction in a register, as well as manipulate more complex data types, such as arrays, records and objects, by storing the **base** address of a structure, then adding the **offset** to an element or field.

The Register Machine is itself a virtual construct built up from a deeper layer consisting of *boolean circuits*. These are constructed of several kinds of "gates": **and, or**, and **not**, whose meaning is made explicit by **truth tables**. These gates are joined to form **boolean circuits**. Though it may look complicated, everything done in a digital computer can be reduced to combinations of these boolean gates. By using truth tables, one can in *principle* specify the behavior of any desired circuit. (In practice, for all but relatively simple behaviors, such tables are far too large to construct!) Then, by taking appropriate combinations of inputs and their negations, feeding them into generalized **and**-gates, and feeding their outputs into generalized **or**-gates, one can obtain multiple-level compound circuits which realize these behaviors.

The truth table for the RM will have multiple input columns for the accumulator, the buffer, and for each register (the exact number of columns depending on the bit-capacity of each), as well as multiple output columns for each. It will also have enough columns to express each instruction as a binary number. From such a truth table, in a three-step process, one can construct circuits with the desired behavior. The trick in doing this is first to construct a sub-circuit for each instruction, having the desired behavior when *that particular instruction* code is input (with no particular constraints on the sub-circuit's behavior when another instruction code is received). Next, each of these is modified (using **not**-gates and **and**-gates) so that when *any other* instruction code is received, the output consists uniformly of **0**'s. Finally, corresponding outputs of all these circuits are **or**-gated together to make a single set of outputs. In this way, the entire behavior of the RM can be realized in a single boolean circuit.

The CPU is only a part of the computer. Other components include main memory and a variety of input/output devices. Main memory is slower than register memory, so computer architects use faster cache memory to speed up processing. Other techniques designed to overcome the von Neumann bottleneck include **interrupt-driven I/O, direct memory addressing**, and **multiprocessing** with many processors in parallel.

Chapter 6
Operating Systems, Networks and Security
Our program, who art in memory,
"Hello" be thy name.
Thy operating system come,
Thy commands be done,
At printer as they are on screen.
Give us this day our daily data,
And forgive us our I/O errors,
As we forgive those whose logic circuits are faulty.
Lead us not into frustration,
And deliver us from power surges.
For thine is the algorithm,
The application and the solution,
Looping forever and ever.
—anonymous computer humor from the World Wide Web

In chapter 5, we peeled the computer onion down through the level of a von Neumann register machine to the boolean logic circuits. This chapter will go back up to a layer that represents the computer as most users think of it—the **operating system (OS)**, *a collection of programs that manage the resources, including the processors, memory, and input/output devices of a computer.* To use an analogy, an operating system is like the conductor of an orchestra, directing the many parts so that they all work together to "make music." Music to a computer user's ear is *convenience*, so users tend to think of an operating system as primarily an interface that controls how things get done, such as executing an application program or printing a file. Music to a computer scientist's ear, on the other hand, is *efficiency* of performance, getting the system to make optimal use of its resources. Users wind up appreciating these issues when they notice that a system can do more for them, performing tasks more quickly or performing several tasks, such as printing a file while compiling a program, seemingly at the same time.

Here's another definition for **operating system**: *a virtual machine that lets a user accomplish tasks that would be difficult and time-consuming to perform directly with the underlying actual machine.* For example, your computer can interact with a user through a graphical user interface, even though the underlying machine only understands obscure machine code; it can give the illusion of having much more memory that it actually has (through the use of *virtual* memory); and it can even run more than one program at a time, even though the underlying machine is actually doing one thing at a time at any particular time. Operating systems are an excellent example of the power of abstraction, hiding the details of how a physical machine gets such complicated things done behind a *relatively* simple and user-friendly interface. Do take note, though: an operating system is much more than a pretty face! A lot goes on behind the user interface, most of which has little or nothing to do with the interface.

This chapter will open with a brief history of operating systems, tracing major developments in their functionality. The second section will recapitulate some of this history by explaining what happens when a personal computer "boots" (starts) up a modern OS. The third section will study basic concepts of OS architecture. The fourth section will turn to computer networks, support for which is now incorporated into modern operating systems. The final section will examine issues of computer protection and security.

Exercise 6.1: We have compared an operating system to the conductor of an orchestra. How might you also compare an OS to the foreman of a work crew? Explain this analogy in terms of what an OS does, both from a user's point of view and a system designer's point of view. Or think of another analogy and explain it.

Exercise 6.2: What do you learn about the nature and purpose of operating systems from the two different definitions given in the chapter overview?

Exercise 6.3: Give several examples of activities that illustrate each of the two definitions of operating systems given at the beginning of this chapter.

6.1 A brief history of operating systems

During the first generation of machines (roughly 1945-1955), it was basically every person for him(her)self. Time on a computer was precious: sign up sheets reserved a machine for blocks of time—days or even weeks in advance. During a session, all machine operation was "hands on"; the only "operating system" was a person. That person would show up in the machine room carting in programs as trays of punched cards and/or reels of magnetic tapes, load the programs into memory, punch some buttons on the console to set the starting address of the program, and hope that the machine would produce expected results. The next programmer might often be impatiently waiting for the previous one to wrap up, since—as you may have figured out by now—it's not always easy to get a machine to do what you want in an allotted amount of time!

The second generation of machines (roughly 1955-1965) introduced **batch operating systems**. Since the learning curve for operating a computer was steep, it made sense to train a computer operator to do the job. Moreover, since a computer was expensive equipment (costing millions of dollars in those days), it made little sense to let it sit idle while a programmer was setting up a job or thinking about what to do next. Instead, system administrators decreed that programmers would submit a program, usually a deck of cards, along with any special instructions, to a human operator. The operator in turn would group a "batch" of programs (from several different programmers), copy all these programs from cards to tape (using a special purpose machine), feed programs and data from these tapes into the "big" computer's mass storage, and finally punch the appropriate buttons. The programmer would get printed results—perhaps a few days later.

Batch processing streamlined computer usage by having the operator put "jobs" (programs to run) into a storage system called a "job queue". In busy amusement parks, people line up into "queues" between railings waiting to get onto popular rides, one person at a time. Similarly, a **queue** is a *data structure which imposes an order of events in which the first item that comes into the queue will be the first one out ("first in first out" or "FIFO" for short)*. A **job queue** is a storage structure which makes each computer job wait until the system is ready to execute it, one job at a time. The process was further streamlined by eliminating most of the handwritten notes from the programmers to the operator. Instead, batch operating systems included the ability to interpret a special **job control language (JCL)**, *in which programmers would encode specific instructions to the system or the operator*. Figure 6.1 shows a typical batch job, along with JCL instructions, for compiling and executing a FORTRAN program.

The $JOB card specified the maximum run time in minutes, the account number to charge (computer time was money!), and the programmer's name. Next came a $FORTRAN card, to which the system responded by loading a FORTRAN compiler from tape, followed by

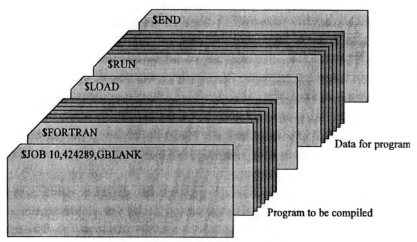

Figure 6.1: Batch Job with JCL

the program to be compiled. The $LOAD command invoked a loader to put the just compiled program into memory, followed by a $RUN command to execute it, using the input data which followed next. As operating systems became more sophisticated, they took over carrying out more and more of these JCL instructions without the aid of a human operator. As a result, there were fewer buttons to push, fewer human glitches, and faster turnaround time.

As integrated circuits sped up CPUs, it became apparent that processors were spending more and more of their time waiting for much slower input/output devices to complete their work. Rather than waste those idle milliseconds, the third generation of operating systems (about 1965-1985) introduced **multiprogramming**—*switching between many different programs in memory*. Whereas earlier systems just loaded just one program into memory at a time, a multiprogramming system loads several, as shown in figure 6.2.

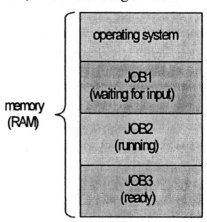

Figure 6.2: Multiprogramming

Suppose JOB 1 requests input. The system sends the request to an input device (with its own processor), then selects one of the other jobs that are ready for execution, say JOB 2. When that program pauses, processor attention can switch back to JOB 1, if it's done with input, or go on to JOB 3. The trick is to keep the processor busy, maximizing its utilization.

Multiprogramming sets up the possibility of **time-sharing**, *dividing processor time up into small slices*. The OS can try to allocate "fairly" among competing jobs. Multiprogramming also allows for **interactive processing** *letting users interact with a computer hands-on*, rather than wait for each complete job to finish. Batch processing works fine for applications for which all data can be provided up front, such as scientific computation or payroll processing, but not so well for applications with less predictable data such as making airline reservations or debugging programs. Interactive processing permits *on-line* data entry, accelerating transaction turnaround, but depends very much on a multiprogramming system that can switch between many different users, while many of them may be scratching their heads about what to do next.

Batch and interactive processing both can make use of time-sharing, a technique for letting several different jobs share processor time. A time-sharing *batch* operating system can actually improve total throughput by finding a mix of jobs that make judicious use of a machine's resources. For example, suppose a job queue contains a payroll job, which requires significant use of a tape drive, as well as a number crunching job which primarily manipulates data in main memory. The number crunching job can be running during those time intervals in which the payroll job is waiting for data from the tape drive. The total elapsed time of the two jobs, running together, will be much less than if they had executed separately.

Multiprogramming and time-sharing led to the development of **multiuser** operating systems (such as UNIX), *which let many different users share the same machine*, and **multitasking**, *which lets many different tasks share processor time*. If the system divides up its time slices small enough (say, a millisecond) and can switch between jobs fast enough, then it can give several users the illusion that they each have their own machine. A millisecond may not seem like much time to you, but it's long enough for a processor to execute several hundred thousand machine instructions. Of course, if too many users log onto the same system, there may be annoyingly long lags as the system devotes too much time managing the users and not enough time running their programs. An overloaded system can seem rather like waiting for service in a busy restaurant with too few waiters! They spend more time scurrying about than they do serving food. The number of simultaneous users that a time-sharing system can service depends on (1) the speed of the processor, (2) the length of the time slices, and (3) how many users perform operations that perform a full time slice and how many stop before that. For example, a reasonably fast machine that acts as a "mail server"—facilitating access to e-mail and related services—could conceivably serve several dozen users comfortably.

In the 1980's personal computers (PCs) arrived. At first, many PCs were regarded as simply terminals providing access to a central time-sharing system. As PCs became more powerful, people saw that computing could be done more conveniently and cheaply on their desks than in the computing center. Computing rapidly changed from the **centralized environment** of *a time-sharing main-frame computer* in highly secured, air-conditioned rooms to a **distributed environment** of *workstations and personal computers sharing resources over a network* in a laboratory or office building. Workstations offered all the strengths of a multiprogrammed operating system, supporting multiple users, multitasking and connections to other workstations over a network. On the other hand, PCs for the most part initially used simple single user operating systems (notably MS-DOS™), giving their users total access to all the resources of a single machine. Since PCs were so inexpensive, there was no need to share their processing time with other users, so time-sharing and multiprogramming became less important.

As the processors in PCs became more powerful, operating systems designers realized that multiprogramming could still have applications for single-user operating systems: **multitasking**, or *switching between tasks*. For example, rather than wait for a long document to print or a file to transfer through a relatively slow modem, a multitasking operating system will also let you do something else at the same time. Early versions of Windows™ (through version 3.1) supported **cooperative multitasking**, which *only switch if programs explicitly cooperate* *with the system*, by signaling that they are not using the processor; otherwise, task switching simply *suspends* one task altogether while running a different user-selected task. In practice, pressing <Alt-tab> would switch from one window to another, and usually just suspend all processing in the background windows. On the other hand, Windows95™ (and successive versions of Windows and other operating systems) incorporate **preemptive multitasking**, which *lets the OS switch between tasks at its own discretion* (much as time-sharing multiprogramming systems had been doing on larger computers for some time). Preemptive multitasking is to cooperative multitasking as a dancer who "cuts in" is to one who politely waits for his partner of choice to become available. Preemptive dancers keep things hopping on the floor; similarly, preemptive tasks do not need permission from another task to start processing again. You can print a file, search for information on the Internet, and compile a program, all at the "same time." The payoff of preemptive multitasking becomes more obvious as users run a wider range of complex applications on ever more powerful processors.

PC users discovered that peripheral devices, such as laser printers, tape backup units and special-purpose software packages, were relatively expensive compared to the dropping cost of the computers themselves, so they began looking for ways to share these supporting resources. Moreover, PC users wanted to communicate via electronic mail. The late 1980's ushered in a fourth generation of **network operating systems**, which *manage resources for many computers communicating with each other*.

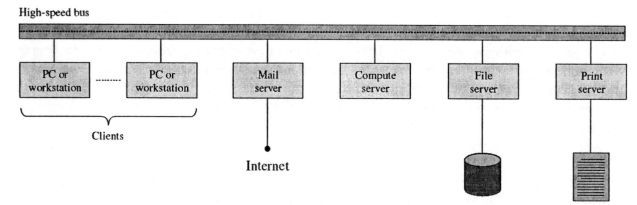

Figure 6.3: A local area network

Figure 6.3 shows a configuration of computers communicating with each other in a **local area network** or **LAN**. A LAN is a network located in a geographically contiguous area such a laboratory or building. It consists of many personal computers and workstations for individual use, called **clients**, plus specially designated machines called **servers**, so-called because they *provide access to common services* such as electronic mail, printers, etc. All of these are connected via a high-speed (ranging from millions to billions of bits/second) **bus** (a bundle of wires), typically made of copper coaxial or fiber-optic cable.

Each **client** *performs computations for its local tasks locally*, pretty much oblivious to the network. Thus the core of a network OS is a single-user OS. What makes a network OS particularly useful is that each client can access any of the shared network resources (e.g., printers, licensed software) just as if they were attached to the local computer. A network OS will hide all the details involved in communication with (and possibly competition for) shared resources, giving the network user a powerful virtual environment.

Servers come in several flavors. A *print server* gives all the clients on a network access to shared network printers. The server is itself a computer which receives and processes print requests. It can allow a user to choose between different printers, perhaps on the basis of print quality or availability. A *file server* provides access to a large disk storage facility. Besides taking advantage of an economy of scale in mass storage (a large capacity device costs much less per byte of storage than a small one), a file server provides a place to share information and software packages, and also facilitates regular backups to tape or other media. A *compute server* is a more expensive machine which provides more processing power or number crunching capability. Since personal computers are pushing the envelope of processing power, a compute server will likely be a machine that consists of multiple processors churning away on a problem *in parallel*. A *mail server* routes electronic mail to the international **wide area network (WAN)** known as the Internet. Modern operating systems integrate support for access to and browsing on the Internet, making a personal computer a virtual machine whose resources encompass documents and programs anywhere in the world.

The future of operating systems appears to have two major thrusts at this time: 1) more powerful, multimedia interfaces and 2) parallel processing. Users of our multimedia as well as cool sites on the Internet can begin to see the expressiveness of multiple media for interacting with a larger community of potential users. Multimedia, particularly speech, animation and video, put increasing demands on processing and memory, which in turn drives the need for efficient use of available resources as well as more powerful resources. More computer horsepower can come from either breeding faster horses (processors, disk drives, etc.) or from yoking several horses together. The latter possibility is what we mean by parallel processing, or **multiprocessing**—discussed at the end of the previous chapter. Instead of just one processor, *many processors in close communication* can share a common bus, memory, peripheral devices, power supplies and cabinets. While the speedup using *n* processors is not *n*, because of the overhead incurred in getting the processors to work together, getting close is certainly a goal. In a **symmetric multiprocessing OS**, each processor has its own copy of the OS, so that many processors can run at once without any deterioration of performance. An **asymmetric multiprocessing** OS is centralized so that a master processor controls a configuration of slave schedules and allocates work to a configuration of slave processors. In a **distributed OS**, multiple processors are more *loosely coupled*, no longer sharing memory or devices. A distributed OS can exploit the resources of many computers via a network.

Exercise 6.4: What are some examples of queues in everyday life, both for people and for machines? Are there situations, for each example, in which the queue order is (or should be) first-in-first-out (FIFO) violated or modified?

Exercise 6.5: Cite three examples of applications that batch processing can handle efficiently. Cite three examples of applications that require an interactive environment.

Exercise 6.6: How does the $JOB card in the JCL example above use parameters? Why might it be useful to allow for parameters on other JCL cards? How could the possibility of optional parameters make the job control language obscure? (Indeed, JCL was notoriously obscure!)

Exercise 6.7: In a time-sharing operating system, why is the value of the time slice crucial to system performance? What system behavior is likely to occur if the value of the time slice is too large? What system behavior is likely to occur if the value of the time slice is too small? What other factors play into the performance of a time-sharing system?

Exercise 6.8: Define multiprogramming and multitasking. Explain how one supports the other.

Exercise 6.9: Find a personal computer or workstation. Does it support multitasking? How can you tell? If it does support multitasking, is cooperative or preemptive? How can you tell? What are the advantages of multitasking? Illustrate with an example that you have tried out.

Exercise 6.10: How can a multitasking operating system achieve higher throughput than a batch operating system that insists on performing each task completely before starting the next. Use an example (not the same one as in the book) to illustrate.

Exercise 6.11: What is the difference between the roles of a client and a server in a network?

Exercise 6.12: Find a personal computer or workstation on a network. What services are available to the local computer via the network? Are those services supported by other servers? Are these services supported by application programs or by the operating system on your local machine? How can you tell? (If you're not sure, ask around!)

Exercise 6.13: Define multiprocessing. Why is it useful? What are the differences between symmetric and asymmetric multiprocessing?

Exercise 6.14: What's the difference between multiprogramming and multiprocessing? Would it make sense to incorporate multiprogramming in a multiprocessing OS? Why or why not?

Figure 6.4: The Altair 8800 hobbyist computer

6.2 Booting an operating system

These days, starting up a computer may not seem to require much more effort than flipping a power switch, but you probably have noticed a flurry of activity that goes on before the system is ready to accept any input from you. It can be useful to understand some of what is going on (for example, just in case something goes wrong). It can also provide a perspective on what we have learned about operating systems so far; for the process of starting up a modern computer recapitulates much of the history of operating systems.

To give you a better appreciation of that flurry of activity, consider how users of the first microcomputer, the Altair 8800 (shown in figure 6.4), got it going, *circa* 1975. (By the way, "Altair" was a destination of the Enterprise in the original *Star Trek* series.) The hobbyist-user first manually entered a startup program, by flipping the switches on the front panel, one bit at a time. Flipping a switch up was a binary one and down a zero. The machine stored this program in its memory (RAM) and reported the results by flashing lights. Once this startup program was loaded, the machine was ready to load a larger program into memory from a paper tape reader (a device, rather like the head of a Turing machine, that reads binary information as holes in a long stream of paper). This larger program might, if successful, allow the use of a keyboard. (The Altair was quite unaware of any peripheral devices until an appropriate program for interacting with it—nowadays known as a **device driver**—had been loaded into memory.) Once the machine was aware of the keyboard, the user could type in a still larger program, such as one that would be able to interpret programs written in the BASIC language. Once the BASIC interpreter was loaded, the user could start entering BASIC programs so that the machine could actually do something useful! Are you remembering that onion we peeled? The Altair user essentially reconstructed the onion, layer by layer, every time its power went on.

This reconstruction explains the expression "booting up a computer". In the old west, cowboys pulled up their boots by the straps (little tabs for grabbing). To pull someone (or something) up by the bootstraps means to start from almost nothing. Similarly, to boot up a computer means to start from a simple program, which in turn reads a larger program, and so on.

Personal computers got rid of the need to flip switches to load in the first, lowest-level program by storing it in Read-Only-Memory (**ROM**). Unlike RAM, which is **volatile** (i.e., its contents dissipate when the power is turned off), ROM is **permanent** (i.e., retaining its content even when the power is turned off).

As figure 6.5 shows, the first thing a personal computer does is read one or more programs from ROM, which allow it to use its floppy drives and hard drives, then look for another program (called COMMAND.COM on PCs) stored on one of these devices, starting the search with one of the floppy drives. If this program is not on the floppy (or if there is no disk in the floppy drive), then the ROM program will look on the hard drive. If it's not there, you've got a problem! (The possibility of misplacing or having an error in COMMAND.COM on the hard drive is, by the way, one reason the ROM program always looks on a floppy first. That way a user isn't stuck if the system files on the hard drive have gone bad.) Once this program has been

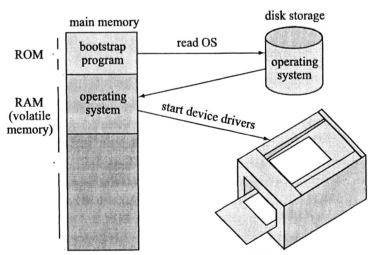

Figure 6.5: Booting from ROM

loaded from a drive into memory, the core or **kernel** of the OS is up and running.

At first, the operating system runs in batch mode, running a sequence of other startup programs. (DOS, for example, automatically sequences through commands in the files CONFIG.SYS and AUTOEXEC.BAT. Unix environments typically run several startup files with names like .login, .profile, and .bashrc. Windows invokes WIN.INI.) Some of these startup programs are drivers for communicating with other peripheral devices, such as a mouse or a CDROM drive. Others have to do with memory management. (DOS only recognizes 640K of memory, but memory management drivers allow some programs to reside in "high" or "extended" memory, above the first 640K. Windows makes considerable use of this extra memory. This 640K ceiling, which seemed high enough when DOS was designed in the early 1980's, doesn't exist in other operating systems, such as OS/2, Macintosh and Unix.) Still others may enhance the operating environment. (For example, in DOS, loading a program called "doskey" will enable you to recall previous commands by pressing the up arrow and edit the command using the left and right arrows, Backspace and Insert keys. Windows XP builds this capability into its cmd processor. Unix environments can load in alternative "shells" to enhance a command-line environment.) Still others may enable a local computer to connect to a network.

Once an operating system has booted, you may want to boot up another operating system! For example, if a computer has Windows 3.1 available, from the DOS command-line prompt you can enter "win" to boot up Windows.[1] Similarly, from Unix, you can boot into X-windows or a related windowing environment. From Unix or Macintosh (the latter always puts you immediately into its own windowing environment), it is possible to start up a program that will simulate Windows. In each case, the higher level OS will have its own initialization procedures, with files directing it how to access drivers and other programs. Each higher level system is another virtual machine, adding new capabilities to the machine. For example, from DOS you can boot into a network operating system.

Once an operating system is up and running, it is effectively "looping forever," waiting for user input. On occasion, the system or an application that it is running will cause the environment to become unresponsive to your actions. (This tends to happen more often on single-user systems than multiuser environments, which are designed to be more robust.) If so, you may need to "reboot." One way to accomplish this is to turn the power switch off then back on, triggering a "cold boot,", restarting from ROM. (Computers generate heat when running, even when they are running unresponsive programs, but cool off when they are turned off.) You may not need to be quite so drastic, however. A "warm boot" (which may be achieved by pressing a reset button or, on PCs, the key combination <ctrl-alt-del>) just reloads the complete OS from disk into memory. A warm boot is preferable because it avoids the shock of power surges which may eventually damage physical components of your computer.

Exercise 6.15: Why do most computers use ROM for the bootstrap process? Explain what ROM is and how it is used.

Exercise 6.16: Can you think of analogy between starting up a computer and a car? Explain in as much detail as you can.

---

[1]Windows95/98/ME/2000/XP will usually automatically boot itself without stopping at the DOS level. It is possible, however, to get Windows to stop the boot process at DOS, by pressing F8 during the boot process.

Exercise 6.17: Examine the lines in the startup files on your computer (e.g., CONFIG.SYS and AUTOEXEC.BAT) and explain, in English, what each line does. (You could print out the file and annotate the listing with a pen.) If you're not sure, ask around for documentation (or search on the web) describing the DOS operating system.

6.3 Operating system architecture

You may have been tempted to think of the operating system as basically the program running the interface—that is, the command-line interpreter (CLI) or graphical user interface (GUI). By now, perhaps you are beginning to realize there are lots of things happening behind the scenes. Figure 6.6 shows the major components of an operating system that jump into action when a user initiates a task (or job).

The **command processor** is an interface that interacts with one or more users, watching the keyboard, mouse, and any other input devices attached to the machine. It *receives commands, whenever an input device notifies it about an* **event**—that is, whenever a user enters a new-line or clicks on a mouse. The command processor interprets the event and determines whether it is an executable command. For example, `dir /w` is a legal DOS command (displaying the names of all the files in the current directory in column format), but `dir /e` is not—the DOS command processor will complain, "`Invalid switch -/e`".

If the event turns out to be a request to run a program, the command processor asks the **scheduler** to *arrange for the execution of programs*. First, the scheduler would place the program in a job queue. In a batch system, the scheduler might take into consideration the possibility of **priorities** of jobs. Higher priority jobs should have a better chance of getting processor time, so they can get done sooner. In an interactive multitasking environment, the

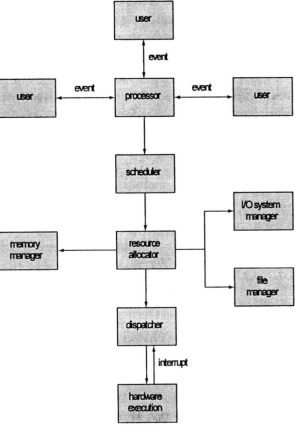

Figure 6.6: Operating system components

scheduler creates a **process** to execute the program, sharing CPU time and other resources with other processes. A process is an active copy of a program, in memory, with its own **program counter** indicating the next instruction to execute. Note that there may be more than one process for the same program. For example, you can invoke the same editor program, perhaps to look at two different text files. Each process will maintain its own running copy of the program working with its own data, progressing on its work at its own rate.

The scheduler in turn invokes a **resource allocator**, which *makes sure that each process has secondary resources*—memory, files, and peripheral devices—that it may need. The **memory manager** coordinates the use of the machine's memory, keeping track of which areas of memory are being used by which processes. Note that it is important that processes have their own distinct region of memory. Some operating systems (though not DOS) have managers that will protect memory, aborting processes that attempt to access memory outside their allocated region, rather than let them corrupt other programs. A memory manager may also support **virtual memory**, a scheme that *gives a process the illusion of working with a large block of contiguous memory space* (perhaps even larger than real memory) when much of it is actually in a "swap file" on disk. As needed, the memory manager reads in pages (fixed-size blocks) from disk into memory. The memory manager must determine just how much actual main memory to allocate to each process and which page should return to disk ("swapped out") to make room for an incoming page. Efficient virtual memory managers try to anticipate which pages a process will need by exploiting the likelihood of "locality of reference"—a process is likely to keep referring to the same or nearby pages of memory. On the other hand, overloaded memory managers can get stuck in a vicious cycle of reading and storing the same few pages. This bothersome behavior—known as "thrashing"—can tie a machine up in knots!

The **I/O system manager** *coordinates the assignment of peripheral devices (through specific device drivers) to processes*. The **file manager** *keeps track of information about files on your disk* and protects against unauthorized access. In a multiuser operating system, each user can selectively make his or her files accessible to others. Suppose a program attempts to write information on a file to which its user only has read access (only permission to read from the file). The file manager will report the problem to the scheduler, which will in turn report the problem back to the command processor, which will in turn chastise the offending user! As another example, if a word processor is modifying a file, the Windows95 file manager will prohibit other programs from accessing it at the same time, generating an error message, e.g., "Sharing violation reading drive C".

Finally, the **dispatcher** *monitors processes and decides when to switch execution from one process and another*. We will describe how process switching works in a moment. When a process completes executing, the dispatcher reports back to the scheduler, which in turn notifies the resource allocator that it can release any resources held by that process. The scheduler then reports completion to the command processor, which in turn may inform the user.

Process switching responds to a feature, built into the hardware, known as an **interrupt**, *which causes a CPU to stop the current process, save its state in memory, then start an interrupt service routine, starting at some fixed location in memory*. Consider an analogy. Suppose you are reading a book when the telephone rings. The ringing phone is an interrupt signal. Before you pick up the phone, you save your place in the book, so that you can resume reading from that page later. Of course, after you get off the phone, something else will demand your attention! But when you eventually return to the book, you continue reading from the bookmark, but you must first remember the context up to that point. Similarly, saving a state of a process involves more than saving the particular instruction that was in the machine's program address register; it also involves storing the contents of the machine's registers into memory. A dispatcher can later restore a process's state by copying values from memory back into the registers, including the program address register. *The work of saving one process state to memory and reloading another process state from memory* is known as a **context switch**. Reducing the amount of effort required to do a context switch can speed up operating system performance. Too much context switching can lead to "thrashing"—too much time spent moving processes in and out memory.

Single-user systems let input devices, such as a keyboard, trigger an interrupt, in order to get the processor to notice and respond to user input. Time-sharing systems also rely on interrupts to signal the end of an allotted time slice. Consider the situation shown in figure 6.7. Suppose there are two processes scheduled for execution, both stored in memory. The dispatcher starts process A by executing a jump (setting the machine's program address register) to the first instruction in A. Just before doing so, the dispatcher also starts a timer circuit that will generate an interrupt after a fixed period of time—the time slice. When the timer circuit sets off the interrupt, the machine suspends process A, storing its state in memory, then starts executing the dispatcher again. The dispatcher in turn sets the timer again and then jumps to the first instruction of process B. When the next interrupt occurs, the dispatcher restores process A so that it will continue execution from where it had left off. And so forth. Thus the dispatcher works together with interrupt and timer circuitry in hardware to coordinate the execution of several processes by the same processor. So long as the length of a time slice is short enough, and the time it takes to make a context switch from one task to another is not too great, and the number of slices not too great, an interactive time-sharing system can give a number of users the illusion that they each have their own virtual machine.

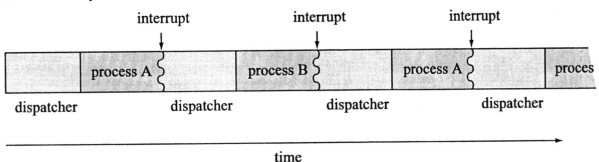

time

Figure 6.7: Interrupts and time-sharing between two processes

Now that we've seen how the dispatcher coordinates CPU activity, let's consider how the resource allocator coordinates the activity of other hardware devices. Suppose two or more processes want to print a job. Imagine how jumbled printer output will look if it tried printing characters coming from two or more interleaved processes! Or imagine the havoc if two different processes were allowed to modify the same data on disk "at the same time." Clearly, certain resources must not be simultaneously shareable. The resource allocator must make sure one process has completed its work with a device before allowing another process to have at it.

This business of controlling access to non-shareable resources is analogous to railway systems that let different trains (possibly traveling in opposite directions!) share the same stretch of track. To guarantee that just one train is on the critical stretch of track at a time, a railroad man would set a signal or flag known as a **semaphore**, *signaling that the* **critical region** *is in use*. A train cannot enter the critical region unless the semaphore is clear (green light), sets it (red light) before entering the critical region, and clears the semaphore (back to green light) when it leaves the region, so that another train can use it. Similarly, a process must check a semaphore (in this case, a bit where 1 means "set" and 0 means "clear") for each resource it is about to use, set it, and clear it when it has completed its task with that resource.

Let's consider a couple of subtle situations that can arise with semaphore checking. Since the activity of testing and setting a semaphore flag itself requires several machine steps, it is possible that a process may be interrupted *after* detecting a clear flag but *before* setting it. For example, suppose process A requests a printer, checks the flag for this device and finds it clear. Before it can set the flag, however, A gets interrupted by process B, which also requests a printer. Since the flag hasn't been set yet, the resource allocator lets B start printing. Later, process A resumes execution, at the point where the resource allocator had found the flag for the printer clear. Oops: now two processes are using the same supposedly nonshareable printer! The overall system must avoid this situation by guaranteeing that testing and setting the flag occur without interruption. For this reason, most machine languages feature **interrupt-disable** and **interrupt-enable** instructions, where an interrupt-disable instruction causes the CPU to delay recognition of interrupt signals until an interrupt-enable instruction executes. If the resource allocator consistently 1) executes an interrupt-disable, 2) tests a semaphore, 3) sets the semaphores, and 4) executes an interrupt-enable, then it will avoid collisions in a critical region. An alternative approach to safeguarding critical regions is a **test-and-set** instruction, in which the CPU retrieves the value of a flag, notes its value and sets it to a new value, *all in one machine instruction cycle*. Since a CPU always completes a single instruction before recognizing an interrupt, the test-and-set instruction also avoids collisions in a critical region.

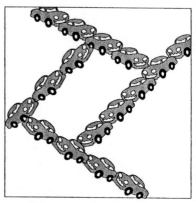

Figure 6.8: Deadlock

Another problem that might arise is the **deadlock** *between two processes competing for the same resources*, illustrated by traffic jam of figure 6.8, in which the cars heading down block the cars going up, and the cars heading up block the cars going down, so that none of them can move.

Suppose process A requests use of printer P. Shortly afterwards, process B requests hard drive D. The resource allocator grants each request, setting appropriate flags. Later, process A needs drive D as well as printer P, but the resource allocator denies the request because D is in use. So A must wait for B to finish using D. Meanwhile, process B reaches a point where it needs printer P. Oops: the resource allocator will deny this request, too. Now both A and B are waiting for each other to finish, which they each steadfastly refuse to do. The competing print processes are in a deadlock, stalling the printer resource indefinitely. Operating systems must avoid deadlock in order to avoid degrading system performance. Various techniques for removing deadlock have been developed. One approach is to convert nonshareable resources into shareable ones. For example, instead of sending data to an actual printer, a nonshareable resource, an OS could send data to disk storage, until it knows that a printer is available. Figure 6.9 depicts how this widely used technique, known as **spooling**—*holding data for output on disk until the device is ready*—lets each process act as if it has use of its own printer (actually, it's a *virtual* printer), thus avoiding any collisions.

Exercise 6.18: In terms of the components of an OS shown in figure 6.6, describe what the system does, step by step, when a Windows or Macintosh user a) starts working on a document with a word processor, b) asks the word processor to print the document, then c) continues editing it.

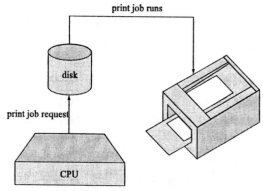

Figure 6.9: Spooling

Exercise 6.19: Why does an interrupt capability have to be implemented in the hardware of a computer? What three things does an interrupt do? How does the software of a dispatcher interact with this hardware feature?

Exercise 6.20: Describe a situation in which a process does not use the entire time-slice allotted to it by a time-sharing system. What component of the system should take note of this situation? What should it do about it?

Exercise 6.21: An engineer designs a single-lane tunnel with a signal system. A car entering either end of the tunnel triggers red lights above both tunnel entrances. The lights turn off when the car exits the tunnel. Approaching cars will wait until a red light is turned off. Unfortunately, this system can allow cars to collide in the tunnel. Explain how this could happen. Can you come up with a better solution?

Exercise 6.22: As the cost of hardware (processors and memory) dropped during the 1980s and 1990s, time-sharing became less and less attractive for operating systems. Explain why.

Exercise 6.23: How does spooling solve a deadlock problem? How does it illustrate the power of virtual machines?

6.4 Networks

What are computer networks for? Local area networks allow users to share resources, such as a disk storage system, which in turn provides common access to shared data and software packages. Some vendors will sell "floating" licenses of a program, which can run on a fixed number of platforms (machines) on a network as users request it. If, for example, there are 10 floating licenses, then when 10 users are running the program, the 11th user will be denied use of the program until one of the original 10 finishes using it. Electronic mail and shared calendars facilitate communication and scheduling of meetings. Computer scientists at large corporations are developing effective **groupware** to facilitate people trying to work together on projects. Wide area networks allow some users to share the power of an expensive supercomputer and other users (such as travel agents) to perform transactions on an on-line database.

Nowadays, it is fairly easy for any computer to connect to the Internet, giving users access to information from any other computer already connected, from news and weather to stocks and sports. Electronic "bulletin boards" allow a community of users to post and read messages. You can do your banking or get your photographs delivered in digital form over the network. Digital telephony lets users literally talk or even see each other over the network.

How do networks work? Enter the onion metaphor again. This time let's work inside out. At the lowest level, a network is a configuration of computers (also known as **nodes** or **sites** or **hosts**) communicating with each other by sending bits over wires (or wireless media). There are many possible topologies for connecting nodes, with different tradeoffs with respect to physical cost (the expense of actually connecting hosts), communication cost (the time it takes to send messages from one site to another), and reliability (the ability to keep communicating if a host or link between hosts fails). Figure 6.10 shows some common network topologies.

A **fully connected network** (6.10a) links every node directly with every other node. The physical cost of putting in so many direct lines is high, with the number of links growing as the square of the number of nodes. On the other hand, the communication cost is low, since messages transmit directly from host to host, and reliability is high, with so many possible indirect paths available should a direct link fail.

A **hierarchical network** (6.9b) organizes sites as a tree. Each node (except the root) has a unique parent and some number of children. The military and many corporations organize

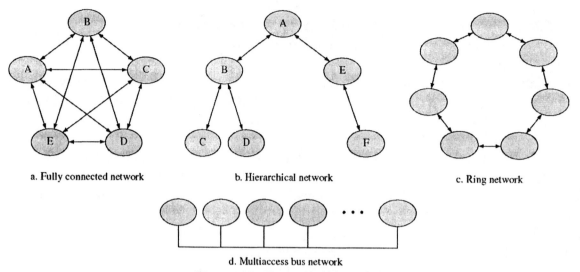

a. Fully connected network   b. Hierarchical network   c. Ring network

d. Multiaccess bus network

Figure 6.9: Network topologies

things hierarchically, with individual offices linked to a regional office in turn linked to corporate headquarters. The physical cost of this structure is relatively low (the number of links is equal to the number of nodes minus one), but the communication cost is relatively high (siblings can only communicate with each other only via common parents, and cousins require even more message passing). Failure of any node or link (except a leaf that no node relies on) partitions the network into disjoint subtrees. The command structure of the army is efficient, but rigid—imagine how it would be if a general were *never* allowed talk to a lieutenant, let alone a private!

A **ring network** (6.10c) connects each node to two other nodes, so that messages travel around a ring until they reach a desired host. IBM popularized token ring networks for early LANs. The physical and communication costs of a ring are comparable to that of a hierarchy, as are the reliability problems, since the number of links is the same as the number of nodes. However, a ring topology makes a refinement possible at relatively low cost. If the network is bidirectional (that is, each host can communicate to both of its neighbors), then communication speed doubles (since the number of transfers required to send a message is at most $n/2$ rather than $n - 1$) and reliability also doubles (since two links would have to fail in order to prevent any node from communicating with any other node).

A **multiaccess bus network** (6.10d) lets every site communicates with every other site via a shared wire (bus). The physical cost is low, so long as one can lay a single highspeed bus between hosts. (Devices called **repeaters** may be necessary to boost transmission over distances such as between buildings.) The communication cost is also low—so long as there isn't too much traffic on the bus, in which case it becomes a bottleneck. Since the failure of one site does not affect communication among the rest of the sites, reliability is as good as the reliability of the bus. The **Ethernet** standard has popularized the bus model for LANs worldwide.

No one configuration rules the world. The Internet is a **hybrid network**, connecting many different kinds of networks. Networks talk to each other through **gateways**, hosts that figure out how to translate information sent between different local networks, which can be tricky since each individual network may have its own language for communication.

The Internet grew out of an experimental network called ARPANET, originally funded by the Defense Advanced Research Projects Agency (DARPA) in the 1970s and the National Science Foundation (NSF) in the 1980s. Now completely weaned of governmental subsidies, the Internet now really belongs to no one and everyone, with much of its internal infrastructure being continuously maintained and upgraded by large communications companies such as long-distance telephone carriers, with access supplied by hundreds of small and large companies. The Internet is really a network of networks. To get access, you buy (or someone, such as a university computing center, buys for you) the right to connect to a local network, which in turn links to the international network of networks.

Moving to the next layer of the onion, above the physical level of a network is the level of messages. Just as the envelope you drop in a mailbox has to have a mailing address uniquely identifying its recipient, so every message on the Internet needs a **host name** *uniquely identifying its destination*. Just as mailing addresses are hierarchical (a residence in a city in a state in a country), so are host names on the Internet (a host in a department in a locale in a domain). For example, "cimel.cse.lehigh.edu" identifies a particular workstation, arbitrarily named "cimel", in the "cse" department at "lehigh" in the "edu" or educational domain. Other top level domain names include "gov" for government, "com" for commercial sites, "org" for other organizations, and two letter domain names for countries other than the USA (where the Internet started), e.g., "uk" for United Kingdom, "ru" for "Russia", etc.

Symbolic names are, as you might expect, primarily for human consumption. Machines munch on numbers, so every host on the Internet also has a unique 32-bit address, such as "128.180.14.37", which is also a hierarchical structure. (The dots give a hint of the hierarchical structure and of the 32 bits. The hierarchy has four levels, each labeled with an 8-bit byte. Thus each of the four labels ranges from 0 to 255. A 32-bit version of an address is 01000100001110100000011100010010. We like the dot notation better!). Just as with tokens in programming languages, a machine needs to translate or *bind* symbolic names to numeric codes. Once upon a time, every host maintained its own table of name bindings, rather like a telephone book associating names with phone numbers, but this soon became untenable. Now the Internet relies on the **domain name service (DNS)**, *which distributes name bindings at many hosts around the world*. When your local machine connects to a network, it connects to a name server which maintains all the bindings in your department (a LAN). If you want to talk to a host outside your department, your name server will request a binding from a name server for the locale or domain you want (unless it already happens to be a host that maintains that information locally). Name servers quietly trade name bindings to keep each other up to date. An advantage of a distributed DNS is robustness: if one name server goes down, there may be others available.

Most network topologies (except for strict hierarchies or unidirectional rings) allow multiple paths between nodes. Network software must determine a particular route for a message, node by node, then add this information to the message. A **router** is a host computer or special-purpose device which uses this information to *route messages through a network*.

Once two hosts have connected, they may maintain a communication **session** for some duration to exchange a message. Like goods on the Interstate Highway system, messages move in relatively small units. Cars and trucks may seem like large objects to you, blocking up traffic sometimes, but what would a highway be like if we all had to get on board one huge train? Imagine several thousand people waiting to get on a train at once, or one huge train waiting and waiting for another train to pass through an intersection. The highway system is relatively efficient because vehicles are relatively small. Similarly, data goes through the Internet by a scheme called **packet switching**, *which breaks messages* (which may be large files) *up into smaller, fixed-length packets*. Each packet is a fixed block of your data, say a kilobyte or two, prefixed with a "header," which contains the addresses of the source and destination hosts, plus intermediary hosts along the route, plus information for putting packets back together again, plus information to make sure packets don't get corrupted. If a recipient discovers that a packet has gotten corrupted (we'll see how it does this in the next section), it can ask for it to be sent again.

Systems interacting across a network must agree on **protocols**—*standardized rules for communications*. What would you think if you dialed a telephone number, someone picked up the phone, but said nothing? Saying "Hello" or something similar is a protocol that establishes communication between two people. The high-pitched whine you sometimes get instead is a protocol that enables two fax machines or two computers to establish communication—only there's actually information in that whine! Hosts on a network must agree on a set of protocols for determining host names, locating hosts, establishing connections, ensuring that packets get sent correctly, and so on. Computer engineers have simplified this problem by breaking it down into multiple layers. (There's that abstract, modular onion again.) The International Standards Organization (ISO) has designed the **OSI** (Open Systems Interconnection) model, which partitions the communications process into seven layers, as shown in figure 6.11.

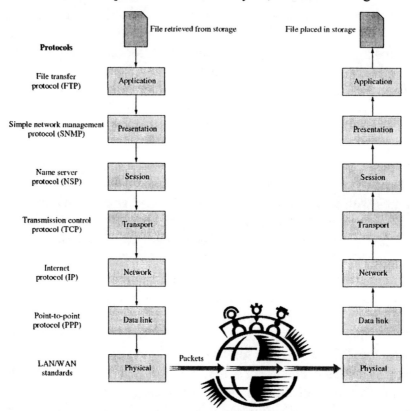

Figure 6.11: OSI layered model of communications

Working bottom up again, the **physical layer** is responsible for the details of transmitting a stream of bits through the hardware of a network. The **data link** layer divides the data stream up into fixed length packets and provides for detection and recovery from errors in transmission. The **network** layer determines how to route packets across networks of computers, host by host. The **transport** layer generates physical addresses of hosts, arranges for the transfer of messages between hosts, maintains packet order, and controls the flow of packets. The **session** layer establishes and maintains communications between two machines. The **presentation** layer may reformat the data to make it compatible between different sites and perhaps securing the data or applying data compression to increase efficiency. Finally, the **application** layer interacts directly with the user through network application programs, such as e-mail and file transfer.

To see how all these layers work together, consider how a package gets from your house to your cousin in another city. You first decide how you are going to send the package (post office or some other parcel service company), then wrap the package in a form acceptable to the post office, with your cousin's name on an address label, then you take it to the post office, where someone adds additional information (such as "sufficient postage paid"). Within the postal service, there are several more layers to go through at one office, before it finally arrives at a post office nearest your cousin. A letter carrier then brings it to your cousin's house, where she opens it. Similarly, suppose you want to transfer a file from your machine (connected to the Internet via modem) to your cousin's host. A small army of software protocols jumps into action behind the scenes. The application layer runs FTP (file transfer protocol), which in turn invokes software at the presentation and session layer—such as SNMP (simple network management protocol) and NSP (name server protocol)—to arrange data for transfer and establish communication with a remote host. The transport layer, usually TCP (Transmission Control Protocol) translates the symbolic name of the host into an Internet address and also starts breaking your file up into packets, each one with a TCP header on it providing information about how to put the packets back together again on the other side. The network layer, IP (Internet Protocol), figures out how to route information between the two machines, possibly via many machines on the net. Once the connection has been made, the data link layer, which might be PPP (Point-to-Point Protocol), gets each packet ready to go through the modem and over the telephone line to the next host. Each packet gets information from higher layers, such as the source, destination, and intermediate hosts, so that once the physical layer has transmitted all the packets, the complete file can be reassembled, with each layer contributing, at the destination.

If by now you are one of the few people on the planet who haven't been "surfing" on the World Wide Web, the multimedia that comes with this book encourages you to do so. A web browser lets you navigate information around the world by simply clicking on highlighted text or pictures on the screen. Obviously, there's a great deal of abstraction going on behind the scenes here! A browser is another program at the highest, application layer. When you click on a "hot" part of a page (screen), the browser automatically invokes other applications such as HTTP (hypertext transfer protocol), which figures out how to format and navigate hypertext on a screen, FTP to arrange for file transfer, NSP to look up host names, etc. Network access can be viewed as a suite of programs, running just like other applications on top of an OS, or as a built-in extension of an OS. Building network capabilities into an OS has two major advantages: efficiency and convenience. System providers realize that they can tune network performance by incorporating lower layers of the network hierarchy into lower levels of the OS itself. Users find it convenient to view the facilities of the network as if they were part of the virtual machine that comes out of the box—just plug it in (including the modem or Ethernet card) and it works!

Exercise 6.24: What network topology would best suit the following environments?
       a. A dormitory floor.   b. A university campus.   c. A country.
Justify your answers in terms of physical cost, communication cost and reliability.
Exercise 6.25: In a ring network, what are two drawbacks to limiting the transfer of messages to a single direction?
Exercise 6.26: In a multiaccess bus network, why is the bus a non-shareable resource? Propose a scheme for avoiding deadlock between machines trying to use this resource.
Exercise 6.27: What is packet switching? Explain how different layers in the OSI model contribute to this process.

Exercise 6.28: What is a protocol? Name three or four protocols and explain what they contribute to computer networking.

Exercise 6.29 (*explore*): The current generation of the Internet uses a 32-bit addressing scheme for identifying hosts. Why do you suppose ISO has proposed a 128-bit addressing scheme?

Exercise 6.30 (*explore*): What is **peer-to-peer** networking? Get on the web and find a definition, contrast it with client-server networking, and discuss a couple of different p-to-p applications.

6.5 Protection and security

Once upon a time, computer security was a matter of putting up walls and locked doors around the computer room. To get into the inner sanctum, you had to tell a human security guard a secret password. Then came time-sharing with remote terminals and telephone dial-up. After that came personal computers which were isolated machines on which you could only run one task at a time. Somewhat later came networking and multitasking. Multiple processes and multiple users opened up opportunities for conflicts and collisions, sometimes accidental, once in a while malicious, sometimes harmless but occasionally disastrous. A need arose for **protection**—*preventing processes (running programs or users running them) from doing unauthorized things.* In an world increasingly reliant upon complex operating systems and networks, computer scientists are devoting more attention to increasing **security**—*a measure of confidence in the protection of a system and its data.*

When multiple processes are running virtually at the same time, there may be a need to protect access to CPU time (for example, not allowing a process to hog time unfairly) or to memory (for example, preventing one program from accessing—and possibly altering—data that another program is using), or to input/output devices (for example, keeping two processes from writing data to the same device at the same time), or to files (for example, not allowing a process to modify another user's data). Since these resources are all managed by operating systems, why not incorporate measures for protecting them in operating systems? DOS, Windows and Macintosh OS, originally designed as single-user systems on hardware which was not designed to support any protection (aside from some with physical locks on the cases), all provide little security. But multiuser operating systems, such as Unix, and multitasking operating systems running on more advanced hardware, seek to provide increased measures of security.

For example, Unix provides protection for files. Each file has access modes permitting *(in any combination) read, write, and execute* access to the original user, to other members of a designated group of users, or to any other user on the system. One might want to hide some files (such as a grade book) from other users altogether or make other files just read-accessible to others, e.g., for Internet browsing. The operating system must maintain this access scheme for its users. Moreover, it must also prevent *indirect* violations of file access permissions, say, by a process Q that process P starts (that user U initiates).

Things get more complicated if multiple processes *are* allowed to modify the same files. Suppose programmers are working on a project together. If they both modify the same file, their work will inevitably get out of sync. SCCS (Source Code Control System) is a facility that enforces a policy of letting just one user at a time check a file out for modification purposes. Similarly, suppose many travel agents have access to the same airline database. If two different agents can reserve the same seat at the same time from two different terminals, two different clients are going to be very unhappy! Note that preventing access collision is a matter that can be handled at different levels of abstraction—at the OS level or at the application software level (such as a database management system).

Multiuser systems (and even some single user system in open offices or labs) put up their first wall of defense by authenticating passwords during a login procedure, something like this:

```
login: asb0
password: ******
```

The OS automatically hides the entry of the password so that a passerby cannot read it over your shoulder. However, passwords are not foolproof, especially for users who make poor choices of passwords, such as familiar names, dates or words. Beware of 'hackers'. Earlier, we introduced one sense of 'hacker' in computing as one who solves problems by a trial and error method. Informed hackers, who have already built up considerable specialized knowledge, develop a reputation for getting things done this way. Yet another kind of hacker is someone who breaks into computer systems—for gain, spite or fun. In the movie *War Games*, a young hacker breaks into a military computer and starts launching nuclear missiles! He actually gets in through a "trap door"—a login program which notices a specific user identifier and circumvents normal security procedures for that user. Until then, we see him engaging his personal computer in password guessing by repeated trials. A 4-digit password provides 10,000 variations—reasonably safe for automatic teller machines which require entry by hand. But computers can be programmed to enter passwords automatically. A program, trying a different password every millisecond, could try all 10,000 4-digit different passwords in 10 seconds and would be guaranteed to crack a users password. Longer passwords, including alphabetic and special characters ('@', '#', etc.) greatly increase the time needed to guess a password. This increase in time may make the method impractical. Most of us are not ready to wait 500 years to learn someone else's password.

Of course, to match passwords, the OS must maintain them, in a password file. This file is kept hidden (unreadable) from most users, except a "superuser" or system administrator. Nevertheless, if a hacker could get access to this file, he'd strike gold. So there is clearly a need for further protection of the password file, as well as other sensitive data, from government classified information to personal medical or financial records. Network operating systems also introduce a need to *transmit* data—such as credit card numbers—securely, especially when the transmission channels themselves are unprotected from eavesdropping.

Encryption is a systematic algorithm which encodes "clear text" to another form called "cipher text" which, though still a string of characters, is undecipherable without a corresponding **decryption** (decoding) algorithm. Encrypted data can thus be safely stored or transmitted just like unprotected data. The Roman general Julius Caesar developed one of the first known encryption schemes. The **Caesar cipher** replaces each character in a string by a character that appears j positions later in the alphabet. In Julius's original version, j was 3, so he would have encrypted the string "IDESOFMARCH" like this:

```
IDESOFMARCH    (clear text)
|||||||||||
LGHVRIPDUFK    (cipher text)
```

The cipher text looks like gobblygook. Yet it can be readily decrypted by reversing the process, replacing each character by one that appears j positions *earlier* in the alphabet. Suppose j is 8? Since there are only 7 letters after 'S', how should this character be encoded? The encryption algorithm does a "wraparound" to the first character, encoding 'S' as 'A', 'T' as 'B', etc.

The Caesar cipher may have befuddled barbarian scouts, but it is fairly easy for a systematic sleuth or computer algorithm to break it, by simply trying all possible values of j. Modern encryption schemes incorporate many substitutions and permutations, whereas the Caesar cipher performs a simple substitution. A more sophisticated substitution scheme uses a user-supplied keyword. The **Vignère cipher** scheme adds the numerical value of each character in a keyword to each character in a plain text. For example:

```
IDESOFMARCH   (clear text)
||||||||||||
CAESARCAESA   (repeated text)
||||||||||||
LEJLPXPBWVI   (cipher text)
```

A different user-supplied keyword would produce a different cipher text. On the other hand, a permutation rearranges the characters in an input text. For example, one might divide a string into blocks of four characters (adding a random character to complete the last block), then permute the letters in a block as follows:

```
1 2 3 4   (clear text)    → IDES OFMA RCHZ
3 4 2 1   (cipher text)   → ESDI MAFO HZCR
```

The **Data Encryption Standard (DES)**, developed by IBM and adopted by the National Institutes of Standards and Technology, consists of a permutation followed by 16 different keyword substitutions and a final permutation. However, two Israeli scientists (E. Biham and A. Shamir) have discovered a mathematical technique that can break a DES code under certain circumstances. The current best hope for encryption, especially on wide area networks, is a **public-key encryption scheme**. You actually make your encryption key public to anyone who wants to send you a message, but keep your decryption key, for messages you receive, private. By using fairly large (several hundred digits long) prime numbers as decryption keys, breaking this scheme, while conceivable, becomes infeasible in a reasonable time frame. Unfortunately for this scheme, computers continue to get faster. While it may take years for today's computers to break a public-key encryption scheme using 200 digits, it may take seconds for tomorrow's computers to break the same scheme. To further complicate matters, the current algorithm for breaking a code encrypted with a public key is of exponential complexity, some mathematician may discover an algorithm of lower complexity for breaking the code.

Another threat to computer security is the proliferation of computer **viruses**, programs which are to computer hosts what the infectious micro-organisms are to biological hosts. Once planted in software, a virus can replicate itself, and also spread from computer to computer, either on floppy diskettes or through a network. It might activate itself as soon as it arrives in a new host, or, just to give folks a nasty surprise, wait for some event such as a particular date, before it wakes up and starts doing something on its own, possibly just annoying or possibly seriously damaging data or system integrity.

The Lehigh virus, discovered at the authors' own Lehigh University in 1987, could migrate from an infected floppy disk to a PC's hard disk. Once on a PC's hard disk, it would copy itself onto any other floppy disks with uninfected system files. When an infected disk was copied for the fourth time, the virus would destroy all data on the hard disk! It took several frustrating months to eradicate the virus from the campus. The culprit responsible for the virus is still officially unknown.

On November 2nd, 1988, Robert Morris, Jr., launched a computer "worm" which reproduced itself from one host to another across the Internet. It gained access to hosts through a security flaw in Unix network software at the time—the `sendmail` program code still contained debugging code left by its designers for testing. The worm program searched files for sites that would allow remote execution without a password. The worm would then login anonymously into a new site, upload itself and execute anew. To make matters worse, it would try discovering user passwords, starting with common ones. The very connectivity and cooperative spirit of the

Internet which facilitated the spread of the worm also facilitated its discovery and eradication within a couple of days. Morris's worm did no serious damage except tying up resources on the net, but he was sentenced to 3 years probation, 400 hours of community service and a $10,000 fine; his legal costs were estimated in excess of $100,000.

The security measure for viruses is the use of "vaccines" and "disinfectants." A software *vaccine* scans your disk for viruses and notifies you of any viruses. A *disinfectant* will then eliminate the virus. Often it is necessary to delete the infected program. Software vaccines and disinfectants are available on the Internet as well as from private vendors.

Exercise 6.31: What is the relationship between protection and security? Explain in terms of an example, such as password protection or virus vaccines.

Exercise 6.32: Suppose a computer center insists that all passwords at least be at least five characters long, four of which must be digit and the fifth an alphabetic character. What is the minimum number of possible number of possible passwords assured by this policy? How much more security does this policy give, mathematically?

Exercise 6.33: Can you recommend a significantly better policy for passwords than the 4-digit policy discussed in the text? How much more security does your policy give, mathematically?

Exercise 6.34: Why would it be a bad idea to give Internet browsers *write* access to files?

Exercise 6.35: A program has been developed that scans a particular computing environment for possible security holes, alerting the user to potential problems. What are the potential hazards of such a program for security? How can these problems be avoided?

Exercise 6.36: What does the Caesar cipher produce from plain text "HELLOWORLD" if *j* is 5?

Exercise 6.37: A Caesar cipher produces a cipher text "DKTVJFCA". What is the plain text? How does this exercise affect your confidence in this encryption scheme?

Exercise 6.38: Use the Vignère cipher scheme to encode your last name, using your first name as the key.

Exercise 6.39 (*social/ethical*): Develop an argument for and another argument against the sentence handed down against Robert Morris, Jr, for his creation and spread of an Internet worm.

Exercise 6.40 (*explore*): What is the Secure Sockets Layer (SSL) and what does it do? Does it increase your confidence that web-based transactions can protect your private information?

Exercise 6.41 (*explore*): Some web site start with the address (URL) *https* rather than *http*. What's the difference, i.e., what does *https* add and how does it work?

Chapter review. Are the following statements true or false? Explain why or why not.
a) An operating system is a virtual machine.
b) An operating system is a resource manager.
c) Job control language (JCL) described the employment of computer programmers.
d) Batch operating systems streamlined usage of computer resources.
e) Multiprogramming makes both multi-user and multi-tasking systems possible.
f) Multitasking is when several users can send tasks to the same machine.
g) Preemptive multitasking is when users determine which task is using the processor.
h) In a LAN, a client is a person who is requesting services.
i) Access to the Internet typically requires access to a network server.
j) Booting a system is giving a recalcitrant machine a swift kick.
k) To enable a PC to run Unix instead of DOS, you must reprogram the ROM.
l) The scheduler responds to events—such as when a user clicks on a mouse.

m) A program counter is similar to the program address register, only every process has one.

n) Virtual memory is limited by the amount of RAM a machine has.

o) A dispatcher responds to interrupts by switching from one process to another.

p) Thrashing is when a frustrated user is shaking a keyboard or a mouse.

q) A spool can make more effective use of high quality printers and other resources.

r) A fully connected network has a higher connection cost than a ring or hierarchical network.

s) Only hosts, which are servers for other machines, require their own unique host name.

t) A domain name service (DNS) provides names for users on the Internet.

u) HTTP, FTP, NSP, SNMP and TCP are examples of network protocols.

v) Computer security has to do with keeping unauthorized users out of a computer room.

w) Protection and security are more important for networked than stand-alone computers.

x) Obscure words like 'ROM' or 'cipher' or 'gnostic' make good passwords.

y) A public-key encryption scheme is unsuitable for securing data over the Internet.

z) Viruses and other malicious software spread via floppy diskettes or over networks.

Summary

An **operating system** is a collection of programs that manage the resources, including the processors, memory, and input/output devices, of a computer. From a user's point of view, an OS is a *virtual machine* letting users accomplish tasks that would be difficult and time-consuming to perform directly with the underlying actual machine.

Early **batch operating systems** streamlined computer usage by having a human operator put "jobs" (programs to run) into a storage system called a **job queue**. Programmers could specify instructions to the system or operator in a **job control language (JCL)**. Whereas earlier systems just loaded one program into memory at a time, a **multiprogramming** system would load several programs and switch between them when one became idle, perhaps waiting for a response from a slower I/O device. Multiprogramming sets up the possibilities of **time-sharing**, dividing processor time into slices that the OS tries to divide "fairly" among competing jobs; **interactive processing**, which lets a user interact with a computer hands-on; **multiuser** operating systems (such as UNIX), which let many different users share the same machine; and **multitasking**, or switching between tasks. With the 1980's came **network operating systems**, which manage resources for many workstations or personal computers communicating with each other. A local area network or **LAN** is a network located in a geographically contiguous area such as a laboratory or building, while a wide area network or **WAN** is spread over a larger area with connections at generally slower speeds. Support for networks, including the various **servers** of a local network and the vast resources of the **Internet**, is incorporated into many modern operating systems, making each computer appear to be a very powerful virtual machine indeed!

A modern computer **boots** or starts up by reading an initial program from Read-Only-Memory (**ROM**), which then looks for the rest of the OS on a disk drive. The OS then runs a sequence of device driver routines that recognize input/output devices and set up memory management. Once the OS has booted, it may in turn boot into a higher level OS, such as a graphical user interface and/or a network OS. Thus the boot process may recapitulate the evolution of operating systems though increasing layers of abstraction.

The major components of an OS include the **command processor**, which interprets user-triggered events as (possibly) executable commands, the **scheduler**, which starts up programs as executable **processes**, the **resource allocator**, which makes sure that each process has the secondary resources—memory, files, and peripheral devices—that it may need, and the

dispatcher, which monitors processes and decides when to switch execution from one process and another, for example when a hardware **interrupt** stops a process in order to signal input from a user or the end of a **time slice**. OS design must consider how to get processes to cooperate in sharing resources, for example by controlling access to nonshareable resources using flags known as **semaphores**, avoiding **deadlocks** between processes competing for the same set of resources, and holding data on disk until a printer is ready (**spooling**).

A computer network is a configuration of computers (known as **nodes, sites** or **hosts**) communicating with each other by sending bits over wires (or wireless media). There are many possible topologies for connecting nodes, with different tradeoffs with respect to physical cost, communication cost, and reliability, including **fully-connected**, **hierarchical**, **ring**, and **bus** networks. The Internet is a **hybrid network**, connecting many different kinds of networks. The Internet relies on the **domain name service (DNS)**, which distributes bindings between symbolic and numeric host names. Data go through a network by means of **packet switching**, which breaks messages (possibly large files) into smaller, fixed-length packets. Systems interacting across a network must agree on standardized rules for communication called **protocols**. Hosts on a network must agree on a set of protocols for determining host names, locating hosts, establishing connections, ensuring that packets get sent correctly, and so on. Computer engineers have simplified this problem by breaking it down into layers. The OSI model partitions communications into seven layers, each with standardized protocols.

Multiple processes and multiple users opened up opportunities for conflicts and collisions. A need arose for **protection**—preventing processes (running programs or users running them) from doing unauthorized things—and increasing **security**—a measure of confidence in the protection of a system and its data. A modern OS may try to protect memory, for example by not letting one process tamper with memory in use by another process, or files, for example by designating access privileges for different communities of users. Hackers trying to break into systems for profit or other motives and snoopers looking at data transmitted over networks have made security increasingly important to the rest of us. While users can help by choosing non-trivial passwords, system administrators can secure password files and other sensitive data by means of **encryption**, where clear text gets encoded into unintelligible cipher text. Another threat to computer security is the proliferation of computer **viruses**, programs which can replicate themselves and spread from computer to computer, either on floppy diskettes or through a network.

Chapter 7
Analyzing algorithms
"...such loyalty to ideas, such sublime irrecognition of the unessential."
James Russell Lowell, on the poet Dante

Strings, arrays, files, lists, tables and various collections let programs perform computations on aggregates of data. The most common way of processing these elements is in loops, operating on all or a subset of the elements, in order. This kind of activity can add up to significant processing time. In this chapter, we analyze several important algorithms, notably searching and sorting elements. We will then analyze their efficiency, introducing the "Big O" analysis of algorithms, and consider the practical tradeoffs between different algorithms.

7.1 Searching and sorting
Searching, or *looking for a particular value in a particular collection,* is a common activity from looking up a name in a telephone directory to finding the host computer of a web site on the Internet. The collection might be an array of values in memory or a file or database of records on disk. **Sorting** *rearranges a collection's elements into some prescribed order.* For example, the names in a telephone directory are in alphabetical order. Although these two tasks are quite different, there is an important connection between them, as we shall see shortly.

7.1.1 Linear search
The simplest way to search an array or collection of elements is a **linear** search—trying all the possibilities, serially, starting with the first element, then the second, and so forth, until either finding what you are looking for or reaching the last value of an array. (We introduced arrays in chapter 3, p. 66). In the simplest case, the process continues until either the target is found or the last array element is reached without a hit. Here is the algorithm for a linear search through an array:

LinearSearch(array A,value)	//1	function with parameters
set index to 0	//2	initialize array counter
LOOP until reaching the end of A	//3	an array has a size
if A[index] == value then return index	//4	found the value, exit function
else increment index	//5	then go back to LOOP
return notFound	//6	loop didn't find value in A

The algorithm returns either the index or subscript where it found the desired element or returns a flag notFound a value that is outside the range of possible subscripts of the array (such as -1). To see how it works, let's suppose array A is initialized as A[0]=9, A[1]=4, A[2]=5, A[3]=6, A[4]=8. Now let's trace what the algorithm does, when searching for the value 4. To show our trace systematically, we'll generate a table, with line numbers and variables as columns, and a new row each time a variable gets a new value:

line	array A	value	index
1	9 4 5 6 8	4	
2			0
3	not at end of A		
4	A[0] is 9, not==4		
5			1
3	not at end of A		
4	A[1] is 4, 4==4, return 1		

In line 1, we enter *LinearSearch* with parameters *A* and *value*. Line 2 initializes the array *index* to 0 (the first subscript value for arrays in many languages). There are five values in *A*, so the loop condition of line 3 is true. The conditional expression of line 4 is false, because the value at *A*[0], which is 9, does not equal *value*, which is 4. So we take the *else* in line 5, incrementing *index* to 1, then go back to the top of the loop, in line 3. The second time through the loop, since *index* is 1, *A*[1], which is 4, does match the *value*, 4. So we exit the loop and function, returning the value of *index*, 1, to the caller of *LinearSearch*.

Exercise 7.1: Suppose the caller wants to find the value 6. Extend the trace above to show what happens, step by step, when searching for this. Then trace what happens when searching for 3.

Exercise 7.2: What if an item appears more than once in an array? Modify the algorithm above so that it returns *all* of a target's locations.

The algorithm above loops until it either finds the element and exits or reaches the end of the array. But suppose an array can contain a hundred elements but a user only enters eighty—the array is only **partially filled**. Does it make sense to search the last twenty elements, which may contain uninitialized values, one of which might inadvertently be the one we are looking for? Obviously not. Therefore, it would be better to provide the number of *actual* entries in the array as a parameter, then modify the algorithm so that the loop stops when it has seen this number of entries:

<u>LinearSearch(array A,value,numEntries)</u>	//1	numEntries is number of actual entries
set index to 0	//2	
LOOP while index < numEntries	//3	test for numEntries instead of end of A
if array[index] == value then return index	//4	
else increment index	//5	
return notFound	//6	

Exercise 7.3: Suppose the size of *A* is 100 and we initialize the first five elements as we did above. Under what circumstance would the revised algorithm be more efficient?

Exercise 7.4: How might the revised algorithm avoid an error?

Exercise 7.5: The CDROM supplies an implementation of the linear search algorithm in Java (in `chap7\LinearSearch.java`). Does the implementation assume a full or partially filled array? How can you tell? How does the program load values into the array? What would have happened if `LinearSearch` had used this test instead:

```
while (index < a.length)
```

(If you're not sure, try it, by modifying program `LinearSearch.java`.)

Exercise 7.6: Modify the program mentioned in the previous exercise so that each time through the loop it displays the value of `index`. How many times does the program go through the loop if the value happens to be the first element in the array? How many times if the value is not in the array?

Exercise 7.7: Generalize the empirical observations you may or may not have made doing the prior exercise. What is the best possible scenario? What is the worst case scenario?

7.1.2 Sorting

Linear search is not particularly efficient. When you look up a name in a phone directory, you don't start at the beginning and look at every single entry. Since you know that the directory is already in alphabetical order, you can start looking somewhere in the middle of the book, then finger forward or backwards depending on the first letter of the name. Searching is much more efficient if the data is already sorted. (We'll discuss just how much more efficient later in this chapter.)

There are many well-known sort algorithms. We will examine simple one, the **selection sort**. There are three key ideas: 1) *selecting* the element with the *lowest* value (in this case, 44):

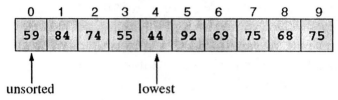

Figure 7.1a: Selecting the lowest value

2) *swapping* it with the first *unsorted* value in the array:

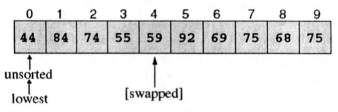

Figure 7.1b: Swapping lowest (44) with first unsorted (59)

and 3) *advancing* the index of *unsorted* in the array to the next element.

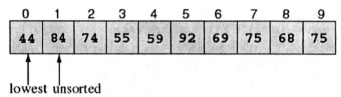

Figure 7.1c: Advancing unsorted index

The algorithm has two loops: one finds the *lowest* value (figure 7.1a) and another swaps and advances the *unsorted* index (figure 7.1b-c). Since we want to swap and advance each time we select the lowest value, the first loop is nested within the second. Figure 7.2 shows the pseudocode.

```
swap(first, second)                                      //1  swap first and second in array
  set temp to first                                      //2  hold value for swap
  set first to second                                    //3
  set second to temp                                     //4  complete the swap
sort(sortArray[], numEntries)                            //5
  set unsorted to 0                                      //6  first unsorted index in array
  LOOP while unsorted < numEntries-1                     //7  Outer loop: sort and advance
    set lowestSoFar to unsorted                          //8  look for lowest item index
    set i to unsorted+1                                  //9  reinitialize i for inner loop
    LOOP while i < numEntries                            //10 Inner loop: find lowest value
      if (sortArray[i] < sortArray[lowestSoFar])         //11
        set lowestSoFar to i                             //12
      increment i                                        //13
    swap(sortArray[unsorted], sortArray[lowestSoFar])    //14
    increment unsorted                                   //15 advance to next slot
```

Figure 7.2: Selection sort algorithm

Before doing the following exercises, you may want to go through the multimedia for this chapter first—it includes a trace of this algorithm.

Exercise 7.8: What is the purpose of the parameter *numEntries* in line 5?

Exercise 7.9: Explain, step by step, how the above algorithm sorts the first two elements of the array in figure 7.1. Make a table as we made for tracing the *LinearSearch* algorithm above.

Exercise 7.10: Why is *lowestSoFar* set to unsorted, in line 8? Why isn't this line before line 7, where it would only have to be initialized once?

Exercise 7.11: Why is *i* initialized to *unsorted*+1 rather than just *unsorted*, in line 9?

Exercise 7.12: What is the conditional expression in line 11 comparing? Discuss examples for when it would succeed and fail.

Exercise 7.13: What is line 14 swapping? Discuss an example.

Exercise 7.14: Why does the outer loop stop at *numEntries*-1 rather than simply *numEntries*?

Exercise 7.15: Modify the algorithm so that it arranges elements in largest to smallest order instead of smallest to largest.

Exercise 7.16: If there are 10 elements in *sortArray*, how many times will line 6 be executed? How many times will line 8 be executed? How many times will line 11 be executed? How many times will line 14 be executed? If there are 100 elements, how many times will line 11 be executed?

Exercise 7.17: Write an algorithm in pseudocode that reads in a list of names from the keyboard and sorts them alphabetically. Optional: implement and test your algorithm as a program.

7.1.3 Binary Search

Now that we have a way to sort elements of an array, we can conduct a more efficient search, reminiscent of finding names in a telephone directory. A **binary search** repeatedly divides the sorted array into two smaller arrays until it homes in on the subscript of the desired item. Suppose we are searching for an occurrence of 75 in the sorted array shown in figure 7.3a:

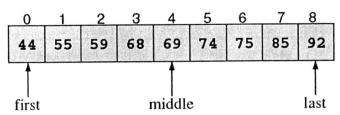

Figure 7.3a: Look at middle element

Binary search first examines the middle element, by dividing the number of elements in two (hence "binary" search). Since that's not it, another comparison reveals that it must be in the upper half:

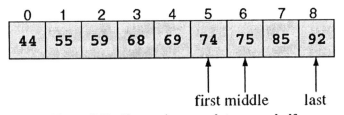

Figure 7.3b: Narrowing search to upper half

Dividing the upper half in two happens to locate the target as the middle element (at subscript 6—note that the "middle" is found through integer division). So in this case binary search finds the desired element in just two cycles—better than seven cycles for a linear search. Here's the algorithm:

BinarySearch(key, sorted[], numEntries)	//1	look for key (item to find) in sorted
set first to 0	//2	starts at 0 but may move with search
set last to numEntries	//3	last may also move with search
LOOP while first <= last	//4	
set middle to (first + last) / 2;	//5	find middle index (integer division)
if sorted[middle] == key	//6	match?
return middle;	//7	return index #
else if sorted[middle] < key	//8	key above middle?
set first to middle + 1;	//9	move first past middle
else set last to middle - 1;	//10	move last below middle
return NOTFOUND;	//11	key is not in sorted array

Figure 7.4: BinarySearch algorithm

Again the multimedia traces this algorithm in detail. (We think multimedia makes it easier to visualize the dynamic behavior of algorithms than static text.)

Exercise 7.18: Write a comment explaining line 4 above.

Exercise 7.19: What do lines 2 and 3 do? When, as the comments for these lines suggest, do the variables first and last change?

Exercise 7.20: What does the computation of line 5 accomplish? How does it rely on the behavior of integer division? Give an example.

Exercise 7.21: Trace *BinarySearch(59,quizScores,9)* where *quizScores* is the array shown in figure 7.3. Make a table as we made for tracing the *LinearSearch* algorithm above.

Exercise 7.22: The program `BinarySearch.java` reports the number of comparison steps it takes to find the key. Run the program with several different keys and describe the results, compared with what you would expect with a linear search.

Exercise 7.23: Modify the pseudocode for *BinarySearch* so that instead of *NOTFOUND* it returns a value indicating where one might want to insert the key value that was not found in the array. (Optional: modify and test program `BinarySearch.java` to make sure your algorithm works.)

Exercise 7.24: Modify the pseudocode for *BinarySearch* so it finds all the occurrences of an element. Return an array with the indices of the element's occurrences and a sentinel (e.g., -1) to mark the end of the array. (Optional: modify and test program `BinarySearch.java` to make sure your algorithm works.)

7.2 Recursion

If a function can call another function, you may wonder, can a function call *itself*? The answer in most modern programming languages is yes. **Recursion** occurs *when a function calls itself* (either directly or indirectly). Modern programming languages implement recursion because it can be a powerful problem solving technique, a favorite of mathematicians. Charles Babbage had something like recursion in mind when he colorfully described the capability of his Analytical Engine "to eat its own tail." Let's start out with a simple example. The factorial of a positive integer is the product

$$n \cdot (n - 1) \cdot (n - 2) \cdot \ldots \cdot 1.$$

So 3! is 3·2·1, which is 6; likewise 4! is 24. A mathematician, noting that (n-1) · (n - 2) · ... · 1 is (n-1)!, would typically define factorial, written *n*! (pronounced "n factorial"), recursively:

$n! = 1,$ for $n = 1$

$\quad = n \cdot (n\text{-}1)!,$ for $n > 1$

In English, if n is 1, $n!$ is 1; else $n!$ is n times the factorial of n-1. In English, the algorithm for computing n! can be stated, "To compute n!, compute (n-1)! and multiply the result by n. A pseudocode version looks like this:

```
factorial(n)                    //1    Given n, return n!
if n == 1 return 1              //2    Base case
else return factorial(n-1)* n;  //3    Recursive case
```

The pseudocode is a straightforward rewrite of the mathematical notation. A recursive function *call* occurs each time the execution reaches the last line of the function and executes factorial(n-1). Note that we have defined factorial in terms of itself—eating its own tail.

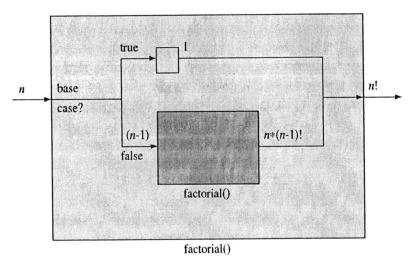

Figure 7.5: Recursive call in factorial()

As figure 7.4 shows, if the base case is true (n==1), then *factorial()* just returns 1; but if the base case is false, then it calls *factorial()* again. You might object, "but this is a circular definition!" Indeed, this is a danger of recursion that must be avoided: a circular definition never ends and leads to infinite recursion! In this case, however, the recursive definition actually makes progress, since it applies itself only after subtracting one. Eventually, it will "bottom out" with the first case (called the **base case**), for n=1. Consider, for example, 3!. Since 3 > 1, the **recursive case** of the definition applies, asking for 2!. Again, since 2 > 1, the recursive case applies, asking for 1!. This time the base case applies. So you can see that in this case the recursive definition does bottom out.

Exercise 7.25: Can you think of a case in which the above definition of $n!$ will never bottom out? (Hint: what values of n are not explicitly considered.)

The solution for the base case is always 1. Where does this solution go? Remember that 3! didn't invoke the base case directly but only recursively. Recursion implies remembering previous states of functions. Figure 7.5 illustrates the situation.

Each function call preserves its own copy of its local variables and parameters—in this case, the parameter n. The outermost call, factorial(3), preserves its copy of n with the value 3 (shown in

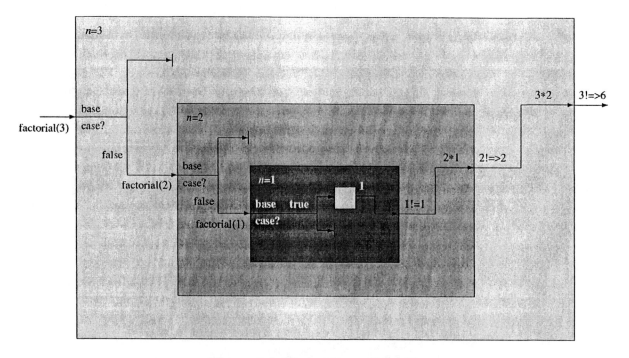

Figure 7.6: Recursive call for 3!

the upper left corner). The first recursive call has a copy of *n* with the value 2 and the second, innermost recursive call has a copy of n with the value 1. The innermost *factorial*() "bottoms out" (the grey box), returning 1. Because the first recursive call has kept the value of *n* as 2, it is able to now able to compute the product *factorial*(2-1)*2, which is 2. Similarly, when *factorial*(2) returns 2, its caller, *factorial*(3), with *n* as 3, can now compute *factorial*(3-1)*3, which is 7.

Earlier programming languages, such as FORTRAN and COBOL, didn't support this ability to keep track of subprogram states. Instead, their compilers would pre-allocate the space for local variables and parameters. Java and other modern programming languages arrange for the dynamic (run-time) allocation of an **activation record** or **frame**, storing the state of the machine before each subprogram call. Such a record must copy the content of processor registers, parameters and local variables, and the instruction pointer, so that processing can continue where it left off when the subprogram finishes. Bear in mind, though, that allocation of a frame for each function call takes time and space. Indeed, there is a practical upper limit for any recursive function—the amount of memory available to a program on a particular machine.

Exercise 7.26: Trace each step of *factorial*(4). Add a line to your table for each level of recursion, starting with 0, then 1 with the first recursive call, etc.

Let's look at a slightly more complicated example which illustrates the usefulness of recursion as a problem solving technique. The "Towers of Hanoi" problem that has its origin in an ancient oriental legend. Deep in a cave under Benares, India, a version of the story goes, are three large pillars of diamond and 64 disks of gold of decreasing size, which fit over the pillars. Once upon a time—long, long ago—the disks were all arranged in order on a single one of the pillars, with the largest disk on the bottom and the smallest disk on top. Each day, one of the attendants moves one of the disks from one of the pillars to another, subject to the condition that no disk can be put on top of a smaller one. The goal is to transfer all the disks from the first pillar to one of the others—at which point the entire universe and everything in it will vanish into nothingness!

Not to worry, it will take a very long time to finish this task! But simpler versions—with fewer disks—are solvable in shorter time. Figure 7.7 shows the simplest case (a basic principle of recursive problem solving is to reduce a complex problem to a simple one). The solution for moving just one disk from peg A to peg B is trivial: just do it.

The next most simplest problem is set up in figure 7.8 on the left: *two* disks. After the initial setup, there are just three steps, shown progressively in figure 7.8 from left to right:

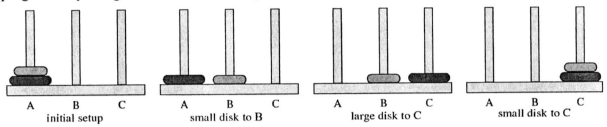

Figure 7.8: Two-disk Towers of Hanoi problem

First, move the top disk, the smaller one, from peg A to peg B (to get it out of the way). Second, move the remaining, larger disk from peg A to peg C (to start the new pile). Third, move the smaller disk from peg B to peg C (solving the problem).

The three-disk version of this problem, set up on the left side of figure 7.9 sets up, is harder.

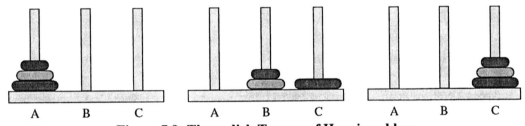

Figure 7.9: Three-disk Towers of Hanoi problem

Thinking analogically, we recall the blocks world problem, shown in figure 2.11 (p. 41). These two problems are nearly *isomorphic* (which means, literally, "of the same shape"): three blocks there, three disks here. (They are not quite isomorphic, because of the constraint imposed by disk size.) The same danger of *interacting dependencies* can occur if one attempts to "hack" a solution together. For example, in the two-disk problem, it would accomplish nothing to put the smaller disk back on top of the larger one; nor would it be productive to start by putting the smaller disk on peg C. (Do you see why?) The latter observation shows that the first step matters: putting the smaller disk on peg C would get in the way of getting the *larger* disk on peg C. It's important to start out using peg B as a temporary storage for the smaller disk(s). This knowledge guides our solution of the three- (or more) disks problem. In fact, the solution to the two-disk problem will be part of our solution to the three (or more) disk problem.

Let's break the three-disk problem down into major subgoals. The first subgoal is to move the *largest* disk to goal peg C, as shown in the middle of figure 7.9. To get there, first move the smaller disks to storage peg B, using the two-disk procedure, only this time, we'll use peg C as the storage peg for the smallest disk. Second, let's move the largest disk to goal peg B, also shown in the middle of figure 7.9. Finally, move the smaller disks from B to C, again using the two-disk procedure, only this time using peg A as temporary storage. Voila!

Perhaps you can see a pattern emerging. The three steps to solving the three-disk problem are the same as the three steps as for the two-disk problem, with one difference: *using the two step solution* to help solve subproblems along the way. We just had to generalize the two step solution to use *any* empty peg as temporary storage.

The solution is similar for the four disk problem.

1) move the top three disks to peg B (using the three-disk solution)
2) move the largest disk to peg C
3) move the top three disks to peg C (using the three-disk solution)

The three-disk solution, in turn, uses the two-disk solution. Do you see some recursion here?

Figure 7.10 shows (spectacularly short and elegant) pseudocode which solves the Towers of Hanoi problem, for any number of disks, followed by a trace of the three-disk solution.

```
Hanoi(nDisks, fromPeg, toPeg)                      //1
if nDisks > 0                                       //2    recursive case?
    xtraPeg = 6 - fromPeg - toPeg                   //3    compute xtraPeg
    Hanoi(nDisks-1, fromPeg, xtraPeg)               //4    recursive call, to storage peg
    write "move disk  from " fromPeg " to " toPeg   //5    trace progress
    Hanoi(nDisks-1, xtraPeg, toPeg)                 //6    recursive call, to goal peg
                    Enter number of disks to move: 3
                    Move disk from 1 to 3
                    Move disk from 1 to 2
                    Move disk from 3 to 2
                    Move disk from 1 to 3
                    Move disk from 2 to 1
                    Move disk from 2 to 3
                    Move disk from 1 to 3
```

Figure 7.10: The Towers of Hanoi program and sample run

When developing the pseudocode we found it more convenient to number the pegs rather than lettering them. Instead of hard-coding the pegs as constants, it treats the start and goal pegs as *parameters*. Then it computes the "extra" peg inside the function, by observing that the sum of the three peg numbers is 6 (1+2+3=6). Now the function can vary which peg it uses as temporary storage for each recursive sub-problem. While solving the three-disk problem, the value of *xtraPeg* starts out as 2, but becomes 3 and 1 for recursive two-disk problems. The values of *fromPeg* and *toPeg* also vary, correspondingly. This use of parameters (rather than global variables) is crucial to recursive problem solving, and indeed to the power of functions in general.

Switching from lettering the pegs to numbering the pegs illustrates an important principle about data structures. The right choice of data structure can facilitate the solution of a problem. Using letters for the pegs makes the computation of the extra peg more complicated. Numeric parameters avoid a tangle of if statements (if (fromPeg=='A' and toPeg=='B'), etc.).

A non-recursive solution for the Towers of Hanoi problem is quite hard. We admit that we don't know how to solve it. But why bother? The recursive solution is so easy!

As a third example of recursion, consider how the Knobby's World translator parses program source code. In chapter 3, we described the syntax for Knobby instructions as syntax diagrams (see figure 3.4) and also introduced an equivalent textual notation, Backus-Naur Form (BNF). In BNF, boldface terms are "terminal symbols," which correspond to tokens in the language, while italicized words correspond to non-terminal symbols. Figure 7.11 gives the rules for Knobby instructions using extended BNF notation, in which * (Kleene star) means zero or more, † (Kleene cross) means one or more, | denotes alternatives and parentheses group symbols. This amazingly compact set of rules specifies all possible syntactically correct Knobby programs. The first rule shows that a *knobby-program* consists of at least one *define-instruction*. The second rule shows *define-instruction* consists of the keyword **define** followed by an *instruction-name*, etc.

These rules include some recursion. Pause for a moment and see whether you find the recursion in the rules below. Don't read past the rules yet....

knobby-program ==> *define-instruction*†
define-instruction ==> **define** *instruction-name* **as** *compound-instruction*
compound-instruction ==> { *instruction** }
instruction ==> *primitive* | *compound-instruction* | *instruction-name*
primitive ==> *move* | *left* | *read* | *write* | *b1=b2* | *b2=b1*
instruction-name ==> (*letter* | *digit*)*
digit ==> **0 | 1 | 2 | 3 | 4 | 5 | 6 | 7 | 8 | 9**
letter ==> **a | b | ... | z | A | B | ... | Z**
Figure 7.11: Extended BNF rules for Knobby's World

Did you find the recursion? Here it is: we defined *compound-instruction* using *instruction*, then we defined *instruction* using *compound-instruction*. Of course the corresponding syntax diagrams in figure 3.4 are also recursive, but you probably did not notice (unless you did exercise 3.17). You were already thinking recursively!

We could have used recursion in other rules. Here's how we could rewrite the first rule:
knobby-program ==> *define-instruction knobby-program*
knobby-program ==>
These first rule is recursive: a *knobby-program* consists of a *define-instruction* followed by another *knobby-program* (which consists of another *define-instruction* and so forth). It thus gives the effect of † by looping back on its own definition. The second rule says that a *knobby-program* can also consist of nothing; this is the base case, exiting the loop These rules involve **tail-recursion**, occurring at the end or tail of the rule. With tail-recursion, there is really no need to remember anything, hence it is equivalent to iteration († or *). Recursion that appears in the middle of a rule, on the other hand, requires that we keep track of where we left off. For example, the rule for *compound-instruction* involves a center-recursion, since *instruction* is surrounded by curly braces. Recursive definitions are necessary to describe **nested** programming language structures.

Given these rules, it is rather easy to generate the code to parse a program, to determine whether the program satisfies the rules. Here's how:

1. The left-hand side of each rule is the name of a function.
2. Start by calling the function for the top level symbol, in this case, *knobby-program*.
3. The function scans (matches) the current token.
4. Symbols separated by "|" are alternative possibilities for matching the current token.
5. If the current symbol matches a terminal token, get the next token and get the next one, else diagnose error, unless the current symbol is repeating.
6. If the current symbol is a non-terminal symbol, call the corresponding function.
7. For a symbol with an † or *, repeat steps 3 through 6.
8. If none of the rules apply to the current token diagnose a syntax error.

Here's pseudo-code for a few of the functions corresponding to BNF rules for Knobby's World:

knobby-program()
        call *define-instruction* once, then repeatedly if possible
        if not at end of file, diagnose error: "Unknown token at end of program."
define-instruction()
        match("define")   //scan for token: if match fails, it diagnoses an error
        instruction_name()
        match("as")
        compound-instruction()
compound-instruction()
        match(" { ")
        while token is appropriate to *instruction* call *instruction*()
        match(" } ")

As you can see, the pseudocode consists of functions that call other functions or match. As the comment notes, the match function tries to match up the current token, produced by scanning the source file, with its parameter, the expected token. This approach to analyzing a language is called a **recursive descent parser**, because it starts at the top-most rule and descends through other rules until it has either successfully matched the tokens or detected an error in the form of the program. And of course, some of the functions may be recursive.

Exercise 7.27: Trace each step in the sample run shown in figure 7.10, explaining how it observes the constraints on the problem yet moves toward the ultimate solution. (In addition to line numbers and parameters, your trace should keep track of the level of recursion, starting at 0.)

Exercise 7.28: Predict the first move of the Hanoi program for a four-disk problem and explain why. Then confirm it by compiling and running `Hanoi.java`. Explain each of the program's first five moves, how it observes the constraints on the problem yet moves toward the ultimate solution.

Exercise 7.29: How many moves does the 2-disk problem require? The 3-disk problem? The *n*-disk problem? Hint: if you cannot figure it out by studying the algorithm, try running `Hanoi.java` a few times. At one move a second, roughly how many years will it take for the 64-disk problem?

Exercise 7.30: Modify `Hanoi.java` so that it shows a picture of each move rather than text.

Exercise 7.31: Write pseudocode for a recursive function that performs multiplication using the addition (+) operator. For example, 3*3 == 3+3+3.

Exercise 7.32: Write pseudocode for a recursive function that computes the Fibonacci series up to some number. The Fibonacci series is 0,1,1,2,3,5,8,13,21, ..., where each Fibonacci number (after the first two) is the sum of the previous two. (This series describes a spiral form that occurs often in nature.) Optional: implement and test this function in a program.

Exercise 7.33: Write pseudocode for a recursive function that finds the prime factorization of a positive integer. For example, the prime factors of 12, in descending order, are 4, 3, 2 and 1.

Exercise 7.34: Write pseudocode for a recursive function that takes a String and reverses it. For example, "star" backwards is "rats". Optional: implement and test this function in a program.

Exercise 7.35: Write pseudocode for the recursive descent parser's function *instruction*().

Exercise 7.36: Write pseudocode for the recursive descent parser's function *instruction-name*().

Exercise 7.37: Can the rule for *instruction-name* be rewritten without a Kleene star? If so, how? Then rewrite the rule. Hint: reread the discussion of tail recursion.

Exercise 7.38 (*explore*): On the web, find another example of recursive algorithm and describe it.

7.3 Complexity of algorithms and Big "O" analysis

Now that we studied a few interesting algorithms, we can introduce a bit of **computational complexity theory**, the study of the potential size of algorithms. We can measure the complexity of an algorithm in terms of its memory requirements or processing time, where the latter is the numbers of "steps" required to perform it. More precisely, since the number of steps in the computation of a function generally depends on the size of the input, we try to express the relation between the algorithm's input-size and its computation-size by some function. We might find, for example, that the computation-size of one algorithm might grow as some **polynomial** function of the input size—say $5N^2+3N+2$, where N is the input size—while the computation-size of another might involve some **exponential** function of the input size—say 3^N. Since, for large inputs, the value of an exponential function is much greater than that of a polynomial function, this would show that the second algorithm is more complex (and probably less desirable) than the first.

Exercise 7.39: For the polynomial and exponential examples given above, for small values of N (say, N=3), which algorithm is more efficient? At what size does the other algorithm become more efficient? Why do we judge comparative efficiency by *large* values, rather than by *small* values?

When we compare two algorithms, especially two algorithms for accomplishing the same task, we can find that in some sense, one is more efficient than another. One algorithm may require less storage space or less computing time than another, and so will be more efficient. Clearly, efficiency is desirable, but it is not the only criterion by which a program may be judged. In the early days of computing, space was scarce and computers were slow, as compared to today. Over the years a PC's RAM capacity has increased from 64K (the top of the Apple II+ line) to 640K (the first IBM machines) to well over a gigabyte in today's machines—an increase by a factor of 10000, or five orders of magnitude. Meanwhile, processor speeds have jumped from megahertz to gigahertz.

These changes have had profound effects on the "aesthetics" of programming—the standards of what makes a "good" program. "Once upon a time," economy in the usage of space and time was paramount. Clever programmers went to all sorts of lengths to minimize these factors, jumping here and there throughout the program to make the maximum use of each individual instruction, doubling data structures in the same memory. Unfortunately, these kinds of program are also maximally difficult to debug or update. (Remember our discussion in the chapter on software engineering about how maintenance dominates the costs of real world software.) Especially in today's programs written by teams of programmers and running thousands or millions of lines, efficiency in space and time may not be as important as clarity and reusability.

Nevertheless, all other things being equal, algorithm efficiency does matter. Nested loops multiply the time needed for a computation. For example, if an outer loop performed 10 times contains an inner loop performed 20 times, then as the entire program runs, the inner loop will be executed 200 times. Now consider the case in which the outer loop is performed 1000 times and the inner loop 2000 (neither an overly large number for some sorts of computations)—2 *million* executions of the inner loop! So some evaluation of execution time is worth considering. But how does one evaluate an algorithm's execution time (since that will generally depend on the input data)? Two measures are often used—a **worst-case** scenario (in which the given state of the data is as far as possible from the goal state) and an **average-case** scenario (in which the distance of the given state from the goal state "randomly" varies). (Of course, there is also a **best-case** scenario, in which the given state is already the goal state, but this is usually of little help, since that is rarely the case!)

7.3.1 Searching efficiency

In searching, one specifies a *key* value, then compares this value with values in an array. Depending on the purpose of the search, the process may terminate as soon as a *hit* occurs (i.e., the array element value matches the target), but it may also search the entire array—an **exhaustive** search. If the array is not already arranged in any particular fashion, the only effective search strategy is a **linear** or **sequential** search. Compare the key value with the first element in the array, then if necessary with the second element, then if necessary with the third, ..., etc. The *worst case* is when the key is not in the array. If the size of the array is N, the worst case is N comparisons. To determine the *overall average performance*, we would need to know: (1) how often on the average the key is present and how often it is absent, (2) the average performance when the key is present, and (3) the average performance when the key is absent. The first piece of information is often unavailable, so we often can't say what the overall average behavior will be, other than to say it lies between the two individual average performances. For the second piece of information, assuming random positioning of the key in the array, the average position will be in the middle of the array, so this will involve approximately N/2 comparisons. For the third piece, note that the average performance when the key is absent is just the worst case—i.e., N. So the overall average performance lies between N/2 and N, and depends on how often the key is or is not present in the array. We say that such an algorithm takes **linear** time, i.e., time proportional to the size of the array.

Exercise 7.40: Suppose we know that on the average a key is in an array *half* the time. What is the overall average performance? What if the key is in the array only *one-tenth* of the time?

Pre-arranging array elements can improve search efficiency. One approach is **hashing**: given an element value, such as a string, compute an index at which to store it. Then one can reliably expect to find this element by recomputing its subscript the same way. One possible hash function might be to multiply the ASCII values of all the letters in a string, say for "Bob" it's 2*15*2 = 60 and for "Glenn" 7*12*5*14*14 = it's 82320. Since these values may be larger than the size of the array (say it's 50), we can take the remainder after dividing by the size of the array, 10 for "Bob" and 20 for "Glenn". Recomputing this hash function will always produce the same subscript. This can be very efficient. In the best case, the time to find an element is just one computation—**constant** time. However, hashing becomes more complicated if multiple values happen to compute the same index. In this case, we need a **collision resolution** scheme. One possibility is to store multiple values in *neighboring* slots. Another is to add values to a *chain* of values hashing into a particular slot. After computing a hash function, we'd have to look for the value we want among the neighbors or in the chain, one at a time. In the worst case, all the values might just happen to compute the same index, which would reduce a hashing scheme to *linear* time. In practice, the efficiency of hashing depends on the effectiveness of the hash function at distributing values at distinct subscripts.

Exercise 7.41: In the worst case, is hashing worse, the same, or still better than linear search? Why? How can the possibility of the worst case be minimized?

Exercise 7.42 (*explore*): On the web, find an application of hashing and explain why it was used.

Probably the most common way to pre-arrange the elements of an array is by *sorting* it. For a sorted array, if the key occurs in the array, the average-case behavior of a linear search is the same as for the unsorted array—that is, N/2—since in general the correct position of the key may vary just as randomly as in an unsorted array. When the key is *not* in the array, however, the performance of a sorted array is better. To find that a key is *not* in the array, we need search only until we have *passed* the correct position—that is, found a stored value *beyond* the key value. Since the correct position is on the average still N/2 when the key is absent, the average behavior is again N/2. Since the average behavior is the same in the two cases, the overall average behavior is also N/2—in general, better than for the unsorted array, which we saw earlier was N.

This average-case improvement is minimal compared to the efficiency of a binary search, which exploits a sorted arrangement. As with unaided linear search, the worst case is when the key is not in the array. In this case, there are roughly $\log_2(N)$ repetitions and in each repetition there are *two* comparisons (key==value and key < value), so the number of comparisons needed is roughly $2*\log_2(N)$. If the key is found, on the average it will be halfway through the search, roughly $2\log_2(N/2)= 2\log_2(N)-4$ comparisons. As figure 7.12 demonstrates, for large values of N, $\log_2(N)$ is much less than N (or even N/2). So binary search is much better than linear search for large arrays.

N	$\log_2(N)$
1	0
10	3
100	7
1,000	10
10,000	13
100,000	17
1,000,000	20

Figure 7.12: Magnitudes (rounded to the nearest integer)

Exercise 7.43: Why does repeatedly dividing the array in half require roughly $\log_2(N)$ comparisons to ensure that a key is not in the array? Hint: Any N which is a power of 2 is equal to the product $2*2*..*2$ (where there are $\log_2(N)$ factors).

Exercise 7.44: Under what conditions should we sort an array before searching it?

7.3.2 Sorting efficiency

A variety of sorting algorithms are available for use with arrays—*selection sort, bubble sort, insertion sort, quick sort*, etc. All involve repeated comparisons and swaps. Thus we can get some kind of efficiency measure by counting the numbers of comparisons and swaps performed in sorting an array of size N. The **bubble sort** is relatively easy to understand. It repeatedly passes through an array and swaps adjacent elements that are out of order. After many swaps, an unsorted element will appear to "bubble up" to its correct position—hence the name. The sort terminates when a pass completes without a swap. Here is a pseudocode outline of this algorithm:

```
Bubble Sort                                      //1
initialize onceMoreFlag on                       //2  first pass is needed
LOOP while onceMoreFlag is on                     //3
   toggle onceMoreFlag off                        //4  assume no more passes
   initialize i to 0                              //5  start at beginning of sortArray
   LOOP while i < N-1                             //6  pass through sortArray
      if sortArray[i] > sortArray[i+1]            //7  elements out of order?
         swap sortArray[index] and sortArray[index+1]   //8 swap two elements
         toggle onceMoreFlag on                   //9  not sorted yet, need another pass
      increment index                             //10
```

The key to analyzing this algorithm is the loops. There is an inner loop nested within an outer loop. For the inner loop, if N is the size of the array, there are N-1 comparisons in each pass. What about the outer loop? The worst case occurs when the elements of the array happen to be in reverse order, so we have to make N passes through the outer loop. (The first pass through the array has to move the element in the first position all the way to the last position (N-1 swaps); the second pass moves the new first element up to the next to last position (N-2 swaps); etc. Each pass moves the element currently in the first position all the way to its proper position. Thus in the worst case, there are N-1 passes in which elements bubble through the array, followed by one final pass in which no swaps are made, for a total of N passes through the array.) Each pass involves N-1 repetitions of the inner comparison/swap loop, for a total cost of N*N-1 or roughly N^2 steps. Figure 7.13 shows some worst cost values for different values of N.

N	worst case
1	3
10	492
100	49,902
1,000	4,999,002
10,000	499,990,002
100,000	49,999,900,002
1,000,000	4,999,999,000,002

Figure 7.13: Bubble sort costs

Exercise 7.45: How much of a difference do the last two terms (N+2) make in the costs shown in the table? Do you think we could just ignore them? From this exercise, what generalization can you make about measuring the efficiency of algorithms?

Exercise 7.46: Write a bubble sort program to sort a 100-element array. Test it on best- and worst-case scenarios. Are these arrays large enough for you to observe a difference in run-time? If not, experiment a bit with array size.

So the bubble sort, though perhaps the easiest to understand, is perhaps the least efficient, and should be avoided for large arrays or sequences. Let's analyze another algorithm—the selection sort, described in section 7.1.2. The main idea of this algorithm is to *select* or find the element which properly belongs in the first position (say, because it's the smallest value in the array), and then swap it with whatever element happens to be already there. The same process then repeats for the second position, the third position, ..., and finally the next-to-last position, whereupon the array is in order. So in the selection sort, there are always N-1 passes, in each of which there is a selection and a single swap afterward—thus N-1 swaps.

Like the bubble sort, the selection sort involves a nested loop. And like the bubble sort, the inner loop requires N-1 comparison/swap steps, and the outer loop requires up to N iterations, in the worst case. So the selection sort is also an N^2 algorithm. The details of these two algorithms are slightly different. Figure 7.14 tabulates all the approximate behavior of the selection in the worst, best and average cases. Compare these with the results for the bubble sort above.

N	worst case	best case	average case
1	2	2	2
10	200	150	175
100	20,000	15,000	17,500
1,000	2,000,000	1,500,000	1,750,000
10,000	200,000,000	150,000,000	175,000,000
100,000	20,000,000,000	15,000,000,000	17,500,000,000
1,000,000	2,000,000,000,000	1,500,000,000,000	1,750,000,000,000

Figure 7.14: Selection sort costs

Exercise 7.47: Try out the selection sort program, `selsort.java`, to sort a 100-element array. Test it for best and worst-case scenarios. Are these arrays large enough for you to observe a difference in run time? If not, experiment a bit more with array size.

Exercise 7.48: As the comment notes, the algorithm given sorts elements in ascending order, that is, from the smallest to largest element values. Modify the algorithm so that it sorts in descending order instead. Is there any change in the cost of the algorithm?

A third sorting algorithm is the **insertion sort**. In a sense, an insertion sort is the exact opposite of a selection sort. A selection sort repeatedly considers a *position* in the array; the inner loop determines which *element* properly belongs there. An insertion sort repeatedly considers an *element* in the array; the inner loop then moves that element to its proper *position*. A pseudocode outline is as follows:

```
Insertion Sort                          //1
set firstUnsorted to 1                  //2   Start by comparing 0th and 1st elements
LOOP while firstUnsorted < N            //3   Outer loop: until all elements sorted
    set i to firstUnsorted              //4
    LOOP while i > 0 and sortArray[i] < sortArray[i-1]  //5 Inner loop: swap elements
        swap sortArray[i] and sortArray[i-1]  //6
        decrement index                 //7
    increment firstUnsorted             //8
```

Exercise 7.49: Based on the structure of the algorithm, what is its approximate cost of the insertion sort? (Hint: look at the loops.)

Exercise 7.50: The inner loop could be written with a simple repeat condition (index > 0) and a conditional swap statement as the first step in the loop body. What would the outline look like in such a case? However, in some cases, the algorithm is more efficient as it is written. How and why? Hint: when does the inner loop terminate in the algorithm as originally written? as rewritten?

Exercise 7.51: However, if the code for the algorithm as outlined is not written carefully, the compound continuation condition for the inner loop poses a danger. What is it? How can it be avoided? (Hint: think about precedence of operators.)

Exercise 7.52: Write an insertion sort program to sort a 100-element array. Test it for best and worst case scenarios. Are these arrays large enough for you to observe a difference in run time? If not, experiment a bit with array size.

Exercise 7.53: We can improve the insertion sort algorithm by reducing the number of swaps.

Instead of moving the key element into place by repeatedly exchanging adjacent elements, we can: (1) copy the key element into a temporary holder, (2) repeatedly compare it with its predecessors in the array, moving each of them up one position, until the proper position for the key element is found, and (3) copy the holder value into the proper position. Write a pseudocode outline for this version of the insertion sort.

A casual glance at the big numbers in the three preceding figures makes it pretty obvious that for large arrays, in all but the near-best cases, these functions are unacceptably slow. So computer scientists have set out in search of the holy grail of a sort algorithm that doesn't grow polynomially (N^2 or worse). The **Quicksort** is one of several algorithms with substantially lower costs, in terms of computation (though its cost is higher in terms of memory requirements). Quicksort initially divides an array into two partitions or segments. It then arranges for all the elements in the first segment to precede all the elements in the second segment. The array is now "semi-ordered" in the following sense: those elements that actually precede the search key are exactly those which *should* precede it in the desired ordering, and those elements which follow the key are exactly those which *should* follow it in the desired ordering. However, the two segments themselves—the elements preceding the key and those following the key—are not yet ordered. The same process is then recursively repeated on each of the segments, until the segments are unit size, at which point the entire array has been sorted.

Below is the pseudocode outline of Quicksort, using the last element of any segment of the array as its key. Quicksort is a **recursive** procedure: near the bottom of the algorithm, it calls itself again, in two different ways. Each call receives segment bounds (bottom and top) as parameters.

```
Quicksort(bottom,top)                                      //1  initial call will be with 0 and N-1
if bottom < top                                            //2  segment has at least two elements
    set pivot to top                                       //3
    set bottomIndex to bottom                              //4
    set topIndex to top-1                                  //5
    LOOP while bottomIndex < topIndex                      //6  outer loop: more to sort
        LOOP while sortArray[bottomIndex] < sortArray[pivot]    //7  lower inner loop
            increment bottomIndex                               //8
        LOOP while sortArray[pivot] < sortArray[topindex]       //9  upper inner loop
            decrement topIndex                                  //10
        if bottomIndex < topIndex                          //11 elements need swapping
            swap sortArray[bottomIndex] and sortArray[topIndex]  //12
    //bottomIndex now is >= topIndex, so no more internal swapping needed
    swap sortArray[pivot] and sortArray[topIndex]  //13
    //the key element now precedes everything that should come after it
    Quicksort(bottom,bottomIndex)                  //14
    //next level lower call--sorts segment preceding the key
    Quicksort(bottomIndex+1,top)                   //15
    //next-level upper call--sorts segment following the key
```

Figure 7.15 shows the progress of Quicksort for a sample 10-element array (the same as figure 7.10). (In the process, the last element in any segment of the array is chosen to be its key element.)

a)	(59	<u>84</u>	74	55	44	92	69	75	<u>68</u>	**75)**
b)	(59	68	74	55	44	<u>92</u>	<u>69</u>	75	84	**75)**
c)	(59	68	74	55	44	69	*92*	75	84	**75)**
d)	(59	68	74	55	44	69	**75**	75	84	*92)*
e)	(59	68	74	55	44	69)	75	(75	84	92)
f)	(59	68	<u>74</u>	55	<u>44</u>	**69)**	75	75	84	92
g)	(59	68	44	55	*74*	**69)**	75	75	84	92
h)	(59	68	44	55	**69**	*74)*	75	75	84	92
i)	(59	68	44	55)	**69**	(74)	75	75	84	92
j)	(<u>59</u>	68	<u>44</u>	**55)**	69	74	75	75	84	92
k)	(44	*68*	59	**55)** ·	69	74	75	75	84	92
l)	(44	**55**	59	*68)*	69	74	75	75	84	92
m)	(44)	55	(59	68)	69	74	75	75	84	92
n)	44	55	59	68	69	74	75	75	84	92

Figure 7.15: Stages in a run of Quicksort

Line a) gives the original unsorted array. The entire array, between parentheses, is the segment for the first call. The key element, shown in **boldface**, is therefore the last element in the array (in this case, a far from optimal choice). The <u>underlined</u> elements are the ones to be swapped. Line b) shows the result of the first swap and underlines the next pair to swap. Line c) shows the result of that swap; there are no other swaps to be made, so the key and the *italicized* element, which will become the first element of the upper segment are swapped, giving line d). The first pass is complete; the algorithm now divides the array into the segment preceding the key and the segment following it. (Of course, *we* can see that the upper segment is arranged—the computer cannot, so it will continue processing the segment's elements until all the segments are single-element.) In the lower segment, line f) shows the selection of a new key and the first two elements to be swapped. Line g) shows the result of that swap; no further swaps are necessary. Therefore, the key swaps with the first element to follow it, resulting in line h). Two new segments are now defined in line i). The upper one consists only of a single element, so it is sorted; in the lower segment, the key is chosen and the first two swap-elements are marked, as in line j). The result is shown in line k), and the key and the element to follow it are ready for their swap. In line l), that swap has been made, and in line m), the new segments laid out. One segment consists of a single element, and the other segment is now arranged, so the process is essentially complete, as in line n).

It should be clear that the efficiency of Quicksort depends on the relative sizes of the two segments, so a particular method of choosing the key may produce a good sort or a bad one, depending on how central to the array's elements the chosen key is. Assuming the elements of the array initially occur in reverse order does not ensure a worst-case scenario, as various choice methods will produce better or worse choices of the key. For simplicity in the above example, we assumed the final element of the array to be chosen as key, and in the reverse-order case, this is indeed a bad choice. A "middle" element choice would be optimal choice for that ordering. But given the array we began with above, choosing the middle element would have been worse.

Exercise 7.54: What lines in the Quicksort algorithm are recursive calls, and what are they for?
Exercise 7.55: Trace Quicksort, step by step, on an unsorted array of five elements.
Exercise 7.56 (*explore*): On the web, find yet another sort algorithm and describe how it works.

From the algorithm outline, we figure that the computation cost at any level is either just 1 (if the array segment is a single element) or else 1+3+O+3+L+U, where O is the cost of the outer loop, L is the cost of recursively calling Quicksort for the lower part of the array, and U is the cost of recursively calling Quicksort for the upper part of the array. The cost of each pass of the outer loop is 1+LL+UL+C, where LL is the cost of the lower inner loop, UL is the cost of the upper inner loop, and C is the cost of the conditional—either 1 or 4. If we assume reverse ordering, the lower inner loop does not execute; since the key is the lowest element, nothing is less than the key, so LL is only 1. On the other hand, the upper inner loop executes N-2 times until topIndex reaches 0, with a cost of 2 for each execution, so UL = 2*(N-2)+1 = 2N-3. Since bottomIndex now equals topIndex, there's no need to swap, so the cost of C is just 1. The total cost of the outer loop is then O = 1+1+(2N-3)+1 = 2N. Since bottomIndex hasn't changed (i.e., still equals bottom), the lower call terminates with a cost of 1. This gives us 1+3+2N+3+1+U = 2N+8+U as the total cost. Since topIndex has decreased to 0, the upper call gets parameters 1 and top. Since it processes N-1 elements in essentially the same way, just in the reverse direction, by the same sort of argument, its cost will be 2(N-1)+8+L'. And the cost of L' will be 2(N-2)+8+U'', and so on. There will be only N calls, the last with cost 2(1)+10. Thus, the total cost is $2*[(N)+(N-1)+...+1]+N*8 = (N+1)*N+8N = N*(N+9) = N^2+9N$.

On the other hand, had our choices for the pivot position continually divided each segment into halves, we would have only approximately $\log_2(N)$ levels, with $2^{(k-1)}$ segments on the kth level, and a cost for each segment about $1/2^{(k-1)}$ of that for any of our levels. Although the sum of the segment costs on the kth level is roughly that of our single segment on the kth level, there are only roughly $\log_2(N)$ levels. Adding these, the total cost for the approximately $\log_2(N)$ levels will be roughly $(N+9)*\log_2(N) = N*\log_2(N)+9*\log_2(N)$. Figure 7.16 quantifies the results, which you can see compares favorably with the results shown for the other three sort algorithms. (That's why Quicksort is part of many standardized libraries.) On the other hand, Quicksort does have a memory cost. Every time it makes a recursive call to itself, the program must keep track of the call, so it can continue where it left off. For very large arrays, this memory cost could be prohibitive. This is an example of a **cost tradeoff** between computation time and space.

N	worst case	best case
1	1	0
10	190	63
100	10,900	724
1,000	1,009,000	10,055
10,000	100,090,000	132,997
100,000	10,000,900,000	1,661,114
1,000,000	1,000,009,000,000	19,931,748

Figure 7.16: Quicksort costs

7.3.3 Efficiency of the Towers of Hanoi Solution

Exercise 7.29 effectively asks you to analyze the efficiency of the Towers of Hanoi algorithm, shown in figure 7.10. Here we'll do that analysis in detail. The algorithm moves n disks from Peg p to Peg m, so the cost of this algorithm is moving n disks, C(n). In the trivial case, if n is 0, the cost is 1, for the comparison, n>0. For n>0, the cost is 1 (for the same comparison) + 1 (for computing xtraPeg) + C(n-1) (for the first recursive call) + 1 (for writing out the move) + C(n-1) (for the second recursive call). Thus, for n>0, C(n)=3+2C(n-1). This **recurrence relation** is easy to solve (although many recurrence relations are dogs). As noted above, C(0)=1. C(1)=3+2C(0)=5. C(2)=3+2C(1)=5. C(3)=3+2C(2)=13. C(4)=3+2C(3)=29. Do you see a pattern emerging? It looks like $C(n)=2^{n+1} - 3$. Suppose that we have the formula correct and verify it for C(n+1). $C(n+1)=3+2C(n)=3+2(2^{n+1} - 3)=3 + 2^{n+2} - 6)=2^{n+2} - 3$. Yes, that's correct. So, the solution of the Towers of Hanoi is of exponential complexity. (Our analysis uses an **inductive argument**—finding a pattern and verifying it.)

Exercise 7.57: What feature of the formula tells us the Hanoi algorithm is exponential?

7.3.4 Here Comes the "Big O"!

Since all these numbers may be a bit dazzling, it would be useful to develop a framework for comparison—something more than the bare numbers themselves. To get the big picture, there's a system of comparison called **order of magnitude** (or simply **order-of**) analysis.[1] The basic idea at work is that in comparing really large numbers, small differences just don't count. For example, suppose one algorithm may take 10 seconds longer than another in some computation. If the time of the faster algorithm is 0.5 seconds, say, the difference is substantial (20 times the time of the faster algorithm), but if it is 5 minutes, the difference may be negligible (only 1/30 the time of the faster algorithm). In order to make these comparisons, we need some systematic measure of the relation between the size of a task and the time that the algorithm takes to accomplish the task. As a task grows larger, the time it takes almost always grows larger. The question is...how fast does this happen? If we get a measure of this, then we can compare these "growth rates" of several algorithms and see how they match up.

There are three kinds of comparisons: additive constant differences, constant factor differences and order of magnitude differences. Two algorithms display an **additive factor** difference if the difference between the two is *independent* of the size of the task (i.e., the measure of the one is always roughly equal to the measure of the other plus some fixed number). So, for example, one algorithm might perform the task in, say, 200 fewer steps or milliseconds than another regardless of the size of the task. And, as we've noted, for small tasks, this might be important, but it will be dwarfed as the size of the task grows to perhaps 10,000 or 100,000 data elements. A **constant factor** difference occurs when the measure of one algorithm is always roughly a fixed multiple of the measure of the other. This is a much more substantial difference—that one algorithm takes twice as long as another may be very important, even for large tasks. But even more striking is an **order of magnitude** (or just "order of") difference. For example, suppose the measure of one algorithm is roughly proportional to the task size, but the measure of the other is roughly proportional to the *square* of the task size. Then the difference itself grows substantially—the difference between a multiple of N and a multiple of N^2 for large values of N approximates N^2 itself. The second algorithm is said to be an *order of magnitude* larger than the first. Generally speaking, the key decimal orders of magnitude are the following: k (constant), log(N), N (linear), N*log(N), N^2 and N^3 (polynomial) and 10^N (exponential). Decimal values are given below for simplicity—to convert to binary orders of magnitude, remember that $\log_2(N)$ is simply a fixed multiple of log(N)—i.e., $\log_2(N) = \log_2(10)*\log(N)$—and $2^N = 10^{\log(2)*N}$.

---

[1] The term 'order of magnitude' also has another meaning—the number of digits in a numeral. The two are related, but not the same thing.

log(N)	N	N*log(N)	N²	N³	10^N
0	1	0	1	1	10
1	10	10	100	1,000	10,000,000,000
2	100	200	10,000	1,000,000	***
3	1,000	3,000	1,000,000	1,000,000,000	****
4	10,000	40,000	100,000,000	1,000,000,000,000	****
5	100,000	500,000	10,000,000,000	1,000,000,000,000,000	****

*** Much too large to show.

**** Don't even try to think about it!

Figure 7.17: Some decimal orders of magnitude

Exercise 7.58: For example, suppose one algorithm's measure is 6N and a second algorithm's measure is $2N^2$. Compute the two values for powers of 10 up to 1,000,000. Compare the size of the two numbers with the size of their difference. What happens, and what is its significance?

As a short-hand for describing the performance of particular algorithms, computer scientists use what has come to be known as **Big-O notation**. An algorithm is **O(f(N))**, where **f(N)** is the function which expresses the algorithm's order in terms of **N**, the size of its task. An analysis of sort algorithms shows roughly that in the worst case the bubble sort is $O(N^2)$ and in the best case, it is $O(N)$. For the selection sort, although there are some differences between best, average, and worst cases, the order is the same—$O(N^2)$ for all. (The differences are constant factor differences, so the selection sort is about twice as good in the best case as in the worst, and the average is about halfway between them.) For the insertion sort, however, there is a significant difference: the order for the worst and average cases is the same $O(N^2)$—in the average case, the insertion sort is about twice as good as in the worst case—but the order in the best case is $O(N)$.

Finally, consider Quicksort. In the worst case, the behavior of Quicksort is somewhere between N^2 and N^3, and in the best case, it is somewhere between $N*log(N)$ and N^2. Discounting constant factors, we can say that the worst case is $O(N^2)$ and the best case is $O(N*log(N))$. Computations for the average case are beyond the scope of this book; however, the average case is generally considered to be $O(N*log(N))$ also.

In general, given cost equations like those we have previously seen, one can obtain a simple order of magnitude using the following principles, where k is any constant:

$O(k) = O(1)$; (constant time reduces to unit time in large computations)

$O(f(x)+g(x)) = \max\{O(f(x)),O(g(x))\}$; (use the larger of two orders)

$O(k*f(x)) = O(f(x))$. (unit time calculations are usually less important than larger orders)

Thus, one can see that for any constants a and b, $O(a*f(x)+b) = \max\{O(a*f(x)),O(k)\} = \max\{O(a*f(x)),O(1)\} = O(a*f(x)) = O(f(x))$.

Note that O(N) or *linear* time is not so hot for searching but would be the holy grail for sorting! That's OK, since we search more often than we sort. There are *tradeoffs*. Algorithms of all different orders of complexity have their place in computing. Indeed, lest you conclude from the numbers that computer scientist must avoid $O(10^N)$ or *exponential* time algorithms like the plague, let us assure you that there are in fact many important and interesting exponential algorithms out there. Think back to the chapter on problem solving, in which we explored search spaces for the fox-goose-corn problem and the like. Do you remember how we showed how a search for all possible ways to solve the problem grows a tree of moves that grows and grows—that's right, exponentially. We concluded that blind search or hacking is something to be avoided, because we discovered the same sort of exponentially growing numbers. Nevertheless, there are many problems that seem to call for consideration of exponentially growing numbers of states—such as chess-playing or language understanding or exhaustive database queries. Artificial intelligence researchers among others study these problems with an eye out for taming exponentially growing monsters.

Exercise 7.59: Confirm the above "eyeball" estimates from the tables for the four sorts by applying these principles to their cost equations. (Hint: $O(\log_2(N)) = O(\log(N))$; why?)

Exercise 7.60: Confirm our claim that blind hacking (see pp. 36-40) is indeed exponential.

Exercise 7.61: Why would chess-playing be a exponential problem? Hint: think about the possible moves that each player can make each turn.

Exercise 7.62: If chess-playing is an exponential problem, and people are relatively slow to consider the consequences of possible moves, why are some people good chess players? Why only recently did a special-purpose supercomputer defeat the world champion?

Exercise 7.64: Algorithms have tradeoffs. When might it make sense to use, say, a Bubble sort, rather than Quick sort, and vice versa?

Exercise 7.65: Given the tradeoffs, when might it make sense to use linear search rather than binary search, and vice versa?

Exercise 7.66 (*explore*): On the web, find the N-queens problem and describe its complexity.

Chapter review. Are the following statements true or false? Explain why or why not.
a) If linear search fails to find a key in an array, a run-time error occurs.
b) Linear search is fine for little arrays, but a *dog* for telephone books!
c) Selection sort swaps the smallest value in an array with the first element of the array.
d) Binary search works by examining the binary values of array elements.
e) A recursive function that cannot match a base case is a logical error.
f) Activation records or frames make recursion possible in modern programming languages.
g) A recursive descent parser solves the Towers of Hanoi problem.
h) Complexity in a program is highly desirable because complex programs are more powerful.
i) A linear search is a highly efficient way to search an array.
j) Hashing is *always* more efficient than linear search.
k) A binary search is substantially more efficient than a linear search.
l) An array should always be sorted before searching in it.
m) A bubble sort is so-called because it was invented by "Bubbles" Ort, an early programmer.
n) A bubble sort is conceptually a very complicated type of sort.
o) A selection sort is roughly twice as efficient as a bubble sort.
p) In the worst case, an insertion sort is about as efficient as a selection sort.
q) In the best or average cases, an insertion sort is a good deal better than a selection sort.
r) All of the sorts we considered involve nested loops.
s) Quicksort is fundamentally different from the bubble, selection, and insertion sorts.
t) Quicksort is more efficient than the bubble, selection, or insertion sorts.
u) An algorithm which is $O(N*\log(N))$ is more efficient than one which is $O(N^2)$.
v) $O(\log_2(N))$ is smaller than $O(\log_{10}(N))$.
w) Order of magnitude is where the biggest payoffs in performance are.
x) Linear time is excellent for a search algorithm.
y) Chess-playing is an example of a problem that can require exponential time.

Summary

Searching and sorting are very common activities with arrays, files and other collections. A **linear search** is a brute force technique: look at every element in order. If a program needs to search for items often, then it makes sense to improve the efficiency of searching by first **sorting** the elements so that they appear in an ascending (or possibly descending) order. The **selection sort** algorithm is a simple technique (there are other more efficient algorithms) that involves selecting the smallest item available, swapping it with the first slot in the array, then doing the same thing to put the next smallest item in the second slot, and so forth. Once the elements of an array have been sorted, a **binary search** is possible, a technique that keeps splitting the space (an array) of possibly matching elements in half until finding the desired element. Intuitively, binary search is more efficient than linear search because it doesn't have to look at every element.

Recursion is a powerful technique for solving some otherwise difficult problems. A recursive function always consists of two cases: a **base** case, which defines a simple solution for basic input which exits the recursion, and a **recursive** case, which defines a solution by reapplying itself to a smaller subset of the input. The **Towers of Hanoi**, **recursive descent parsing**, and **Quicksort** are examples of algorithms that use recursion to solve interesting problems. Most modern programming languages support recursive functions by dynamically storing the state of the machine at the point of each function call in a stack of **activation records** or **frames**, so that a program can resume its state each time it returns from a function.

Computational complexity theory studies the potential size or efficiency of algorithms. We can compare the efficiency of algorithms in terms of the order of magnitude of their "cost" (in terms of basic actions that they perform). Complexity analysis focuses on really large differences, using a system of comparison called **orders of magnitude**. The key decimal orders of magnitude for **Big-O analysis** are, from smallest to largest orders: k (constant), log(N), N (linear), N*log(N), N^2 and N^3 (polynomial) and 10^N (exponential). So for large collections, binary search, a O(log(N)) algorithm in the worst case, is much more efficient than linear search, an O(N) algorithm. **Hashing** is excellent in the base, O(k), where k is the time to compute a hash index from a key. But in the worst case, when the hash index leads to a collision of many elements at the same index, hashing is no better than linear search, O(N). Certain general principles help to simplify "**order-of**" calculations:

O(k) = O(1); (constant time reduces to unit time in large computations)

O(f(x)+g(x)) = max{O(f(x)),O(g(x))}; (use the larger of two orders)

O(k*f(x)) = O(f(x)). (unit time calculations are usually less important than larger orders)

Using these principles we have analyzed various sort algorithms. In the worst case the **bubble sort** is $O(N^2)$ while in the best case it is O(N). The **selection sort** is the same, $O(N^2)$, for all cases. The **insertion** sort, has the order for the worst and average cases, $O(N^2)$, but in the best case it is O(N). Quicksort is usually much better: in the worst case $O(N^2)$, while in the best and average cases O(N*log(N)).

Analysis of algorithms is thus an important aspect of the science of computing. It also has implications for the engineering of software. With these results, software developers can make more informed decisions about which algorithm or combination of algorithms to use for different applications. Often such decisions involve practical tradeoffs. For example, though binary search is more efficient than linear search, it assumes a collection has already been sorted, worth doing if we will search often, but maybe not for infrequent searches or small collections. Quicksort is far more efficient in time than the other algorithms we've studied, its memory requirements (remember, it relies heavily on recursion) may make it prohibitive for large collections such as databases.

Chapter 8
User Interface and Web Design
"You would need an engineering degree from MIT to work this."
Someone puzzling over a new digital watch

Do you know anyone who has had trouble setting the time using the four pins on a sports watch? Some people enjoy figuring out all the features, but how much time and effort should it take people who would rather be doing something else? In *The Design of Everyday Things* (Doubleday, 1988), Donald A. Norman chronicles many examples of artifacts that have been poorly designed for the people who need to use them. Every day people struggle with the controls on VCRs, washing machines, telephones, and computer software. Many people just give up. (Anyone you know?) Norman tells a story that may sound familiar to you:

> In England I visited a home with a fancy new Italian washer-drier combination, with super-duper multi-symbol controls, to do everything you ever wanted to do with the washing and drying of clothes. The husband (an engineering psychologist) said he refused to go near it. The wife (a physician) said she had simply memorized one setting and tried to ignore the rest.

The engineers who designed that machine probably went to a lot of trouble to design those controls. The instruction manual explains how this machine takes into account a wide variety of synthetic and natural fabrics. But the engineers hadn't designed it well for actual users. Perhaps they hadn't actually watched people use it.

Engineers tend to focus on designing machines; software engineers focus on designing programs. Either way, when the emphasis is on what *machines* can do, the emphasis is usually on features and performance rather than on usability. What is efficient or functional for machines is not necessarily so for people. For example, how long is it before PC novices learn to use the key combination Ctrl-Alt-Delete to kill a process, rather than just pressing the power button? (The Ctrl-Alt-Delete is preferable because it's faster to interrupt a single program than restart the whole operating system, it can preserve work in other programs, and a "soft" reboot of the operating system puts less wear and tear on hard drives than a "hard" reboot with the power supply.)

In this chapter, we will study the design of software systems from a human perspective. Instead of algorithms or efficiency for machines, there will be more emphasis on cognitive psychology and efficiency for people. First, we will outline some principles and criteria for user-centered design, then begin to use these to analyze and redesign actual user interfaces. The second section will then look at how professional software developers implement user interfaces and look at some of the high-level tools that facilitate the creation of windowing systems, web pages and multimedia. (You will even learn a bit about how the multimedia that accompanies this book was created; moreover, the multimedia for this chapter includes tutorials that will teach you how to create your own web pages and multimedia.)

8.1 Usability

Why is good user interface design important? Once, at the London Stock Exchange, an inexperienced computer-operator pressed the wrong key on a terminal. The result was chaos. Systems staff were working through the night to correct the problem. People make errors like this routinely; software systems should help people avoid errors and certainly not let slips become

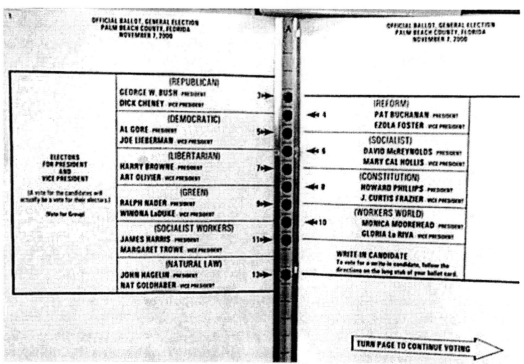

Figure 8.1: Palm Beach county's 2000 presidential ballot
(photo by Scott Fisher, Sun-Sentinel staff photographer)

catastrophes. Figure 8.1 shows an even more famous example: a ballot in the 2000 Presidential election, in Palm Beach county. Apparently, hundreds of voters who intended to vote for Al Gore got confused about which hole to punch. Even though the arrow points to the third button from the top, many voters assumed that the Democratic candidate would be the *second* button (the Buchanan ticket). Lots of people might object that educated citizens should be able to interpret such a ballot. But should a national election come down to a questionable user interface design? The **usability** of an artifact is its effectiveness for users. Various experts have proposed different principles or criteria for usability. Let's start with a few of Donald Norman's principles:

- **Visibility**. How easy is it to understand how to manipulate it? If it's an important or frequently used function, it should be obvious how to do it. For example, Sony has added buttons to its keyboards: MAIL brings up the default e-mail program and INTERNET brings up the default Web browser—and runs a setup program the first time. On the other hand, my telephone has a button labeled FLASH which I've never used and remains obscure to me to this day. It should be obvious what an interface element such as a button or menu item is for.

- **Mapping**. How easy is it for a user to relate a user interface to her mental model? People use models to predict the effects of their actions. For example, people quickly learn how to use scrollbars by clicking on or near the up arrow to move up and vice versa. On the other hand, a user interface may set up a defective model, misleading a user, or no model at all, forcing a user to learn how to do things from rote memory. For example, the scale on many thermostats might give you the impression that if you push it all the way up, the room will heat faster, when in fact, the thermostat is a basically on/off switch, keeping the heating system on until it reaches the desired temperature. Ideally, the user's model should quickly match the designer's model. That's not so easy to achieve.

- **Feedback**. How easy it for the user to determine whether an intended action has been done or whether something else happened? People use feedback to develop their mental model of a system. So it is important that there be feedback, and that it be immediate, descriptive, and accurate. For example, sound effects can act as cues that a learner has done something right or wrong. Better yet, short messages that appear when a mouse rolls over a button (usually called "tool tips") can help a user decide whether to use a feature before committing to use it. On the other hand, too many software systems have been guilty of emitting obscure error messages.

Exercise 8.1: The handles that control burners on a stove are typically arranged horizontally, often in pairs. Have you ever made mistakes with this interface? Which of Norman's principle(s) does this interface violate? How so? Propose a better design.

Exercise 8.2: Have you ever walked into a room and fumbled with the light switches, often turning on the wrong ones? Which of Norman's principles does this interface violate? How so? Propose a better design.

Exercise 8.3: To the left is a graphic of a floppy disk. (A firm plastic case encases this disk; before this design, they really were floppy.) How many ways can this disk be inserted in a drive? How does the shape of the disk affect its use? (Is it a square, or is a rectangle? What are those notches for?) How well does this design support Norman's principles? How so? Can you propose a better design?

Exercise 8.4 (*social/ethical*): When people cannot figure out to use a mechanical or computer system, why do they sometimes apologize, saying things like, "I'm sorry, I'm no good with mechanical things" or "I'm no good at computers"? Who's to blame here? What are the business costs as well as broader social costs of interfaces that discourage users? What if anything can be done to alleviate these costs?

As Norman shows in example after example, a lot of everyday artifacts have flawed designs. Why does this happen? One reason is that engineers (software engineers included) do not adequately take into account the design of human beings. Human memory does not work the same way as computer memory. People can only store a small amount of information in short-term memory—seven things, plus or minus two. Hence, phone numbers with seven digits are generally much easier than those with ten or more. Grouping (or "chunking") things together can help: so people can cope with ten-digit phone numbers if they learn the first three as an area code. In order to transfer information to long-term memory, people have to rehearse the information in short-term memory, which requires effort. With practice, people can learn phone numbers. However, most people (except a few endowed with "photographic" memory) cannot easily reproduce memories verbatim; memories tend to come back as approximations. People do better if they can recall things in multiple modes; hence, people do better at recalling words when they are set to melodies, poetic meter, or rhymes.

That's a very quick summary of what cognitive scientists have learned about human memory and learning. It helps explain Norman's principles. For example, visibility: designers should not overtax human attention (related to short-term memory) with unimportant or obscure features.

People are more than individuals: they are social creatures. Effective user interface design must consider the nature of the target audience. Age, gender, physical abilities or disabilities, educational training, and specific task training all have a bearing. For example, children enjoy more stimulating graphics and sound, which adults may find distracting. Novices may be overwhelmed by technical features, which experienced users may use efficiently. Color-blindness, which affects nearly 8% of males, may make them unable to distinguish color-coded features that other users (and designers) see easily. Taking a bit of human psychology, physiology, and sociology into account, we can derive more principles for user interface design which are more germane to software systems:

- **Real world mapping** (a corollary of Norman's mapping principle): Can user interface features be laid out in a way that things have already been laid out in the world? For example, if a program is presenting a digital movie, use controls that are similar to a VCR's play, fast forward, and reverse buttons. (Other aspects of VCR interface design might not be worth imitating.)

- **Consistency**: What interface features should users always be able to access? These should appear globally, i.e., on every screen of a system, always in the same place. Moving things around just creates confusion. It also helps to standardize on fonts, graphics, and transitions. Gratuitous diversity can distract users from what they really need to accomplish.

- **Less is more**: How many features do users really need? Keep less important functions out of view, perhaps in submenus or keyboard short-cuts. For example, it may be a good idea to have a novice mode that presents essential features first.

- **Anticipation**: Should features be visible when they are not possible? Hide or grey out features when they are inactive. Context-sensitive help can explain what preconditions are required before a feature can be active.

- **Customization**: Can more experienced, "power" users learn how to use subtler features or how to perform frequent functions more efficiently? For example, menus can show keyboard short-cuts. Complex behaviors can run as macro-instructions.

- **Transparency**: What happens when a user interface element covers up other content that a user needs to see? Frustration. For example, Clippy, the animated agent who offers help in Microsoft Word, annoys many users when it gets in the way or distracts them from their work.

- **Contiguity**: If a picture is worth a thousand words, where should the words go? The answer is: place concise, explanatory text as close to the graphics as possible. Avoid scrolling windows with long explanations far removed from what they explain or multiple windows that require users to switch back and forth. Effective examples of contiguity include integrating explanatory text within a graphic and showing tips when the mouse rolls over icons or parts of a graphic.

- **Reduce memory load**: Why make users work hard to remember things that computers can? For example, instead of asking the user to type in a command or a file name blind, present a list of likely candidates, constrained by the context of the user's recent activity.

- **User control**. In a human-computer interaction, who is in charge? Be careful about automatic procedures that make users feel out of control, passive or distracted from the task at hand.

- **Speak the user's language**: Can users understand a system's instructions, feedback, error messages, and online help? Software systems are notorious for cryptic or intimidating language. Is an error truly "fatal" just because the user must "abort" a program or procedure? Error messages should not just tell users that there is a problem; they should help them correct it and avoid it in the future. Online documentation can help users gain confidence, especially if it is context-sensitive. For example, when a user has the mouse over a function that he doesn't understand, clicking on a reference book icon could display a page describing the function.

- **Consider the audience**: User interface designers must take care not to design for themselves. Actual users are likely to have different assumptions, backgrounds or capabilities. For example, what if there are visually- or hearing-impaired users—is the interface accessible to them? Can obstacles be removed or features added to meet their needs?

- **Test with actual users**: What happens when someone other than the designers use the system? Observe what users do when assigned a task, how long it takes, when and why they get stuck. Focus groups can provide feedback to designers about the opinions and experiences of users, leading to further development.

Exercise 8.5: How do these additional user interface design principles follow from the way human memory and learning work? Discuss as many as you can in terms of human cognition.

Exercise 8.6 (*explore, social/ethical*): Do some research on the web to learn about accessible web design. What legislation and court rulings mandate accessible web design? What are a few techniques that web page designers can incorporate to made their content more accessible to hearing- or visually-impaired users?

Exercise 8.7 (*explore*): Do some research about human-computer interaction (HCI). Find a definition of HCI. What is the relationship between HCI, computer science, and psychology? Identify a few principles of user interface design postulated in the HCI literature, a few that may be similar to those discussed in this chapter and at least a couple that are not.

Let's try applying these principles by analyzing an example. Figure 8.3 shows the original prototype of *The Universal Machine* (a precursor of this book).

Figure 8.3: Prototype user interface for *The Universal Machine*

While certainly eye-grabbing, in retrospect it violates many of the user interface principles laid out above. The **Out** button and **Full** buttons on the upper left, though they make interesting features on a spaceship, violate *real world mapping*, since most users would already be familiar with the close and minimize/maximize buttons in the upper right hand corner of most Windows applications. Also, though "out" is a familiar word, its use here to mean "exit" does not *speak the user's language*. The large **Hyperdrive**, **Probe** and **Assistant** buttons violate the *less is more* principle, by drawing attention to functions that learners probably won't use that often. On the other hand, the "Tools" button hides a number of other buttons that scroll up when requested. The smaller red box at the bottom is a model of outer space seen through the viewer window above. Instead of a menu, a user must mouse around in the box below the viewer in order to navigate its content. The original idea was to teach learners that computer scientists create and interact with models that simulate the real world. Separating model and viewer in a user interface, however, violates *contiguity*, making users look at two separate places at once to accomplish a task. (Models do have this kind of indirection, but forcing beginners to do this to get anywhere is probably not effective user interface design.) Also the odd-shaped viewer window, designed to give the feel of a small Jules Vernes space ship, violates *transparency*, since it covers up potential space for displaying content (making life difficult for content designers).Finally, while successful with part of the target audience that the designers especially had in mind—novices, especially women—it was less successful with male users who had more experience with computing. *Speak the user's language* requires that one design for *all* relevant users—experienced users and instructors, too.

Exercise 8.8: Based on our principles and critique, propose a redesign of the user interface for *The Universal Machine*. (And no, don't just point at the newer interface of *The Universal Computer*!)
Exercise 8.9: The multimedia CDROM includes the released version of *The Universal Machine* interface. How well does it improve on the prototype shown above, in terms of UI principles?
Exercise 8.10: How well does the newer user interface of *The Universal Computer* improve on *The Universal Machine*, in terms of the principles discussed above?
Exercise 8.11: Evaluate a user interface for another software system—any application or a web site of your choosing—in terms of the usability principles outlined above. Try to take into account the intended purpose and audience of the program. Write up a report describing both the strengths and weaknesses of the interface. Look for things that work as well as things that don't—effective design isn't easy! This is a good project for groups of students to work on, then present their results to the rest of a class, which can provide feedback on the group's work.
Exercise 8.12: Next, propose a redesign of the interface you just critiqued. You may want to do a mock-up of a redesign on paper or use screen capture and graphics editing tools to manipulate the original design.

8.2 Implementing user interfaces

As the architecture of machines changed, so did the architecture of user interfaces. ENIAC and other early computers were controlled by wires on circuit boards, levers, knobs, and punched cards. The first generation of interactive machines were driven by command line interfaces, where the user typed in commands. In chapter 1, we gave a brief introduction to DOS, which prompts a user to enter commands, then responds. In command line systems, who is in control—computer or human? True, the person gives commands, but she must wait until the computer is ready to accept them. More critically, the user must speak the operating system's command language, which is often cryptic.

Though as early as the mid-1960's Douglas Engelbart had demonstrated a word processor that used a graphical user interface and mouse, it was Apple's Macintosh that popularized GUI-based

Figure 8.4: Apple Macintosh, circa 1985

interfaces starting in the mid-1980's. (It was not until 1990 and version 3.0 that Microsoft Windows began to gain wide acceptance on PCs.) Though GUIs require more computational power, they have opened access to many more users. A picture is worth a thousand words: with GUIs came applications for painting pixels, drawing shapes, and computer-aided design (CAD), WYSIWYG (What You See Is What You Get) editing and desktop publishing, and visualizing data with graphs or animations. User interface elements such as buttons, windows and scrollbars became familiar to users. They have also become easier to program in software development toolkits, as "widgets" or "components" with standardized interfaces.

While windows and buttons show views as output, devices such as mice, mouse balls, finger track pads, pens and good old keyboards wait for user input. A GUI architecture is **event driven**, responding to user-initiated input, represented as events. At the heart of this architecture is the **event loop**:

```
Initialize Application & Window
while (not done) {
        Get next event E
        Dispatch event E
}
```

Once a windowing environment has launched an application in an associated window, it goes into a loop, waiting for and responding to events until the application exits. The windowing environment packages the activity of input devices as events with relevant data describing its context. For example, if a user clicks on a mouse, the windowing environment gets an event, with information about the coordinates of the mouse on the screen, whether it is a single- or double-click or a continuous press, whether there is a modifier, such as a Shift or Ctrl key pressed at the same time, etc. It then dispatches the event to an **event handler**, which then performs any work associated with it. For example, if the mouse click is on a button labeled "quit" or the "X" icon in the upper right corner of a window, an event driven system dispatches an event to a handler associated with that button or icon. The event handler in turn executes code, which in this case quits the application. More complicated events include mouse rollovers (mouse moves with no button activity), mouse drags (button pressed and held down while mouse rolls) and mouse releases (ending a mouse drag). Each of these trigger its own event handler with its own associated action code. In most modern software development toolkits, the event loop is implicit and hidden. When the environment starts, the event loop begins without the programmer doing anything. The programmer associates components (user interface elements) with event handlers (actions).

Next we will briefly examine how to set up these user interface components on web pages using HTML, JavaScript, and Macromedia Flash. A goal is to show you a bit about how web page design has evolved, from static presentation of materials, to animations and interactivity (such as what you see in the multimedia with this book), to dynamic tracking of user interactions with databases. The multimedia supplies tutorials that go into more detail than we will provide in this chapter; the goal here is to show how these high-level programming languages and tools facilitate user interface prototyping and implementation. Once you learn how to use these tools, getting started with implementation is relatively easy. Effective *user-centered design* is still the hard part.

8.2.1 HTML

HyperText Markup Language (HTML for short) is the core language for describing and formatting web pages. In a web browser, you can view the HTML source code for any web page, as an option under the View menu. HTML files (with extension `.html` or `.htm`) contain plain text, so they can be edited with a text editor as simple as notepad, though richer web page development environments such as Dreamweaver, Frontpage, and many others are very helpful. (The multimedia describes HTML development in the context of Dreamweaver.)

HTML encodes all its information in the form of **markup tags**, always enclosed in angle brackets, *which describe elements of the page.* Tags typically occur in pairs, for example, `<b>user</b>` pairs the `<b>` (bold-face) tag with the `</b>` (close bold-face) tag, instructing the browser to display **user**. When tags come in pairs, the closing tag starts with a '/' and everything between the pair is said to be within that tag block, taking on the properties conferred by the tags. So a tag pair may cross over many lines, and encompass other tags.

The first tag in a document is usually `<HTML>`, confirming that the file contains an HTML document. It must ultimately match up with a `</HTML>` at the end of the document. A document has two main parts: a `<head>..</head>` and a `<body>..</body>`. The **head** contains general information about the document as a whole, such as the `<title>..</title>`, which usually appears in the title bar of the browser. The **body** contains the information displayed as the page itself. Tag names are not case sensitive, so `<BODY>` and `<body>` are equivalent. The `<BODY>` tag can also supply additional information as parameters, such as `<BODY BGCOLOR = "silver" TEXT="maroon">`, which causes all the text on a page to be maroon on a silver background. Browsers recognize sixteen predefined color names: blue, fuchsia, gray, green, lime, maroon, navy, olive, purple, red, silver, teal, white, and yellow.

Headings (not to be confused with the aforementioned head structure) set apart sections in the body of a document. A heading always takes its own, separate line. There are six standard levels of headings, from H1 to H6, where H1 produces the largest size. So `<H3>User interfaces</H3>` displays "User interfaces" in a moderately large bold-faced text, on its own line.

Between headings you will usually find a set of **paragraphs**. Each paragraph tag breaks any previous paragraph, inserts an empty line, starts a new line, then displays its content as a continuous block. To start a new line without inserting an empty line, use the `<br>` tag. For example:

```
<p>Four     score</p><p align="center">and seven years ago
<p>our fathers<br>brought forth upon this continent</p>
```

displays as

Four score

                         and seven years ago

our forefathers
brought forth upon this continent

The second `<p>` tag includes an `align` parameter which center-justifies its text. You'll also notice that the third paragraph starts without an explicit `</p>` tag closing the previous one, but most browsers will accept this form. Finally, the `<br>` tag starts a new line without a blank line; note that `<br>` does not take a paired closing tag.

Note that HTML documents ignore extra white space, so only one space appears between "Four" and "score". The format of an HTML file is determined by the tags, not the way information is laid out in the HTML file itself. The idea is to let the browser take care of as many low-level details as possible; you just supply the essential information that you want a page to show.

HTML includes many other useful text formatting tags. **Forced style tags**, such as <i>..</i> (you saw how to do bold-face above) tell the browser exactly what you want, while **logical styles** such as .. for emphasis leaves some discretion to the browser or local rules. Block quotes and various lists give more control over the layout of text, while tables and frames give more control over the layout of pages. The multimedia includes a tutorial that provide more details.

What makes HTML "hyper" is its ability to embed links to other web pages. The tag structure <a href=URL>Description of link</a> sets up a link. A **URL** or Uniform Resource Locator is *a standardized way of telling a browser where to find a resource on the web*. For example:

```
Visit <a href=<http://www.cse.lehigh.edu/~glennb/um>
The Universal Computer</a> site!
Email <a href=<mailto:gdb0@lehigh.edu>the author</a>.
```

Creates a couple of hypertext link on a web page:

Visit <u>The Universal Computer</u> site! Email <u>the author</u>.

If you click on the first hyperlink, the web browser will try to open a window containing the web page for this book. (Note that the link does not necessarily need to contain a reference to an `html` page; the browser automatically looks for a file called `index.html` in the um directory.) If you press the second hyperlink, it will try to open an email program with the address `gdb0@lehigh.edu`.

In addition to hypertext, HTML also supports hyper**media**, by embedding images, which can in turn contain links to other pages. Most browsers support .GIF (Graphical Interchange Format) and JPEG (Joint Photographic Experts Group) files. You cannot use the BMP files produced by the Windows Paint program or PICT files produced natively in Macintosh. The GIF and JPG formats are cross-platform and use compression algorithms to save on file size and hence transmission time. Here is an example of a tag importing and describing a image:

```
<img src="graphics/cimel.gif" WIDTH=200 HEIGHT=50 ALT="CIMEL logo">
```

Since the URL does not begin with `http://`, the browser assumes that it should use *relative* addressing—that is, `cimel.gif` is in a folder `graphics`, underneath the folder containing the current page. The `WIDTH` and `HEIGHT` parameters specify the size of the graphic in pixels, for layout purposes. The `ALT` parameter provides a "tool tip" telling the user what the picture is—a very good idea for usability if a graphic might take some time to load or if it contains a link to another site.

An image can contain a link as a whole or you can segment it as an **image map** containing one or more "hot spots" associated with their own links. Here are a couple of examples:

```
<a href="ucomp.htm"><img src="UcompCover.gif" alt="Contents"></a>
<img src="shapes.gif" usemap="#sample" width="50" height="90">
<map name="sample">
<area shape="rect" coords="20,25,84,113" href="rect.html">
<area shape="circle" coords="130,114,29" href="circle.html">
<area shape="rect" coords="19,156,170,211" href="rect.html">
<area shape="default" nohref>
</map>
```

The first line links the image file `UcompCover.gif` to another web page (`ucomp.htm`) The remaining lines divide one graphic file, `shapes.gif`, and three different clickable regions, each defined by pixel coordinates and each linking to another web page. (Figuring out the pixel coordinates of an image map is tricky; we recommend using a WYSIWYG program such as Dreamweaver.)

For the following exercises, point a browser at http://www.cse.lehigh.edu/~glennb/um/ (the web page associated with this book), then use the menu to **View** the HTML page **Source** code.

Exercise 8.13: What are the first three words after the `<title>` tag and where do these words appear in the browser?

Exercise 8.14: What does each of the parameters of the `<body>` tag do? (If you can't figure them out, check out documentation at http://devedge.netscape.com/library/manuals/1998/htmlguide/.)

Exercise 8.15: Looking back at this page in the browser, what happens when you roll the mouse over the picture of the book cover? What happens when you click on the book cover? Viewing the source code again, how did the page get these effects?

Exercise 8.16: Reload or refresh the page in your browser and notice what Knobby does on the right side of the page. What does Knobby do? What did the web page load in to give this effect? The effect is not something the browser does, it just plays the embedded file. (To learn how the file does it, look at http://www.cse.lehigh.edu/~glennb/mm/gifcon/.) Explain briefly how it works.

Exercise 8.17: There is a button at the bottom of this page that says "Contact Us". What does it do and how does it work?

Exercise 8.18: Navigate to http://www.cse.lehigh.edu/~glennb/um/book/weblinks.htm. What happens when you click on different parts of the graphic on top? Explain how it works, in terms of the HTML code.

Exercise 8.19: Design your own web page. Give it a title, use different text formatting, heading levels, paragraphs and breaks. Include a couple of hyperlinks and a graphic as a link to another page. Use alt tags in your images. Test your work either by having a browser open your HTML file locally, or by uploading your file to a web server and giving a browser the URL for your page. Make sure it is clear and usable.

Exercise 8.20: Add an image map to your page.

Exercise 8.21: Use tables and/or frames to organize the layout of your page.

Exercise 8.22 (*explore*): Do some research on the web to study the differences between GIF and JPG formats and when to use which. Support your conclusions about the tradeoffs with a web page including links to sample images, highlighting the strengths of each format.

Exercise 8.23 (*explore*): Do some research on the web to discover some of the differences between the two major web browsers, and how web designers try to accommodate some of these differences.

Exercise 8.24 (*explore*): Actually there are really more than just one or two web browsers out there. Do some research to learn about other web browsers, their advantages and disadvantages.

Exercise 8.25 (*explore*): Find a web page that you think is particularly well-designed and study its source code. Does it rely primarily on HTML or use additional plug-ins? If so what, and why?

8.2.3 JavaScript and Dynamic HTML

JavaScript, not to be confused with Java, is a language that a web browser interprets and runs directly. Until Netscape developed JavaScript, web pages were fairly static, laying out information only as designed in advance. Snippets of JavaScript code (called scripts) confer on pages the ability to compute dynamic effects, such as rollover effects, animations, and changing their content with information loaded from other sources, such as databases.

We'll start with an example that lets a user change the background color of a browser window. You've already learned how to set the background color in HTML. The difference here is that the color will change dynamically, after the page has loaded, in response to user choices.

```
<HTML>
<HEAD><TITLE>Dynamic background colors</TITLE>
<SCRIPT LANGUAGE = "JavaScript">
<!-- Hide all JavaScript from browsers that don't support it...
     alert("Hello, Universe!")
     function showColors() { //Show background color in hex
         document.colors.hex.value = "hex="+document.bgColor;
         alert(document.colors.hex.value)
     }
     function changeColors() { //Randomly assign new bgColor
         document.bgColor = Math.round(Math.random()*10000000);
         showColors();      //show value in textbox
     }
//end JavaScript code in HEAD -->
</SCRIPT>
</HEAD>
<BODY ONLOAD = "showColors()">
     <CENTER><H3>Show and change the background color</H3>
     <FORM NAME = "colors">
     <INPUT TYPE="button" VALUE="Change" ONCLICK="changeColors()">
     <INPUT TYPE="text" NAME="hex" SIZE=10>
     </FORM></CENTER>
</BODY>
</HTML>
```

Figure 8.5: Dynamic colors in JavaScript (bgcolor.htm)

An HTML file embeds all the JavaScript code between <SCRIPT LANGUAGE = "JavaScript"> and </SCRIPT> tags. The opening tag specifies JavaScript as the language; Vbscript, based on Visual Basic, is another script language with similar capabilities, though JavaScript is supported by more browsers. An HTML file can contain many SCRIPT tags, in both its head and body. Tags are processed in the order in which they appear. So alert("Hello, Universe!") —the first statement in the document's HEAD—appears before anything else on the page. The most common approach is to put most of the JavaScript code in the HEAD, as we have done.

Figure 8.6: Snapshot of bgColor.htm

There are two kinds of comments in our example: everything between <!-- and --> is an HTML comment. Since it is meant for the JavaScript interpreter rather than users, commenting out the code tells the browser not to show it to users; also older browsers unfamiliar with the JavaScript language won't get confused. The second kind of comment, starting with //, is part of JavaScript itself, commenting out the rest of a line. JavaScript also supports comments between /* and */.

The body of the script above consists of two functions. We introduced the idea of functions back in chapter 3, comparing them to programmer-defined instructions in Knobby's World. When function changeColors() gets called, it executes the statements in its body. The first statement changes the background color of the current window and the second invokes another function, showColors(), which displays the hexadecimal value of the background color in a text field as well as in another alert box. Figure 8.6 shows a snapshot at this point, with white as the background color, and white's hex value in both the text field and alert box. When showColors() completes its work, control returns to changeColors(), then returns control to its caller.

So where does this chain of function calls get started? In the body of the document, you'll notice two **event handlers**, ONLOAD and ONCLICK, which the browser will execute when a corresponding event occurs to a page element. Note that there is no main in a JavaScript program; it's implicitly in the browser itself, which in turn watches for events, either directly or indirectly initiated by the user. Each event handler is an attribute of an HTML element. The ONLOAD handler is an attribute of the BODY tag; as you might expect, this event occurs when the page gets loaded, invoking showColors() to show the hex (base 16) values of the page's initial color. The ONCLICK handler is an attribute of an INPUT element, in this case a button. HTML typically uses INPUT elements to gather information for forms. When the user clicks this button, it sets off the chain of functions described above, changing the page's color and displaying the hex value of the new color.

Let's look a little closer at the function bodies. Both use dot notation, borrowed from object-oriented languages like C++ and Java, to access elements of a page. The current page itself is called document. All parts of a page are arranged in a hierarchy, which we can visualize as a tree structure, with document as its root. This structure is called the **Document Object Model**, or **DOM** for short. Hanging off document like branches are its attributes, such as bgColor, as well as components of the page such as the FORM to which we have given the name colors. (We do need to give HTML components names if we want to access them using the DOM.) Hanging off the document's branches, like twigs or leaves, are more components or attributes. For example, document.colors.hex.value refers to the attribute value of the hex element (a text field) of the colors FORM of the document.

Function showColors assigns this value as a new string, created by concatenating (that's what the + operator does in this context) the string "hex=" and the value of document.bgColor. HTML represents this value as a hexadecimal number, which JavaScript automatically converts to a string for the concatenation operation. Assigning this new string to the value of hex automatically updates the contents of this text field in the browser.

Function changeColors assigns the result of a slightly more complicated expression to create a new bgColor. JavaScript, like other high-level languages, provides many useful functions in a library. Math.random() produces a pseudo-random real number (pseudo-random because it will always produce the same sequence of values once it is given an initial *seed* value). Since Math.random produces a real (floating point) value between 0 and 1, we multiply it by 10000000 to produce a number between 0 and 10000000, then use Math.round() to round this value off to the nearest integer value. This integer value is what we assign as the new bgColor, which in turn causes the background color of the document to change. Then showColors displays this value.

Exercise 8.26: What is an object in JavaScript? Give a couple of examples.

Exercise 8.27: What is the relationship between dot notation and the DOM? Give a couple of examples illustrating this relationship.

Exercise 8.28: You can find the document shown in figure 8.6 on either the CDROM (in folder chap7) or the web at http://www.cse.lehigh.edu/~glennb/um/book/bgcolors.htm. Load it into a web browser, and experiment with it. What are the first three colors and their hex values? Explain how they are produced. Then press the browser's Refresh or Reload button and repeat the same experiment. Do you get the same three colors? Is this what you expected? Why or why not?

Exercise 8.29: Continuing the previous exercise, use the browser's File > Save As... menu item to save a copy of this page on your local hard drive, then open it in notepad or another text editor. What happens if you remove the `<!–`, save the file, and open it in a browser? What happens if you remove the first `//`? Explain why.

Exercise 8.30: What happens if you remove `*10000000` from the code, save the file, and open it in a browser? Explain why. When you put `*10000000` back, then keep pressing the `Change` buttons, you may notice that occasionally nothing seems to happen. Any idea why not?

Exercise 8.31 (*explore*): We explained two JavaScript event handlers above. There are many more. Use a web search engine to find the other event handlers. Describe what at least three other event handlers do, with what HTML elements they are associated, and discuss how you might use them.

Exercise 8.32 (*explore*): We explained two JavaScript `Math` functions above. Use a web search engine to find more `Math` functions. Discuss what at least two of these functions do. Write a function that, given radius as a parameter, computes the perimeter of a circle (2Πr) and displays its value in a text field.

JavaScript is often used to validate data entered in forms. Figure 8.7 shows an example that validates an email address:

```
<html><head>
   <script type="text/javascript">
      function validate()
      { at=document.myForm.myEmail.value.indexOf("@")
        if (at == -1)
        { alert("Not a valid e-mail")
          return false
        }
      }
   </script>
</head>
<body>
   <form name="myForm" onsubmit="return validate()"
           action="http://www.yahoo.com">
      Enter your e-mail address:
           <input type="text" name="myEmail">
           <input type="submit" value="Send input">
   </form>
   <p>Tests if email address contains an "@" character.</p>
   <p>Should do more thorough testing!</p>
</body>
</html>
```

Figure 8.7: Validating e-mail in a form (emailValidate.html)

This example sets up a form requesting an e-mail address, then invokes function `validate`. This function uses the string function `indexOf` to check for an "@" in what the user enters in the field; `indexOf` returns –1 if it cannot find the substring requested as its parameter. So if you enter "xxx" as my email address, `validate` pops up an alert box pointing out the error, then returns `false`, so that no action will be taken. On the other hand, if I enter "xxx@lehigh.edu", then `indexOf` finds the "@", `validate` does not return `false`, and the form performs its action, in this case opening an arbitrary web page. "Real world" forms typically perform more thorough testing, then submit valid data to a program running at another site. JavaScript thus handles some processing on the client side, leaving further processing for more complex programs on the server side. Figure 8.8 shows an example of script that might appear on the server side:

```
#!/bin/bash
echo Content-type: text/html
echo "<pre>"
# next line gets rid of characters myEmail=
mailid=`echo $1 | cut -b9-`
# writes a line of html to the user...
echo "You are going to send a message to " $mailid "."
# canned message to be sent to user
mailmessage="This is a great book!"
# The actual send of the mail message
echo $mailmessage | Mail -s "Book review" $mailid
echo "</pre>"
```
Figure 8.8: A simple CGI server-side script

This script receives an email address, from the client (the JavaScript program above running in a browser), edits it slightly, opens a mail program and sends a message to this address, with the message "Book review" as the subject and "This is a great book!" as the body of the message. Our system administrators note that this is a very simple server-side script, (not to mention an open invitation to spammers, who could use this program to send lots of junk email!). It does give an idea how client and server scripts cooperate to solve problems.

JavaScript is also useful for creating animations. Figure 8.9 shows code that produces a simple rollover effect.

```
<html><head>
   <script type="text/javascript">
      function bulbOn() { document.images.bulb.src="bulbOn.gif" }
      function bulbOff(){ document.images.bulb.src="bulbOff.gif" }
   </script>
</head>
<body>
   <a OnMouseOver="bulbOn()" OnMouseOut="bulbOff()">
      <img id="bulb" border="0" src="bulbOff.gif">
   </a>
</body>
</html>
```
Figure 8.9: A rollover effect in JavaScript (rollover.html)

When this page loads, it displays `bulbOff.gif`—a dim bulb. When you roll your mouse over it, the `OnMouseOver` event handler invokes function `bulbOn()`, which in turn changes `bulb.src` to `bulbOn.gif`—and a bright bulb appears. When you roll your mouse off it, `OnMouseOut` calls `bulbOff()`, which sets `bulb.src` back to `bulbOff.gif`. Voilá! A rollover effect.

Exercise 8.33: Explain what `at=document.myForm.myEmail.value.indexOf("@")` does.

Exercise 8.34: What additional testing should a better email validation function do?

Exercise 8.35: Rewrite `emailValidate.html` to perform more through testing of user input.

Exercise 8.36: Explain how function `bulbOff()` gets invoked and changes the bulb image.

Exercise 8.37: Some web pages speed up the rollover effect a bit by preloading the image files into variables in memory. Why would this preloading speed up the effect?

Exercise 8.38: Taking into account the user interface design principles introduced earlier in this chapter, when is a rollover effect a good idea and when might it not be such a good idea?

8.2.4 Flash animations

HTML and JavaScript have the advantages of being built right into web browsers and free. Nevertheless, Macromedia's Flash (see figure 8.10) has become a de facto industry standard for adding richer animations and interactivity to web pages, including the multimedia associated with this book. Flash is now used to create all kinds of content both on and off the web, such as interactive games, animated cartoons, and movie trailers.

Animation works because of a phenomenon that biologists call persistence of vision. An object seen by the eye remains mapped onto the retina for a brief time, before it can refresh for a new object. A series of images that change slightly and rapidly will thus give the illusion of movement.

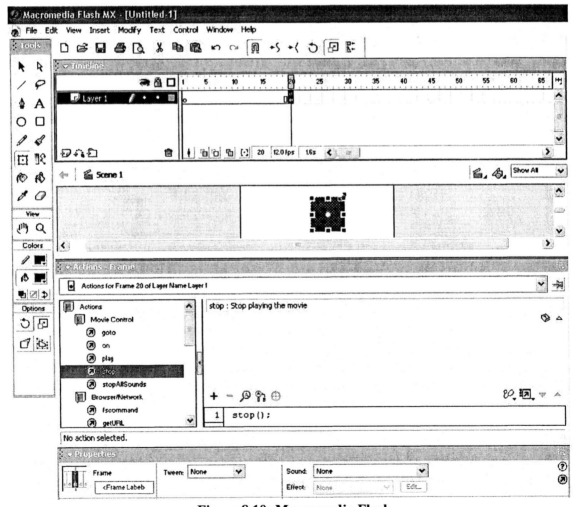

Figure 8.10: Macromedia Flash

Television builds 30 frames per second on a screen, while cinematic film is shot at 24 frames/second; movies appear to have a higher quality in part because the projector flashes through each image twice, for an effective rate of 48 frames/second. Transmitting such a large number of frames/second through the web would be highly data-intensive, but it turns out that for simple animations a smaller rate is acceptable. Flash defaults to 12 frames/second (see the box below the red vertical line in figure 8.10), which you can change.

When Disney and other artists made cartoons, they would make a different **cel** (short for celluloid sheet) for each frame. GIF animations (see exercise 8.16) bring this approach to computer animation, storing and playing an animation as a sequence of distinct frames, each hand-constructed in a graphics program. Needless to say, this approach is labor-intensive. The best cartoonist would focus on making key frames, showing the major steps of a motion, letting their apprentices fill the gaps in between. Flash automates this process: you create the **keyframes** and Flash performs **tweening**, an automated process of interpolating the frames needed between the keyframes.

As figure 8.10 shows, the Flash is primarily a visual programming environment rather than text-based. It is divided into many sub-windows: the **stage** in the middle, where the performance takes place, the **Timeline** near the top, where we control the timing of movies as a sequence of frames in layers, the **Tools** palette on the left, which supply graphics and text editing facilities, the **Actions** window near the bottom, where we can add ActionScript code for interactivity, and the **Properties** inspector at the bottom, where we can set properties of the objects currently in focus.

Currently the Timeline has about 20 frames, of which the first and last ones are keyframes. Flash automatically sets up the first frame as a keyframe. We then created the second keyframe by selecting a frame, then selecting Insert>Keyframe from the menu. Flash then automatically inserts the content of the first frame (the box) in all the frames up and including to the new keyframe.

The Tools palette show some of Flash's graphics capabilities. **Bitmapped** (rasterized) **graphics** tools, such as Adobe Photoshop, Paint Shop Pro or Fractal Painter, "paint" the color of each pixel (picture-element) of a graphic, then store a binary representation of every pixel in BMP (bit map) files on PCs or PICT files on Macintoshes. Formats such as GIF and JPG reduce the file size of bitmapped images with compression/decompression (**codec**) algorithms, thus speeding up file transfer through the web. Scaling or resizing bitmapped graphics is difficult, however, requiring interpolation of all pixels. **Vector-based graphics** tools, such as Adobe Illustrator, Corel Draw and Macromedia Freehand and Flash, "draw" pictures using mathematical formulas such as those for polygons, circles and lines. E.g., a vector representation "RECT 0,0,300,200,RED,BLUE" says "Draw a rectangle starting at **0,0** (upper left corner of screen) going **300** pixels horizontally right and **200** pixels downward, with a **RED** boundary and filled with **BLUE**." For a vector-based program such as Flash, scaling the size of such an image is just a matter of changing one or two parameters and redrawing it. By right-clicking on the graphic, we brought up a menu, then selected Scale. We can now drag a corner inward to make it smaller (note that the cursor changes to a double arrow, shown at the upper right corner in figure 8.10). Or we can distort is shape, change its color, or move it to another place on the stage. Now keyframes 1 and 20 will hold different graphics.

Right-clicking on any frame between the two keyframes brings up another menu, from which we select Create Motion Tween. This option tells Flash to "tween" all the frames between the two keyframes: an arrow appears in the Timeline to show that there is a motion tween. When we play the movie (by either pressing Enter to see it play on the Stage or by pressing Ctrl-Enter to see it play in a separate window), we see an animation effect: the box gradually moves or changes in size. In addition to location and size, motion tweens can also change the color and orientation of a graphical object. Simple motion tweens move in straight lines, but by adding a **motion guide** layer, Flash lets a developer create arbitrary movement along paths of points.

Flash also supports **shape tweens,** which automatically morph one image into another. So if we distort the shape (another option selected by right-clicking on the shape) in the second keyframe, Flash will tween one shape, in the first keyframe, into the other, in the second keyframe. Shape tweens can also be used to change the transparency or "alpha" of an image. Tweening to a keyframe with an alpha value of zero will cause it to gradually fade out.

Exercise 8.39: Why is Flash's default rate of 12 frames/second usually acceptable and also practical for its computer-generated animations?

Exercise 8.40: Assuming 12 frames/second, how long is the movie in figure 8.10? Would you expect the animation produced in this movie, as described above, to be smooth or jerky? Why?

Exercise 8.41: Why are GIF and JPG files smaller than corresponding images in BMP format? What does this difference imply about why these formats are popular on the web?

Exercise 8.42: The faces of the personae in the multimedia, originally produced as a bitmapped photos, were vectorized in Flash (by selecting Modify > Trace Bitmap). Which would you expect to be smaller, the original bitmapped files or the vectorized versions? Why?

Exercise 8.43: What is a *motion guide* for? Explain how to use it to get an animation effect you couldn't get without it.

Exercise 8.44: How would you cause the box in figure 8.10 to vanish gradually?

Exercise 8.45: If you have access to Flash (note that you can freely download a trial version from macromedia.com for thirty days), create a box that moves across the screen, then vanishes.

Exercise 8.46: If you have access to Flash, experiment with motion tweens (changing the location, size, color and orientation of different images) and shape tweens (morphing between images and changing the alpha transparency of an image). Put each effect on a different layer (you create a new layer on the timeline by clicking on the + icon at the bottom of the timeline area).

Exercise 8.47 (*explore*): Find a couple of web sites that use Flash animations, one well and one maybe less effectively. Explain your judgments in terms of usability principles discussed earlier.

Figure 8.11 depicts the relationship between the Flash authoring environment and its web player. The authoring environment, which we began to describe above, creates, edits and stores files in FLA format. It also translates files into a SWF (Shock Wave Format)— this happens when you press Ctrl-Enter. You can view SWF files either in the Flash player in stand-alone mode, or in a web browser with equipped with a Flash "plug-in" player. A **plug-in** is a program that extends the capabilities of a browser—for

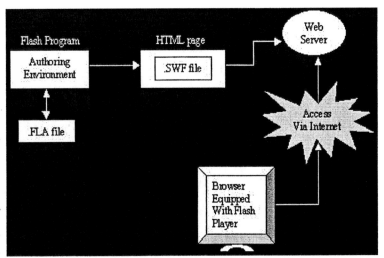

Figure 8.11: Flash authoring and player

example, adding the ability to play audio samples or view video movies from within your browser.

We usually embed SWF files in an HTML file, including lines that look something like this:

```
<OBJECT classid="clsid:D27CDB6E-AE6D-11cf-96B8-444553540000"
        codebase="http://download.macromedia.com/pub/shockwave/cabs/flash/
                swflash.cab#version=6,0,0,0"
        WIDTH="550" HEIGHT="400" id="GDBface" ALIGN="">
        <PARAM NAME=movie VALUE="GDBface.swf">
        <PARAM NAME=quality VALUE=high><PARAM NAME=bgcolor VALUE=#FFFFFF>
        <EMBED src="GDBface.swf" quality=high bgcolor=#FFFFFF  WIDTH="550"
        HEIGHT="400" NAME="GDBface" ALIGN=""
        TYPE="application/x-shockwave-flash"
        PLUGINSPAGE="http://www.macromedia.com/go/getflashplayer">
</EMBED>
</OBJECT>
```

This looks messy, but what it does is not that hard to understand. It checks to make sure the browser has a version of the Flash player plug-in at least recent as 6.0, and if not offers to download it from the Macromedia download site. The reason for both OBJECT and EMBED tags is to allow for both different plug-in conventions of the Microsoft Internet Explorer and Netscape Navigator browsers.

Exercise 8.48: In Flash, use the menu to go to File>Publish as, and study the different publishing options. (If you are not sure what they mean, check out the Help files.) What are the default publishing options and when would you want to use them? What is the "projector" option and when might you want to use that? What does a projector file include besides your SWF content?

Exercise 8.49: Which file format is larger, FLA or SWF? Any idea why there's a big difference?

8.2.5 ActionScript and Flash interactivity

If you make a simple animation in Flash and play it SWF file, it will repeat indefinitely. How do you make it stop? Here's how: 1) Go to the last frame in your movie. If it's not open already, open the Actions window (the short-cut is F9) then select Actions > Movie Control > stop. (It's selected in figure 8.10.) Flash inserts action stop() into this frame. In the timeline, you'll also see an *a* in this frame, denoting an action. When you play the movie, it stops when it gets to this frame.

You've just written your first snippet of ActionScript—Flash's programming language, which has much in common with JavaScript, except that it is designed to control objects in Flash. (It can also invoke JavaScript, so it is quite powerful.) Let's consider how we can get a movie to play twice, instead of just once. We want to use another action, gotoAndPlay(), which branches to another frame in a movie and continues playing from there. Here's a snippet of code that accomplishes what we want. After selecting Expert mode (from the pull-down menu in the upper right corner of the Actions window), insert the following to the last frame of your movie:

```
if (firstTime)  //set true in frame 1
{ firstTime = false;
  gotoAndPlay(2);
}
else stop();
```

As the comment explains, this movie assumes that a variable, firstTime, has been set to true in frame 1 of the movie. It will then be true when it arrives at the last frame for the first time. So it sets firstTime to false, then goes to frame 2 (so it will not reset the variable again!) and continues from there. The second time through, firstTime is false, so our snippet stops the movie. Voilá!

Exercise 8.50: After experimenting with the ActionScript described above, try writing a script that will play a movie *three* times.

So far, we have used ActionScript to control the behavior of a movie. The primary use of ActionScript is to create interactivity. Let's create a button that opens a web page. We start by creating a graphic, by clicking on the rectangle tool in the Tools palette, then drawing a box on the stage. OK, now that we have a box, we want to convert the box into a button. Use the pointer tool to double-click on the box; its appearance should change to a cross-hatch. Select Insert > Convert to Symbol (or the shortcut, F8). In the Convert to Symbol dialog box, change the name to URL, leave the behavior as Button, and press OK. Flash stores all symbols in a library. You can have many instances referring to the same symbol in the same or different movies. Thus symbols are one way that Flash conserves on file size as well as promotes consistent design.

With the button still selected on the stage, open the Actions window again, then insert the following code:

```
on (release)
{ getURL("http://www.cse.lehigh.edu/~glennb/um"); }
```

The `on` control structure, like JavaScript's `ONCLICK`, is a mouse event handler—only this one observes when a user releases the mouse button. When that happens, action `getURL` will open a new web page, directed at the URL we have provided as its parameter (the home page for this book).

Exercise 8.51: The default behavior of the above ActionScript is to open the specified URL in a *new* browser window. To open the URL in the same browser window, you need to add a parameter to the action. Use Flash's context-sensitive help facility (a little reference book icon with a question mark on it near the upper right corner of the Actions window) to learn more about `getURL` and its parameters. Then write the ActionScript that opens a URL in the same window.

Exercise 8.52: So far, the button we designed doesn't give indication that it is aware of the mouse, until you click it and something happens. In terms of user interface design principle design, why would it be a good idea for the button's appearance to change when you roll on and off the button?

Exercise 8.53: Having established that changing a button's state is a good idea, here's how to do it: Once you have a button as a symbol, double-click on the button, and Flash will opens another timeline. Here you will see four different frames representing four possible states of a button: **Up** (when the mouse is not on the button), **Over** (when the mouse is rolling over it), **Down** (when the mouse is pressing down on it), and **Hit** (when the mouse is in anywhere in a region defined as the button—this state is useful if a button has an irregular shape). You can change the appearance of your button graphic (for example, by changing its color) in each of the first three states. Try it!

The multimedia tutorial goes over many more examples of Flash interactivity. As we said above, our goal in the text is give you an idea what it can do. In fact, the multimedia itself should give you an excellent idea what is possible, since it is just about all implemented in Flash, with lots of ActionScript, especially the user interface and interactive exercises.

Exercise 8.54: After going through the multimedia tutorial, create a Flash movie with its own interactive drag and drop interaction. A couple of design questions: 1) Why is it important to provide clear instructions explaining what the user should do to successfully perform this exercise, without giving away the solution? 2) Why is it important that the draggable object return to its original position if the user drags it to the wrong place? And technical questions: 1) Why do we need to use movie clips to create this exercise? Why do we need to give the movie clips instance names?

Chapter review. Are the following statements true or false? Explain why or why not.

a) Engineers tend to focus on machines, software engineers on user interfaces.

b) The function keys on most keyboards violate usable design, specifically visibility.

c) The scroll bars on the sides of windows are effective because of real world mapping.

d) Including alt tags in HTML are a good example of the feedback principle.

e) Clippy, Microsoft's help agent, is annoying to some users because it violates transparency.

f) Scroll bars are also effective because they can include more material than fits on a screen.

g) The prototype for *The Universal Machine* (figure 8.3) succeeds at speaking the user's language.

h) It is a good idea (too often forgotten) to test a user interface by observing actual users.

i) JavaScript, Flash and other language run-time environments all assume an event-driven loop.

j) When you look at a web page in a browser, you are viewing the source code of an HTML file.

k) Most markup tags come in pairs, for example <br> and </br>.

l) Many tags, such as <body> or <p>, can take optional parameters.

m) Most browsers ignore extra white space in HTML files.

n) A URL is the name of a file.

o) An image map is how HTML supports the idea of "hot spots" in graphical images.

p) JavaScript is a subset of the Java language that web browsers know how to interpret.

q) An event handler embedded in an HTML form can invoke a JavaScript function.

r) Document and Math are examples of objects built into JavaScript.

s) JavaScript can do forms validation on both the client and server side of a web transaction.

t) Persistence of vision requires that animations have at least 30 frames per second.

u) GIF and Flash animations both support automatic tweening.

v) JPG is a popular format for web graphics because of its codec.

w) Vector-based graphics tools typically "paint" pixels in an image.

x) Unlike Dynamic HTML, Flash requires a plug-in to play movies in a browser.

y) You can use ActionScript to jump to specific pages on the web.

z) It's a good idea to differentiate the states of a button in a Flash timeline.

Summary

As with all the chapters, there is of course much more that we could say about user interface and web design (for example, designing for accessibility, so that users with disabilities are not shut out, see exercise 8.6). User interface design looks at software systems from a human perspective. What is efficient (or effective) for people is not necessarily the same as what is efficient for machines. Software engineers need to consider the tradeoffs. The study of **Human Computer Interaction (HCI)** is relatively new, its findings are still rather soft, and too many software engineers haven't studied them. So it is little surprise that many applications and web sites are not terribly usable. But there is a significant payoff. For example, IBM found that redesigning its sales web site according to effective HCI principles led to a 400% increase in its rate of converting hits to actual sales, in the first month (J. Battey, "IBM redesign results in kinder, simpler site," *InfoWorld*, April 18, 1999). We introduced some user interface principles (by no means a definitive list), and looked at how to apply them, both in critiquing and redesigning existing applications. Keep these principles in mind as you apply these principles to web sites in HTML, JavaScript and/or Flash.

Chapter 9
Social and Ethical Issues
"War is too important to be left to the generals!"
René Clemenceau, premier of France 1912-1920

Technology accelerates social change. One hears much about "The Computer Revolution" But has the computer really *revolutionized* anything? That is, anything beyond the manufacture and use of the machines themselves? Opinions are still divided, because seeing into the future is a tricky business. Let's begin by attempting to clarify some of the issues relating technology (specifically, computers) and society. What is a "revolutionary change"? And have computers really brought about this kind of change? And what does it matter to us? After an initial exploration of the idea of "The Computer Revolution," we will look at the general changes in our society that have come about over the last two hundred years, and the key role of the computer in social change today. We then consider several aspects of a particular issue that has broad implications for society: namely, the concept of *privacy*—what it is, how it has been affected by computers, and what may be the outcome. We'll also consider some of the other legal issues that have arisen with the growth of the computer industry--*software protection, software failure*, and *censorship*.

Figure 9.1:
**Computers pose social
and ethical dilemmas**

Finally, we consider ethical implications of all these changes and see how they affect both professionals and citizens. Dilemmas of "computer ethics" are dilemmas, because they are not straightforward choices between good and bad, but between "good" and "better" or "bad" and "worse." Difficult decisions like these are rarely made well by blind hacking. It is therefore important to equip both professionals and citizens with skills and ideas—analogous to the problem solving skills we have developed in earlier chapters for programming—which will help them in cases of ethical deliberation.

9.1 Computers and Society

Geography, population, customs, and beliefs all play a part in shaping the nature of a society. But a society's technology also has a hand in shaping its character. An agricultural society based on the ox-drawn plow is quite different from one in which farming relies on heavy agricultural machinery. A society in which transportation or communication is difficult and expensive is also quite different from one in which both are commonplace. When a new technology becomes pervasive in a society—as computers have become—it has an impact that goes well beyond the technologists. Social change begins to affect the rest of us—whether we like it or not. The motto "Sit back, and enjoy the ride!" is not always a good idea, when the ride is a rapidly changing society. Where is it taking us?

Exercise 9.1: Think of some technological development (other than computers) that has had a profound effect on the nature of society. How and why has it had this effect?

9.1.1 New technology brings changes

That new technology brings changes is obvious. Not so obvious are the *kinds* of change and the *degree* to which these changes permeate and reshape society. Some changes in the last 25 years spring to mind readily. Twenty-five years ago, touch-tone phones were common but were by no means as widespread as today. Twenty-five years ago, automatic teller machines (ATMs) were quite rare. Both of these have made life simpler and more convenient, but socially, just how significant are either of these two technical innovations? It is hard to answer such a question, in part, because the effects of separate technical developments build on each other, so that the joint effect is far greater than the effect of either separately. In such a case, it is impossible to evaluate the effect of one without considering the other.

Let's consider the "Computer Revolution." Is it really a *revolution*? How does it stack up with other historical revolutions, such as the American and the French Revolutions, or perhaps most relevantly, the Industrial Revolution. One important feature of all these, that went beyond the recorded events themselves, was that they fundamentally changed the way people saw themselves and their relation to their society. In the United States, Americans began to see themselves as their own people, with their own national destiny, not as an appendage of England. Moreover, they had launched a great social experiment in constitutional democracy that would eventually become a model for other nations, including many new nations. In France, the overthrow of the monarchy enabled the people to reject the "divine right of kings" to rule nations as they pleased (even to bankrupt them). In both Europe and the United States, the Industrial Revolution changed the society from one in which people largely grew and made their own food, clothes, and tools (or purchased them from their makers locally) to one in which factories churned out products which were distributed over a wide area. In chapter 1, we saw that the Industrial Revolution played a role in suggesting to Charles Babbage the very idea of automated computation. A "revolution" is a movement that brings on sweeping changes in the relationship between a society and its members.

Exercise 9.2: Give reasons that touch-tone phones may have a greater impact on society than ATMs will. Give reasons that ATMs may have a greater impact than touch-tone phones. What kind of effects can you see that the two together might have?

Exercise 9.3: Consider the automobile. Do you think that the automobile has created a revolution? What reasons might one have for thinking it has or has not? Has it fundamentally changed the way people see themselves and their relation to society, and if so, how?

Is "The Computer Revolution" really a revolution? Have computers brought on sweeping changes in society? At a meeting of the American Society for Information Science in 1984, Professor Barnes argued that they haven't. Although computers had made a substantial impact, a reorientation might not have happened yet. In fact, despite their widespread use, computers were then still generally seen only as calculating devices. (Recall in Chapter 1, our emphasis that computers are *not* just calculating devices. Do you now agree?)

In less than a generation since 1984, though, computers had begun to make these pervasive social changes. Applications of AI have become common enough that many financial and management decisions can be made by computers, not managers. Medical diagnostic programs are in a position to provide at least substantial assistance to physicians, and in some cases to make diagnoses themselves. Computer-based ATMs now appear in retail stores, and banking can be done so easily over the telephone that the idea of actually *going* to the bank for a transaction is beginning to vanish. Corresponding or doing business with persons halfway across the world, instantaneously, no longer seems strange; indeed, web applications can even do rough translation between human languages. If a genuine computer revolution has not been accomplished, it is certainly in the making.

The depth and pervasiveness of these changes have also called a number of concepts into question. James Moor, in an essay entitled "What is Computer Ethics?"[1], gives a number of ways in which some of our ordinary concepts—privacy, property, theft, among others—have had to be modified as a result of the computer revolution. For example, it is now possible by consulting many computer data bases, to obtain an immense amount of information about someone without that person's even being aware of it. Is that an infringement of the person's privacy, or not? Again, it is now possible to access a person's private files and "remove" information, while still leaving it apparently untouched (for example, secretly copying a file). Since the original owner still has the information, does this count as theft? there is a strong tradition that the ideas behind inventions and literature are in some sense protected—granting patents and copyrights to creators protects "intellectual property." But there is also an equally strong tradition that mathematical ideas and natural phenomena are free for all to use. In some sense a computer program is a creation, like a machine or a book, but in another sense, it is simply a mathematical process. So do computer programs count as intellectual property or not?

From all this, perhaps you can begin to see another aspect of the "universal machine": its universal impact on the shape of society. In addition to providing instruction in a programming language, the previous chapters have shown the broad outlines of the discipline. At this point, we want to explore the areas where the discipline and the society at large tend to merge. As we do, keep in mind what you have learned in those chapters which have been aimed at describing the discipline of computer science, as we shall refer to them again.

Exercise 9.4: Prof. Barnes argued in 1984 that despite all the hype there hadn't really been a computer revolution yet. Do you agree? Or would you think the sweeping social change of a revolution is more apparent now? If so, how? Either provide at least three reasons one way or the other, or argue both ways.

9.1.2 Understanding technological change

It might be easier to evaluate the social impact of computation if we step back and look at an older technological development. Consider the steam engine, which helped to launch the Industrial Revolution.[2] As you do, keep in mind what is said in general about technological change and apply it to the social impact of computation. Essentially, engines of the day were devised to serve as a power source—initially, where other power sources were unavailable or inefficient. Water, wind, or muscle had been the previous sources of mechanical power, but both water and wind power where and when one finds a usable power source. Muscle power is a much more flexible power source, because it is movable, but it is relatively weak unless large numbers of animals are available, and then food and shelter become inconvenient necessities.

---

[1] In the journal *Metaphilosophy* 16:266-275. Blackwell (1985). Reprinted in *Computers, Ethics and Social Values*, by Deborah Johnson and Helen Nissenbaum. (Prentice Hall (1995))

[2] Today the steam engine has been superseded by the internal combustion engine so that it no longer has much of an impact. Nevertheless, its applications were many and varied. For example, it's seldom realized today, but the "Stanley Steamer"—a steam-engine powered automobile—was the first car to exceed 100 miles an hour (setting a world speed record of 127 mph in 1906), in a day when most cars' limits were under 50 mph.

Often, a new technological development is initially used in a straightforward way as a *replacement* for some previous device or technique. The first practical steam engines were used to pump water from coal mines—a task that had previously required muscle power. Later, steam engines replaced water, wind, or muscle power in grinding grain. Similarly, they were used in the textile industry to power cotton gins, spinning devices, and looms—again, a fairly direct replacement of water or muscle power.[3]

After this first stage, however, comes the *adaptation* stage, when technology is adapted to provide novel ways to perform old tasks. For example, we saw the adoption of steam engines to power boats and ships—not just as a replacement of wind power on sails or muscle power on oars, but as an adaptation to propel a craft by propellers or paddle wheels. In general, the adaptation stage represents an analogous rather than straightforward replacement. A steam engine to run a ship does not directly replace the motive power which drives sails or oars, but replaces it through an analogous device (the propeller or paddle wheel).

At some point, however, genuinely *new* uses appear. Often this is combined with the development of some other invention, and the two combine in their effects. For example, using steam engines to generate electricity could scarcely have been imagined until the use of electricity had developed to the point that it was desirable to generate it at a central location and distribute it over power networks. At this stage, another kind of effect occurs: besides new applications of the given technology, these applications generate other new applications, and often sow the seeds for other new inventions. In this way, at a certain point, technology nourishes itself.

As our society evolves technologically, it is important that we understand it in order to have some control over the process. For this, a narrow technical understanding of our technology is not enough. Here, we must keep in mind Clemenceau's warning "War is too important to be left to the generals!" But why should this be so—aren't the generals the experts in war? An important reason is that the generals' highly specialized training[4]—in the art of war—may make them blind to other dimensions than the military. (Remember our remarks in Chapter 2 about "blinders.") For much the same reasons, one might say that "Highway design is too important to be left to the civil engineers," because the design of highways can have environmental, economic, and social effects. This is not to say that civil engineers should have nothing to say about the design of highways, or even that they must become experts in all the dimensions of highway design. It does say that good highway designers must be aware of and sensitive to the demands of these issues. Of course, the same could be said of the design and construction of computer systems. If we do not remember this, we shall find that our highways and computer systems hurt us more than they help us.

Exercise 9.5: List at least four ways in which the design of a computer network can have effects other than simply providing data a way to get from point A to point B. What disciplines might therefore be needed to evaluate the effects of a proposed network?

Exercise 9.6: Pick some kind of computer system with which you are familiar (it needn't be a technical one; it could be your watch or your credit card), and list what its effects might be other than its intended ones. What disciplines might therefore be helpful to consult in the design and development of this kind of computer system?

---

[3]In much the same way, nylon replaced rayon, which had replaced silk or linen in fine fabrics.

[4] Today, general's training is far less specialized than it once was. But war is still too important...

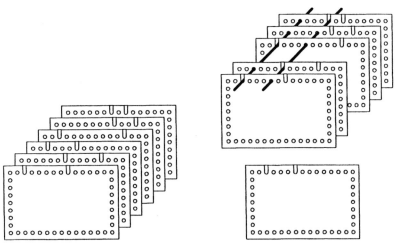

Figure 9.2 Information processing with edge-notched cards

9.1.3 Understanding the computer revolution

How does the model of social change that we have outlined in terms of the steam engine apply to the computer revolution—if it is a revolution? The early stage of computer use was in terms of mathematical computation. In fact, at one point, a prominent electrical engineer argued against the creation of "Computer Science" departments on the grounds that a computer's function was essentially the same as that of a slide rule. Having a "Computer Science" department in a university, he argued, would make no more sense than having a "Slide Rule Science" department. Of course this reaction is perfectly in accord with our earlier remarks about the initial stage of any technical advance—*replacement*—so it might almost have been predicted.

The next stage is *adaptation*. Rather than simply performing computation, computers were adapted to other tasks, such as **information management**, compiling and comparing various sorts of information, such as census data. Henry Hollerith founded what eventually became the International Business Machines (IBM) corporation because of a need to automate information—half a century before the development of electronic computers. The tool used for such tasks was **edge-notched cards**, shown in figure 9.2. Information was placed on large cards with holes punched all around the edges, through which thin metal rods could be run. Clipping out the edges of a specific hole on a card would mean that when the rods were run through that hole on a deck of cards, those cards on which the hole was *not* clipped could be lifted up by the rod, while those cards whose hole had been clipped would remain behind. This allowed the user of this system to select cards according to various criteria.

Suppose the census bureau needed to record information about a person's gender. The procedure would be to designate one hole on each card for that—clipping it out only for males. Then, using a rod in that hole to lift cards, it's easy to select all the cards representing females. For logical conjunction—say, of males over 21—using two rods, one raising female cards and another raising cards on a hole representing age (clipped if and only if over 21), would leave behind the cards for all the males over 21. Logical disjunction (e.g., those under 21 *or* unemployed) would require two selections—not quite as simple, but not overly difficult.

Exercise 9.7: Suppose the first hole is clipped for males and left unclipped for females, the second hole is clipped for employed and unclipped for unemployed, and the third hole is clipped for those with driver's licenses and unclipped for those without. How would one find all employed females who do not have driver's licenses? All unemployed males with driver's licenses?

Exercise 9.8: What are some disadvantages of edge-notched cards for information processing? Hints: (1) How would one represent a person's age? (2) What if an unemployed person becomes employed? What if an employed person becomes unemployed?

Though certainly an improvement on early hand-based computation methods, mechanical card processing was still very cumbersome. Adapting the logical process of sorting and selecting information to computer programs was a major breakthrough, not only making it faster, but making it possible to gather and easier to "mine" data for more complex information. The introduction of punched cards, decks of which could be mechanically sorted on machines called *sorters* was a major improvement, but still no match for computer processing. The development of **database** software, involving the application of boolean operations to data, made really large-scale information processing not only possible but practical. In fact, the computer really ushered in what has been called the "Information Age," an era in which intangible information has become a valuable commodity. But information processing at least started as both a replacement of non-computer processes on computers and an adaptation to computers.

The final stage—the development of genuinely *new* applications—came later, and in fact is still going on. One of the first of these new applications was the use of computers to translate high-level computer languages into the low-level languages which computers can execute. The deployment of FORTRAN and COBOL, making it much easier to program computers, soon made software development a major industry. Once the basic design of stored program machines was well understood, and integrated circuits brought the cost of implementing these processors down, it became possible for hobbyists and homeowners to build or buy their own computers, albeit at first primarily for playing games. But now these "microprocessors" are more powerful, both in terms of space and in terms of speed, than the main-frame computers of a generation ago, and their power has been unleashed to understand speech, simulate virtual reality, make information from around the world available at our finger-tips, tutor children, let the dumb speak (the brilliant physicist Stephen Hawking communicates and even writes books and multimedia software with the aid of computer-generated speech), and the lame walk (with computer-aided prostheses). Reaching this third stage is what leads us to believe that a genuine computer revolution is underway. The ways in which people see themselves, in relation to each other and to computers, have fundamentally changed.

Like a good highway designer, a good computer scientist needs to have an appreciation of the non-technical, social issues spinning out from the computer revolution. But not just the computer scientist—the rest of us as well. Political leaders insist that our society must make sure that every school and every child has access to the Internet—but at what bandwidth, and at what cost? Should children have unimpeded access to pornography? Should anyone? Should we put a human being on Mars, or be content to let robots do the exploring for us? Should we trust "expert systems" with decisions about our wealth or our health? Should foreign countries have access to America's encryption technology and thus be able to intercept sensitive information on computer networks? Should the federal government be able to intercept any information (say, to fight crime or terrorism)—even what private citizens want to keep private? Wise decisions in these areas cannot be left to the specialists; educated citizens need to understand them as well.

What are these key issues? They are many and complex, and a single chapter cannot cover all of them, or even any of them in complete detail. However, this chapter will introduce you to four currently "hot" areas: (1) computers and social change; (2) computers and privacy; (3) computers and legal issues; and (4) computers and professional ethics. We will explore the background in each of these four areas, then touch on some of the major issues of today, and finally raise questions concerning the future. In all of these areas, as well as in the multimedia for this chapter, you will also be pointed in some directions for you to explore on your own.

9.2 Computers and Social Change

Technology in general has been around for centuries, so before we look at the effect of the computer, we should first look at the effect of some other technologies. To do this, we might go back long before the time of Christ, when technological developments first created the agricultural society. But we need not go that far back to see how technology can change society. We need only look at the Industrial Revolution and its impact on a hitherto largely agricultural society.

Although the eighteenth century is generally seen as the time of the Industrial Revolution, the United States remained primarily an agricultural economy for some time after that. Not until around 1915 did more people work in factories than on farms. This change—occurring earlier in England than here—significantly changed the nature of society. In an agricultural society, the key to wealth and power was land; the central tool was the plow. Although not every family was entirely economically independent—shoes were seldom made at home, for example, but were bought or traded for from the shoemaker—industrial commerce was on a low scale. There were no merchandising combines to sell shoes on a wholesale scale.

In the ensuing industrial society, the key to wealth and power was capital; the central tool was first the steam engine, later engines and motors of other sorts. The invention of machine technology affected society in many ways—some obvious, some subtle. An obvious one was that central factories, rather than dispersed sources of production, became the norm; this resulted in the rapid growth of the towns and cities where those factories were located. Many jobs were created, and the resulting new opportunities brought immigrants to the industrialized countries. A subtle effect was that peoples' concept of time changed—the clock, not the sun, became the measure of time. Efficient use of factories required the work force to arrive and leave at given times. Also, as transportation networks spread, dependable arrival and departure times became more important. "Time is money" is no longer a metaphor but a way of life, part of the way we perceive the world.

In today's information age, information has also become a resource or a product with a price tag, and the information factory is the computer. It would be difficult to imagine how large information-intensive organizations such as insurance companies, pollsters, or intelligence agencies could operate today without computers. Police departments are increasingly making use of computers and computer networks. When you are stopped for a traffic violation, the officer remains in the police car, running a check of your car plate to see if it is stolen. Banks now seldom if ever actually transfer funds back and forth—everything is done by computer in terms of credits and debits. Recently, not only has the number of people using the Internet increased dramatically, the amount of business conducted "on-line" is growing, as well. One need no longer work at an office, but can telecommute from home, or even from a resort. Our society has changed to the point that the computer revolution is a true revolution.

Exercise 9.9: Think back as far as you can remember. What is the greatest technological change you have experienced? What have been its benefits? Have there been accompanying disadvantages? Could they have been avoided with some foresight?

9.2.1 Dislocations in a changing society

At the time of the early Industrial Revolution, when power looms and devices for knitting and spinning came into use, many independent producers were thrown out of work. Bitter social struggles resulted, and the term 'Luddite'—originally applied in the early 19th century to bands of unemployed who roamed the country destroying machines—now refers to any opponent of new technology. A particularly poignant folk song of the time tells of a young hand-weaver who is disgrace because has fallen in love with a "factory girl" (who works at a power loom in the weaving factory). Not only did substantial unemployment result from the widespread adoption of these inventions, but the working conditions in the factories and mills were often hard and dangerous, and children were often exploited as workers. The conditions of laborers moved Karl Marx to develop the economic theories which resulted in the Communist movement. In the long run, however, the increased productivity brought about increased employment and a higher standard of living for most of the society, and now most people judge the Industrial Revolution as socially beneficial, on the whole. Nevertheless, it has had subtle consequences. Discovering the efficiency of centralization, "social engineers" have built "factories" for health care (hospitals), care of the elderly (nursing homes), education (public schools), caring for the poor (welfare), and so forth, removing these activities (along with employment) from the home. Though these institutions are indeed more efficient, they also tend to depersonalize and devalue relationships among people. Modern, techno-industrial society is indeed more efficient at producing wealth and preserving health, but it has also contributed to greater psychological depression, family disintegration, and spiritual alienation. Yet it is not so easy, or even necessarily desirable, to go back to the "good old days" on the farm!

As the industrial society gives way to the information society, many similar dislocations have resulted. The automation of industrial plants has resulted in substantial "downsizing" of the work force, with unemployment and the shifting of personnel from one type of job to another. Forty years ago, the tradition of working in the mines or the steel mills or the automobile factories was often handed down from father to son. Imagine the effect on a worker with a family tradition of that sort who, at age 50, finds himself replaced by a computer-driven machine. According to a joke concerning automation, the "the factory of the future" would be run by one man and a dog. The man's job was to feed the dog; the dog's job was to keep the man away from the machines!

This clearly hasn't occurred, nor will it soon. But we are more recently seeing another kind of dislocation, as expert systems are incorporating more and more human expertise into their decisions. Programs to assist medical diagnosis have been around for years, and other programs have been developed which duplicate the decisions of judges. After seeing the workings of a program designed to simulate a psychotherapist, some people argued the desirability of doing this for real cases. What directions will these efforts lead?

An optimistic view looks back to displacements of the Industrial Revolution and argues that again new technological developments will create new jobs. A more pessimistic view is that the new jobs created will be substantially less rewarding—both in terms of money and a sense of accomplishment. (It seems that many of the jobs in the "Information Society" will be positions in the service sector of the economy. And these are substantially less well-paying than those in the manufacturing sector.) Another pessimist points out that the well-paying jobs (e.g., computer design or programming) will be fewer and will require an advanced educational background—that the days in which a high-school graduate, or perhaps even a new college graduate, could be assured of a productive job are over. (In fact, in order to graduate from high school today, students often must absorb much more knowledge than their parents had to.) A still more radical view is that the accomplishments of artificial intelligence are coming closer to "take-off" and that at some point they will enable even highly skilled intellectual labor to be replaced by computers. All these views take issue with the argument that the move from the Industrial Society to the Information Society will be similar to the move from the Agricultural Society to the Industrial Society.

How will computers will further change the society? Probably the two greatest issues deal with employment and education. The first is simply the question we touched on above: What impact will the computer have on the economic structure of the country? Will it create large-scale unemployment? If so, will the earlier pattern of the Industrial Revolution—an ultimate increase in productivity and the creation of new jobs, leading to even more employment—be followed? The second issue deals with the changing demands on the educational system: What, if any, changes in the educational system will be needed to keep pace with the changing nature of society and the job market? Will a highly technical education be a "must" for employability?[5]

The "downsizing"of the American manufacturing sector is now obvious. The growing area in the economy is the service area. It seems likely that the increasing capabilities of computers will further increase the downward trend of the "blue collar" sector of the economy. But the "white collar" sector may be affected as well. For example, the widespread use of word-processing and feasibility of speech recognition technology has meant that dictation to secretaries is becoming rare. Sophisticated computer-aided design packages, usable by almost anyone, are replacing drafting equipment and its users. On the other hand, the service economy seems at first not to be affected. People are needed to provide services, no matter what. But are they? Telephone operators are certainly being replaced by automated systems. "Record your message at the tone" and "For product information, press 1 now; for customer service, press 2; for ..." are commonplace. Who (or what) will receive the drive-in orders at the "Burger Palace" of the future? Automobile repair is becoming more and more a matter of removing and replacing a microprocessor-based unit than of repairing a malfunctioning part. Nils Nilsson, at the Stanford University Artificial Intelligence Laboratory, has even argued that *employment* as such will cease to play a significant part in our lives, and that most people's economic support will be in the form of what is now called "welfare". The present political mood of the country makes this seem unlikely, however. So what will happen?

The educational system of the future will also be harder pressed. As computer technology comes to play an increasing role in the society, schools will have to equip their students to deal with it. This in itself poses two problems. The first is that technology is expensive. Although the cost of computational power has decreased greatly, much of this decrease is eaten up in increasing the capacities of individual machines. Although the computational power of a moderately high-powered desktop has increased many times, its cost has decreased slightly. Providing the needed computing capabilities for every school may be very difficult for already financially stressed school systems. A second problem is that adding new material to the curriculum would seem to require that something be removed. Or will increasingly computer-based instruction be so much more efficient in terms of time that the additional material can be incorporated without affecting school schedules?

A computer-based school will face other problems. Different people have different learning styles. (This is a major reason why we have included the multimedia with this book—we hope that it is helpful for students with different learning styles.) Some learn by reflecting on ideas, others require a more participatory approach. Some are comfortable with abstract concepts as such, while others need concrete examples for understanding. Good teachers can vary approaches for individual students. At present, computers are not this flexible; they appeal to just a few learning styles. (Some researchers in artificial intelligence are exploring the possibilities of developing computer-based

---

[5]On the other hand, many educators argue that education at *all* levels should concentrate on teaching the skills of critical thinking, which are certainly not unique to a technical education, rather than technical knowledge, which may quickly become obsolete. (What about "problem-solving"?)

tutoring systems that adapt to students' individual needs, learning speeds, and learning styles. Will we have someday have "super-teachers" with inexhaustible patience?) Computers typically appear to have a fixed agenda, based on the assumptions of the program being run. In large part, the goal of the educational process is the empowerment of the student, but computer-based instruction often empowers the student to do only what the computer wants or expects. Much research on how computers affect learning remains to be done before we can simply say that adding computers to schools will solve the educational problems computers pose.

Exercise 9.10: If you have access to them, talk to people who do career counseling. What do they see as important computer-related trends in the job market?

9.3 Computers and Privacy

Privacy is a rather strange thing. We all want at least some of it, but when someone seems to want "too much" of it, we wonder if something is being hidden. Moreover, different societies and different cultures want different amounts of it. What is friendly attention in one culture is "snoopiness" in another. What is decent regard for others in one culture is "stand-off-ishness" in another. Even in the U.S., the amount of privacy differs from a small town to a large city. In a small town, almost everybody knows almost everybody, and privacy is relatively scarce. In a large city, you may not know the person in the next apartment or across the hall. But in spite of these differences, we all think at times that we want some privacy. Exactly what is it that we all want?

Whether or not you realize it, computers and privacy are intricately related in a variety of ways. In this section, we'll explore some of the issues and see just what's happening to privacy out there in this computer-based world. The key to all the relationships between computers and privacy is the immense power of computers to manipulate information. Information-processing tasks that once would have been virtually impossible or impractically expensive can now be done easily and inexpensively. And whether you know it or not, whether you like it or not, some of the processing going on out there involves information about *you*.

9.3.1 What is "privacy", anyway?

We all *know* more or less what "privacy" is, but we may find it difficult to *say* exactly what it is. Our right to privacy has been described as "the right to be let alone".[6] But we must not confuse the notion of **privacy** itself with the **right** to have privacy. Of course, if there were no such thing as privacy, it would be odd to speak of having a *right* to it. And if no one, under any circumstances, had *any* right to privacy, we would say that under these circumstances, privacy (although a concept) was non-existent. Still, there is a difference. Therefore, to distinguish the two, rather than speaking of privacy as a *right*, it makes more sense to speak of privacy as a *power* or *ability* to say "no" in certain ways to the outside world. But in what ways?

Sometimes we simply want to be by ourselves, and may say "I'd like some privacy, please!" What we seem to mean is that we want other people to stay away from us, we want to be alone. This we could call **physical privacy**. But we might well have physical privacy—no one at all is near us—yet we are being observed by powerful cameras or telescopes. Does this mean we *don't* have

---

[6]The phrase, found in a famous article "The Right to Privacy" by Samuel Warren and Louis Brandeis in the Harvard Law Review (1890), is due to Judge Thomas Cooley of the Michigan Supreme Court. The article is reprinted in *Computers, Ethics and Social Values*.

physical privacy in such a situation? If all we want to do is to be by ourselves, this observation might not matter, so we would not say that we did not have our (physical) privacy. But we might want more than that. Denying physical access would not be enough if we did not want to be *watched*. So we need to distinguish physical privacy from what we can call **observational privacy**.

There are yet other kinds of privacy. Suppose you discover that someone has taken pictures of you doing something when you thought you were in private—making silly faces in the mirror, say. This person has clearly violated your observational privacy—and that's bad enough! But even worse, you find out that copies of the pictures have been handed out to a number of people you know. This is no longer a matter of simply infringing on your observational privacy, it's something that goes above and beyond that. And still worse yet, you find that these other people you know have made copies and given them to still other people, who have made copies and ...! These other people have not infringed on your observational privacy at all, since they did not watch you. But surely there is *some* kind of infringement on your privacy, since you cannot say "no!" to them. What the others, as well as the original distributor, have done is to violate your **information privacy**. You have lost control of *information* about you. Here is where the tie between computers and privacy begins to emerge, since as we have noted, computers are information processors *par excellence*.

Exercise 9.11: Do you know someone whose information privacy ever been invaded? How was that person harmed? How could it have been prevented?

A fourth kind of privacy, somewhere between observational privacy and information privacy, is something we shall call **communications privacy**. By this we mean the ability to deny others access to your communications—mail, phone calls, telegrams, e-mail, etc. This is closely related to information privacy, as once you have received a letter, someone who steals it has certainly violated your information privacy, but it is importantly different in certain ways—particularly in its legal implications. It is also related to observational privacy, since reading your mail, or listening in on your phone calls is observation of a sort. But again, different legal implications make important differences, so we consider this a distinct kind of privacy. A few moments' reflection on e-mail should remind you of the increasingly numerous and increasingly vast computer-based communications networks. When we discuss communications privacy further, we'll also see another important issue that arises: free speech and censorship.

9.3.2 The value of privacy

As we remarked above, in some places privacy is pretty minimal, and people get along pretty well, so one might wonder just how important privacy is. It's sometimes said that privacy is a refuge for scoundrels—if you're not doing anything wrong, you don't need it. This is particularly true when we see some court case being thrown out because of improper procedures used in gathering evidence. But in fact, even when we are not doing anything wrong, the thought of being closely scrutinized makes us a bit uncomfortable. If you doubt this, peer closely—say, at a range of a foot or less—for several minutes at someone doing perfectly ordinary things. (Best to do it to close friend, though!) Moreover, most of us, reading George Orwell's futuristic novel *1984*, would find the thought of living in that society—with little if any privacy whatever—pretty horrible. Privacy, then, does have some value—but just what is it? And why does it have this value?

One common theme is that privacy is necessary for democratic values to flourish. One of the first things that a totalitarian government tries to do is to place its citizens under nearly total surveillance. In Nazi Germany and Communist USSR, children were encouraged to report on their parents' beliefs and activities. In George Orwell's novel *1984*, "Big Brother" seemed to know everything about everyone, and the slogan "Big Brother is watching *you!*" was everywhere. The Chinese government wants to regulate the flow of information through the Internet by demanding that all of it flow through computational gates overseen by Beijing. Even today in the U.S., holders of socially unpopular ideas are often subject to sanctions—ostracism, threats or even violence—and so value their privacy highly.

Another claim is that privacy is necessary for one's sense of individuality—the sense that one has the right to be one's own person. One of the objections to some of the early very large housing developments after World War II was that the houses were all alike, so one couldn't be different from all the others there. Of course, the desires for conformity and nonconformity are probably both in everyone, to different degrees. But if everything about you is known—and in small communities, that often seems to be the case—it is difficult to be one's very own person. It is especially hard, in communities with little privacy, to hold unpopular social or political beliefs.

A third view argues that the very idea of being a person involves one's having a variety of relationships with other persons. This requires control over the degree of intimacy that we have with other people. We tell our secrets to our nearest and dearest that we would never tell to casual acquaintances. If these secrets are passed on to others, we feel betrayed. (Think of a person who took pictures of you and distributed them wholesale!) If one's whole life is open to everyone, you lose control—there are no "secrets" to tell. This view makes privacy a very important human value.

9.3.3 The cost of privacy

But privacy has a cost. As the saying goes, "TANSTAAFL!"[7] People who move from a small community to a large city often enjoy the increased privacy, but moan the loss of "community." In a classic case, the inhabitants of an apartment house heard the cries of a woman being raped and murdered in the parking lot, and no one even called the police. *There's* privacy for you! On the other hand, giving up one's privacy may provide certain benefits. Some people with special medical problems—severe diabetes or penicillin allergy, for example—wear bracelets or neck medallions to advise of this fact if an accident occurs. And imagine the advantage, if you are sick or injured far from home, if a physician could tap into a large data base which has all your medical information in it. But this would involve a loss of some of your privacy.

The extreme complexity of society at large also encourages some loss of privacy. The police officer who stops you for running a red light is happy to be able to check your car's license plate to see who is the owner of the car and whether it is stolen. This, too, is to some degree an infringement on your privacy, but surely it is worth that small cost. Consider another example: if you have an unlisted number, you may still receive telephone solicitations, since a computer can be programmed to call all the numbers in a particular area. This is, of course, very convenient for marketing whatever product is being sold, but you will probably consider it an invasion of your privacy. On a still larger scale, various social programs confer benefits on those who have various disabilities, but to prevent fraud, waste, and duplication, it is important to know who is receiving what benefits. Of course this, too, infringes to some extent on these individuals' privacy.

Exercise 9.12: One view about privacy is that the only people who need it are people who have something to hide. Do you agree? Why or why not?

---

[7] **"There Ain't No Such Thing As A Free Lunch!"**

9.3.4 Information privacy

For all these reasons, we need to balance any loss of privacy against gains that will result. Let's consider information privacy. This, as we noted, is the privacy that lets you control information about yourself. Of course, some of this information is a matter of public record—such as when you were born, and who your parents were. But your grades in school, for example, are another matter. The Family Educational Rights and Privacy Act (1974) ensures your privacy by making it illegal to post students' grades by name. Your salary when you are in the workplace—what about that? Well, it depends. If you are in a private business, that is private information. But if you are an employee in the public sector, that may be a matter of public record, since you are being paid with public funds. Does this infringe on your privacy?

Much more information about you is public than you probably realize. For example, when you last bought software—or a stereo or television set—one of the first things you may have done was fill out a warranty card and send it in. Along with that you probably filled out a questionnaire about where and why you bought this product, and you probably answered some personal questions as well—interest, income, and so forth—nothing *really personal*, of course, just to help the company market its products. But suppose that all this information were combined into a single data base. What would it say about you? This is the idea of an *information mosaic*—just like a real mosaic, with lots of little insignificant pieces put together to form a grand overall pattern. In fact, before the computer era, one of the major sources of information in the intelligence agencies of various nations was the daily newspapers of the world. Just imagine many intelligence analysts, scanning many newspapers, clipping out item after item (to be mounted on edge-notched cards, of course). Afterwards, the collection of cards, and even the discarded newspaper itself, would become classified information, subject to security regulations.

Here is a concern of many people. Many government offices—federal, state, county, local— have extensive files about the people who are their "clients," each for its own purpose. The Internal Revenue Service is an obvious example, with extensive files on many people's incomes and expenditures. The Federal Bureau of Investigation, also, has files on many persons (not only those who have committed crimes). A number of agencies—county, state, and federal—have files about those who receive various kinds of welfare. Surely it would be advantageous if all these files could be combined in one master file! Income tax evasions could be more easily identified, criminals could more easily be located, fraudulent or duplicate welfare applications could be eliminated, violators could be more easily located, and activities could be made more efficient.

Such a proposal periodically surfaces, but so far strong enough opposition has put off attempts to have a single national data base of all these kinds of records. Why would one oppose such an obviously useful resource? For a number of reasons. One is that errors almost invariably occur in any collection of data. If data are divided among many collections, any error will have a much more limited effect, but with a single master data base, any error could have an almost unlimited effect. Imagine faulty data about you indicating (non-existent) criminal activity becoming available nationwide! Another reason arises from your providing certain kinds of data for specific reasons, so that to use them for other purposes breaches a trust. Again as an example, imagine your complete medical history available to any banker, policeman, employer, or anyone else who has a legitimate interest in certain other information about you. A third reason to oppose a national data base is that such information may be used improperly. Administrative decisions may be made about you on grounds that you may never know, but which are based on inappropriate or inaccurate information. You might be denied a scholarship because you once stole candy from a drug store. A fourth reason, which applies only to governments, is based on our Fourth Amendment rights to be free from improper search and seizure. When the Constitution was written, this was an important inclusion in the Bill of Rights. Today, court cases are often dismissed when crucial information has been obtained in violation of these rights. Such an all-embracing "master file" of information would make these abuses easier. A final argument is simply that an individual ought to have some control—the right to say "no!"—over the availability or use of any personal information, as long as he or she is willing to take the consequences. While this cannot be an unlimited right, the idea does seem to have more than a grain of truth to it. Without some rights of control over information about ourselves, we feel powerless.

One example of the force of such opposition was the cancellation of a large project called *Marketplace: Households*. In 1990, the Lotus Corporation and Equifax, a large credit organization, planned the release of a large data base of customer information. It was to have demographic information—ranging from simple (name and age) to complex (buying habits and lifestyle)—on the residents of 80 million households. Much of the information was taken from public sources, but some items were inferred from other data—gender was inferred from name, for example. There was such substantial public objection to the project that the offer was made to allow objectors to remove their names from the data base. Eventually, there was so much opposition and so many people did remove their names that the project was canceled.

In sum, it is clear that information privacy is important enough that it must be guarded, and designers of computer projects involving the acquisition and processing of information must be aware of the dangers. (The Association for Computing Machinery, a major professional organization in computer science, regards this issue as important enough to address it specifically in its code of professional ethics.) If these concerns are not heeded, people's increased opposition to their loss of information privacy may jeopardize uses that are otherwise perfectly appropriate and useful.

Exercise 9.13: It is common practice before hiring people for certain jobs to run background checks on them. The White House has been using FBI files for this purpose. Is that okay? Why or why not? Hint: what sort of material goes into FBI files? Should this data be available via the web?

9.3.5 Communications privacy

Communications privacy, as we have noted, concerns the accessibility of information as it is transmitted from one point to another. In a sense, it is a sort of dynamic version of information privacy. Before information is transmitted and after it is received, the issue is one of information privacy, but the privacy of information during transmission is another matter. The important differences lie in the way that communications systems are regulated by the government. The U.S. Mail system is a case in point: interfering with the delivery of any item in the mail, including opening it, is a federal offense; opening someone else's mail after it is received is not. Wire-based communications like telephone systems also offer legal guarantees of privacy. In order to wire-tap telephone lines, warrants must be obtained through fairly elaborate court procedures. Electronic communications, such as e-mail and other Internet operations, are quite another matter.

In the first place, federal law distinguishes between *wire* and *electronic* communications in the protections it offers. Wire communications are not quite what you might think. They are defined as those which contain the human voice in whatever form—oddly enough, cellular telephone calls are thus wire communications, and are protected as such. Telegrams and faxes, though sent over telephone lines, are not; neither are e-mail, or most other transmissions over the Internet. (By definition, voice transmissions over the Internet *would* be considered wire communications.) Second, as noted in chapter 6, the Internet is a network of networks. E-mail messages sent across it may go along complicated pathways. In fact, because of the general use of packet switching on the Internet, a single message may follow many different pathways, which makes infringements of privacy that much easier.

Communications privacy becomes even more important as the number of business transactions over the Internet increases. Whether the volume of net-based business ever reaches the level some predict, the number of on-line credit-card purchases even now makes communications privacy important. One answer, of course, involves encryption (see the end of chapter 6), or encoding sensitive messages so that only intended recipients can decode them (ideally). But "bad guys" as well as "good guys" desire privacy. The danger of terrorist threats, for example, raises the question of whether law enforcement agencies should be enabled to read all enciphered material. So the federal government advocated a "Clipper chip" which would be required to be used for encrypting communications, sot that the government would have a "peephole" into encrypted communications. The proposal was roundly attacked as invasive of privacy and equally as vigorously defended as necessary for the prevention of crime and the pursuit of criminals.

Exercise 9.14: Leaving aside credit card information or other very personal information, do you think it's okay for your employer to read all your ordinary e-mail messages? Why or why not?

9.4 Computers and legal issues

In our discussion of privacy, we have repeatedly referred to legal protections of privacy. In today's computer-intensive society, it would be surprising if this were the only way in which computers and the law are related—and it is not. In fact, an entire book would be needed to cover the whole range of ways in which computers and the law can interact. We'll look only at three in some detail: the *legal protection* for computer software; the *legal liability* for computer failure; and the *legal control* over information available on computer networks. Before that, though, let's touch very briefly on a somewhat more glamorous topic: **computer crime**—that is, crime in which use of the computer is an *essential* element. Thus, if I hit you over the head with a computer, that's a crime, but it doesn't count as *computer* crime, since I might just as well have used a stool, or even just a rock. Although computers offer new ways to commit crime—theft, say—for the most part, these crimes don't pose *conceptual* problems. Breaking into someone's house to rifle files is a crime, even if you don't take anything; so is breaking into one's computer system. If you take money, that's a crime; taking money by computer (say, by altering a bank's records) is also a crime. Even copying information of certain sorts is a crime, whether you do it with or without a computer. So, oddly enough, although it gets good press, most computer crime is not really a very different sort of thing. What we want to look at are the kinds of issues that require some careful thinking in order to understand them, and that's why we've chosen the ones we'll look at.

9.4.1 Protection for computer software

Material property—at least until someone invents a matter duplicator—has the feature that if I take something from you, you no longer have it. Information is strikingly different—although I take it from you, you haven't necessarily lost it. This means that legal protection must be different for this kind of intangible property, which over the years has become known as **intellectual property**. Although some argue that ideas should be free, and so intellectual property should not be protected, most people think that the ideas of the author of a book or the inventor of a new device deserve protection from those who would copy them. In general, three kinds of protection have been developed: *trade secrets, copyrights*, and *patents*.

Trade secrets protection is the simplest and least complicated, so we'll consider it first. Suppose you develop a secret formula for a new soft drink. If you keep the formula secret, then it qualifies for protection as a **trade secret**. Someone who steals it from you can be legally punished for violating trade secrets laws. But the essence of a trade secret is that it is a *secret*. If it can be shown that you have not treated this information as a secret—if you have shown it about, or have not appropriately protected it—then it will no longer qualify as a trade secret. This makes most computer software not a good candidate for trade secret protection, since it is generally developed to be widely distributed. Only proprietary software—software which a company develops for its own use—would qualify. New programs which an engineering firm develops for structural calculations might be of this sort, or a program to project expenses of an engineering project. But the vast majority of all software is developed for sale, and when you sell a piece of software it ceases to be a secret. In fact, taking a finished product and trying to find out how it is made and how it works is common enough that it is called "*reverse engineering*", and this is common in analyzing computer software and hardware.

A more practical approach is to treat software as something like a piece of literature and **copyright** it. This means that as the author, you have legal control (at least in principle) over who may copy it. Copyright was originally for works of literature, and in fact for some time it was held that material qualified for a copyright only if the material was in a form readable by humans. But over the years copyright has also been extended to designs, music, and a whole variety of things, so this restriction has lost most of its force. In any case, in 1980, Congress passed a law explicitly making computer programs eligible for copyright.

A crucial restriction is that copyright cannot apply to an *idea* itself, but only to the *expression* of an idea. So you cannot obtain a copyright to your idea for a novel, symphony, or program—only to the way you *expressed* that idea in an actual novel, symphony, or program. If someone else wrote another work based on the same idea, as long as it is not too similar to yours, it would not be a copyright violation. What's behind this restriction is the notion that ideas should be free, but someone who expresses the idea should have that creation protected. An interesting consequence of this view is that if an idea were only expressible in a single way, then the idea and the expression would be said to have **merged**, and even the idea's expression could not be copyrighted.

Another feature of copyright is that it does not prevent one from *duplicating* your work, only from *copying* it. If a person could prove that he or she did not actually copy your work, that would not be an infringement on your copyright. (Of course, if a very long and complicated work were to be duplicated *exactly*, it would surely be difficult to convince a judge that it had not been copied!) What this means is that the date of creation of a work can be important, since the first author obviously has not copied the work of the later author. For this reason, authors seeking to protect their work *register* copyrighted materials with the U.S. Copyright office.[8]

Another method of protection is a **patent**. A patent is an exclusive license granted by the government and protects against much more than mere copying—unauthorized duplication or use, for example, is also prohibited. Originally, patents were issued on inventions—machines, (non-natural) substances, and processes—but have been extended to cover a variety of other things. What cannot be patented, however, are natural phenomena and mathematical procedures. The extension

---

[8] It is a common but mistaken belief that you must register a work to obtain a copyright on it. You actually have a copyright on a work as soon as you have created it. However, to ensure your right, you must display a copyright notice on all copies of your work, and of course, registering it gives even stronger protection.

of patents to computer programs has had a rockier road than with copyright. For some time programs could not be patented, since the underlying algorithm could be described as a mathematical process.[9] The requirements for being patented are also stricter than for being copyrighted: the invention must be *useful*, *novel*, and *non-obvious*, and patent examiners have not always been experienced enough to know whether programs met the last two criteria.

Partly because the criteria for being patented are more complex, the process for obtaining a patent is more complicated than that for a copyright. The application must describe the specific qualifications the invention falls under. This can be crucial, as something may not be patented under one description, but be patented under another. Also, an exhaustive search for pre-existing patents is required to demonstrate novelty and non-obviousness. In general, the process is both expensive and time-consuming. As a result, copyright is more often used than patent as a protection for programs, though the rate of program patenting is increasing.

An alternative to either copyright or patent (or as a supplement to copyright) is the *licensing agreement* often found on software. According to this, the user does not actually *buy* the software, but only the right to use it under given conditions. This is often accompanied by a statement to the effect that opening the package counts as an agreement to abide by the licensing conditions. Violation of these conditions is a violation of a contract, and the violator is subject to legal penalties. However, there are questions whether these "shrink-wrap" contracts can be enforced, so that there is no clear view of how legally significant the agreement may be.

These are the mechanisms for protecting software, but the discussion so far has not been directed at the underlying question: *Ought* software to be protected at all? The amount of illegal software copying suggests that many software users think not. Why should this be? Some influential programmers argue that, like information, software is a social good and so should be free to all. Richard Stallman, in an article "Why Software Should be Free," speaks for this position, as well as for the position that making software freely available promotes technological progress.[10] On the other hand, most computer scientists argue for at least some protection, also on two grounds. First, they argue that software production is a major business in the United States, which is seriously harmed by unauthorized copying. Without any protection, the economic underpinning of the industry will collapse, and we shall have less software, less sophistication, and less user support—not more. Second, although one can scarcely argue for people having *complete* control over their own ideas, the idea of *fairness* requires that someone's ideas should not be taken without some sort of compensation; that is the goal of copyright and patent protection.

Whatever the virtues of these two positions, it seems clear that both copyright and patent protection *will* continue to be available for software, but that modifications may be made when either

---

[9] A frequent sequence of events has been: (i) the patent application for a program was denied by the Patent Office; then (ii) the individual's appeal to the Court of Customs and Patent Appeals was successful; but (iii) on the Patent Office's subsequent appeal to the Supreme Court, the patent was denied, but without the Court's specifically saying that programs could not *per se* be patented. The first program patent was granted only as a part of a process for curing rubber (*Diamond v. Diehr* (1981)).

[10] Stallman's article *is* copyrighted by his Free Software Foundation, Inc., but "Verbatim copying and redistribution is permitted without royalty; alteration is not permitted." The article itself is reprinted in *Computers, Ethics and Social Values*. The authors and many other computer scientists are of course grateful to Stallman and his associates for developing valuable software, including the C++ compiler that we distribute on our CDROM, in compliance with the "GNU LIBRARY GENERAL PUBLIC LICENSE."

under- or over-protection seems to be the case. And for those programmers who do not wish to use them, the development of freeware or shareware, legally unprotected software, is an interesting alternative.

Exercise 9.15: What limitations would be placed on the copyrighting of certain software if the requirement of human readability were still in force? (Hint: Think about the translation from source code to object code.)

Exercise 9.16: What reasons can you give to support Stallman's arguments? the opposing arguments?

9.4.2 Liability for computer failure

When products fail and consequent harm results, lawsuits always follow. Here's another intertwining of computers and the law. Failure of computer hardware is in principle like the failure of any other complicated electronic instrument and poses no special problem. Failure of computer software is quite different, however. Software systems, especially the very large programs mentioned at the beginning of Chapter 6, are intrinsically unreliable.[11] Why is this? For several reasons. First, programmers make errors, and anything short of exhaustive testing will fail to uncover all of them. Yet exhaustive testing of complex systems may be prohibitively expensive and impossibly time consuming. Moreover, in correcting identified errors, one often introduces new errors. Second, the sheer size of major software packages makes it impossible for a single person to write them, and even if one person could write the entire program, it would take so long that by the end, the beginning would have been forgotten. (Hence we advocate documentation, assertion-checking, the development of re-usable code, etc., as matters of social responsibility as well as technical cost-effectiveness.) Third, when software fails, it fails in a way that is different from most types of hardware failure. In part this is because hardware is largely analog and continuous, while software is digital and discrete. This means that there is no "margin of error." A mistake in a single character of a program may change the entire behavior of the program. Fourth, it is easier to protect against hardware failure. Hardware failure has a greater degree of randomness, for example, so having several processors working independently makes it likely that not all of them will go down at the same time. Software failures are often caused by the failure of particular common assumptions (about the nature of input, for example), so running multiple programs does not give the same assurance that they will not all crash.

Unfortunately, the legal system which has developed to handle liability is not well adapted to handle liability for software failure. In general, there are two kinds of liability when something goes wrong. The one most often heard about is **negligence**—the failure to exercise due care. When the provider of a good or service is negligent, both *consequential* and *punitive* damages may be assessed by a court.[12] **Consequential** damages are basically *reparations*—damages assigned to repair the harm done. **Punitive** damages are basically what they sound like—*punishments* for not having fulfilled the duty of due care. Therefore, the size of punitive damages may run many times

---

[11]This is emphasized in Fernando Corbato's article "On Building Systems That Will [!] Fail," in *Computers, Ethics and Social Values*.

[12]The term 'damages' used here (always in the plural) is a legal term. It has a special meaning something like "payments".

the size of consequential damages. Another kind of liability is **strict liability** (often called *product liability*). As the alternative name suggests, this can be assessed only when a *product* is defective. Interestingly enough, strict liability can in principle be assessed even though the product is defective through no fault of the producer—it is often spoken as "no-fault liability".[13] Under strict liability, only *consequential* damages may be assessed (since there may be no "fault" to punish).

In applying these concepts to software failure, three problems arise. First, the traditional assumption has been that in the absence of negligence, a product failure is unlikely, so the rationale for strict liability will not cause undue harm. But as we have seen, the failure of computer software is highly likely, even in the absence of negligence. Second, as its alternative name ("product liability") suggests, strict liability is applicable only to products, not to services. Computer programs in one way seem like products, but in another way are like services in that they perform tasks. It is unclear how they should be treated? Third, in cases of negligence, the failure to exercise due care must be specifically proven. With programs of great size, actually locating the specific error and demonstrating the failure of due care may be impossible, practically speaking. So the recourse of consumers in cases of defective software is extremely uncertain.

9.4.3 Censorship on the Internet

As the use of the Internet broadens, it is put to stranger and stranger purposes. These days, practically any person with any particular interest of any sort can find a kindred spirit. The problem is that not all of these individuals' interests are in the public interest, and there is much concern over whether some of these activities should be banned. Issues of pornography, particularly child pornography, led to the passage of a federal Computer Decency Act.[14] Threats of international or domestic terrorism seem to be aggravated by the availability of explosives "recipes" on the net. Reasons other than terrorist possibilities have also been advanced as justifying censorship of material on the Internet. In Pennsylvania an honors high school student was killed when a "project" he was working on, with directions obtained from "The Anarchist's Cookbook," exploded. On the other hand, the history of the Internet has been one of free and open communication, and many are reluctant to see this change. What are the legal issues involved in this area?

The Internet is vast but unorganized in scope. We hear almost daily about the huge number of sites and computers on it, yet the Internet does not exist as a unified entity—it is best described as a network of independent networks. Many of these are located in other countries whose laws are strikingly different from our own, so it would seem that any single source of control over what happens on the net is simply impossible. Moreover, even within the U.S., many activities are not governed by federal law, and the relevant laws differ from state to state. Behavior that is at least tolerated in one state can be illegal in another—"community standards" are often invoked in defining obscenity. But what is the relevant "community"?

In the Bill of Rights, the First Amendment secures the right to freedom of speech. Free speech is not, however, an unlimited and absolute right—falsely shouting "Fire!" in a crowded theater is a classic example of something that does not fall under that guarantee. But a standard

---

[13]This may seem unfair, but a full rationale is more than can be given here. Suffice it to say that through a rather interesting series of legal cases, strict liability has become accepted over the years.

[14]The Supreme Court eventually struck down this legislation as unconstitutional. Members of congress have since been crafting new legislation that they hope may pass constitutional muster.

requirement for the government to take any action that verges on affecting constitutional rights is that the action must be *minimal*—there is no other alternative with a lesser effect. Whether such alternative solutions are possible, and what they might be, will be debated for some time.

Exercise 9.17: Does a university have the right to censor material it makes available over its computer network (for example, to prohibit hate mail or other undesirable material)? On the one hand, it's the university's network. On the other hand should not universities, of all places, stand for the free expression of ideas? Give reasons for both positions.

9.5. Issues of professional ethics

Recall the argument about whether software should be given legal protection. Both sides brought forth social and ethical claims to support their conclusions. What at first might be seen as a purely technical issue—whether legal protection of software furthers or hinders technological development—itself has a socio-ethical underpinning, because both sides assume that further technological development is good for society, and that we ought to do what is good for society. Moreover, one side argues that for ethical reasons we ought to make the benefits of software freely available, while the other side argues that for ethical reasons we ought to recognize and protect programmers' rights over their software. Here we have an excellent example of an *ethical dilemma*—both sides may well agree on the desirability of both these goals, but for one reason or another disagree over which should take priority.

**Figure 9.3:
Balancing ethical
priorities**

The more complex issues of professional ethics are of this sort. Thoughtful professionals disagree less often over the basic ethical status of one act or another than they disagree about ethical priorities. That is, as in the software argument, the real disagreement is about the relative merits of one course of action or another, generally because people place different priorities and values on different conditions and outcomes. Nevertheless, ethics does generally assume some common values or standards (as old as the Ten Commandments), and professional societies promulgate standards for their members. Professional training needs to include a review of these standards and their application to straightforward as well as difficult choices.

For example, college students presumably have already learned that plagiarism is unethical; it is also a violation of most university codes. But what counts as plagiarism in software development, especially when both faculty and textbook encourage software reuse? Clearly, students should learn from examples and from each other, but they also need to learn that there is a Rubicon over which they cross at their own peril—copying or excessive cooperation on an assignment (unless explicitly authorized as a team project) is unethical.

Exercise 9.18: How would *you* formulate plagiarism guidelines for students who work together with friends to think how to do a computer program? When is working together good? When is it okay? When is it bad?

9.5.1 What *is* "professional ethics?"

"Once upon a time," professional ethics was seen quite differently than it is now. As various professions began to codify what were seen as their ethical obligations, there resulted in general merely a commitment to high professional standards of performance. Surely this is an ethical requirement of a professional—it is unethical to conceal a lack of one's qualifications for professional activities. But over the years, many professions have come to view commitment to mere **competence**, as only a beginning step. This narrow view of professional ethics was satirized by comedian Tom Lehrer's 1960's song about a German rocket scientist: "'When the rockets go up, who knows where they come down? That's not my department!', says Werner von Braun."

Beyond mere competence, many professions have come to believe that an ethical requirement is also a commitment to understanding the profession's **context**—that is, the way the professional's activities have impact on other aspects of society. Here we see an echo of Clemenceau's concern about war and the generals, and our paraphrase about highways and civil engineers, or computer systems and computer scientists. But we believe there is even more to be said about professional ethics. In terms of a homely analogy, the commitment to competence might be like a commitment to see that a hole is dug as well, as efficiently, and as safely as possible. The commitment to context, then, would be like a commitment to an awareness of the *consequences* of the hole's being of this shape or that, or of being dug in this place or that. But there must be more than that.

We believe that professional ethics in the richest sense extends even farther—to what we call **concern**: in this case, an interest in *why* and *whether* the hole should be dug. More generally, this would mean that ethical professionals should have a concern for what the profession can contribute to the richness of human life, without the professional blinders that lead them to assume that a professional accomplishment leads always to a social advance. Had that been the case in the Industrial Revolution, perhaps its dangers and exploitations might have been lessened, if not avoided. But this is a partisan view—that professional ethics extends beyond competence to context, and beyond context to concern. Others would disagree about the scope of professional ethics, limiting its range substantially, though still considering it important. At the other extreme is the view is that there is, properly speaking, no such thing as "professional ethics" at all. In a provocative paper prepared for the American Academy of Arts and Sciences,[15] a prominent philosopher John Ladd has argued that professionals have no particular "corner" on ethical issues, that professionals are humans and that "professional ethics" is no more than human ethics. If this is so, all one needs to do to be an ethical professional is to be an ethical person. A counter-argument to Ladd's position is provided by the following scenario:

A is a well-established member of a certain profession, whom B consults for professional reasons. The transaction goes well, and between the two there develops a social relationship which soon becomes a sexual relationship. Rate this behavior on a scale of 1 (highly ethically negative) to 5 (ethically neutral) to 9 (highly ethically positive), under the assumption that A is a(n):

         (a) physician;
         (b) attorney;
         (c) dentist;
         (d) psychiatrist;
         (e) engineer;
         (f) professor.

Over many years in a course one of the authors has taught, the profile of students' responses has been quite different with respect to the six professions, but quite consistent in the judgment of each

---

[15] "The quest for a code of professional ethics: An intellectual and moral confusion", *American Academy of Arts and Sciences Professional Ethics Project, Professional Ethics Activities in the Scientific and Engineering Societies*. AAAS (1980). Reprinted in *Computers, Ethics and Social Values*.

professional. This seems to make clear that, although the hypothetical situation is the same across the professions, the ethical obligations are not. If this is correct, all professionals need to consider the ethical demands of their own disciplines.

Exercise 9.19: Evaluate for yourself the six situations described above. Then take a poll of, say, twelve of your classmates. What are the results? Is there agreement or not?

9.5.2 Ethical underpinnings of social issues

Social issues often involve factual issues. For example, does welfare encourage the breakup of families? These questions can only be settled by empirical research. But they often involve more than factual issues, they also involve questions of what *ought* to be the case—not in the sense of expectation ("John ought to be here about 4:30"), but in the old-fashioned sense of one's duties ("John ought to pay you what he owes you").[16] Sometimes we fail to see these factors because what ought to be the case is generally agreed and obvious—shattered families are not good, for example. But too often there are questions about what ought to be the case that are not asked. For example, are broken families *worse* than domestic violence? Social issues must thus be approached with an awareness of both facts and expectations—or to use the terms introduced back in chapter 2, givens and goals. A knowledge of what *is* the case provides our givens; a sense of what *ought to be* the case gives us our goals. Understanding givens and goals gives us a start toward applying what we've learned about problem solving to social and ethical issues.

At the bottom of social goals generally lie ethical positions. The abolition of slavery, for example, was seen as socially desirable because of an ethical view of the immorality of slavery. The prevalence of domestic violence is deemed a social evil because of our ethical views of a person's human rights. Differing views about the desirability of certain welfare programs are based on a number of differing principles—social and economic, and ethical as well. Many technical matters of computing also pose ethical problems. How one approaches privacy issues depends on how much privacy one believes is an ethical right or responsibility. Both sides in the argument over software protection have ethical arguments to support their positions. Similarly, in debates over liability and censorship, ethical views play a role—often hidden, but always there. So in thinking about social issues, we need to be able to dig these out and think about them, too,

9.5.3 Thinking about ethical issues

Difficult ethical problems are dilemmas, where we must choose between the "good" and the "better" (or, if we are unfortunate, between the "bad" and the "worse"). In problem solving, it helps to identify the resources available to make progress from givens to goals. The resources of programming are the primitive instructions, structures, functions or classes available for constructing a solution. The resources of ethical problem solving are *moral standards*. These standards are generally provided by some **ethical theory**. Whether we are aware of these theories or not, they affect what decisions we make every day.

In contrast to most of human history, many people now espouse an ethical theory which is essentially **relativism**—saying that there are no absolute standards of ethical rightness or wrongness. "Right" means "right for me" or "right for you" or "right for ...". Though relativism harmonizes well

---

[16]Although in principle, this distinction is clear, here is sometimes a confusion between the two. Consider, for example, a case in which we might say John ought to arrive at 4:30 because he promised to.

with individualism, it has also has major weaknesses. For instance, no matter how great an atrocity some act may seem to you, you can't say it's *wrong* (except for *you*). Under this theory, the Holocaust was wrong for us who condemn it, but it was presumably right for those who committed it. Or, boiling babies in their bath water, too, is only wrong for those who think it wrong.

Many people prefer some kind of theory that will say that some things are simply better than others and forbid at least certain things as simply wrong. After all, there seem to be many ethical problems that have fairly obvious solutions. But on what grounds are they obvious? For many, what makes one course of action "better" than another are the *consequences* of the two actions. Judging an act solely by its consequences is a type of ethics called **consequentialism**. A consequentialist theory has some of the appeal of relativism, since a certain act may have some consequences for me but other consequences for you, and so may not in itself be absolutely good or bad.

But consequentialism, too, has its limits. In the first place, it is often difficult, if not impossible, to see the full range of consequences of an act. Second, it goes against an ingrained feeling of most of us that there are certain things that are good or bad in themselves, no matter *what the consequences may be*. That is to say, the intrinsic nature of certain acts makes them good or bad, or one act better or worse than another. An ethical theory based the intrinsic value of acts is called **deontological** (from the Greek roots meaning roughly, 'duty' and 'discussion'). Religiously based ethics are of this sort, with a divine origin of the "thou shalt"s and the "thou shalt not"s, but one may also have deontological approaches which are not religious.

Exercise 9.20: Does relativism seem attractive to you as an ethical theory? Why or why not?

Exercise 9.21: It is easy to see how a religious tradition can provide the authority for a deontological ethics. Can you see how one might have a deontological approach to ethics which is *not* grounded in religion? Hint: It's been said "If there is no God, then everything would be permissible." Do you agree? Why or why not?

Each of these approaches seems to have advantages and disadvantages. Many people have ethical views that are a mixture. Terry Winograd, a computer scientist at Stanford University, argues against two views of ethical practice and advances a third. Winograd rejects an "angel-devil debate" view, in which ethical thought is a struggle between conflicting desires to do good and to do bad. He also rejects a view that ethics provides a "morality computer" (see figure 9.1), with specific rules which govern what should be done; all a "user" has to do is to read out the answer. Winograd suggests that ethical reflection is more like being a member of a juggling team, as in figure 9.4—constantly tossing knives, torches, and clubs back and forth to one another. It is a constantly changing activity occurring in a social context. As a result, acting ethically is not a matter of merely learning and applying one or more theories—it is a matter of constant reflection and participation, a blend of thought and action.

Figure 9.4: Ethical "decision-juggling"

9.5.4 Professional ethics codes

Several computer professional societies have published ethical codes. It is instructive to "compare and contrast" the several codes. The ACM is the major professional organization focused on computing. Figure 9.5 gives the ACM's code of ethical standards.

1. **General Moral Imperatives**
    1.1. Contribute to society and human well-being
    1.2. Avoid harm to others.
    1.3. Be honest and trustworthy.
    1.4. Be fair and take action not to discriminate.
    1.5. Honor property rights, including copyrights and patents.
    1.6. Give proper credit for intellectual property.
    1.7. Respect the privacy of others
    1.8. Honor confidentiality.
2. **More specific professional responsibilities**
    2.1. Strive to achieve the highest quality, effectiveness, and dignity in both the process and products of professional work.
    2.2. Acquire and maintain professional competence.
    2.3. Know and respect existing laws pertaining to professional work.
    2.4. Accept and provide appropriate professional review.
    2.5. Give comprehensive and thorough evaluations of computer systems and their impacts, including analysis of possible risks.
    2.6. Honor contracts, agreements, and assigned responsibilities.
    2.7. Improve public understanding of computing and its consequences.
    2.8. Access computing and communication resources only when authorized to do so.
3. **Organizational Leadership Imperatives**
    3.1. Articulate social responsibilities of members of an organization unit and encourage full acceptance of those responsibilities.
    3.2. Manage personnel and resources to design and build information systems that enhance the quality of working life.
    3.3. Acknowledge and support proper and authorized uses of an organizations' computing and communications resources.
    3.4. Ensure that users and others who will be affected by a system have their needs clearly articulated during the assessment and design of requirements. Later the system must be validated to meet the requirements.
    3.5. Articulate and support policies that protect the dignity of users and others affected by a computing system.
    3.6. Create opportunities for members of the organization to learn the principles and limitations of computer systems.
4. **Compliance with the Code**
    4.1. Uphold and promote the principles of this code.
    4.2. Treat violations of this code as inconsistent with membership in the ACM.

Figure 9.5: Professional ethical standards of the ACM

The IEEE, although its name refers only to electrical and electronics engineers, is another professional organization to which many computer scientists and engineers belong.

We, the members of the IEEE, in recognition of the importance of our technologies in affecting the quality of life throughout the world, and in accepting a personal obligation to our profession, its members and the communities we serve, do hereby commit ourselves to the highest ethical and professional conduct and agree:

1. to accept responsibility in making engineering decisions consistent with the safety, health and welfare of the public, and to disclose promptly factors that might endanger the public or the environment;

2. to avoid real or perceived conflicts of interest whenever possible, and to disclose them to affected parties when they do exist;

3. to be honest and realistic in stating claims or estimates based on available data;

4. to reject bribery in all its forms;

5. to improve the understanding of technology, its appropriate application, and potential consequences;

6. to maintain and improve our technical competence and to undertake technological tasks for others only if qualified by training or experience, or after full disclosure of pertinent limitations;

7. to seek, accept, and offer honest criticism of technical work, to acknowledge and correct errors, and to credit properly the contributions of others;

8. to treat fairly all persons regardless of such factors as race, religion, gender, disability, age, or national origin;

9. to avoid injuring others, their property, reputation, or employment by false or malicious action;

10. to assist colleagues and co-workers in their professional development and support them in following this code of ethics.

Figure 9.7: Professional ethical standards of the IEEE

1. Thou shalt not use a computer to harm other people.

2. Thou shalt not interfere with other peoples' computer work.

3. Thou shalt not snoop around in other peoples' computer files.

4. Thou shalt not use a computer to steal.

5. Thou shalt not use a computer to bear false witness.

6. Thou shalt not copy or use proprietary software for which you have not paid.

7. Thou shalt not use other peoples' computing resources without authorization or proper compensation.

8. Thou shalt not appropriate other peoples' intellectual output.

9. Thou shalt think about the social consequences of the program you are writing or the system you are designing.

10. Thou shalt always use a computer in ways that insure consideration and respect for your fellow humans.

Figure 9.7: "Ten Commandments of Computer Ethics"

Finally, the Institute of Computer Ethics is a broadly based organization, including among its members many non-professionals as well as computing professionals. Figure 9.7 gives their "Ten Commandments of Computer Ethics."

Exercise 9.22: Find and discuss at least three similarities and two differences among the three codes of ethics above.

Exercise 9.23: For each category in each code of ethics, judge whether it addresses an issue of *competence*, *context*, or *concern*.

Many ethical problems have straightforward solutions once one understands their givens and goals, and the resources (standards) for dealing with them. Dilemmas are more difficult because one has to weigh many different issues, examine their importance and priorities. That's why scales, which appear in a couple of our figures as well as the multimedia, have come to be a metaphor for justice. The Bible itself, a source of moral standards for many people, points out, in Proverbs 16:11, that "honest scales and balances are from the LORD." If you cannot apply ethical resources straightforwardly to solve a dilemma, try using the problem solving strategies you have learned about. You could try decomposition—divide the dilemma into its components, then deal with each subproblem in turn. But then you must consider the possibility of interacting dependencies between subproblems. Or you could try reasoning by analogy—looking at how others have solved similar problems. Professional societies are a good resource here. Sometimes you can apply principles learned from resolving analogous dilemmas in non-technical domains. Examples of effective ethical problem solving abound in history and great literature. We close this section with a few harder ethical problems for you to work out. For each of the following exercises, consider:

1) What are the key features (givens and goals) of the scenario?
2) What are the ethical issues (subproblems) of the scenario?
3) What ethical resources (standard) could apply to each issue?
4) Does this scenario remind you of other similar situations? What is similar and what is different? How can you adapt an old case to this new scenario?
5) What ethical decision do you recommend and why?

Exercise 9.24: While "surfing the net" one day, Harry discovers a tightly secured file. After finally penetrating it, he discovers that it seems to be a file of highly personal information about quite a large number of people, including many he knows. He peruses the information and discovers, among other things, that a girl he used to date a lot in high school has had a baby and given it up for adoption, that the high school principal has been treated a number of times for sexually transmitted diseases and that the current mayor of his home town subscribes to a number of pornographic magazines. He also finds that a neighbor of his is wanted in another state for child abuse. Harry reports this fact to the police, they investigate, and the neighbor is arrested and extradited to another state for trial. The newspaper thinks that Harry is a hero for uncovering this information and bringing a criminal to justice. Others aren't so sure.

Exercise 9.25: For some time Sam has been considering the purchase of SuperSoftWare's "Office Everything," an integrated software package for offices, but finally concludes that it is too expensive. Since a friend has bought it, Sam copies the software and proceeds to use it freely. One day, while working with the copied software, Sam notices a really useful feature and sees that it could be applied in many other ways. He writes several software packages incorporating the key feature, and finds that they work quite well and they become successes on the commercial market as hot-selling packages. Suddenly his sales fall off—almost to nothing. Sam is mystified, until as he is "surfing the net" one evening, he finds a bulletin board offering pirated copies of all his software products. Sam thinks he has been ripped off and threatens to sue the SysOp of the offending board unless he shuts it down.

Exercise 9.26: Alyce owns a small firm that writes custom software and over the years her products have developed a reputation for quality. She has gotten her first really big job—a 100,000 line program for an engineering firm to assist in formulating bids on projects. The overall design and some of the programming are Alyce's, but most of the programming is done by her small staff, which was at first overwhelmed by the task and begged for more programmers. Both for reasons of economy and personal conviction that the current staff would be adequate, Alyce refused to hire any additional help and pressed her programmmers to increase their output. After initial difficulties, things finally swing into high gear and program was well under way when the engineering firm discovered that they would need the program significantly earlier than they had envisioned. Realizing that this change in schedule makes it a new ball game, they have offered to release Alyce's firm from its commitment and pay her a small fee, but that isn't enough. Under great pressure, the package is completed and delivered to the engineering firm on time. Unfortunately, there are apparently errors in the program. The firm drastically underbids on a multi-million dollar project and loses vast amounts on the deal. But it is not apparent where the blame lies. Alyce says that: (1) any program that large will inevitably have bugs, and there was not enough time to eliminate them all, and (2) the design of the program was based on the engineers' own specifications, so any defect in the program is not her company's fault. Alyce resents the engineering firm's charge that her software was at fault.

9.6 Issues for exploration

There are many social, ethical and professional issues than we have touched on in this chapter. We introduce a few more as exercises for exploration, on the web or elsewhere. Two useful sources for *more* issues to explore are the ACM's Special Interest Group one Computers and Society (SIGCAS) and the Computer Professionals for Social Responsibility (CPSR), both on the web.

Exercise 9.27 (*explore*): In the 90's, Congress passed legislation keeping Internet commerce tax-free. But many states are looking forward to the sunset of these provisions so that they can get income from e-commerce. Should e-commerce remain tax-free? Do e-commerce firms and their typical clientele have an unfair advantage over brick-and-mortar counterparts? What are some of the difficulties of taxing e-commerce and how might they be overcome?

Exercise 9.28 (*explore*): Microsoft once required that all clients of its MSN and Hotwire services to sign up for Passport identity authentication service, and Windows XP strongly implied that all its users should do so as well. Yet Passport has had significant security flaws, which software pundits had predicted would happen when it was first introduced. Is uniform identity authentication a good idea or not? Discuss several pros and cons and give your conclusions.

Exercise 9.29 (*explore*): Speaking of Microsoft, the federal government recently settled an anti-trust suit, but a couple of states and Europe are still holding out. Is Microsoft violating anti-trust law? What are some of the arguments on each side of the case? What should be done about it?

Exercise 9.30 (*explore*): You may have heard that RIAA (Recording Industry Association of America succeeded in their suit against Napster's practice of free peer-to-peer distribution of copyrighted music. Recently RIAA sued four undergraduates students for similar practices, and each student settled out of court (paying $15,000 each). What's the fuss all about? What is peer-to-peer distribution and why it such a concern to RIAA and many of the artists they represent? Why did the students believe what they were doing was justifiable? What's your conclusion?

Exercise 9.31 (*explore*): At the best of several large software companies, many state legislatures have been considering adoption of UCITA (the Uniform Computer Information Transactions Act) to standardize software licensing agreements. Many software pundits and advocates think UTICA is a bad idea for consumers. What are the pros and cons of UCITA and what's your conclusion?

Chapter review. Are the following statements true or false? Explain why or why not.

a) Computers has so revolutionized our daily lives that nothing is as it was 20 years ago.

b) Technological change begins as new technology replaces the old to do the same job.

c) "War is too important to be left to the generals" because they don't understand it.

d) Edge-notched cards pioneered information processing and thus were a boon for government bureaucracies.

e) The development of compilers such as FORTRAN was an example of the second stage of technological change—adaptation.

f) The computer is the steam engine of today's technology.

g) Industrialization produced social dislocations, but computerization will not.

h) Employment and education are two major areas for concern as computerization continues.

i) Everyone needs and wants privacy of the same sort and in the same way.

j) Privacy is just "the right to be let alone".

k) In today's society, privacy is gone forever, and we shouldn't worry about it.

l) Information privacy and communication privacy are pretty much the same thing.

m) There are really no reasons to oppose the creation of a national data base.

n) The legal issues involving computers are pretty much the same as legal issues without them.

o) Copyright protects your ideas from being copied.

p) The requirements for patenting a device are that it is useful, novel, and non-obvious.

q) Some have argued that software should not be protected at all because it is a social good.

s) There are two kinds of liability—negligence and strict liability.

t) Punitive damages can be assessed under strict liability, but not under negligence.

u) Censorship on the Internet is greatly complicated by the Internet's international nature.

v) Ethical decisions generally involve balancing good against bad.

w) Professional ethics is merely a matter of ensuring technical competence.

x) As an ethical theory, relativism says that what your relatives say is right, is right.

y) The ethics codes of the IEEE and the ACM are essentially the same.

z) The "Ten Commandments of Computer Ethics" were carved into tablets of stone.

Summary

The development of the computer and all its manifold applications have clearly affected modern society. The "computer revolution" has brought about a change from an industrial society to an information society, just as the steam engine triggered a transition from agricultural to industrial society. There are similarities and differences between these two transitions, which raise a number of questions about the directions for the future of our society. The computer has enhanced our awareness of **privacy** and what questions we need to address to protect this right. We have also looked an several other important areas where computers have affected legal concepts and issues—protection of software, liability for software failure, and censorship. Finally, we have developed a framework of ideas in **professional ethics**, and seen how at present, many professionals have come to see their professional responsibilities as having a larger ethical component—beyond **competence** to **context**, and beyond that to **concern**.

Chapter 10
Artificial Intelligence

"True art selects and paraphrases, but seldom gives a verbatim translation.
We were discussing you, not me. How ya doin, judge?"
Whimsical Conversation (winning computer entreé at the first Loebner contest)

Is artificial intelligence (AI) science or science fiction? AI inspires the imaginations of many —and not just science fiction fans, but scientists and entrepreneurs speculating about the outer limits of computing. Because AI is a science of the frontier of possibilities, it can be slippery to define. Is artificial intelligence an imitation of natural or human intelligence, or something else altogether? Or is it possible at all? One textbook defines AI as "the study of how to make computers do things at which, at the moment, people are better."[1] Clearly, this makes AI a moving target. At one time, spelling correction was considered AI, but now that's just word processing. At one time, getting a machine to beat humans at chess was AI, but now that's just a game in a box—grandmaster play is, for now, not AI but a more expensive box! (HITECH won a game from grandmaster in 1989; after a draw in 1996, IBM's Deep Blue stunned the reigning world champion, Garry Kasparov, in a 1997 match; Deep Junior and Kasparov played to a draw in 2003.) Another textbook defines AI as "the branch of computer science that is concerned with the automation of intelligent behavior."[2] Computer science I know, and automation I know, but what counts as intelligent behavior?

In this chapter we first look at AI as a way of answering one of the "Big Questions" of philosophy—"What is thinking?"—only to find that AI raises *more* interesting questions, such as "What would count as an intelligent machine?" Next we will explore AI as a science of developing algorithms that reason about complex problems—perhaps as humans do, perhaps not. In the third section we will survey applications of AI as cutting-edge technology, and in the fourth section we will examine an alternative approach to AI, which tries to model networks of neuron-like processors. The chapter closes with a look at the potential for intelligent robots.

10.1 Big questions

"What is thinking?" is a question that has puzzled people for hundreds of years. Do animals think? (You'd think so, the way some people talk to their pets.) Do people think? (The answer is not as obvious as you might suppose.) Do, or could, machines think? People often speak of computers as "thinking" about a problem, say, when an hourglass appears on a screen, when it would be more accurate to say that the machine is "processing." Some computer scientists believe such anthropomorphism (attributing human attributes to a non-human being) should be discouraged because it is sloppy thinking. Ah, but what *is* thinking? The great French philosopher René Descartes (1596-1660) contended that although humans thought (as he concluded by reasoning, "I think, therefore I am!"), animals were essentially mere machines, and so could not think. On the other hand, the English philosopher Thomas Hobbes (1588-1679) argued that all reasoning was merely a sort of arithmetic based on definitions. A later French philosopher, Julien de la Mettrie (1709-1751), argued that humans were nothing more than machines, and so of course, since humans think, machines *could* think.

Is thinking something that requires a *thinker*? If thinking is, as Hobbes argued, merely a sort

---

[1] E. Rich and K. Knight, *Artificial Intelligence* (McGraw-Hill, 1991).

[2] G. F. Luger and W. A. Stubblefield, *Artificial Intelligence: Structures and Strategies for Complex Problem Solving* (Benjamin Cummings, 1993).

of arithmetic, then all that it requires is a sort of calculator or ... computer. Shortly after Descartes, Gottfried Leibniz (1646-1716) aimed at developing a universal formal language in which all ideas could be expressed. Then, he hoped, when people disagreed, their disagreements could be settled: "Let us calculate!" Leibniz was one of the first to see thinking as something that could be carried out formally or mechanically. In the nineteenth century, there was much speculation about just what machines could do, especially among writers of romantic fiction. Then in the early 1900's, the American writer Ambrose Bierce wrote a story "Moxon's Master," in which an undefeated chess-playing machine became so angry at its owner's cheating that it strangled him. Of course, in more recent science fiction, we have Arthur C. Clarke's HAL and Commander Data of *Star Trek* fame.

10.1.1 The Turing Test and the Chinese Room

Quite early in the era of electronic computers, Alan Turing (introduced in chapter 1 in connection with his ideas about the universal machine) concluded that the question "Could machines think?" was meaningless, since there was as yet no real understanding of what 'thinking' might be. So Turing proposed a *behavioral* test, an imitation game, depicted in figure 10.1.

The "imitation game," Turing explained, "is played with three people, a man (*A*), a woman (*B*), and an interrogator (*C*) who may be of either sex. The interrogator stays in a room apart from the other two. The object of the game for the interrogator is to determine which of the other two is the man and which is the woman." With a variant of this game, Turing is ready to pose a different question: "'What will happen when a machine takes the part of *A* in this game?' Will the interrogator decide wrongly as often when the game is played like this as he does when the game is played between a man and a woman? These questions replace our original, 'Can machines think?'"[3] The interrogator is allowed to ask any sequence of questions, such as: "How is the weather over there?" "What is the square root of π?" "What do you think of Robert Redford?" If the interrogator cannot tell the computer from the

Figure 10.1: The Turing Test

person, then we would have to say, Turing contends, that the machine has demonstrated intelligence. He went on to speculate that a machine would pass his test within 50 years. (This was the first of many bold predictions for AI that were made before the field had really gotten going and that perhaps blurred the distinction between science and science fiction.) Will a machine ever pass the Turing test? When one does, its creator will win $100,000! The Loebner Prize Competition, inspired by the "Holy Grail" of the Turing test, started in 1991, and is held annually at The Computer Museum in Boston. (Read all about the first contest in the Summer 1992 issue of *AI Magazine*, or check out the multimedia to see if a more recent prize-winner can stump *you*.)

Although the test has yet to be passed satisfactorily, whether the test itself is a legitimate one is still debatable. A number of arguments for and against the Turing test have been given. Perhaps

---

[3]Alan M. Turing, "Computing Machinery and Intelligence," *Mind*, 59 (October 1950), 433-460.

one of the more interesting ones is John Searle's Chinese Room argument. Searle argues against the claim that passing a behavioral test of the Turing sort would actually show that the machine *understands* our language. To argue that it would not, Searle imagines that he is in a room with some slots in the wall, through which come pieces of paper with squiggles on them. When he receives such a piece of paper, Searle consults some instructions and in accord with the instructions, draws more squiggles and passes them back out through the slot. What all this is about is a mystery to Searle, but in fact, the squiggles are all Chinese characters, and the pieces of paper have questions in Chinese written on them. For the sake of argument, Searle further asks us to imagine that the answers he responds with do in fact pass the Turing test—i.e., they are indistinguishable from the answers that a native speaker of Chinese would give. So Searle passes the Turing test! But does this mean that Searle understands Chinese?

Not at all, he says. In fact, not only does he *not* understand Chinese, he doesn't even know that he is playing the Turing test! *Searle* can't by himself say anything in Chinese. The only way he can respond is by laboriously comparing the squiggly inputs with what is in his books, and respond by drawing other squiggles as outputs. Though it is a rather nonintuitive position, some have responded by saying the Searle after all *does* know Chinese—he just doesn't *know* that he knows it. Others have taken the *system response*—that although *Searle* does not know Chinese, he is a part of a *system* (Searle plus all the books and rules) and it is the system that knows Chinese. This is in effect to say that although Searle himself does not know Chinese, the system creates a *virtual* Searle who does know Chinese. Searle argues against this, too, as follows. Suppose, he says, that I memorize all these rules and internalize them, so that the 'system' is no longer part me and part something else. I am all there is, now. But I *still* don't understand Chinese!

Why does Searle say that he still doesn't understand Chinese? Is it possible that he really *does* understand Chinese? Well, think what we generally mean when we say that someone understands a language. Very small children may repeat things they have heard, but that scarcely means that they understand what they are saying. If I say to you "Look out—a car is coming!" as you step off the curb, and you reply "Wow, thanks, I didn't see it," but go right ahead to step off the curb, surely I will conclude that you didn't really *understand* me. Language is a part and parcel of our daily life, and understanding it involves using it in the normal ways.

10.1.2 Strong AI, Weak AI and Cognitive Science

Perhaps, as Searle and others have suggested, there is something about the way humans experience the world that is essential to their intelligence. "When Kasparov lost Game 1 [in 1996], he was gloomy. Could Deep Blue ever feel deeply blue? Does a face-recognition program have the experience of recognizing a face? Can computers—even computers whose data flow precisely mimics human data flow—actually have subjective experience?"[4] While a few AI scientists and philosophers take a "strong AI" position that machines can and will duplicate conscious intelligence, many others are content with a "weak AI" position that makes no claim about the inevitability of machine consciousness, just that machines can be designed to behave *as if* they were intelligent.

Searle's argument may or may not invalidate the Turing test—before a machine even gets close to passing it! However, it does articulate a common feeling that there is more to understanding language and thinking in general than just giving correct responses. For this reason, many distinguish **artificial intelligence** from **cognitive science**. Cognitive scientists put more emphasis

---

[4]Richard Wright, "Can Machines Think?", *Time*, March 25, 1996, p. 53.

on modeling the mechanisms of cognition (language understanding, problem solving, perceiving). AI practitioners, on the other hand, may be content to accomplish the sorts of tasks that thinking humans do, without worrying over whether their program imitates the way humans actually do them. After all, it's hard to see what is going on inside the brain (though cognitive scientists have developed sophisticated experimental techniques, from reaction time studies to CAT scans, to at least peek at how the brain works). A cognitive scientist studying chess playing might focus on how grand masters store and retrieve patterns from memory. An AI team, on the other hand, is quite willing to use raw processing power to build a machine that wins, such as Deep Blue. The rest of this section will explore a few ideas behind cognitive science; the rest of this chapter will then focus on artificial intelligence.

One key idea of cognitive science is that *cognition is like computation*. This old analogy became clearer when scientists appreciated the role of software in computing. Perhaps the relationship between computer hardware and software could provide insight into the ancient and puzzling **mind-body problem**? The *brain* (as part of the body) is a physical object, located in space, and working by physical, chemical, and electrical principles. The *mind*, whatever it is, does not seem to be spatially located at all and it seems to work on non-physical principles. In fact, the mind and the body seem to have quite different properties altogether! So how can the mind affect the body, and how can the body affect the mind? For it certainly seems that each affects the other. A blow to the body creates a pain in the mind, and an emotional experience makes the heart beat faster.

There are several traditional answers to these questions. One—the **dualist** position—is that the mind and the body *are* altogether different things. One is material, the other is not. Although dualism has many adherents, how mind and body affect each other is quite mysterious. (Descartes thought that the mind-body connection was effected through the pineal gland, which then was also mysterious.[5]) It is as if an electrical circuit, whose behavior is described in terms of resistance, voltage, and current, were somehow to become sensitive to the time of day. We would somehow suspect that there was some physical factor we had not identified; but the very essence of the dualist position is that the mind *has* no physical factors. These difficulties with the dualist position gave rise to an opposite view—the **monist** position. Monism comes in a couple of flavors. One says that the mind is merely the brain, that mental states are merely brain states (although, of course, they don't *seem* to be). This **materialistic** view of course leaves open the question of why mind and brain seem so different, which itself begs for a solution. Another flavor is that there is a compound brain-mind, which simply has two kinds of properties. An analogy might be that an athletic team has two kinds of properties—those that apply to the individuals and those that apply to the team as a whole.

The **cognition-as-computation** analogy tries to finesse the mind-body problem: the mind is to the brain as a piece of software is to the hardware it runs on. Thus our brain (and body) are material objects, like a computer. On the other hand, although a program can be *implemented* in one computer language or another, programs are not material objects. In fact, it is much easier to understand the workings of a computer program if it is seen as an abstraction, independent of the particular hardware it is running on. Could this also be true of intelligent behavior? Could programs that model intelligent behaviors give insight into how humans solved such problems? Or would it be useful to build programs that confirm or even predict the results of psychological experiments?

---

[5]Curiously enough, Descartes may have had something in that idea. It has been known for some time that lack of sunshine can produce depression. Apparently, it may be that the pineal gland, in response to sunshine, produces a chemical that helps to ward off depression. But how?

Cognitive science lends itself towards designing models of human cognition that can be implemented as programs. A good example is natural language processing. Consider this sentence:

The horse raced past the barn fell.

Are you having difficulty understanding it? Cognitive scientists call this curious phenomenon a "garden-path" sentence—because the human sentence processor gets "led down a garden path" to the wrong interpretation of the sentence. Believe it or not, it *is* a perfectly grammatical sentence. Its syntactic structure is just like a sentence that should give you no trouble:

The horse taken past the barn fell.

The difference between these sentences is that *taken* leads to just one interpretation, whereas *raced* is ambiguous: a horse can *race* (intransitive) or *be raced* (transitive, passive). The human sentence processor apparently tries the intransitive interpretation first and then gets stuck when it encounters another verb, *fell*. Several computational models have been developed to try to account for this behavior, including one developed by one of the authors of this book.[6] According to the boundary backtracking model, the human sentence processor has just a fixed and finite set of registers, modeling human short term memory. Each register is associated with grammatical boundaries such as Topic, Subject, Predicate, NP (head of noun phrase), PP (prepositional phrase), and so forth. The processor saves its state in a register whenever it crosses one of these boundaries, and if it gets stuck, it can backtrack to one of the states it has saved in a register.

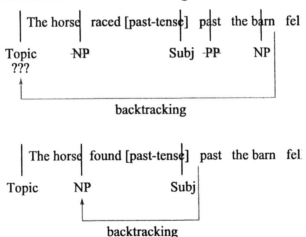

Figure 10.2: Boundary backtracking

For both sentences shown in figure 10.2, the processor saves states in the Topic boundary register, at the beginning of the sentence, in the NP boundary register, just past the head of the noun phrase (*horse*), in the Subj boundary register (after seeing both a noun phrase and a tensed verb, *raced* or *taken*), and in the PP boundary register (the preposition *past*). At this point there is a difference between the two sentences. The first one continues processing and, after *barn*, saves another state in the NP boundary register, clobbering the old one (since boundary backtracking saves

---

[6]Glenn D. Blank, Paul A. Kogut, Kirk Mousley and Edwin Kay, "Semantic Interpretation in Linear Time in the ATIS Domain," Applied Intelligence, 5 (October 1995), 319-395.

just one NP per clause). As a result, when the processor encounters the second verb, *fell*, and needs to backtrack, it will not find the state it needs in the NP boundary register.

For the second sentence, on the other hand, *found* is a transitive verb, expecting a direct object. In the sentence "Sue found a friend," *friend* is the direct object. As soon as the processor encounters the preposition *past*, it starts to backtrack (since *past* is not a direct object). In this case, it can still find the state it needs in the NP boundary register, and can reinterpret *found* as a modifier (a passive participle) of *horse*. Thus, as in the first sentence above, reusing a small set of registers occasionally causes a garden-path effect, since the processor cannot backtrack to a lost state. However, the good news is that putting an upper bound on the number of state registers guarantees efficient, real time sentence processing; it may also closely emulate how humans process language.

The boundary backtracking model also predicts that the following sentences, which are structurally just a little different from the garden-path sentence above, should be easier to process:

> Did the boat floated on the river sink?
> Has the horse raced past the barn fallen?

In the interrogative mood, an auxiliary verb, such as 'did' as 'has', appears *before* the subject. Since a tensed verb has already appeared, the processor can confidently identify the head of the first noun phrase as the grammatical subject, and therefore save a state in the Subject boundary register. This state should still be available for backtracking later. An undergraduate ran an experiment with human subjects to test this prediction (and others), and sure enough, it was borne out, suggesting that the human sentence processor is doing something like what the computational model is doing.[7] Thus a computational model can give us some insight into how human intelligence works, which may in turn help computer scientists develop more efficient algorithms for intelligent machines.

Exercise 10.1: Discuss at least two possible objections to Turing's test. Develop possible refutations to these objections. Hint: Turing himself discusses several possible objections and refutations in his own paper, "Computing Machinery and Intelligence," *Mind*, 59, 433-460.

Exercise 10.2: Turing predicted that by the year 2000, a computer would have a 70% chance of passing his test, convincing an average interrogator for at least five minutes. Do you think this is reasonable? Would passing this test under these conditions convince you that a machine has achieved intelligence? Or that a machine can think? Why or why not?

Exercise 10.3: The Loebner Prize contest modifies the rules of Turing's test slightly. Instead of judging between one human and one machine, interrogators interact with ten contestants, of which at least two are human and at least two (actually all the rest) are computers. Each interrogator then judges how "human-like" each terminal is. If a computer gets a higher median rank than either human confederate, that computer will have passed a variant of the Turing test. (Meanwhile, the computer with the highest median rank wins that year's consolation prize.) Why was it necessary to change the rules of the game? Do these changes remove any objections you might have to the test (see Exercise 10.1 above)? If a machine won the Loebner prize, would you be convinced it is an intelligent machine? Or that machines can think? Why or why not?

Exercise 10.4: To what parts of a computer (e.g., I/O devices, memory, CPU, etc., are parts of

---

[7]Eugene Foss, "An Investigation of Robust Parsing in Human Sentence Processing, *CogSci News*, 8:2, 7-10. *CogSci News* is available by contacting gdb0@lehigh.edu.

Searle's Chinese Room analogous? Discuss Searle's argument that none of these parts actually understands Chinese (or even C++, for that matter). Discuss a counter-argument that *the system as a whole* does understand Chinese.

Exercise 10.5: Joseph Weizenbaum reported a conversation between ELIZA—a program that feigned the behavior of a Rogerian psychologist shown in upper case—and a neurotic (imagine the neurotic on a couch, even though she is typing in a computer terminal, shown in lower case):

> All men are alike.
> IN WHAT WAY
> They're always bugging us about something or other.
> CAN YOU THINK OF A SPECIFIC EXAMPLE
> Well, my boyfriend made me come here.
> YOUR BOYFRIEND MADE YOU COME HERE
> He says I'm depressed much of the time.
> I AM SORRY TO HEAR YOU ARE DEPRESSED
> It's true. I am unhappy.
> DO YOU THINK COMING HERE WILL HELP YOU NOT TO BE UNHAPPY
> I need some help, that much seems certain.
> WHAT WOULD IT MEAN TO YOU IF YOU GOT SOME HELP
> Perhaps I could learn to get along with my mother.
> TELL ME MORE ABOUT YOUR FAMILY
> My mother takes care of me.
> WHO ELSE IN YOUR FAMILY TAKES CARE OF YOU
> My father.
> YOUR FATHER   WHAT RESEMBLANCE DO YOU SEE
> You are not very aggressive but I think you don't want me to notice that.
> WHAT MAKES YOU THINK I AM NOT VERY AGGRESSIVE
> You don't argue with me.
> WHY DO YOU THINK I DON'T ARGUE WITH YOU
> You are afraid of me.
> DOES IT PLEASE YOU TO BELIEVE I AM AFRAID OF YOU
> My father is afraid of everybody.
> WHAT ELSE COMES TO YOUR MIND WHEN YOU THINK OF YOUR FATHER
> Bullies.
> DOES THAT HAVE ANYTHING TO DO WITH THE FACT
> THAT YOUR BOYFRIEND MADE YOU COME HERE

ELIZA uses **pattern matching** rules to match certain words in input and generate appropriate sentences. For example, one rule matches pronouns in the first person ("I" or "my") and transforms them to second person("you" or "your"), producing "YOUR BOYFRIEND MADE YOU COME HERE". Can you reconstruct other rules that ELIZA must be using in the above dialogue? What subject(s) does the program seem to be especially interested in having the patient talk about? Does the use of such rules imply that ELIZA actually understand Rogerian psychology? Does the fact that several neurotics actually called ELIZA and believed it was an actual psychologist mean that a machine has actually passed the Turing test?

Exercise 10.6: There are well-known classes of problems that are intractably difficult for computers, and other classes that are provably undecidable by any computer. Describe at least one AI problem of each kind, and explain why it is so. What do these results imply about the feasibility of "strong

AI," i.e., passing the Turing test? Which do you think is a more desirable goal for AI research—strong or weak AI? Discuss both philosophical and computational issues.

Exercise 10.7: Consider the following sentences:

> The boat floated on the lake sank.
>
> The boat left on the lake sank.

Is one of these harder for you (or if not you, a friend who hasn't seen these sentences) to process than the other? Why? Explain how the boundary backtracking algorithm would process each of these sentences, i.e., when it saves and later attempts to backtrack to states in registers.

Exercise 10.8: Consider the following sentence:

> The barn the horse raced past fell.

Linguists describe this sentence as involves *topicalization*—the object ("the barn"), which normally appears after the main verb, here appears in front of the grammatical subject. Why does the possibility of topicalization prevent a processor from identifying the grammatical subject as early in the declarative mood as it can in the interrogative mood? How does this constraint play into the prediction of the boundary backtracking model about why sentences in the interrogative mood don't garden-path as severely?

Exercise 10.9: With which view of *mind* are you most sympathetic: dualism (in which the mind or soul is a non-material part of a person, distinct from the human brain), monism (in which as Searle puts succinctly, "brains cause minds," or mysterianism (a recent philosophical development which frankly acknowledges that the "extraness" of consciousness will always be inexplicable)? The *Time* article cited in a footnote on p. 241 provides a summary of the debate between the monist and mysterianism. Write a short essay explaining your point of view.

Exercise 10.10: How does the cognition-as-computation metaphor facilitate investigations in cognitive science? How, on the other hand, might it possibly mislead such research?

10.2 AI algorithms and engines

Thus far, AI has had more success simulating highly intellectual pursuits such as chess-playing, theorem-proving, or reasoning in specialized domains such as medical diagnosis, than the ordinary sort of things we do every day—recognizing words or faces. It is easier to model formal tasks in narrowly circumscribed domains of knowledge. A machine can play chess without knowing anything else about the world. But a machine that tries to understand everyday human language will soon need to look at context; for example, in order to figure out when I say "ring", whether I meant a verb (as in "I heard the doorbell ring") or a noun (as in "I heard the ring"), or for that matter whether I meant a sound or a circular object or a circus arena or a group of gangsters, it will need to look at surrounding words, sentences, or even background knowledge.

Good Old-Fashioned AI or **GOFAI** usually succeeds with formal tasks by *representing knowledge in terms of symbols and manipulating these symbols (making inferences) by logical rules*. Back in chapter 2, we used such an approach to formalize and solve the fox-goose-corn problem. Recall how we developed a symbolic notation representing the various states (the initial or given state was YFGC| and the final or goal state was |YFGC). Then we formalized rules to describe the possible moves to new states. By now you have had enough programming experience to imagine how explicit symbols can be represented—as strings—and how rules and constraints on applying these rules can be programmed rather straightforwardly—as branching structures.

The chapter on problem-solving also introduced the idea of a **state search tree** and various ways—such as depth-first or breadth-first—to construct one. Let's consider another example of a problem amenable to solution by generating a state search tree: the 8-puzzle, depicted in figure 10.3.

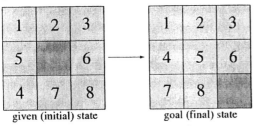

given (initial) state   goal (final) state

Figure 10.3: 8-puzzle

This game, which you may have played in the backseat of the car when you were a kid, features eight numbered tiles, with one slot left empty so that you can slide the others around. The object is to slide the tiles until the numbered pieces are in order. (You may have seen a larger version of this game, with fifteen pieces. The Rubik's cube is more or less a three-dimensional variant.) From the initial, given state shown there are four possible moves: slide tile 2 down into the empty slot, slide tile 5 right, slide tile 6 left, or slide tile 7 up. Figure 10.4 shows a state space tree that starts with these four moves, plus moves of sufficient depth to include the goal state (4th from the left at level 5). See if you can figure out how to generate a few unlabeled moves.

After any of the first four moves, the empty slot is on a side; so from these states there are only three possible moves and of these, one just repeats the previous state, which would not be a practical move. As the tree in the figure shows, after the initial moves, the average **branching factor**—*the number of possible new states to which search could branch from a current state*—is about two. The game shown with the initial state in figure 10.3 happens to take 5 steps, but a typical game takes about 20 steps. An exhaustive or **blind** search for a typical game, trying all possible sequences of moves up to a length of 20, would look at about 2^{20} or over a million states. (If we hadn't eliminated the redundant states there would have been 3^{20} or around three billion states.) That's an awful lot of tile-sliding for such a simple game!

As pointed out in chapter 2, a blind or uninformed search in a state space that grows exponentially is only tractable for small numbers of moves. A little knowledge can cut the state space down to size. There are at most 9! = 362,880 different arrangements of the nine slots, so informing a search to avoid repeating any states is guaranteed not to exceed this upper limit. (Avoiding cycles of moves was the basis for the notion "practical moves" back in chapter 2.) This is better, but there are still too many moves. As you may recall from playing the game yourself, half the time the game has no solution, as would become clear after an exhaustive but fruitless search of of all the possible moves.

Another kind of knowledge that can speed up search is a **heuristic**—*a rule of thumb that helps a search algorithm select the best available move* rather than just choose one blindly. Here are a couple of heuristics for the 8-puzzle:

- h_1: number of tiles in the wrong position. For the given state shown at the root of the tree in figure 10.4, h_1 is 6 (six tiles are in the wrong position, including the empty one). According to this heuristic, of four possible moves, the best is (5→) which reduces h_1 to 5.
- h_2: the sum of the number of moves, either horizontally or vertically, from a tile's current to its goal position. This measure is known as the "Manhattan distance"—the distance in city blocks, rather than "as the crow flies." For example, the Manhattan distance (number of moves) for tile 1 in figure 10.4 (with the number '1') is 0, but the distance for tile 4 (with the number '5' is 1. The sum of the Manhattan distances for the initial state is

$$h_2 = 0+0+0+1+0+1+1+1 = 4$$

Of the first four possible moves, this heuristic yields 5→ as the best move, which produces a configuration with a Manhattan distance of 3.

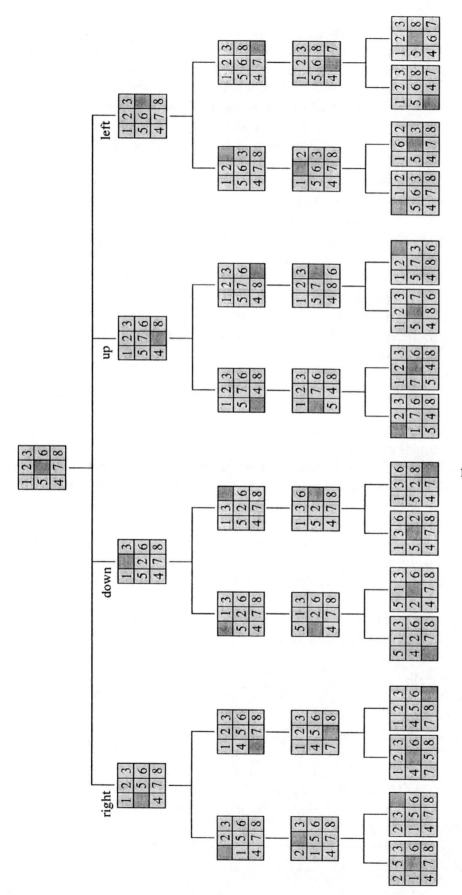

Figure 9.4:
State space search tree
for an 8-puzzle problem

With either the straight-line or Manhattan-distance heuristic, search becomes **informed**: always choose the move that produces the state with the best (lowest) heuristic value. Figure 10.5 shows an algorithm for a state space search guided by a heuristic.

A state space search algorithm generates a **tree** of states. Each state in the tree is a **node**. A **leaf** on a search tree is a node from which new states have not yet been generated. A heuristic algorithm decides which of the available leaf nodes on the tree to expand on the basis of their heuristic costs. (If there is a tie, the algorithm arbitrarily picks the leftmost node.) The multimedia illustrates how this heuristic algorithm goes about solving this particular problem, step by step.

```
while (goal has not been reached)
        generate all possible nodes one level from current-state
        compute cost for each new node (current-state)
        current-state <= leftmost leaf node with smallest cost
        compare current-state to previous states
        if current-state has been generated before then
                calculate path to both states
        current state <= state with the shortest path
```
Figure 10.5: A heuristic state space algorithm

Figure 10.6 compares the search cost for blind vs. heuristic search, using each of the above two heuristics. As you can see, once a search algorithm gets to a non-trivial depth in a search space, blind search becomes prohibitive, but heuristic search can make an otherwise intractable problem manageable. Here's where the quality of the heuristic matters—h_2 is clearly better than h_1. Much of what AI is about is cutting intractable problems down to size.

Search Cost			
depth	blind search (states)	Informed search (h_1)	Informed search (h_2)
2	10	6	6
4	112	13	12
6	680	20	18
8	6,384	39	25
10	47,127	227	73
12	364,404	539	113
14	3,473,941	1301	211

Figure 10.6: Comparison of search costs for 8-puzzle

Exercise 10.11: Using the example state space tree of figure 10.4, point out what nodes a blind search would generate that a heuristic search using h_1 would not. Point out what nodes heuristic h_1 would generate that heuristic h_2 would not.

Exercise 10.12: The algorithm of figure 10.5 is called a **best-first** search, because it *maintains* *heuristic values for all leaf nodes, picking the best* of the lot. Another heuristic algorithm, known as **hill-climbing**, avoids the overhead of maintaining a tree of leaf nodes, instead *just picking the best of the nodes that the current best state can generate*. Which is more like depth-first search—best-first or hill-climbing? Which is more like breadth-first search? For the example of figure 10.4, what happens to a hill-climbing algorithm that uses heuristic h_1?

Exercise 10.13: Consider the game of tic-tac-toe, in which you get to put X's and your opponent O's on squares in a 3x3 playing area. Assuming you go first, what is the branching factor for your first move? What is the branching factor for your opponent's first move in response? Disregarding a win, what is the size of the complete space of possible moves for both players?

Exercise 10.14: Clearly a win, ending the game, prunes the tree considerably. Can you think of any other ways to prune the tree? Hint: think about the 8-puzzle problem.

Exercise 10.15: Can you think of a heuristic for choosing the next best possible move? Give an example of how this heuristic works.

Exercise 10.16: Consider the traveling salesperson problem (TSP), as illustrated in figure 10.7 below. The object is to find the shortest possible tour to all the cities, while visiting each city exactly once. What is the average branching factor for this problem? What is the size of the complete space of possible moves? Can you think of ways to prune the search tree?

Exercise 10.17: Can you think of a heuristic for choosing the next best possible move for TSP? Give an example of how this heuristic works.

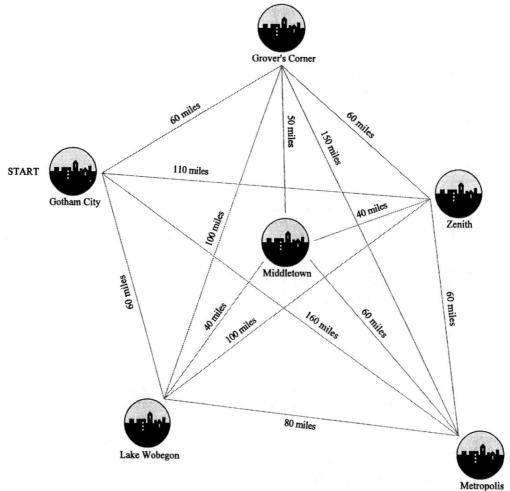

Figure 10.7: Traveling Salesperson Problem (TSP)

10.3 AI engines and AI technology

Here are some "real world" problems that have been tackled using GOFAI:

● Route-finding, like TSP described in the last two exercises, has applications in giving travel advice or getting messages through computer networks. Of course, in a real world application such as air travel, there are more factors to consider in evaluating heuristic cost than simply distance, such as ticket price, seat quality, frequent-flyer miles, etc.

● VLSI design, in which engineers must position and connect millions of gates on a chip, provides opportunity for intelligent computer-aided design.

● Robot navigation seeks an optimal route for a robot traveling through a physical space, such as a hallway or a highway, avoiding obstacles. A robot van has successfully navigated interstate highways at speeds up to 70 mph (and apparently didn't get a ticket)!

● Question-answering allows users to retrieve information from a data base or knowledge base using natural language and possibly speech recognition. A system called LUNAR makes information about rocks that the Apollo missions brought back from the moon accessible via natural language queries. Airline reservation systems are a more mundane application of this technology. A wide variety of more or less successful applications of natural language processing and speech recognition have been developed. For example, several systems have been developed to understand human utterances in the domain of travel planning. A traveler says into a microphone, "I want to go from Boston to San Francisco." A speech recognizer converts a user's analog speech into a digital representation, then words. The natural language processor then takes these words and attempts to understand the sentences they form. Such a system might respond, "What date will you be traveling on?" so that the human can provide additional details. The system then interacts with a database to handle the transaction, resulting in a confirmed reservation that saves the traveler $894 over the regular coach fare. Major software vendors (including Microsoft and Lotus) have incorporated natural language processing into help facilities for their software suites. Instead of plowing through help menus, you can ask, "How can I print a document sideways?" and get advice on printing in landscape mode. Another application of natural language processing is machine translation from one language to another. This has been a very difficult area, but is beginning to yield useful results.[8] More complicated question-answering systems incorporate natural language processing of input information such as short newspaper articles, and permit questions to be asked about their content.

● Domain-specific "**expert systems**" attempt to incorporate the experience of human experts in some specific subject domain, such as medical diagnosis or bridge construction. The MYCIN expert system diagnosed bacterial diseases by reasoning in terms of probabilistic rules. XCON embodied the knowledge of computer systems technicians by transforming customer specifications into custom configurations of VAX computers. Since the payoff of these early systems was high, many new ones have been developed, including several auto mechanic experts, a battlefield tactical expert, an oil-rig drilling expert, a bridge fault diagnosis expert, a space-station control/life support expert, and many more.

---

[8]Early efforts often gave some strange results. A common practice in checking the quality of a translation was to translate a passage back into the original language. On one occasion, after such a re-translation from Russian, the original English sentence "The spirit is willing, but the flesh is weak," became "The whiskey is good, but the meat is rotten"!

Exercise 10.18 (*explore*): Use the web and/or your library to learn more about how AI techniques help computer engineers with VLSI design. Discuss how it works and its benefits.

Exercise 10.19 (*explore*): Use the web and/or your library to learn more about robot vans and trucks driving on the Interstate. Discuss how it works and how you'd feel about a driver-less van!

Exercise 10.20 (*explore*): Use the web and/or your library to learn more about an expert system being used to solve a practical problem. Discuss how it works and its benefits.

These new knowledge-based systems automate many of the problem-solving strategies that we learned about in chapter 2. Many **rule-based** expert systems use **backward chaining** from goals to subgoals, an approach that is very similar to reducing a problem by top-down decomposition. For example, consider the following simple collection of rules:

(1) if X eats meat then X is a carnivore
(2) if X eats grass then X is an ungulate
(3) if X is a carnivore and X has stripes then X is a tiger
(4) if X is a carnivore and X has a mane then X is a lion
(5) if X is an ungulate and X has a long neck then X is a giraffe

Suppose we want the system to answer the query, Is X a tiger? The automated problem-solver (which we call an **inference engine**) searches for a way to prove the goal by matching the goal with the conclusion (the *then* part) of a rule. In this case, rule (3) matches. To prove rule (3), the inference engine needs to prove the premise (the if part) of the rule. This leads to two *subgoals*: X is a carnivore and X has stripes. To prove X is a carnivore, it turns to rule (1). Since there is no rule to prove the premise of this rule, it automatically asks the user: Is it true that X eats meat? If the user says yes, it then goes on to the second part of the premise of rule (3), and asks the user, Is it true that X has stripes? If the user says yes, it has proven rule (3), which proves the goal, X is a tiger. Backward chaining systems, as in this example, are more effective at analysis or diagnosis (such as troubleshooting a car or diagnosing a disease), which involve breaking complex problems down into smaller ones, via the creation of subgoals.

On the other hand, **forward chaining** inference engines *reason from givens to goals*, by matching facts in the current database with rules in the knowledge base. A forward chaining engine tries to prove the *if* part of rules by matching them up with facts in the data base. For example, suppose the user establishes the fact that X eats meat, a forward chaining inference engine would fire rule (1) matching this fact, which in turn adds another fact—X is a carnivore—to the database. It now has one half of the premise of rule (3). After asking the user whether X has stripes (it does), it can conclude that X is a tiger. Since forward chaining engines are more sensitive to changes in the database, they have been useful for systems that monitor other systems, such as the flow of chemicals through a reactor and making necessary adjustments or responding to the error messages generated by an complicated computer operating system. Forward chaining inference is also good at accumulating the facts needed to design systems. The XCON system, which configured layouts for VAX computers, was primarily a forward chaining system. Other forward chaining systems have been developed for the design of elevators and other engineering design tasks.

In many cases, rules cannot be developed that are black and white (i.e., if X then definitely Y). Sometimes there is uncertainty. Therefore, some expert system development environments (also called **expert system shells**) support various kinds of **probabilistic reasoning**. Rules in such shells typically take this form:

IF <evidence for premise> THEN <assert or hypothesize>
WITH <probability or certainty-factor>

For example, one can have a rule

IF X has fins THEN X is a fish WITH certainty .7

(allowing, rather roughly, for the possibility of whales and dolphins). Technically, probability should be based on observed data, but often such data are unavailable or expensive and we have to rely on human expertise. For example, physicians seem to reason probabilistically, yet not necessarily with statistical data. The developers of EMYCIN (a shell which generalized MYCIN-style reasoning for use in other domains) allowed for the use of subjective probabilities called **certainty factors**, provided by domain experts. A key issue for shells that allow probabilistic values is how to combine these automatically. For example, suppose one rule chains its results into another:

rule1: IF a THEN b WITH certainty .6

rule2: IF b THEN c WITH certainty .9

How much should evidence of item 'a' contribute to probability of hypothesis 'c'? EMYCIN and other shells invoke multiplication, e.g., rule1 * rule2, e.g., .54. This combinatory method produces a result that is weaker than the certainty of any of its premises. Though this may seem right, intuitively, it may turn out to be flat out wrong. For example:

IF sprinkler on THEN grass is wet WITH certainty .9

IF grass is wet THEN it rained WITH certainty .8

EMYCIN will therefore infer that, if the sprinkler is on, then combining by multiplying .9 * .8, it rained with certainty .72. Does this conclusion seem a little odd to you? How did this unlikely result happen? The problem is the combinatory method makes an **independence assumption**—each rule's conclusion is independent of the others—but in this case there is actually a causal relationship between the rules. The difficulties associated with probabilistic data makes knowledge engineers cautious about using them.[9]

Perhaps the biggest challenge of AI is giving machines "common sense"—the ability to reason about everyday knowledge of the world. Expert systems and chess programs are clueless about the world beyond their narrow domains. And they are stumped when they reach the limits of their knowledge. So AI researchers have developed richer knowledge representation structures to deal with the default and procedural knowledge that seems to characterize common sense. Semantic networks, such as the one shown in figure 10.8 represent knowledge hierarchically, as in biological taxonomies.

A **semantic network** is essentially a labeled graph, in which some of the arcs have special interpretations. All "isa" links imply a relationship of **inheritance**, in which a type such as "Turtle", in addition to all its own features (such as "haspart shell") also obtains all the properties of its supertype(s), such as "haspart scales" from reptile and "haspart backbone" of vertebrate. Property inheritance provides an economy in terms of memory, because subtypes do not need to replicate properties that they hold in common with a more abstract supertype. Inheritance also gives a concrete notion to the idea of *semantic distance* between concepts; for example, turtle is semantically closer to shells than backbones (one links vs. three)—even though turtles do have both.[10]

Suppose, for example, you (or a robot) walks into a room and sees a large white cabinet (and

---

[9]Actually, there is an AI technology that accounts for this type of cause and effect relationship called "Bayesian belief networks".

[10]Inheritance is also an important concept in object-oriented software, as seen in earlier chapters.

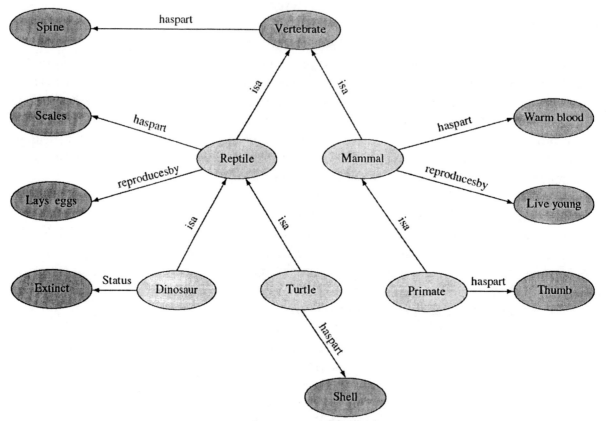

Figure 10.8: A semantic network

hears it humming), next to a flat counter leading to what appears to be a sink with a faucet. By now there's enough information to identify the room as a kitchen. This information in turn sets up predictions about what else we might expect to find in this room: appliances such as a toaster, cabinets containing dishes and food, and so forth. A **frame** can model all this knowledge *as a collection of slots, each of which may have expected default values* (for example, a slot for refrigerator with a default color of white, a slot for appliances with a default instance of a toaster, etc.), or *attached procedures* for filling these slots or performing other behaviors (for example, a slot for clock can compare or set the time using the computer's own internal clock). With this rich structure, frames set up predictive recognition of objects in context. The classes of object-oriented languages are similar in representational power to frames: data members are like slots, representing properties of an object; member functions are like attached procedures, modeling behaviors; constructors can supply default values; and both frames and classes support inference by inheritance.

What distinguishes frames is an emphasis on active, expectation-driven reasoning. When a frame-based system walks into a room and sees balloons and a cake with little candles on it, a Birthday frame kicks into action and predicts the presence of little children and possibly a poster of a donkey. Because it knows what to look for, it can make sense of complex situations.

But what if the predictions are wrong? What if there are grown men instead of children in the room, and a woman suddenly jumps out of the cake? What if a man in the background yells "cut"? What if there seems to be no one else in the room at all? How easily will a frame-based system be able to switch to different expectations? Or will it be easily misled or befuddled? Will the knowledge of expectation-driven systems scale up or be overwhelmed by the rich environment of the "real world" of human interaction? It's questions like these that keep AI on the frontier of computing!

Richer knowledge representation structures like frames have set up the possibility of systems that use something like the analogical approach to problem solving discussed in chapter 2. A **case-based system** tries to match a new case or problem with a similar one in its library of previously recorded cases (represented as frames), then tries to take into account the differences as well as similarities between the known case and the new one. Based on this comparison, slot-filling for similarities and structure-modification for differences, it derives a new solution for the new problem. If it works, this new case can be added to the case library which allows the system to learn! AI systems may not be HAL or Commander Data—but then again, think about how much effort it has taken for *you*, who are "fearfully and wonderfully made," to learn the content of this book, let alone solve complex new computing problems! Nevertheless, case-based reasoning systems *can* provide partial solutions to many practical, limited domain problems. For example, "help desk" operators, who assist customers having problems with products, from printers to coffee machines, can themselves be assisted by case-based reasoning systems which compare a new customer problem with a knowledge base of old cases.

Exercise 10.22: Most college students are adults (at least 18 years old). Most adults are employed. We could write:

> IF college_student THEN adult WITH certainty 0.95
> IF adult THEN employed WITH certainty 0.9

Then, if we are sure that Hank was a college student, these rules would say that Hank is employed with 0.855 probability. Common sense says this is less likely, though. Where did the fallacy creep in? Show how the problem could be fixed by rewriting the rules.

Exercise 10.23: Draw a semantic network that shows that beagles have hair, canaries and robins have wings and can fly, but only canaries are yellow. Allow for inheritance of properties from general classes.

Exercise 10.24: Discuss the problems posed for semantic networks by the following propositions and suggest possible solutions:

> Chickens cannot fly.
> Beagles and canaries make good pets, but robins do not.

Exercise 10.25: Why are everyday tasks, such as recognizing words or faces, though seemingly easy for humans, often surprisingly difficult for AI?

Exercise 10.26: Why would a speech recognition program have difficulty telling the difference between the sentences "He stops at the store" and "His top's at this door"? How do you think humans manage to tell the difference?

Exercise 10.27: AI researchers have proposed many different ways to reason based on knowledge or past experience. One way is to use past cases of problems that were solved (i.e., case-based reasoning) and adapt these to solve a new situation. Another way is to perform a statistical analysis on past data to come to conclusions about a new situation. The first most closely resembles how a human might perform, while the second is more machine-centered. Compare the two approaches. Are they both intelligent? Is one more intelligent than the other? Is it possible to have machine intelligence that does not emulate human cognitive processes? Explain your answers.

Exercise 10.28: In an early episode of *Star Trek: The Next Generation*, Commander Data, an intelligent android, hears a new word and remarks, "Flimflam? Ah! Imposture, or dupe, bamboozle, befool, hoodwink, hornswoggle..." This little remark suggests that Data might not be relying exclusively on logical deduction. What kind of reasoning might be involved in seeing the connection?

10.4 Neural networks

An alternative to GOFAI is the **neural network** approach, which models intelligent behaviors in terms of *levels of activity in an interconnected assembly of neuron-like units or nodes*. As we have seen, symbolic AI and cognitive science explore the **cognition-as-computer** metaphor: the mind (which does cognition) is like a computer. Neural networks advance the **brain metaphor**: what if we built a computer with an architecture more like the brain's? After all, a digital computer is a poor model of the human brain. Though there are efforts in other directions, a typical digital computer works with a central processing unit (CPU), generally of some substantial capability, which can access a large number of memory units, which stores both programs and data. This is not at all how the brain works. In the brain, there are a vast number (several billion) of relatively simple processing units, interconnected in an even vaster number of ways, while in a sense there are no memory units at all. These processing units are the brain cells, or **neurons**. Figure 10.9 depicts a biological neuron and a computational approximation of a neuron, called a **perceptron**.

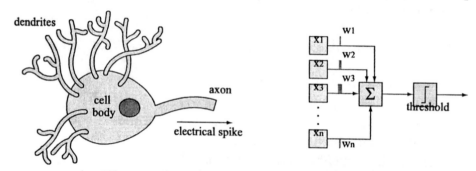

Figure 10.9: A Neuron and a Perceptron

A neuron is a processing element which connects to other neurons via synapses between dendrites (receiving input signals from other neurons) and axons (giving output signals to other neurons). Each neuron receives signals from those neurons which connect across synapses with its dendrites. Depending on the combination of input signals it receives, the neuron either does or does not fire a signal down its axon to those neurons to which it connects across other synapses . After a brief rest, the same sort of thing happens again and again. In large part, the memory of the neural system consists of the firing patterns and their flow throughout the network.

A computational neural network is an approximate simulation of the brain. (Let us emphasize approximate, since neural networks make many simplifications that abstract away interesting and important biological details.) It consists of a number of relatively simple processors connected in a network. Biological neurons are electro-chemical devices, whose processing steps are on the order of milliseconds, whereas digital computer processes are on the order of nanoseconds—at least a thousand times faster! How is it then that humans are so much better at complex, real time activities, such as speech or driving a car or routine problem solving? The power of neurons comes in the volume of their connections. The human brain has billions of neurons with even more billions of connections processing **in parallel**. The brain interprets scenes or understands speech signals in about 100 steps—something current computers cannot do in 10 million steps! Part of the power of human brain is obviously its massive parallelism.

Let's look closer at the perceptron in figure 10.9. The boxes labeled x_1 through x_n are *input* values. These represent an input pattern—such as a pattern of bits representing a pattern of a possible letter of the alphabet—that the network must recognize. Each input has an associated connection *weight*, w_1 through w_n , which are typically real numbers between -1..1. The perceptron computes the sum of weighted inputs: $x_1 * w_1 + x_2 * w_2$ ... (In other words, a perceptron is a polynomial function in which the weights are coefficients.) Finally, output goes through an adjustable *threshold*: if the sum is above threshold, the output is 1, otherwise it is 0. An individual perceptron can gradually *learn*, by training on examples. Learning consists of adjusting weights (using a hill-climbing algorithm) so that the perceptron can better distinguish whether various patterns belong to an identifiable category, e.g., is that letter I scrawled an 'A' or not, or is that image a face or not?

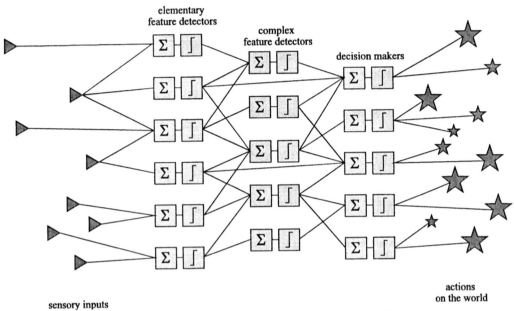

Figure 10.10: Intelligent processing by a network of perceptrons

As figure 10.10 illustrates, it's possible to combine perceptrons into networks that solve recognize more complex patterns or solve more complex problems. The output from one or more neurons can become inputs to other neurons. **Multi-layer networks** organize collections of neurons in distinguishable layers, all of which process at once, in parallel, then send their results along to another layer of neurons. Because neural networks involve so many simple processors, no particular neuron is indispensable; networks as a whole tend to be far more robust than traditional symbolic AI. Once a network has been trained on a set of sample data, it will generally recognize new samples, unseen in the training set, as well as the training data—though it will usually not recognize either perfectly. Indeed, even if some units are damaged, the network will still be able to perform, because its knowledge is distributed, rather than put in a fixed sequence of memory locations.

Research into neural networks slowed for over a decade when AI researchers pointed out that perceptrons could not recognize certain relatively simple patterns. Enthusiasm resumed when researchers began promoting the power of multi-layer networks. The network shown in figure 10.11 has three distinct layers of neurons. The *input units* represent receive the pattern of the digit (in this case, a 7). One output unit reports what the network recognizes (the *output unit* for '7' is on). In between are *hidden units* that neither receive external inputs nor produce external outputs, but perform useful intermediate processing. In learning mode, the **back-propagation** algorithm initializes units to random values, then propagates error values backwards (when the network produces an incorrect result) from output units back to hidden units to input units. As error values propagate backwards, the algorithm adjusts the weights (or coefficients) in units so that their

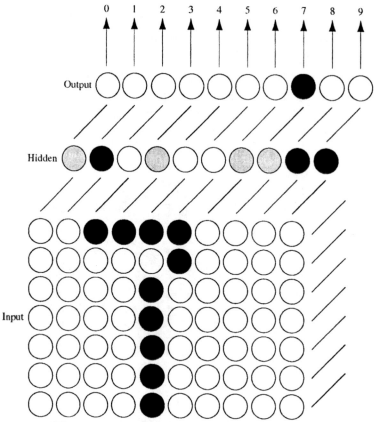

Figure 10.11: Back-propagation network

outputs correspond more closely to the desired result. Then, in recognition mode, processing is **feed forward**, from input through hidden units to output units. If back-propagation has trained the network well, the correct output unit should be activated most of the time.

Much of the interest in neural nets arises not only from the fact that they are simple structural models of the brain, but also that they show certain behaviors that are typical of human brain/mind behavior. One of the features of the human brain is that it is relatively insensitive to the destruction of individual brain cells.[11] So are neural nets. A feature of the human mind is the ease and relative success with which we classify things. We identify adults and children as people, we recognize our friends although they may have changed, and in many other ways, our mental life is constantly involved in classification. Early symbol-manipulating attempts at classification aimed at identifying a set of *distinctive features*, characteristics of the things to be classified, combinations of which would identify each possible pattern or class. Generally speaking, these approaches—some quite ingenious—were unsuccessful.[12] However, neural net approaches not only work quite well on these kinds of problems, but when they fail, they fail in quite human-like ways.

Let's consider how a typical neural net might work in recognizing hand-printed upper-case letters. It is relatively easy to set down a set of distinctive features of which each letter has one or more. But since people print differently, the same letter will not display quite the same set of features

---

[11]And a good thing, too, since our brain cells are constantly dying and generally speaking are not replenished.

[12]This was one of the simple everyday sorts of human activity that early approaches to artificial intelligence could not match.

in each of its occurrences. So an 'A' is somewhat like an 'H' in that both have two more-or-less vertical long strokes, connected in the middle by a short horizontal stroke. In principle, the differences are that the long strokes are exactly vertical and parallel in the 'H' and sloping and convergent in the 'A'. But in practice, the long strokes of the 'H' may not be vertical, or even parallel, and the long strokes of the 'A' may not actually join. In fact, there is a sort of continuous variation from an 'H' to an 'A', with some uncertain specimens in between.

For each distinctive feature we will have an input unit, and we will have 26 output units, one for each letter. We also will have a number of hidden units, perhaps in more than one row; those in the first row receive signals from the input units, those in the second row receive input from those hidden units in the first row; etc. Finally, the output units receive signals from the last row of hidden units. The particular connections (or connection strengths) among the units may be randomly chosen. We now present some letter to the net by inputting its distinctive features to the input units. We then wait and see what the outputs will be; in this case all but one will be wrong, but that is not always the case. In a sort of evolutionary process, we then alter the connections—strengthening those that led to a correct answer and weakening those that led to an incorrect answer. Then we repeat the process again and again, until the behavior stabilizes satisfactorily. (This is known as *training* the net.) After a suitable amount of training, the net is put to work, classifying letters, or photo images, or whatever. For example, the NETTalk neural network system learned, after 50 passes through the training data, how to pronounce written English text, with a 95% accuracy on training data. Starting out as a nonsensical babbler, it developed a speech pattern that sounds remarkably like a four- or five-year-old child.[13]

It's not clear, though, how readily NETTalk would progress to the diction of an adult, nor is it clear that neural networks have solved the problem of scale-up that has plagued AI applications. For example, the Army funded a project to use neural nets to detect tanks. A neural network processor trained on pictures of tanks in the field and it appeared to perform well. When put to the test, however, it failed miserably. Why? All the pictures of the tanks shown during the learning phase had been taken on cloudy days, while pictures without tanks were taken on sunny days. The neural network processor learned to discriminate between cloudy and sunny days, *not* which scenes did and did not have tanks! Since it's not obvious what a neural network is learning, this behavior wasn't obvious until it failed.

Exercise 10.29: Explain how a network learns to recognize a set of patterns such as handwritten letters. How would a network represent input patterns and output results (i.e., how many nodes each and how are they organized)? Why is network learning much slower than recognition?

Exercise 10.30: When we say that a neural network learns, what is it actually doing? Why is neural net learning relatively simple compared to learning symbolic representations such as rules or frames?

Exercise 10.31: Newell & Simon, two pioneers of AI, proposed the **physical symbol hypothesis**. A physical symbol system consists of symbols related in 'physical' ways, such as one symbol being next to each other, in a list structure. A physical symbol system is a machine that produces an evolving collection of symbol structures, by operating on symbolic expressions to produce new symbolic expressions. The hypothesis, then, is that a physical symbol system has the necessary and sufficient means for general intelligent action. Do you think this hypothesis is plausible? Why or why not? Why might a neural network researcher argue that there is a need for a **sub-symbolic**

---

[13]T. J. Sejnowski and C. R. Rosenberg, "Parallel Networks that Learn to Pronounce English Text," *Complex Systems*, 1 (1987), 145-168.

level, for representing and processing below the level of symbols?

Exercise 10.32: If you had an EMYCIN-based (backward chaining) shell, a forward chaining shell, a frame-based shell, a case-based reasoner, and a back propagation neural network tool, which would you choose for simulating the following experts, and why?

    a) An operator monitoring sensors on a nuclear reactor.

    b) A hand writing expert.

    c) A civil engineer designing bridges.

    d) A mechanic troubleshooting Toyotas.

    e) A help desk helping with problems with a company's line of printers.

Exercise 10.33 (*explore*)**:** Use the web and/or your library to learn more about a practical application of neural networks. Discuss how it works and its benefits.

10.5 Agents and robots

One way to pull the many strands of AI together is to view AI "as the study and construction of rational agents," where an **agent** is *an autonomous entity that perceives and acts in a world.*[14] The study of agents refocuses AI onto something like its grand ambition to build intelligent machines yet also puts a helpful and practical emphasis on building machines that interact with the world. (Many early AI efforts were triumphs in **microworlds**, solving problems in *carefully circumscribed environments* such as manipulating blocks, but what was learned did not necessarily scale up to real world environments.) Note that perfect rationality—*always* doing the right thing—is not necessary, nor is it possible in complicated environments. Instead, agent design strives for **limited rationality**—*acting appropriately within real time and finite computational space.*

The first attempt at constructing an intelligent, autonomous robot was Shakey, which rolled around in Stanford Research Institute labs circa 1969. Shakey was GOFAI on wheels. First, it would plan its actions in advance by classical top-down decomposition of goals into subgoals. Then it would attempt to execute its plan—a sequence of actions or operations, some of which controlled the robot's effectors (such as its wheels or grippers). Then Shakey and its creators discovered how demanding the real world is: wheels slipped, measurements were in error, objects (such as people) appeared in the world unexpectedly, etc., so that almost all plans of any non-trivial length failed at some point during execution. Subsequent versions of Shakey made several improvements, especially 1) making planning more efficient by compiling routine sequences of steps as **macro**-operations (just as you can define sequences of Knobby's instructions, only Shakey macro-operations were somewhat more

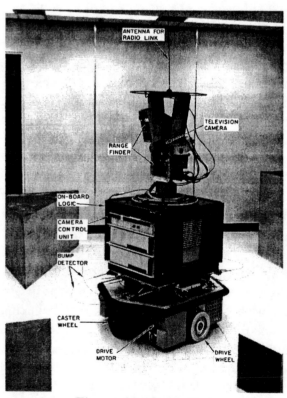

Figure 10.12: Shakey

[14]S. Russell and P. Norvig, *Artificial Intelligence: A Modern Approach*, (Englewood Cliffs, NJ: Prentice-Hall, 1995), p. 7.

general), and 2) letting low-level actions, which controlled the physical robot, include some error detection and recovery capabilities. Shakey was able to move on a flat floor and push large objects with difficulty. For nearly a decade, work continued on Shakey and its descendants, improving the way it developed and debugged its own plans, for example, avoiding interacting subgoals (recall the three blocks problems discussed in chapter 2). Though much was learned about rational problem solving, Shakey was still looking like little more than acting like R2D2 of *Star Wars* fame.

In the 1980's, a new approach to intelligent robotics emerged. Classical robots reasoned by simulating the world in terms of an interior model. The classical approach is formal and explicit, but it is computationally expensive, perhaps too expensive to generate real-time behavior. Instead, Rodney Brooks has advocated what he calls *behavior-based robotics*, which eliminates any centralized representation of world states.[15] For tasks in which sensors can directly determine appropriate effector action, there is no need for explicit representation or reasoning at all. "The world is its own model." Complex behaviors can be modeled in terms of chains of fairly simple behaviors. Instead of relatively expensive top-down planning, behavior-based robotics compose simple, inexpensive behaviors bottom-up into increasingly complex ones, such as a robot that wanders laboratory hallways collecting empty soft drink cans. Perhaps intelligence will involve some combination of neural networks, behavior-based robotics, and GOFAI, just as human activity involves both **automatic** (*unconscious, highly patterned, real time*) behavior—such as walking, a fabulous coordination of joints, muscles and nerves, or driving a car, or recognizing the meaning of a word in a sentence—and **controlled** (*conscious, exploratory, non-real time*) behavior—such as planning your day's activity *while* you are walking or driving a car, or *learning* how to drive a car (with standard transmission), or explicating the meaning of a poem.[16]

Work on rational agents need not necessarily imply the construction of physical robots. A **softbot** is *an agent that senses and acts in a virtual world.* Though this may sound a bit ethereal at first, softbots can turn out to be quite useful and complex in a world that is becoming increasingly virtual. For example, one softbot agent scans online news sources in order to find interesting news items for its customers. Another prioritizes your e-mail. Another retrieves technical reports from archives via the Internet. These critters, which will become increasingly important in this age of information explosion, need some natural language processing capabilities, need to be able to learn what each client is interested in, and need to deal with a dynamically changing world—for example, when a news source or server crashes. Software agents can also inhabit virtual reality. Researchers at the MIT Media Lab[17] have created an environment in which a human can interact with a virtual dog, which "sees" its human "owner" with digital cameras, moves toward or runs away when the human points, and offers its paw or jumps up eagerly in response to human gestures.

Exercise 10.34 (*explore*): How are agents and softbots being used to facilitate shopping and other activities on the web? Do some research on the web and/or in the library.

---

[15]R. A. Brooks, "A Robust, Multi-Layered Control System for a Mobile Robot," *IEEE Journal of Robotics and Automation*, 2 (1986), 14-23.

[16]D. Parson and G. D. Blank, "Automatic vs. Controlled Processing: an Architecture for Real-Time Production Systems," *International Journal of Expert Systems Research and Development*, 2 (3/4), 1989, 393-417.

[17]P. Maes, T. Darrell, B. Blumberg and A. Pentland, "ALIVE: Artificial Life Interactive Video Environment," in *Proceedings of the Twelfth National Conference on Artificial Intelligence (AAAI-94)*, Seattle, Washington, p. 1506.

Chapter review. Are the following statements true or false? Explain why or why not.

a) A number of philosophers and mathematicians, notably Descartes, Leibniz, Hobbes, Boole and Turing, have argued that intelligent thought is simply logical calculation.

b) You believe that intelligent thought is simply logical calculation.

c) Other philosophers, notably Searle, have argued that a calculating machine could never 'think'.

d) A machine has passed the Turing test for intelligence.

e) Programs like ELIZA (exercise 10.5) suggest that machines that can pass the Turing test, at least behaviorally, are around the corner.

f) Weak AI advocates believe that a machine will never achieve intelligent thought.

g) The best chess programs use cognitive techniques that imitate the skills of grand masters.

h) A machine isn't intelligent until it understands sentences like "The horse raced past the barn fell."

i) Because machines aren't limited by short-term memory, they will eventually understand and translate languages better than people do.

j) So far, AI machines are better at playing checkers than recognizing your mother.

k) GOFAI is an attempt to implement the dream of philosophers and mathematicians like Descartes, Leibniz, Hobbes, Boole and Turing.

l) The most successful chess programs can defeat grand masters because they can look at all possible moves in a game.

m) The most successful chess programs use heuristics.

n) Problems like chess and the traveling salesperson problem (exercise 10.16) suggest that much of what AI is about is solving computationally intractable problems.

o) Expert systems, reasoning with formal rules, have achieved success in limited subject domains.

p) Backward chaining inference is especially suitable for engineering design problems.

q) Forward chaining inference is especially suitable for diagnosis or troubleshooting.

r) The independence assumption is why probabilistic reasoning is especially reliable.

s) Semantic networks, frames and classes share a similar technique for inferring common properties.

t) Case-based reasoning systems are better at birthday parties than solving practical problems.

u) A perceptron, like a neuron, packs the power of a CPU into a single small unit.

v) A perceptron learns by asking its trainer to give it more examples.

w) Back-propagation, like a child learning how to talk, learns by propagating error values back to hidden units and input units, causing them to adjust their weights to give better results.

x) Shakey showed that GOFAI-based robots would inevitably have the intelligence and endearing shape of R2D2 of *Star Wars* fame.

y) Automatic behaviors, unlike controlled ones, must have limited ability to search for solutions.

z) A softbot is a virtual robot.

Summary

Alan Turing, ready to envision AI at the dawn of the computing age, proposed a *behavioral* test for intelligence: an imitation game, in which an interrogator must guess which is the man and which is the computer. Many variants of this test, as well as many arguments against its validity, notably Searle's Chinese Room argument, have been proposed. Advocates of **strong AI** believe that the grand project of building a conscious, intelligent machine is inevitable, whereas proponents of **weak AI** argue that machines can be designed to act *as if* they were intelligent, functionally, without necessarily having the biological basis or subjective experience of human intelligence. Even weaker is the claim that AI can model certain aspects of human intelligence, without necessarily achieving the whole grand project. Cognitive scientists put more emphasis on modeling the mechanisms of cognition, using the cognition-as-computation metaphor to finesse the age-old mind-body problem. Evidence for cognitive models may derive from empirical experiments, computational simulations, or convincing philosophical arguments.

Good Old-Fashioned AI (GOFAI) succeeds with formal tasks by representing knowledge in terms of symbols and manipulating these symbols (making inferences) by logical rules. GOFAI automate problem solving techniques studied in chapter 2: **state space search**, whether blind (depth-first or breadth first) or informed (using heuristics or other domain knowledge), backward chaining by reducing goal to subgoals (similar to top-down decomposition), forward chaining from data to conclusions or actions (bottom-up composition), reasoning by analogy (case-based reasoning), and so forth. These techniques have succeeded in getting machines to play games such as checkers and chess at championship levels, navigate through difficult terrains such as battlefields, interstate highways and undersea (autonomous underwater vehicles), understand a subset of natural language, and model the knowledge of domain experts such as an auto mechanic, an insurance claim adjustor, a mainframe computer operator, or a geologist looking for valuable mineral deposits.

As Roger Bacon once said, "Knowledge is power." This axiom is especially true in AI since knowledge representation is a key to its success. **Rule-based systems** encode knowledge in terms of if-then rules (or logical clauses). Expert system shells contain an **inference engine** which automates a process of reasoning (such as backward or forward chaining), given a collection of rules that represent knowledge about some domain and the particular facts of a given problem to solve. Some shells support various kinds of **probabilistic reasoning** for dealing in uncertainty. Alternatives to rules include **semantic networks**, which represent associative knowledge as labeled graphs and introduce the notion of inheritance of properties, and **frames**, which organize knowledge as collections of slots, each of which may have expected default values or attached procedures for filling these slots or performing other behaviors.

An alternative to GOFAI is the **neural network** approach, which models intelligent behaviors in terms of levels of activity in interconnected assembly of neuron-like units or nodes. Like the brain, these networks feature large numbers of relatively simple processors operating in parallel. Each neuron is essentially a function from a set of input values, each multiplied by a weight factor, to an output value which depends on whether the inputs exceed some threshold. Input values can either come from outside the network (a representation of a problem or sensors) or from the output of other neurons (producing a multi-layered network). Neural networks **learn**, gradually improving their performance at some task, by repeatedly adjusting their weights so that their output values most closely correspond to a desirable result. Because neural networks involve so many simple processors, networks as a whole tend to be far more **robust** than traditional symbolic AI, handling unseen data nearly as well as training data. However, it is difficult to get neural networks to explain how they reached a conclusion, or to reason and solve problems as symbolic technologies can do. Both technologies have tradeoffs. Which to use (or perhaps a combination of both) depends on the domain and the nature of the task one a knowledge engineer wants a system to perform.

There is considerable interest now in the construction of intelligent **agents**, which perceive and act in a world. Instead of carefully controlled environments such as fixed industrial settings or laboratory microworlds, **intelligent robots** need to deal with the demands and dynamics of the real world. **Softbots** deal with analogous demands and unpredictability in virtual worlds. Since perfect rationality is not possible in demanding, complicated environments, agent design now emphasizes **limited rationality**—acting appropriately within real time and finite computational space. GOFAI-based robotics emphasize distinct phases of planning (rule-based problem solving) and execution (performing plans and compiled sequences of steps). While making both planning more efficient and execution more responsive, this approach runs into fundamental difficulties in computational complexity. (Faster processors with larger memories make it appear that these difficulties could be overcome, but branching factors will eventually overwhelm faster processors.) Non-symbolic approaches, both using neural networks (which enable a van to navigate interstates at or above speed limits) and bottom-up **behavior-based** techniques, have proven more practical, at least for lower levels of control. The future of intelligent robotics, and AI in general, may lie in some combination of top-down, symbolic and bottom-up, sub-symbolic techniques, analogous to a cognitive distinction between **automatic** vs. **controlled** processing. You can see both kinds of processing exhibited, for example, in the way a toddler learns to walk: leaning on a couch or Daddy's hand, deciding whether to take that step, then wobbling and falling over a lot, but eventually striding around without thinking about it. Then, on to running and thinking about what other kinds of trouble he can get into!

If nothing else, we hope this survey of AI has given you a glimpse, just over the horizon, of both the power and the limits (as well as the risks and responsibility) of the universal computer—and those who use it.